Dance in the Vampire Bund

Age of Scarlet Order

01

story & art by
Nozomu Tamaki

CONTENTS

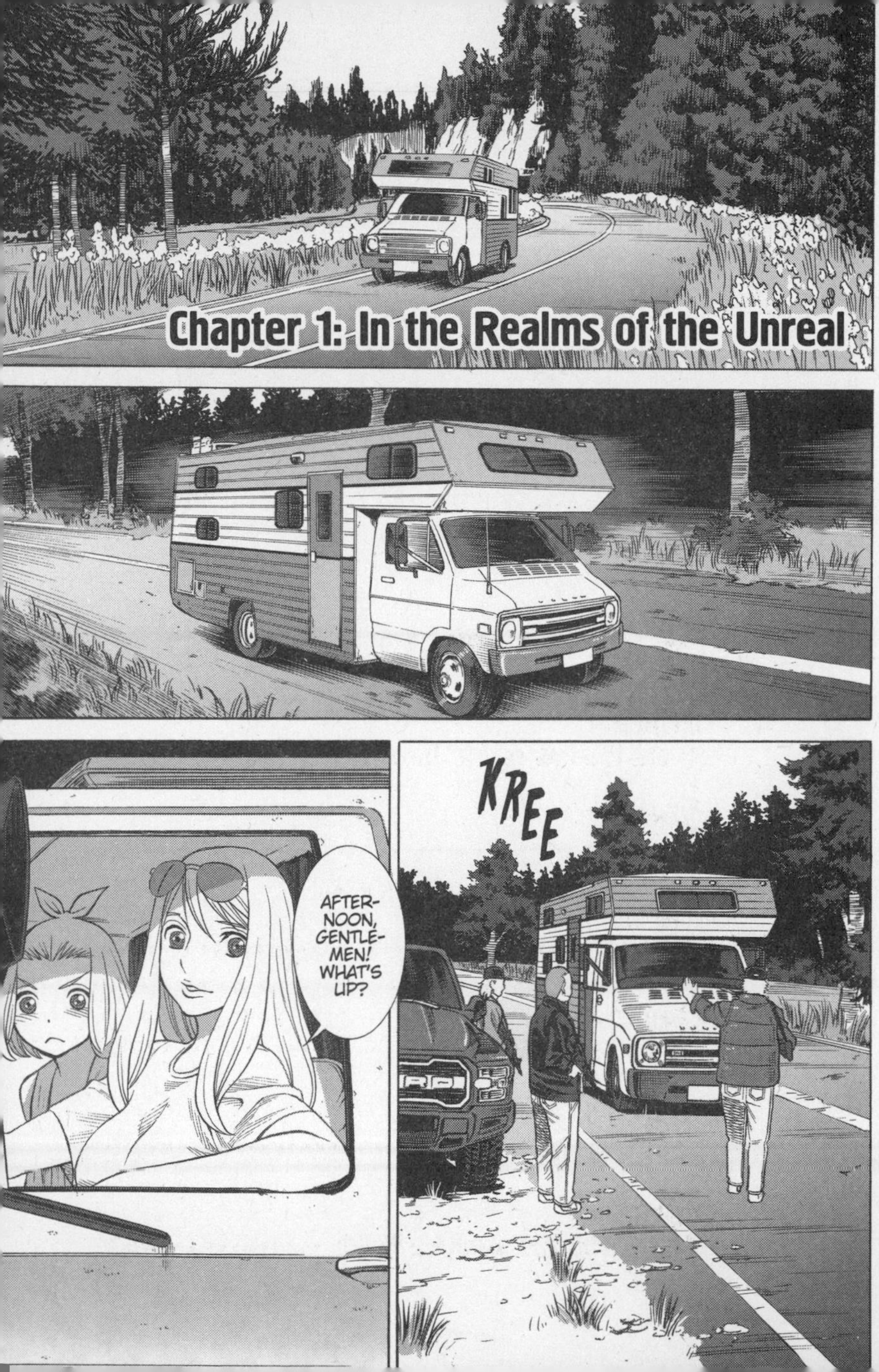
Chapter 1: In the Realms of the Unreal
KREE
AFTER-NOON, GENTLE-MEN! WHAT'S UP?

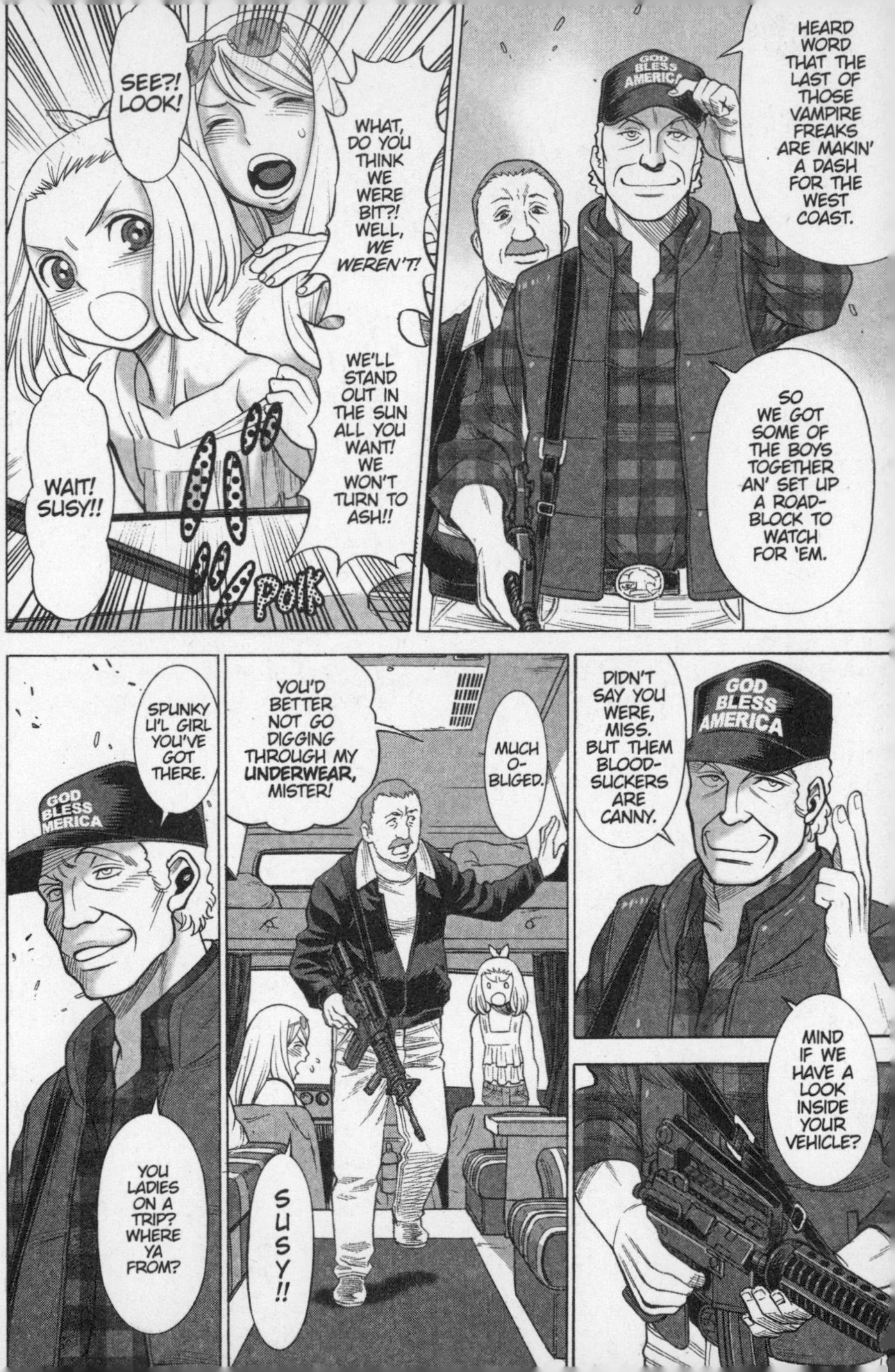
HEARD WORD THAT THE LAST OF THOSE VAMPIRE FREAKS ARE MAKIN' A DASH FOR THE WEST COAST.
SO WE GOT SOME OF THE BOYS TOGETHER AN' SET UP A ROAD-BLOCK TO WATCH FOR 'EM.
WHAT, DO YOU THINK WE WERE BIT?! WELL, *WE WEREN'T!*
WE'LL STAND OUT IN THE SUN ALL YOU WANT! WE WON'T TURN TO ASH!!
SEE?! LOOK!
WAIT! SUSY!!
POK
DIDN'T SAY YOU WERE, MISS. BUT THEM BLOOD-SUCKERS ARE CANNY.
MIND IF WE HAVE A LOOK INSIDE YOUR VEHICLE?
MUCH O-BLIGED.
YOU'D BETTER NOT GO DIGGING THROUGH MY **UNDERWEAR,** MISTER!
SUSY!!
SPUNKY LI'L GIRL YOU'VE GOT THERE.
YOU LADIES ON A TRIP? WHERE YA FROM?

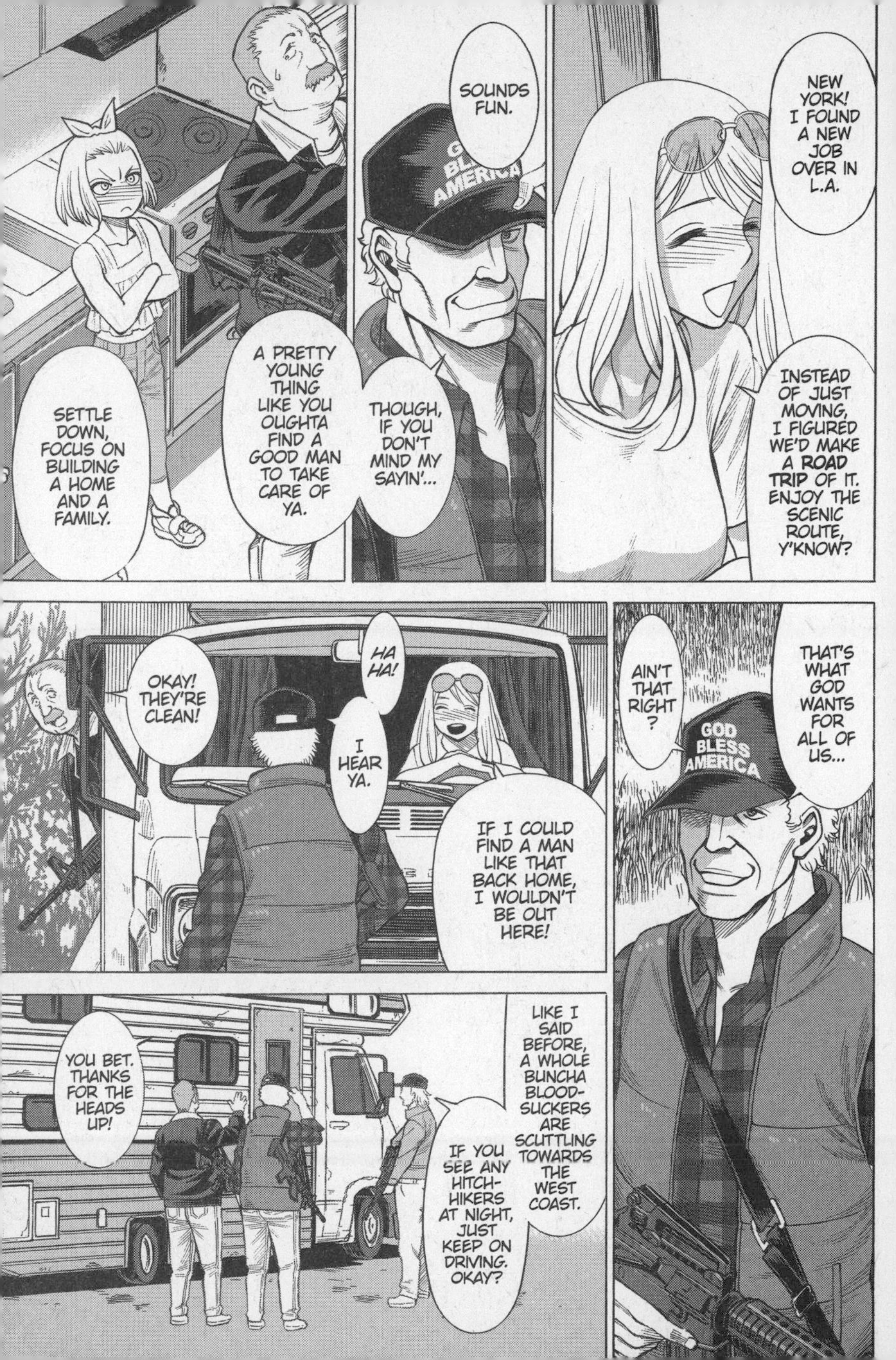
NEW YORK! I FOUND A NEW JOB OVER IN L.A.
INSTEAD OF JUST MOVING, I FIGURED WE'D MAKE A **ROAD TRIP** OF IT. ENJOY THE SCENIC ROUTE, Y'KNOW?
SOUNDS FUN.
THOUGH, IF YOU DON'T MIND MY SAYIN'...
A PRETTY YOUNG THING LIKE YOU OUGHTA FIND A GOOD MAN TO TAKE CARE OF YA.
SETTLE DOWN, FOCUS ON BUILDING A HOME AND A FAMILY.
THAT'S WHAT GOD WANTS FOR ALL OF US...
GOD BLESS AMERICA
AIN'T THAT RIGHT?
HA HA!
I HEAR YA.
IF I COULD FIND A MAN LIKE THAT BACK HOME, I WOULDN'T BE OUT HERE!
OKAY! THEY'RE CLEAN!
LIKE I SAID BEFORE, A WHOLE BUNCHA BLOOD-SUCKERS ARE SCUTTLING TOWARDS THE WEST COAST.
IF YOU SEE ANY HITCH-HIKERS AT NIGHT, JUST KEEP ON DRIVING. OKAY?
YOU BET. THANKS FOR THE HEADS UP!

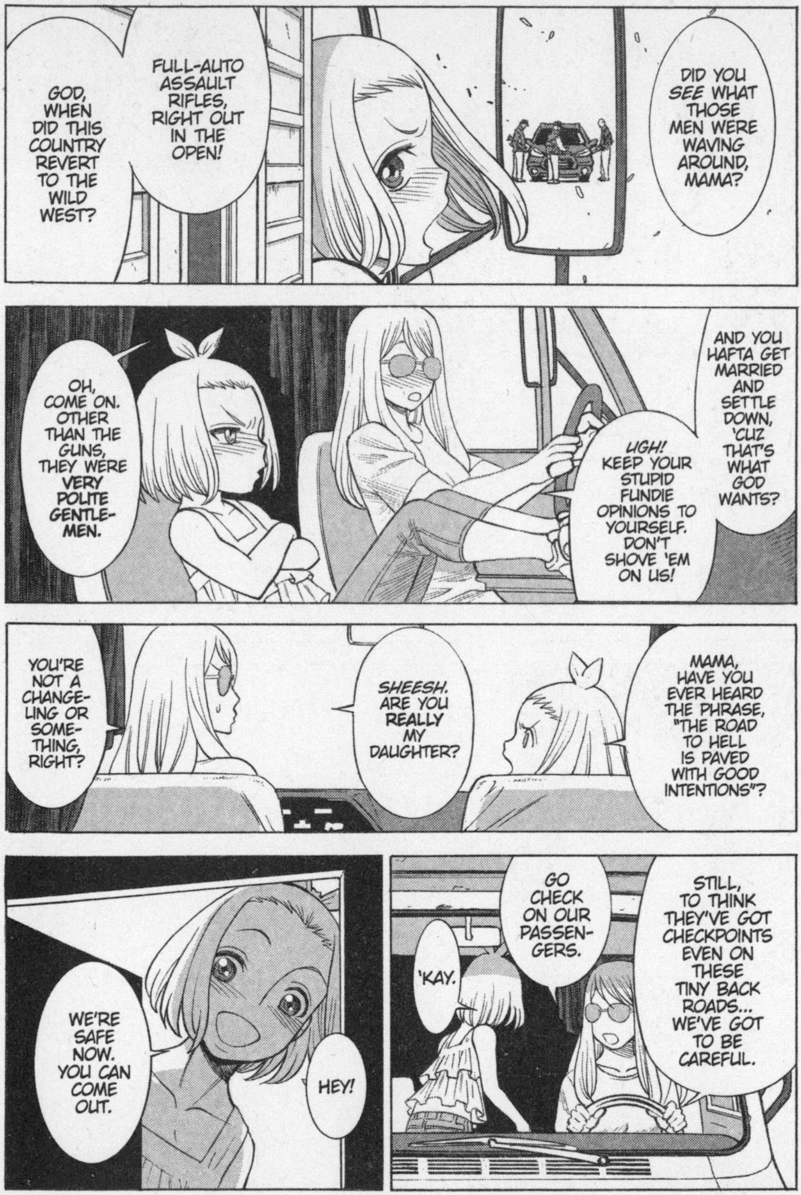
DID YOU *SEE* WHAT THOSE MEN WERE WAVING AROUND, MAMA?
FULL-AUTO ASSAULT RIFLES, RIGHT OUT IN THE OPEN!
GOD, WHEN DID THIS COUNTRY REVERT TO THE WILD WEST?
AND YOU HAFTA GET MARRIED AND SETTLE DOWN, 'CUZ THAT'S WHAT GOD WANTS?
UGH! KEEP YOUR STUPID FUNDIE OPINIONS TO YOURSELF. DON'T SHOVE 'EM ON US!
OH, COME ON. OTHER THAN THE GUNS, THEY WERE **VERY** POLITE GENTLEMEN.
MAMA, HAVE YOU EVER HEARD THE PHRASE, "THE ROAD TO HELL IS PAVED WITH GOOD INTENTIONS"?
SHEESH. ARE YOU **REALLY** MY DAUGHTER?
YOU'RE NOT A CHANGELING OR SOMETHING, RIGHT?
STILL, TO THINK THEY'VE GOT CHECKPOINTS EVEN ON THESE TINY BACK ROADS... WE'VE GOT TO BE CAREFUL.
GO CHECK ON OUR PASSENGERS.
'KAY.
HEY!
WE'RE SAFE NOW. YOU CAN COME OUT.

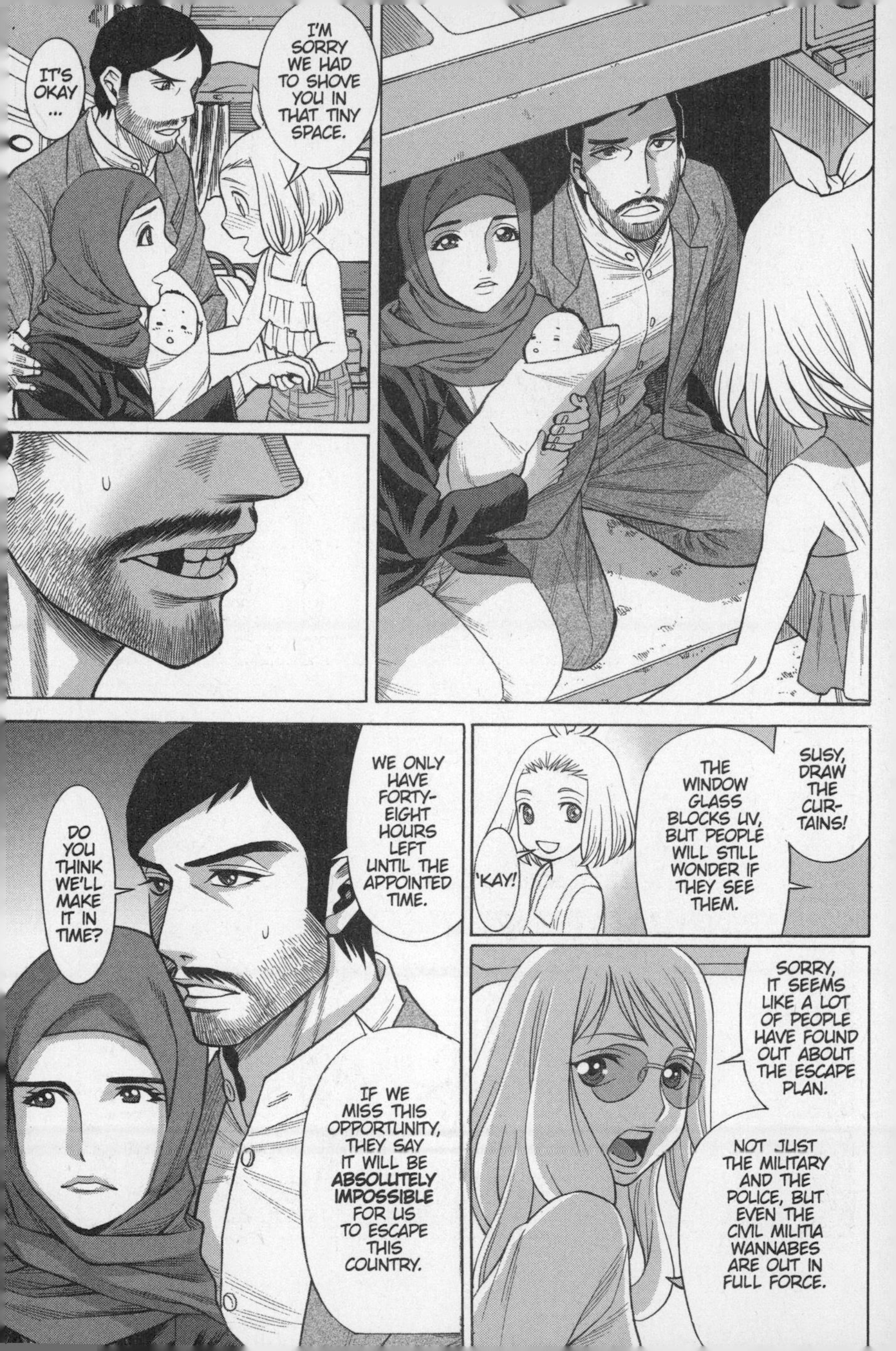
I'M SORRY WE HAD TO SHOVE YOU IN THAT TINY SPACE.
IT'S OKAY ...
SUSY, DRAW THE CUR-TAINS!
THE WINDOW GLASS BLOCKS UV, BUT PEOPLE WILL STILL WONDER IF THEY SEE THEM.
'KAY!
SORRY, IT SEEMS LIKE A LOT OF PEOPLE HAVE FOUND OUT ABOUT THE ESCAPE PLAN.
NOT JUST THE MILITARY AND THE POLICE, BUT EVEN THE CIVIL MILITIA WANNABES ARE OUT IN FULL FORCE.
WE ONLY HAVE FORTY-EIGHT HOURS LEFT UNTIL THE APPOINTED TIME.
DO YOU THINK WE'LL MAKE IT IN TIME?
IF WE MISS THIS OPPORTUNITY, THEY SAY IT WILL BE **ABSOLUTELY IMPOSSIBLE** FOR US TO ESCAPE THIS COUNTRY.

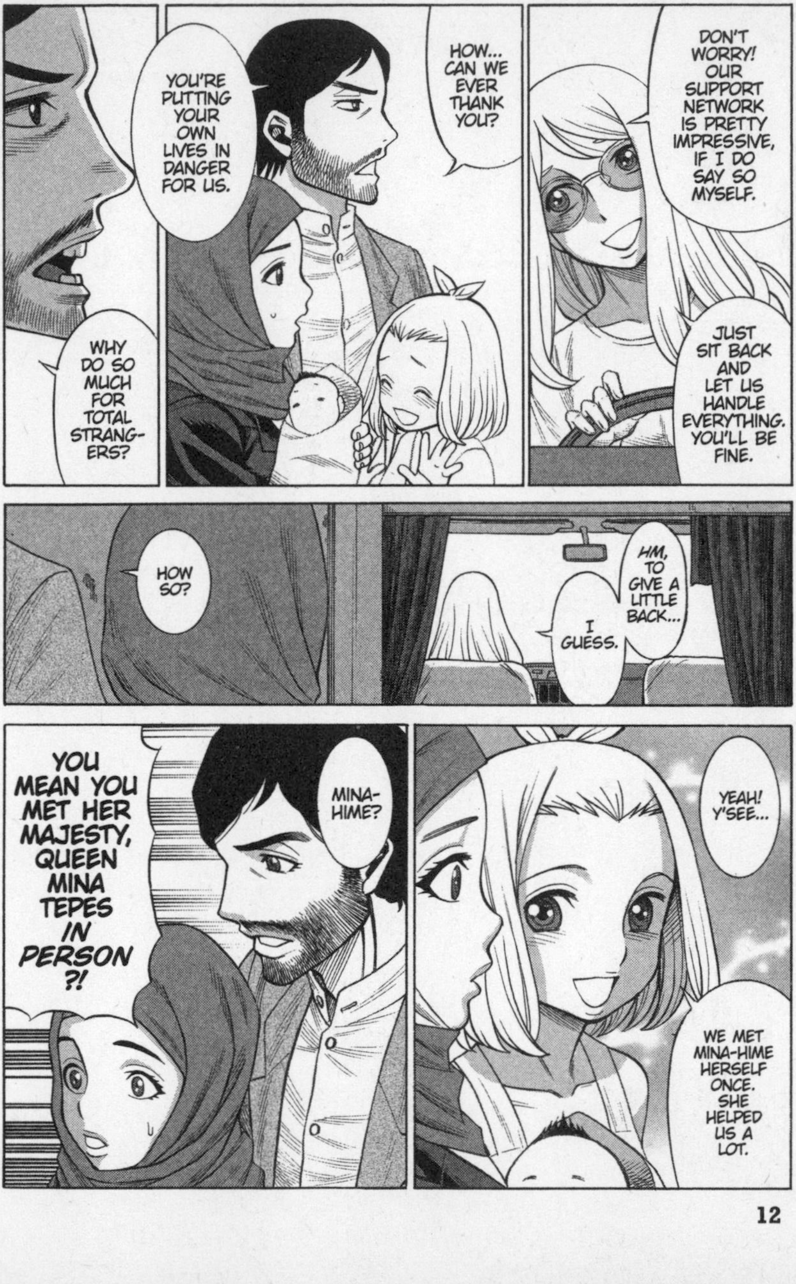
DON'T WORRY! OUR SUPPORT NETWORK IS PRETTY IMPRESSIVE, IF I DO SAY SO MYSELF.
JUST SIT BACK AND LET US HANDLE EVERYTHING. YOU'LL BE FINE.
HOW... CAN WE EVER THANK YOU?
YOU'RE PUTTING YOUR OWN LIVES IN DANGER FOR US.
WHY DO SO MUCH FOR TOTAL STRANGERS?
HM, TO GIVE A LITTLE BACK...
I GUESS.
HOW SO?
YEAH! Y'SEE...
WE MET MINA-HIME HERSELF ONCE. SHE HELPED US A LOT.
MINA-HIME?
YOU MEAN YOU MET HER MAJESTY, QUEEN MINA TEPES IN PERSON?!

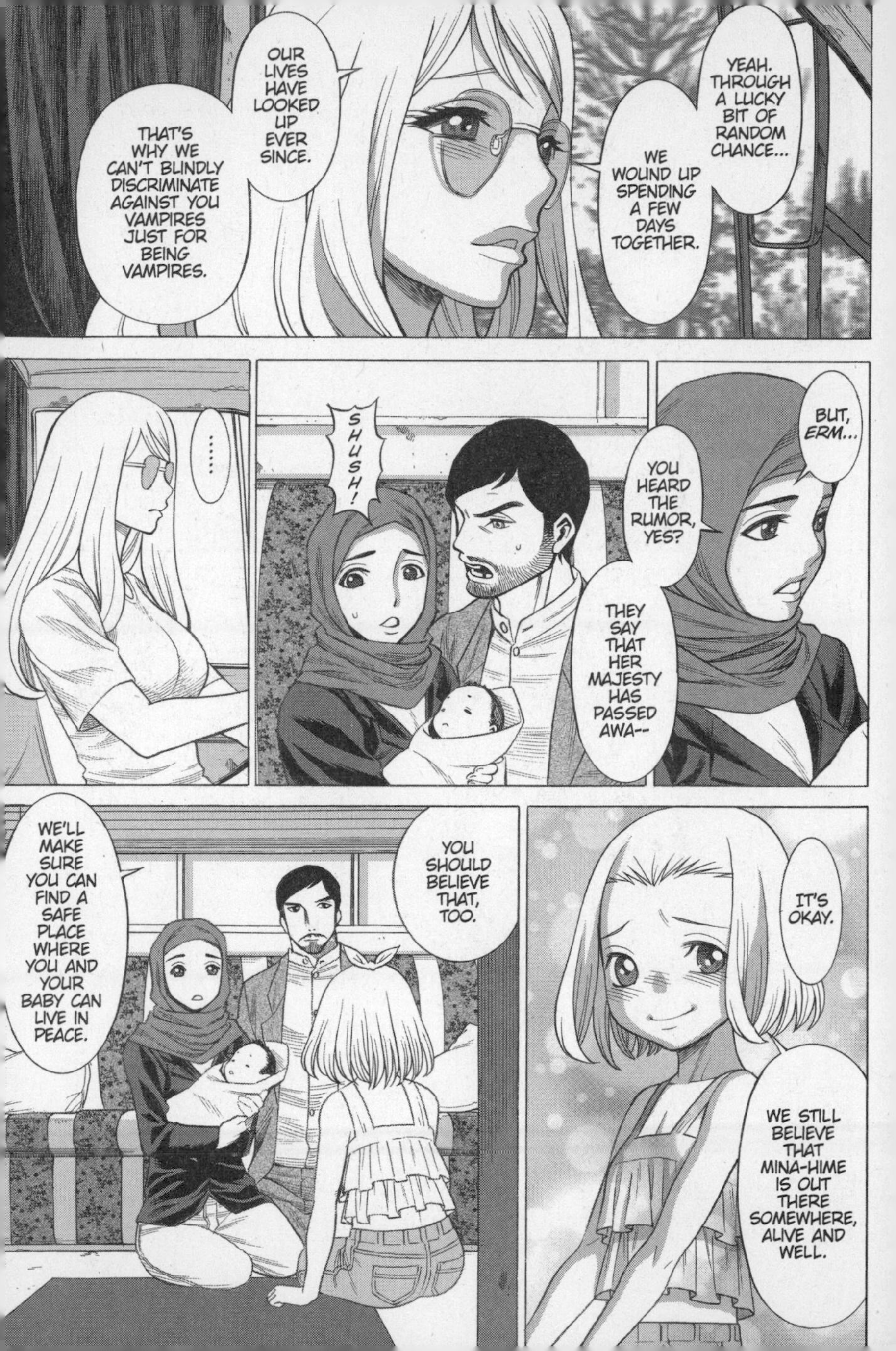

YEAH. THROUGH A LUCKY BIT OF RANDOM CHANCE...
WE WOUND UP SPENDING A FEW DAYS TOGETHER.
OUR LIVES HAVE LOOKED UP EVER SINCE.
THAT'S WHY WE CAN'T BLINDLY DISCRIMINATE AGAINST YOU VAMPIRES JUST FOR BEING VAMPIRES.
BUT, *ERM*...
YOU HEARD THE RUMOR, YES?
THEY SAY THAT HER MAJESTY HAS PASSED AWA--
SHUSH!
......
IT'S OKAY.
WE STILL BELIEVE THAT MINA-HIME IS OUT THERE SOMEWHERE, ALIVE AND WELL.
YOU SHOULD BELIEVE THAT, TOO.
WE'LL MAKE SURE YOU CAN FIND A SAFE PLACE WHERE YOU AND YOUR BABY CAN LIVE IN PEACE.

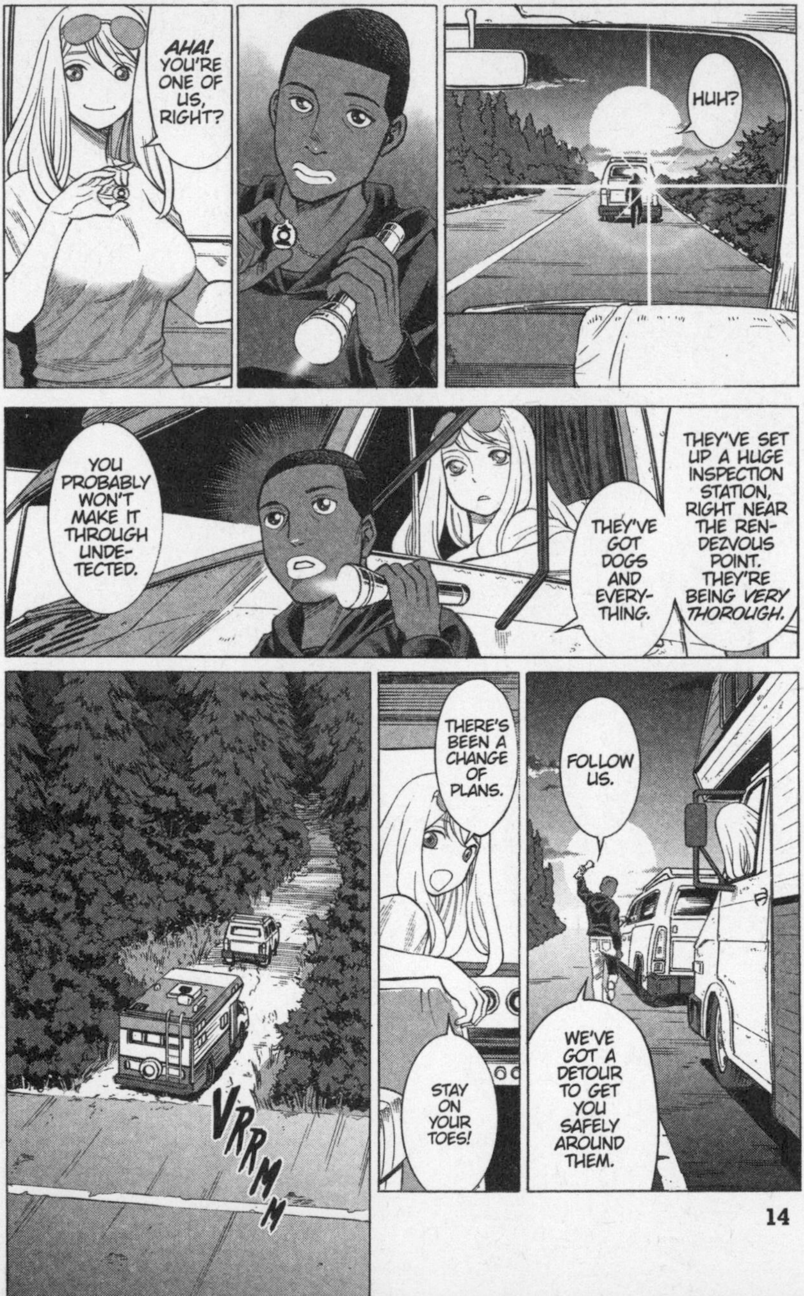
HUH?
AHA! YOU'RE ONE OF US, RIGHT?
THEY'VE SET UP A HUGE INSPECTION STATION, RIGHT NEAR THE RENDEZVOUS POINT. THEY'RE BEING *VERY THOROUGH.*
THEY'VE GOT DOGS AND EVERYTHING.
YOU PROBABLY WON'T MAKE IT THROUGH UNDETECTED.
FOLLOW US.
WE'VE GOT A DETOUR TO GET YOU SAFELY AROUND THEM.
THERE'S BEEN A CHANGE OF PLANS.
STAY ON YOUR TOES!
VRRMM

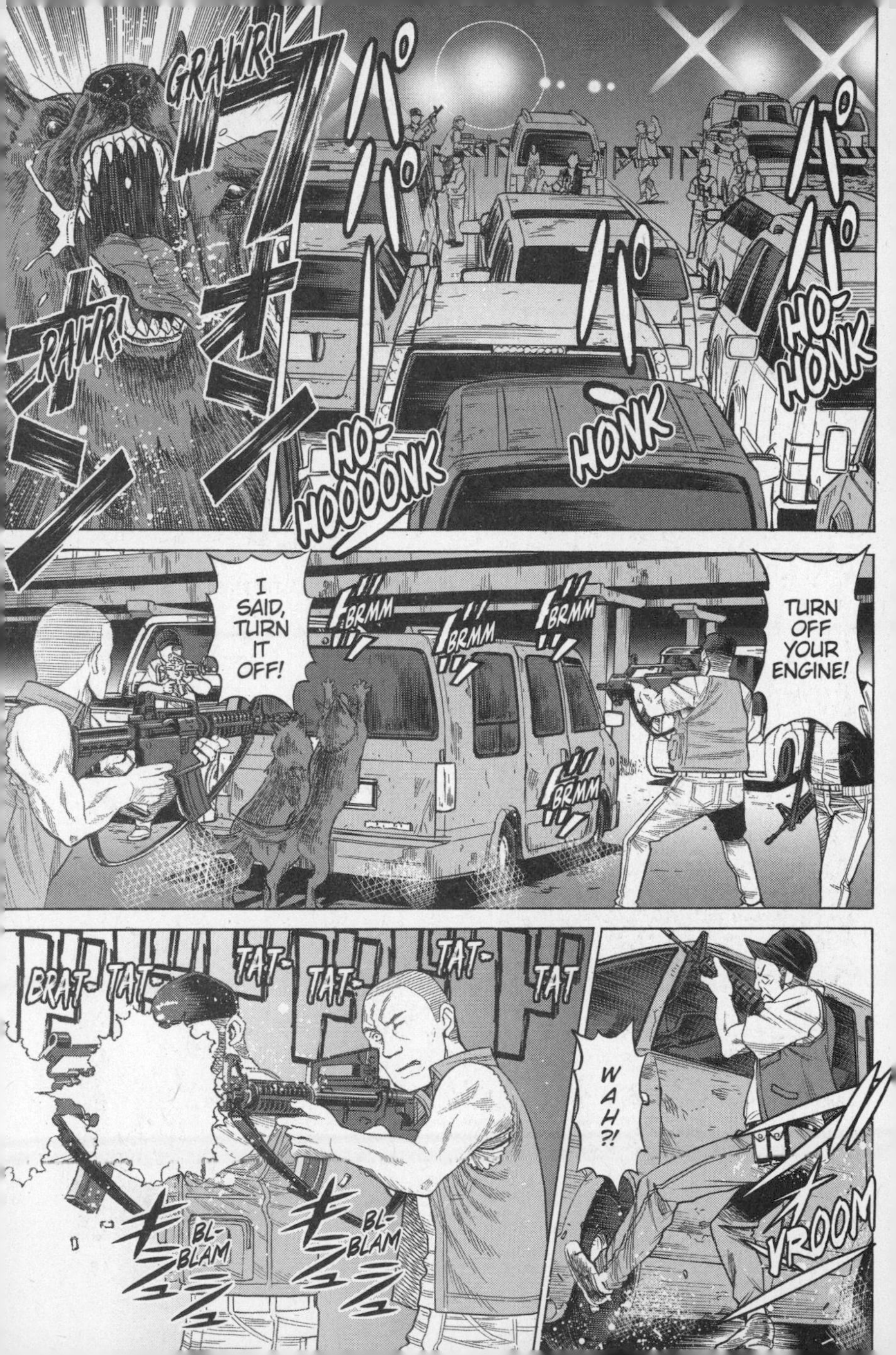
HO-HONK
HONK
HO-HOOOONK
GRAWR!
RAWR!
TURN OFF YOUR ENGINE!
BRMM
BRMM
BRMM
BRMM
I SAID, TURN IT OFF!
WAH?!
VROOM
TAT
TAT-
TAT-
TAT-
BRAT-TAT-
BL-BLAM
BL-BLAM

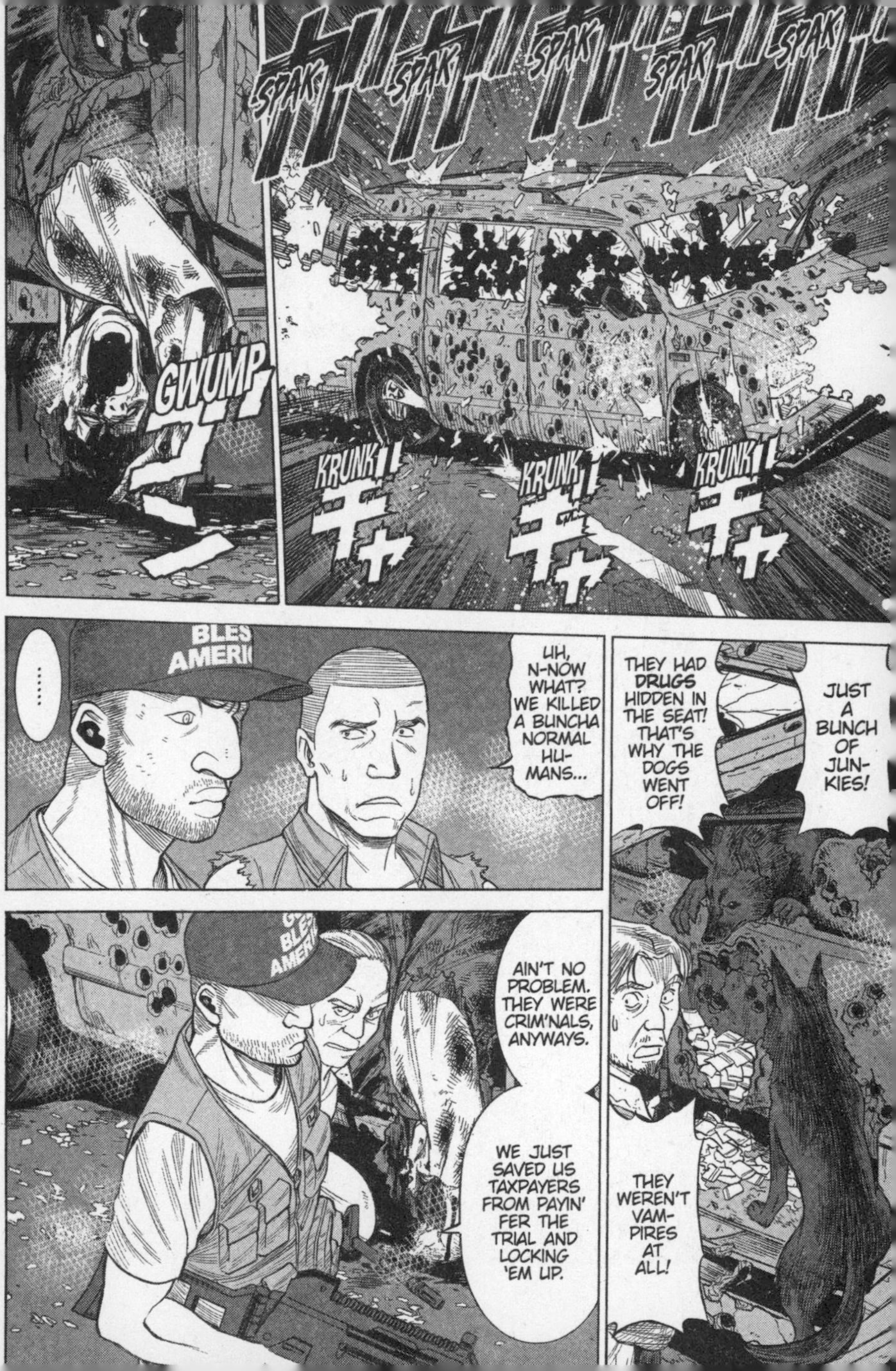
SPAK
SPAK
SPAK
SPAK
SPAK
KRUNK!!
ギャ
KRUNK!!
ギャ
KRUNK!!
ギャ
GWUMP
JUST A BUNCH OF JUN-KIES!
THEY HAD DRUGS HIDDEN IN THE SEAT! THAT'S WHY THE DOGS WENT OFF!
UH, N-NOW WHAT? WE KILLED A BUNCHA NORMAL HU-MANS...
......
THEY WEREN'T VAM-PIRES AT ALL!
AIN'T NO PROBLEM. THEY WERE CRIM'NALS, ANYWAYS.
WE JUST SAVED US TAXPAYERS FROM PAYIN' FER THE TRIAL AND LOCKING 'EM UP.

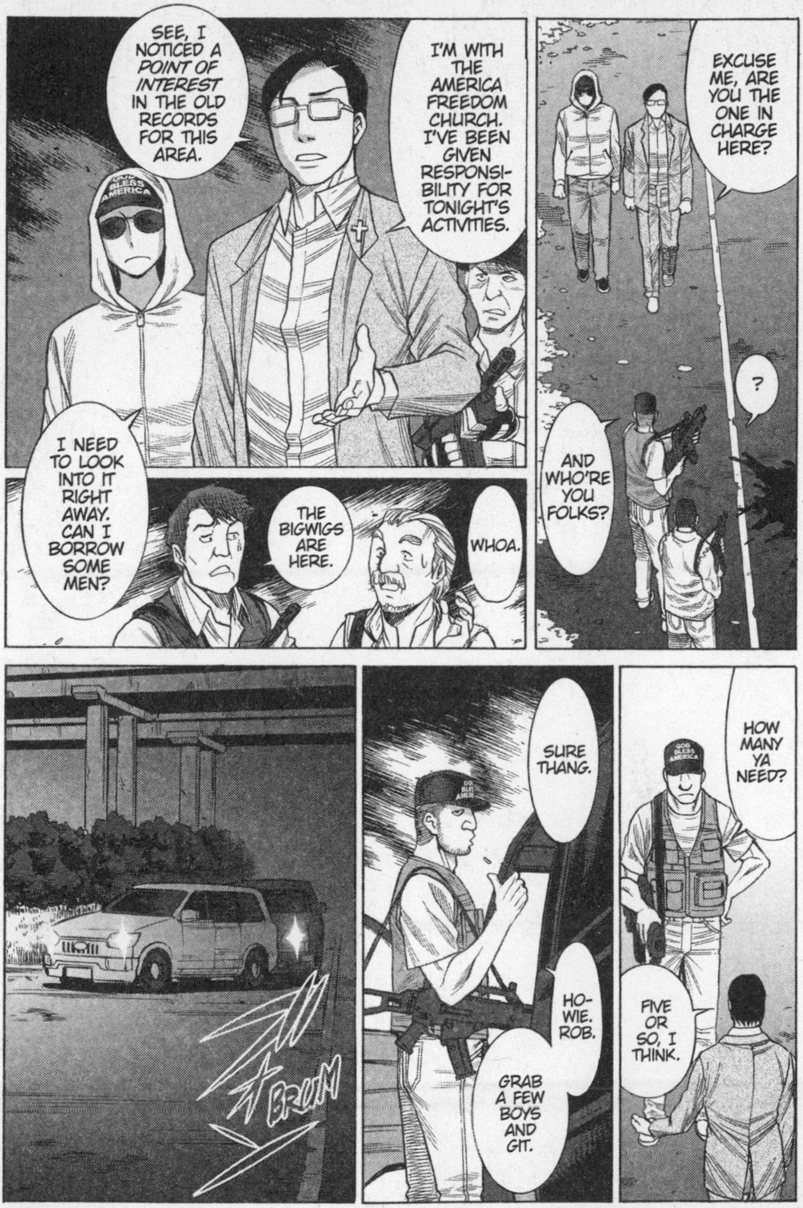
EXCUSE ME, ARE YOU THE ONE IN CHARGE HERE?
?
AND WHO'RE YOU FOLKS?
I'M WITH THE AMERICA FREEDOM CHURCH. I'VE BEEN GIVEN RESPONSIBILITY FOR TONIGHT'S ACTIVITIES.
SEE, I NOTICED A *POINT OF INTEREST* IN THE OLD RECORDS FOR THIS AREA.
GOD BLESS AMERICA
I NEED TO LOOK INTO IT RIGHT AWAY. CAN I BORROW SOME MEN?
WHOA.
THE BIGWIGS ARE HERE.
HOW MANY YA NEED?
GOD BLESS AMERICA
FIVE OR SO, I THINK.
SURE THANG.
HO-WIE. ROB.
GRAB A FEW BOYS AND GIT.
BRUM

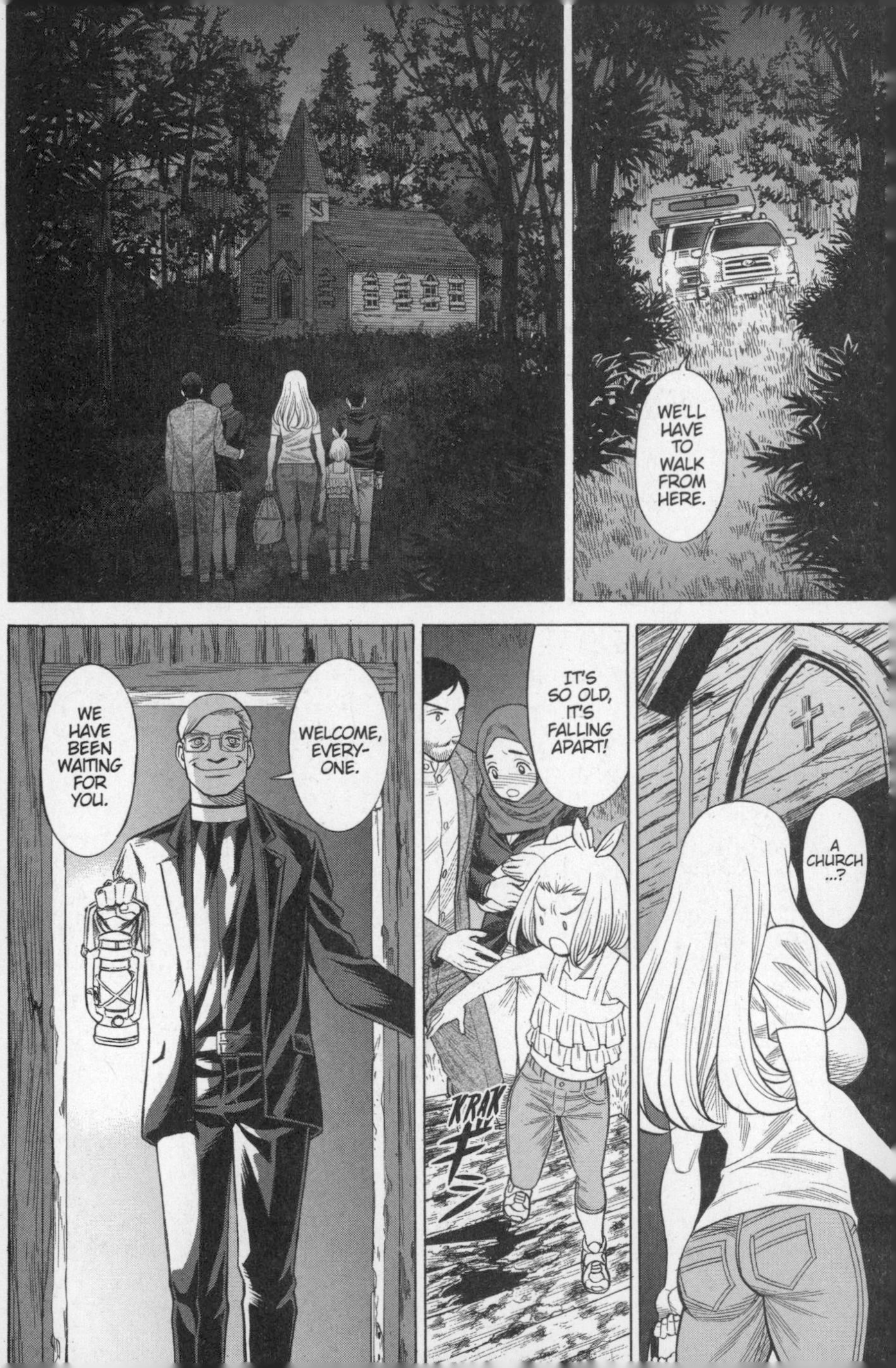
WE'LL HAVE TO WALK FROM HERE.
A CHURCH ...?
IT'S SO OLD, IT'S FALLING APART!
KRAK
WELCOME, EVERY-ONE.
WE HAVE BEEN WAITING FOR YOU.

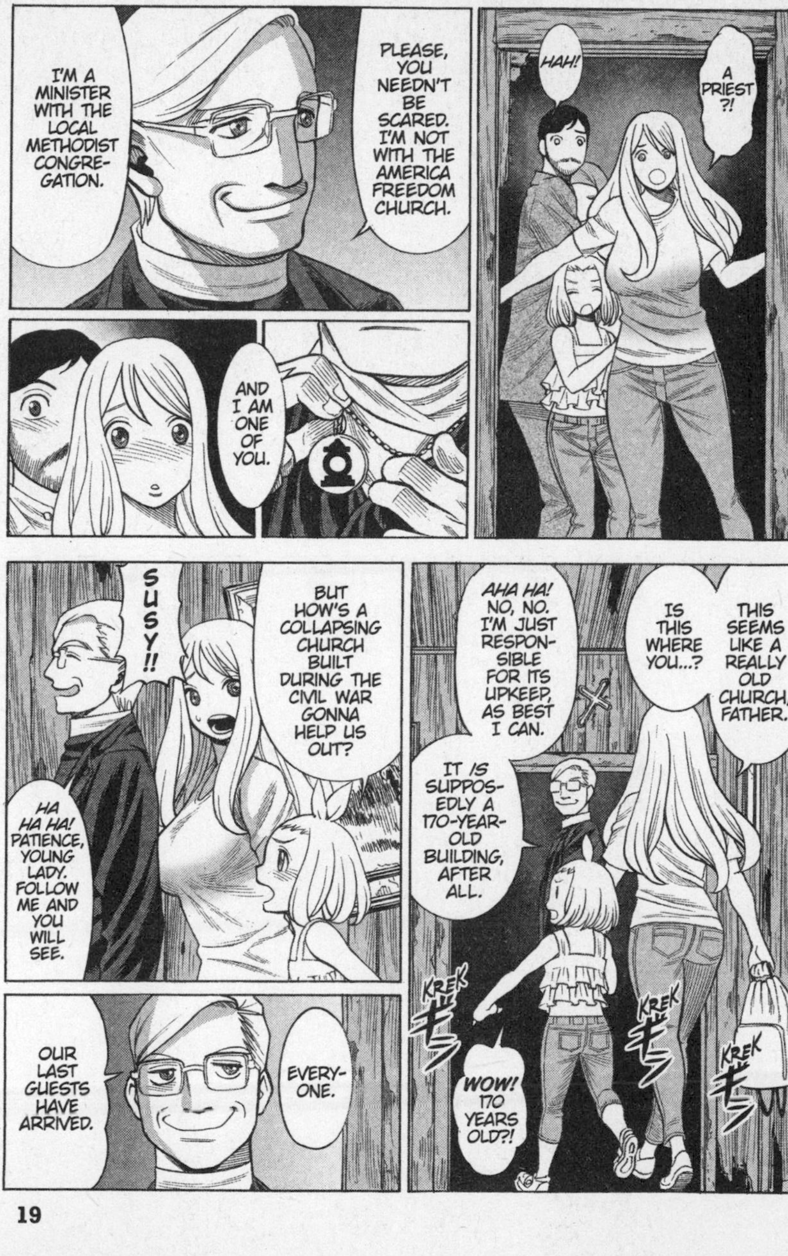
A PRIEST?!
HAH!
PLEASE, YOU NEEDN'T BE SCARED. I'M NOT WITH THE AMERICA FREEDOM CHURCH.
I'M A MINISTER WITH THE LOCAL METHODIST CONGRE-GATION.
AND I AM ONE OF YOU.
THIS SEEMS LIKE A REALLY OLD CHURCH, FATHER.
IS THIS WHERE YOU...?
AHA HA! NO, NO. I'M JUST RESPON-SIBLE FOR ITS UPKEEP, AS BEST I CAN.
IT IS SUPPOS-EDLY A 170-YEAR-OLD BUILDING, AFTER ALL.
KREK
KREK
KREK
WOW! 170 YEARS OLD?!
BUT HOW'S A COLLAPSING CHURCH BUILT DURING THE CIVIL WAR GONNA HELP US OUT?
SUSY!!
HA HA HA! PATIENCE, YOUNG LADY. FOLLOW ME AND YOU WILL SEE.
EVERY-ONE.
OUR LAST GUESTS HAVE ARRIVED.

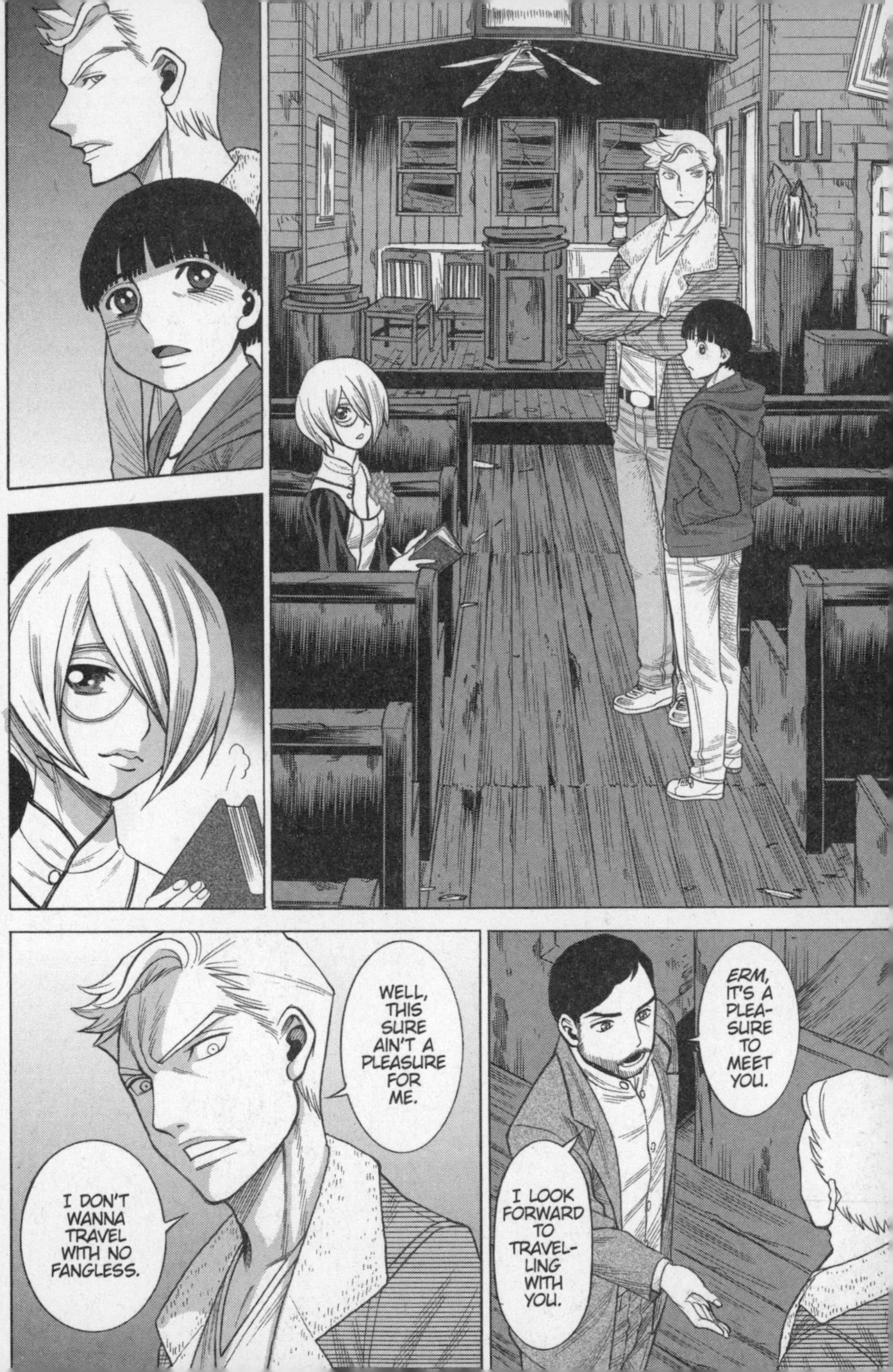
ERM, IT'S A PLEA-SURE TO MEET YOU.
I LOOK FORWARD TO TRAVEL-LING WITH YOU.
WELL, THIS SURE AIN'T A PLEASURE FOR ME.
I DON'T WANNA TRAVEL WITH NO FANGLESS.

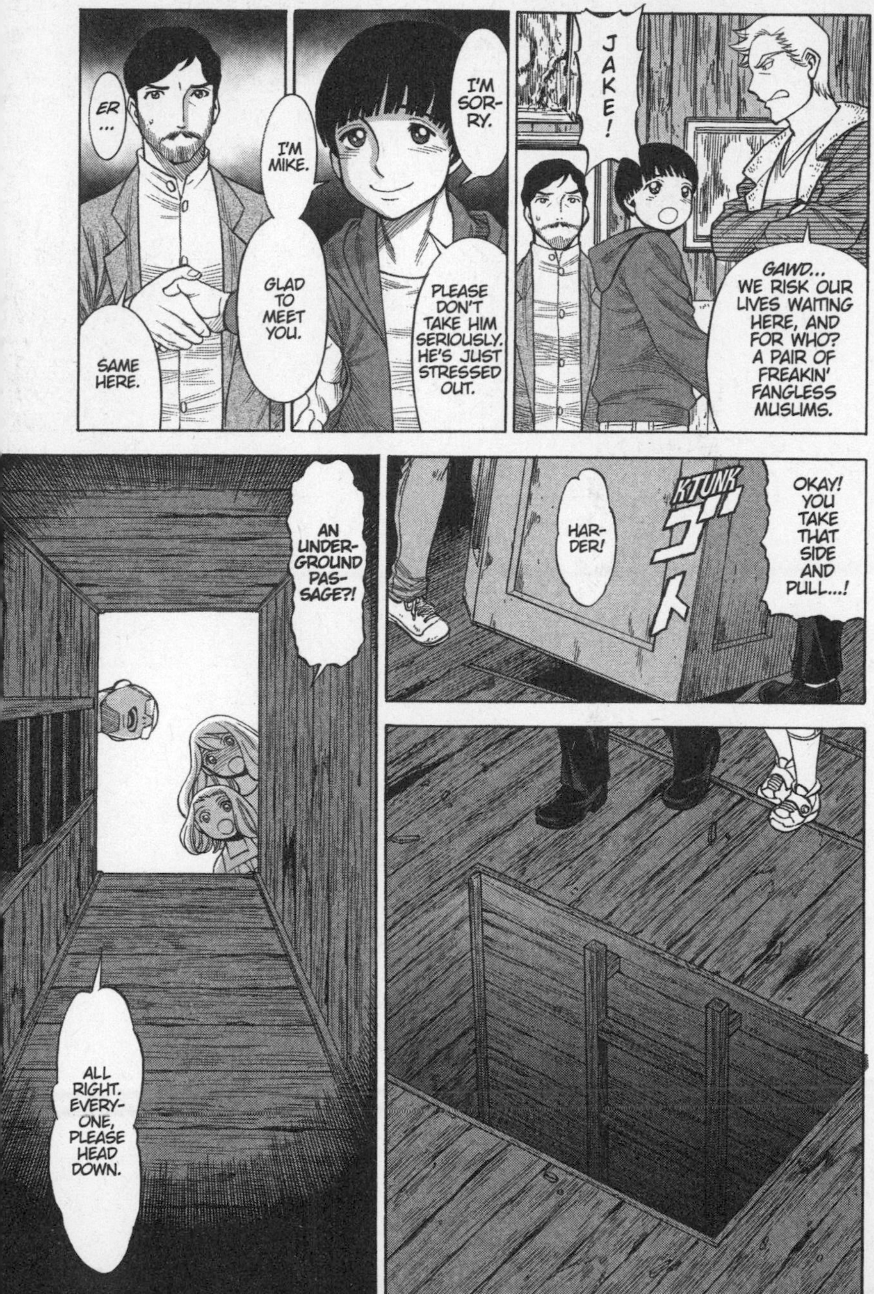
GAWD... WE RISK OUR LIVES WAITING HERE, AND FOR WHO? A PAIR OF FREAKIN' FANGLESS MUSLIMS.
JAKE!
I'M SORRY.
PLEASE DON'T TAKE HIM SERIOUSLY. HE'S JUST STRESSED OUT.
I'M MIKE.
GLAD TO MEET YOU.
ER...
SAME HERE.
OKAY! YOU TAKE THAT SIDE AND PULL...!
KTUNK
HARDER!
AN UNDERGROUND PASSAGE?!
ALL RIGHT. EVERYONE, PLEASE HEAD DOWN.

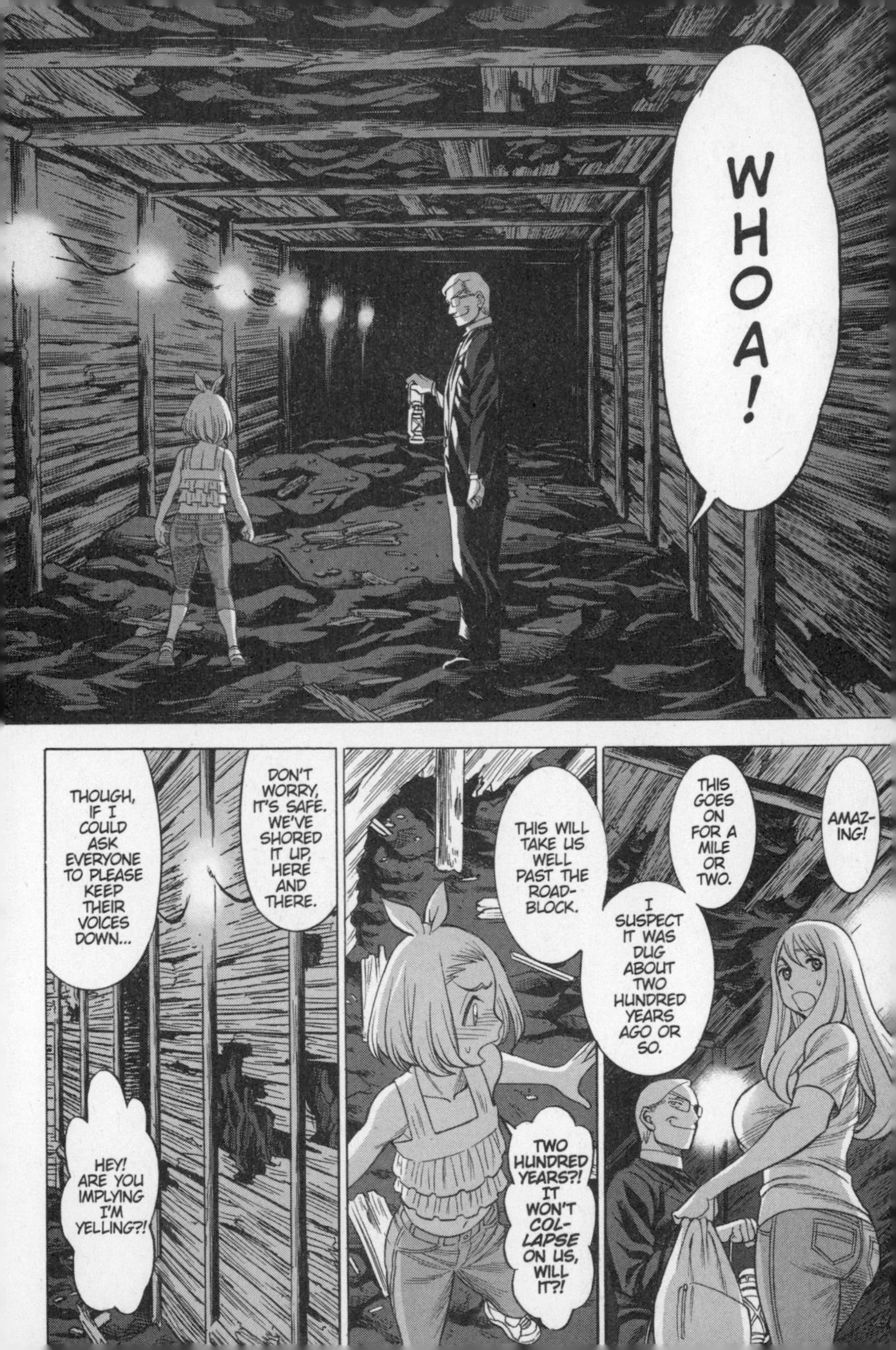
WHOA!
AMAZ-ING!
THIS GOES ON FOR A MILE OR TWO.
I SUSPECT IT WAS DUG ABOUT TWO HUNDRED YEARS AGO OR SO.
THIS WILL TAKE US WELL PAST THE ROAD-BLOCK.
TWO HUNDRED YEARS?! IT WON'T COL-LAPSE ON US, WILL IT?!
DON'T WORRY, IT'S SAFE. WE'VE SHORED IT UP, HERE AND THERE.
THOUGH, IF I COULD ASK EVERYONE TO PLEASE KEEP THEIR VOICES DOWN...
HEY! ARE YOU IMPLYING I'M YELLING?!

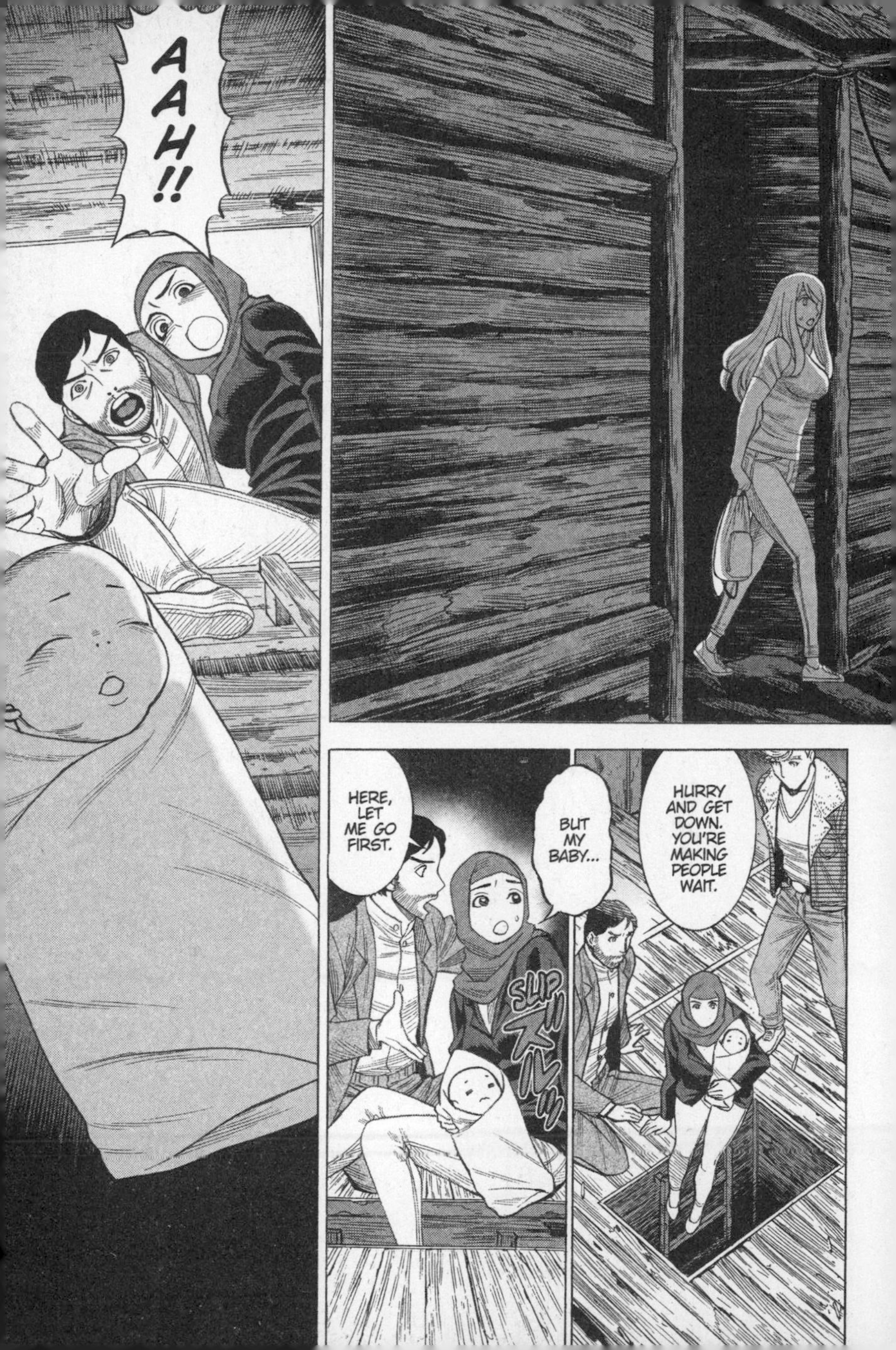
HURRY AND GET DOWN. YOU'RE MAKING PEOPLE WAIT.
BUT MY BABY...
HERE, LET ME GO FIRST.
SLIP!!
AAH!!

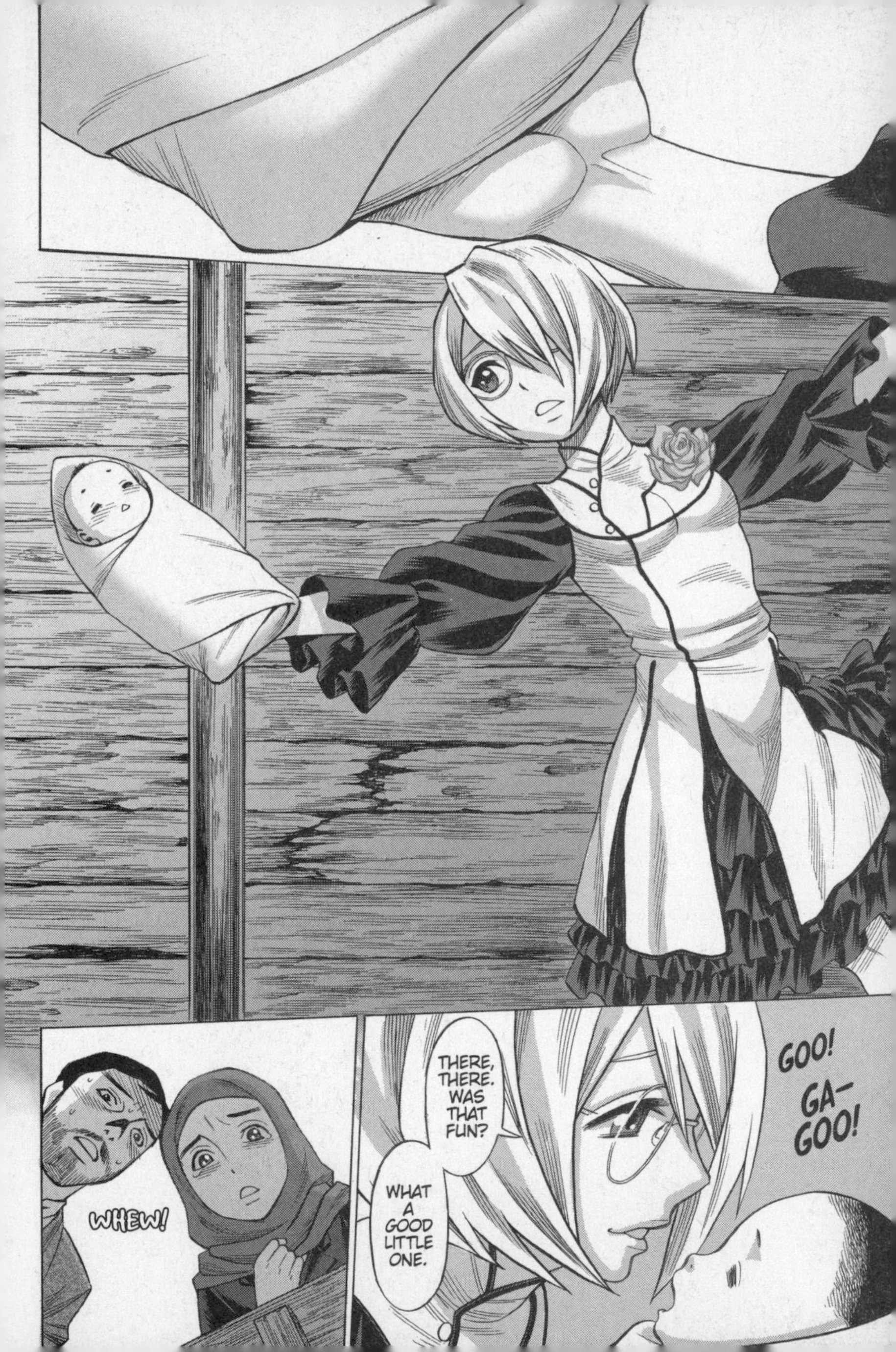
GOO! GA-GOO!
THERE, THERE. WAS THAT FUN?
WHAT A GOOD LITTLE ONE.
WHEW!

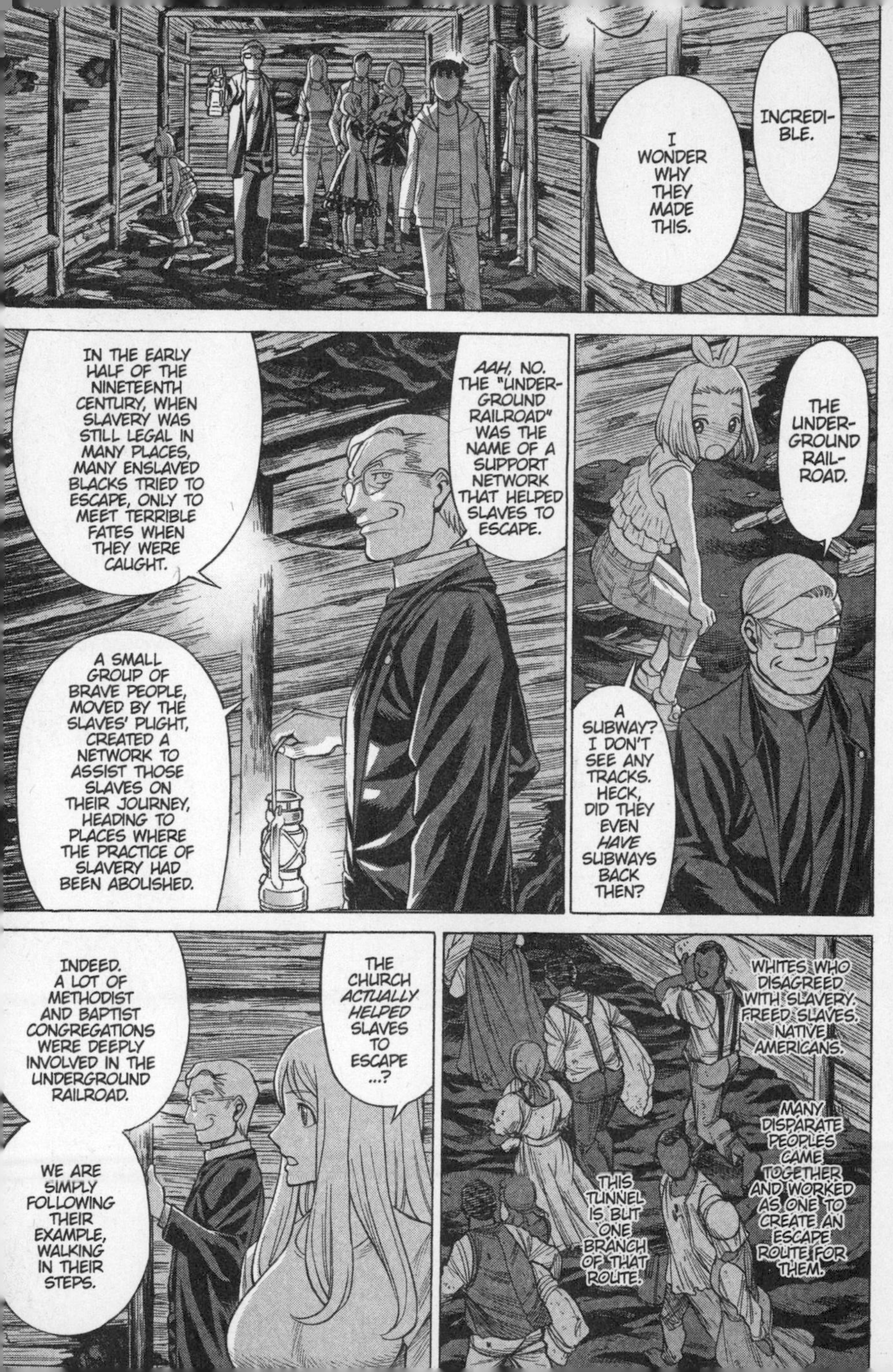
INCREDIBLE.
I WONDER WHY THEY MADE THIS.
THE UNDERGROUND RAILROAD.
A SUBWAY? I DON'T SEE ANY TRACKS. HECK, DID THEY EVEN *HAVE* SUBWAYS BACK THEN?
AAH, NO. THE "UNDERGROUND RAILROAD" WAS THE NAME OF A SUPPORT NETWORK THAT HELPED SLAVES TO ESCAPE.
IN THE EARLY HALF OF THE NINETEENTH CENTURY, WHEN SLAVERY WAS STILL LEGAL IN MANY PLACES, MANY ENSLAVED BLACKS TRIED TO ESCAPE, ONLY TO MEET TERRIBLE FATES WHEN THEY WERE CAUGHT.
A SMALL GROUP OF BRAVE PEOPLE, MOVED BY THE SLAVES' PLIGHT, CREATED A NETWORK TO ASSIST THOSE SLAVES ON THEIR JOURNEY, HEADING TO PLACES WHERE THE PRACTICE OF SLAVERY HAD BEEN ABOLISHED.
WHITES WHO DISAGREED WITH SLAVERY. FREED SLAVES. NATIVE AMERICANS.
MANY DISPARATE PEOPLES CAME TOGETHER AND WORKED AS ONE TO CREATE AN ESCAPE ROUTE FOR THEM.
THIS TUNNEL IS BUT ONE BRANCH OF THAT ROUTE.
THE CHURCH *ACTUALLY HELPED* SLAVES TO ESCAPE ...?
INDEED. A LOT OF METHODIST AND BAPTIST CONGREGATIONS WERE DEEPLY INVOLVED IN THE UNDERGROUND RAILROAD.
WE ARE SIMPLY FOLLOWING THEIR EXAMPLE, WALKING IN THEIR STEPS.

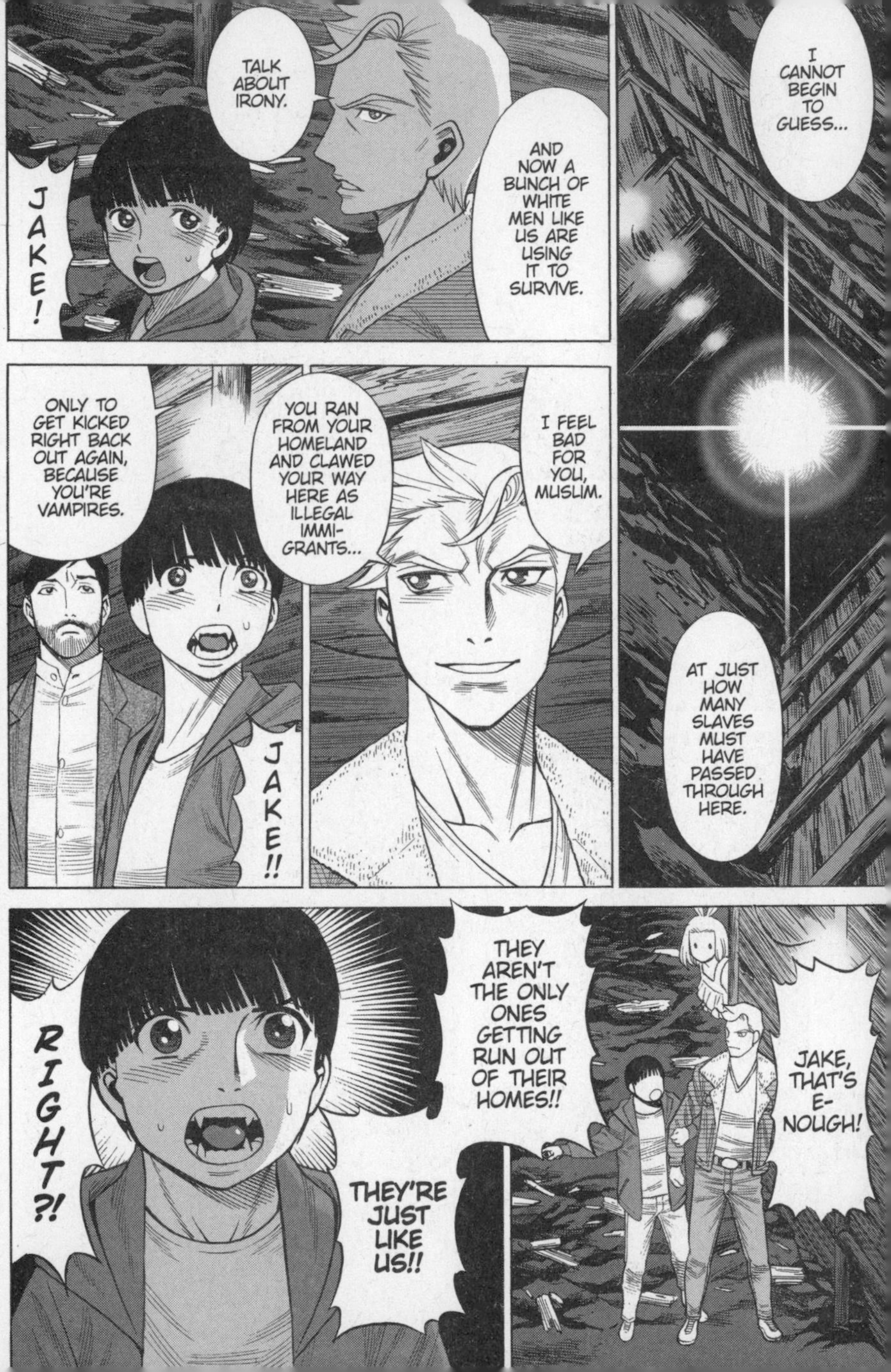

I CANNOT BEGIN TO GUESS...
AT JUST HOW MANY SLAVES MUST HAVE PASSED THROUGH HERE.
TALK ABOUT IRONY.
AND NOW A BUNCH OF WHITE MEN LIKE US ARE USING IT TO SURVIVE.
JAKE!
I FEEL BAD FOR YOU, MUSLIM.
YOU RAN FROM YOUR HOMELAND AND CLAWED YOUR WAY HERE AS ILLEGAL IMMI-GRANTS...
ONLY TO GET KICKED RIGHT BACK OUT AGAIN, BECAUSE YOU'RE VAMPIRES.
JAKE!!
JAKE, THAT'S E-NOUGH!
THEY AREN'T THE ONLY ONES GETTING RUN OUT OF THEIR HOMES!!
RIGHT?!
THEY'RE JUST LIKE US!!

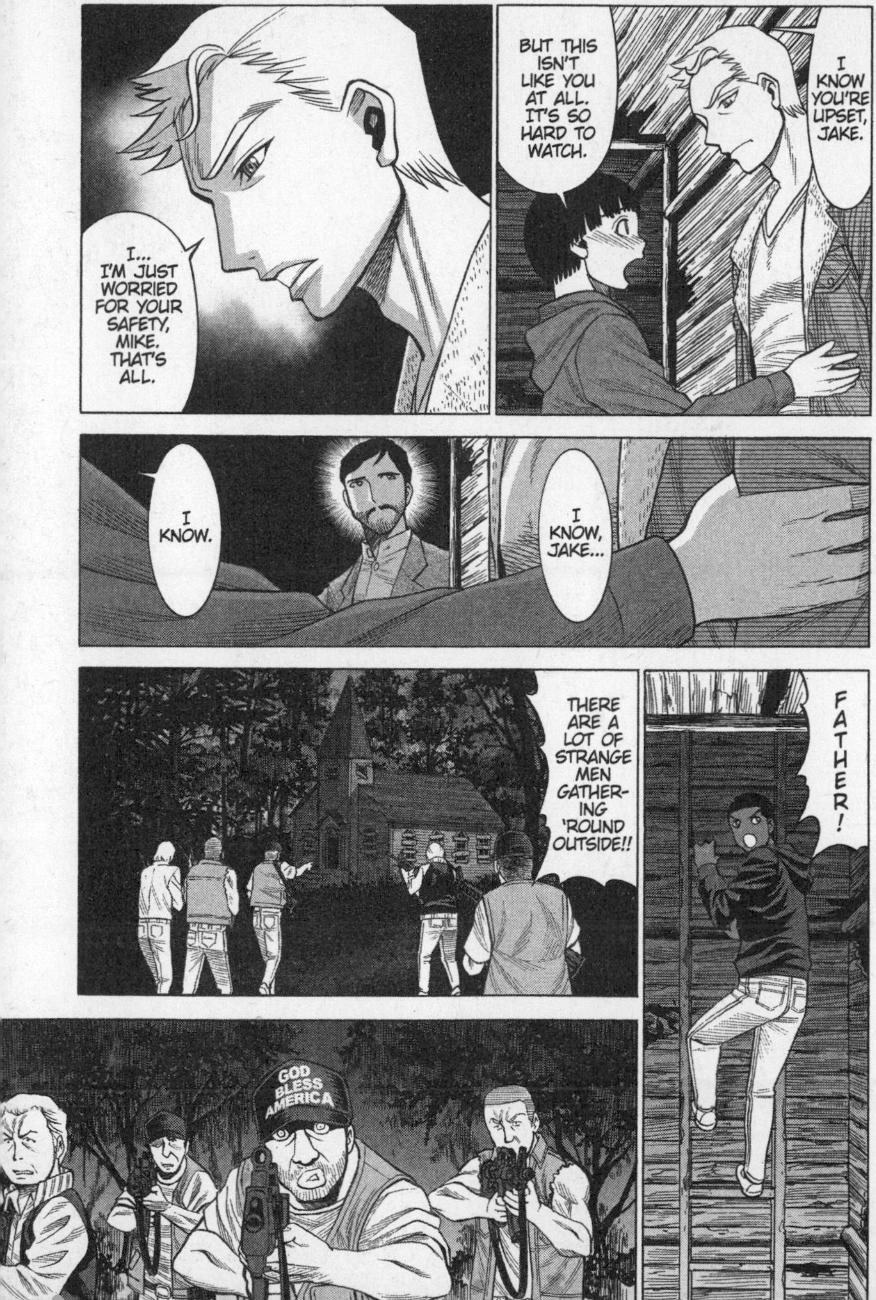
I KNOW YOU'RE UPSET, JAKE.
BUT THIS ISN'T LIKE YOU AT ALL. IT'S SO HARD TO WATCH.
I... I'M JUST WORRIED FOR YOUR SAFETY, MIKE. THAT'S ALL.
I KNOW, JAKE...
I KNOW.
FATHER!
THERE ARE A LOT OF STRANGE MEN GATHERING 'ROUND OUTSIDE!!
GOD BLESS AMERICA

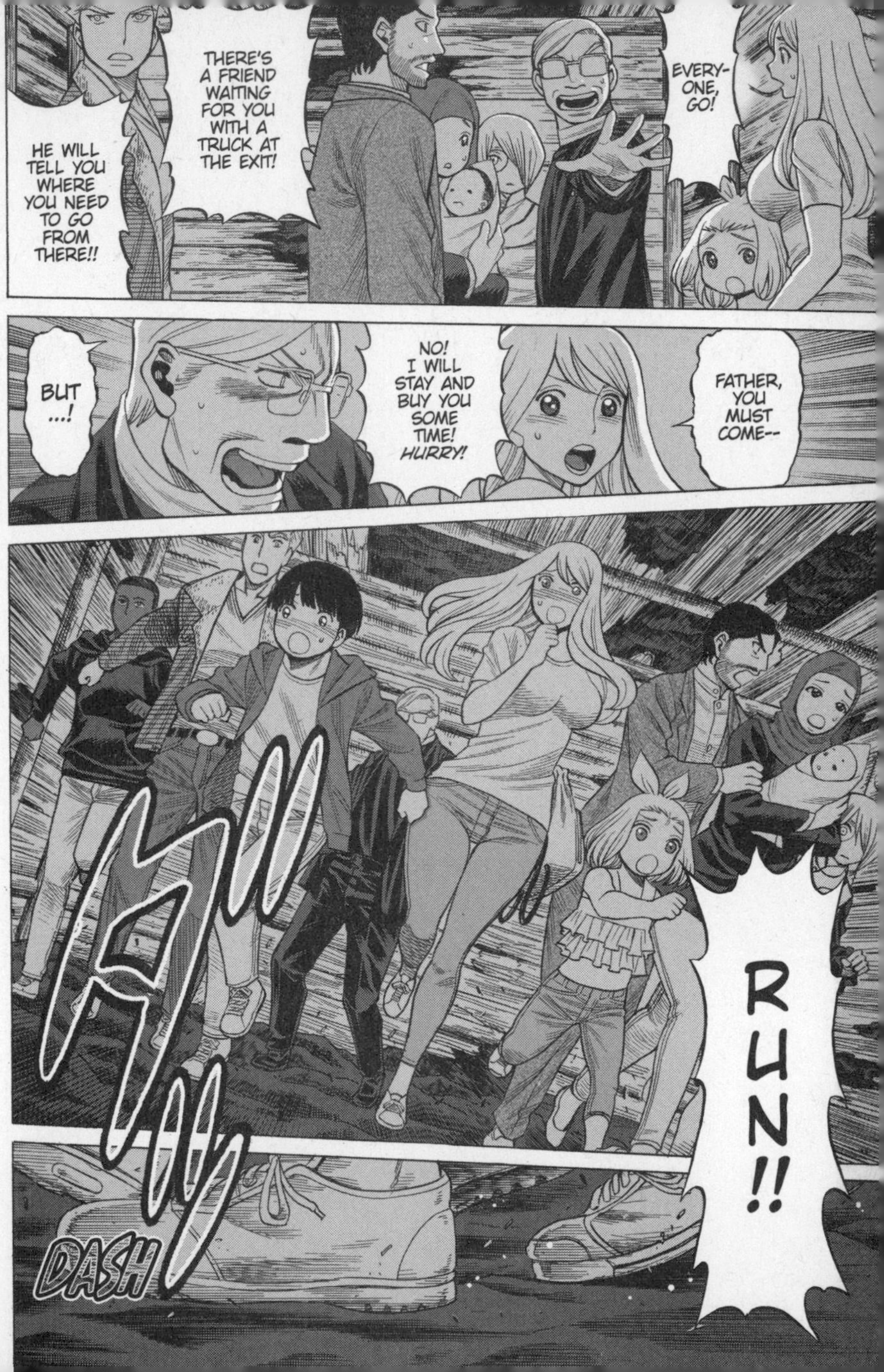
EVERY-ONE, GO!
THERE'S A FRIEND WAITING FOR YOU WITH A TRUCK AT THE EXIT!
HE WILL TELL YOU WHERE YOU NEED TO GO FROM THERE!!
FATHER, YOU MUST COME--
NO! I WILL STAY AND BUY YOU SOME TIME! *HURRY!*
BUT ...!
RUN!!
DASH

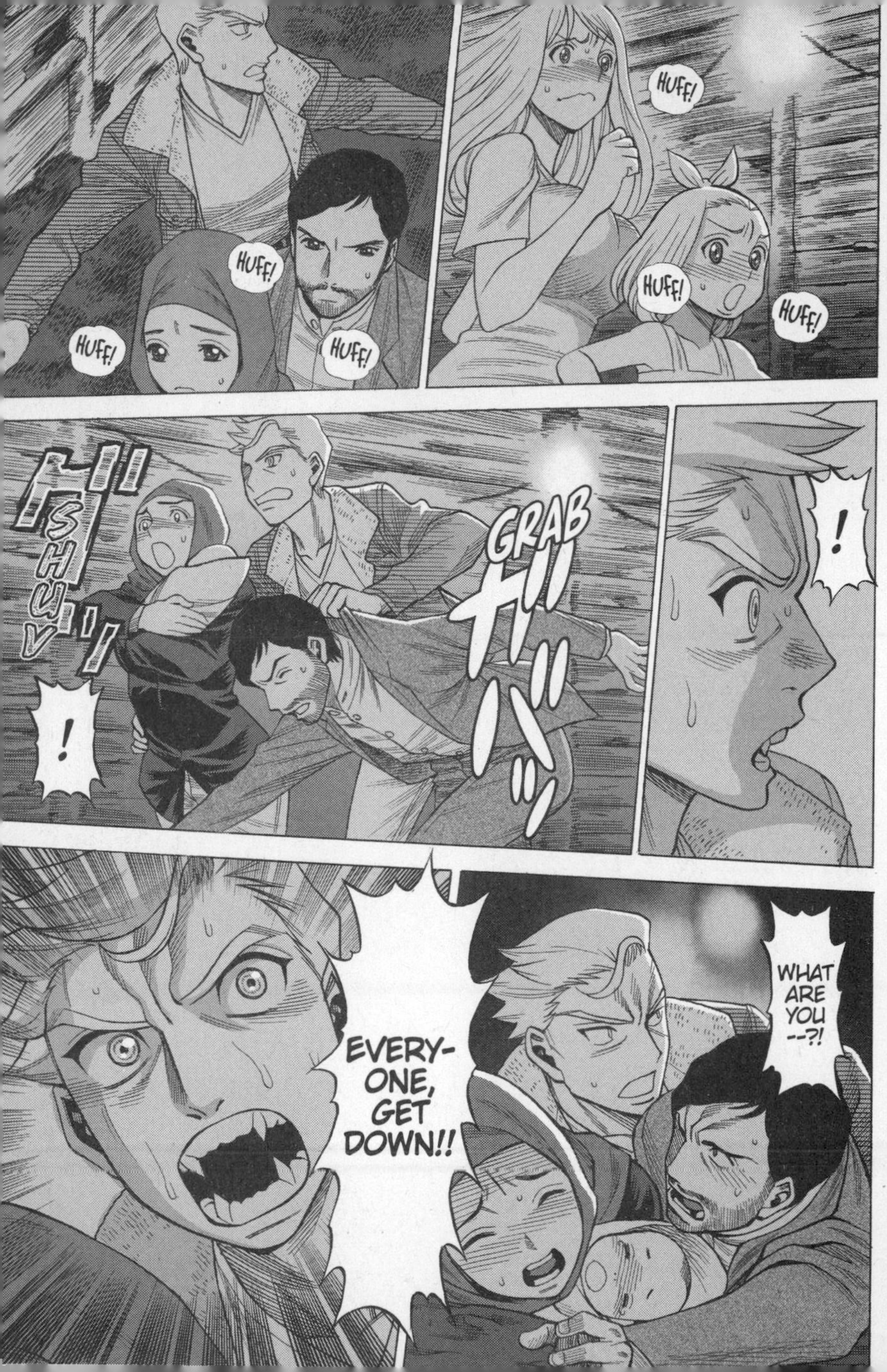
HUFF!
HUFF!
HUFF!
HUFF!
HUFF!
HUFF!
!
GRAB
SHUV
!
WHAT ARE YOU --?!
EVERY-ONE, GET DOWN!!

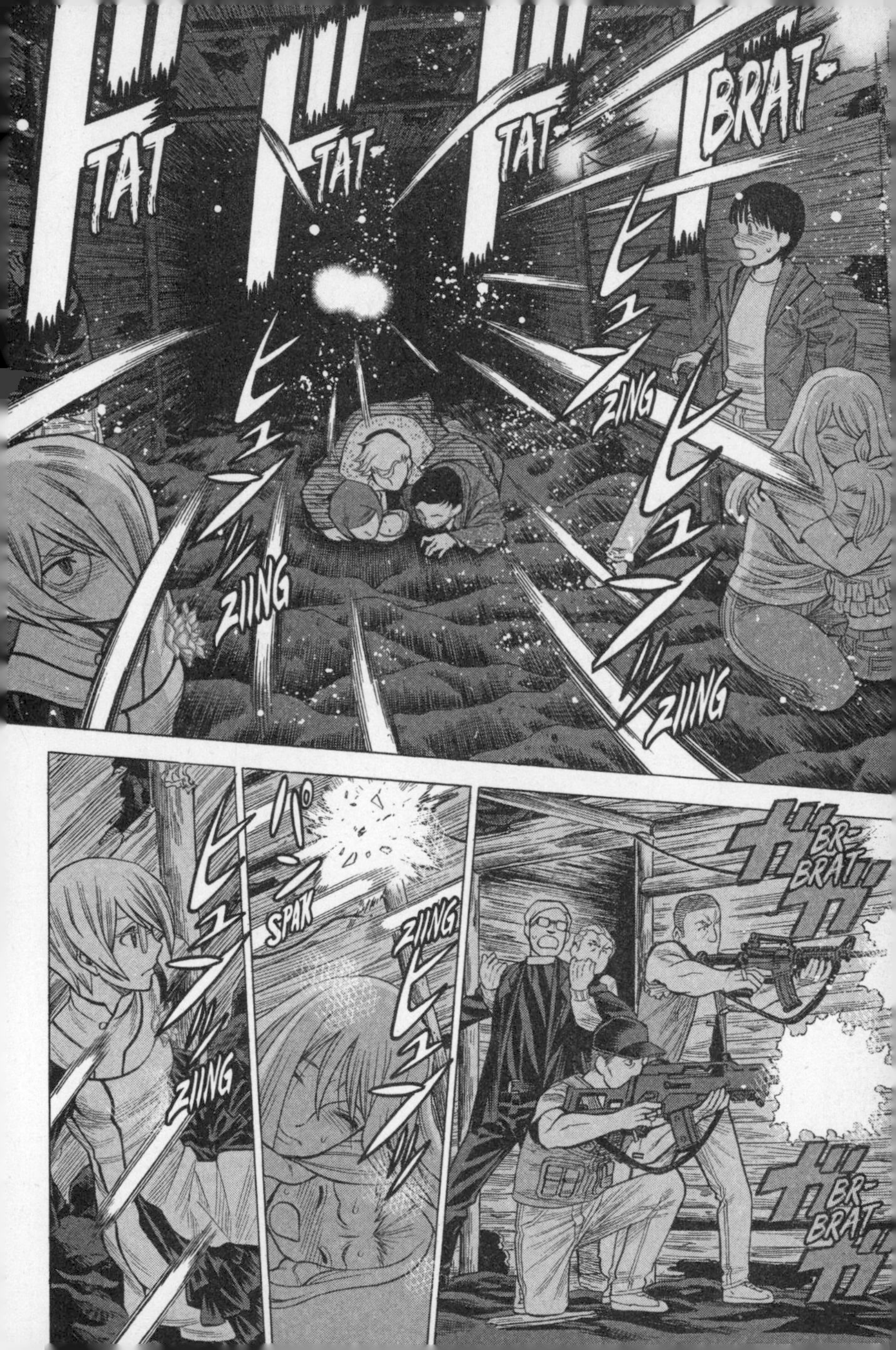

BRAT-
TAT-
TAT-
TAT
ZIING
ZIING
ZIING
BR-BRAT
BR-BRAT
ZIING
SPAK
ZIING

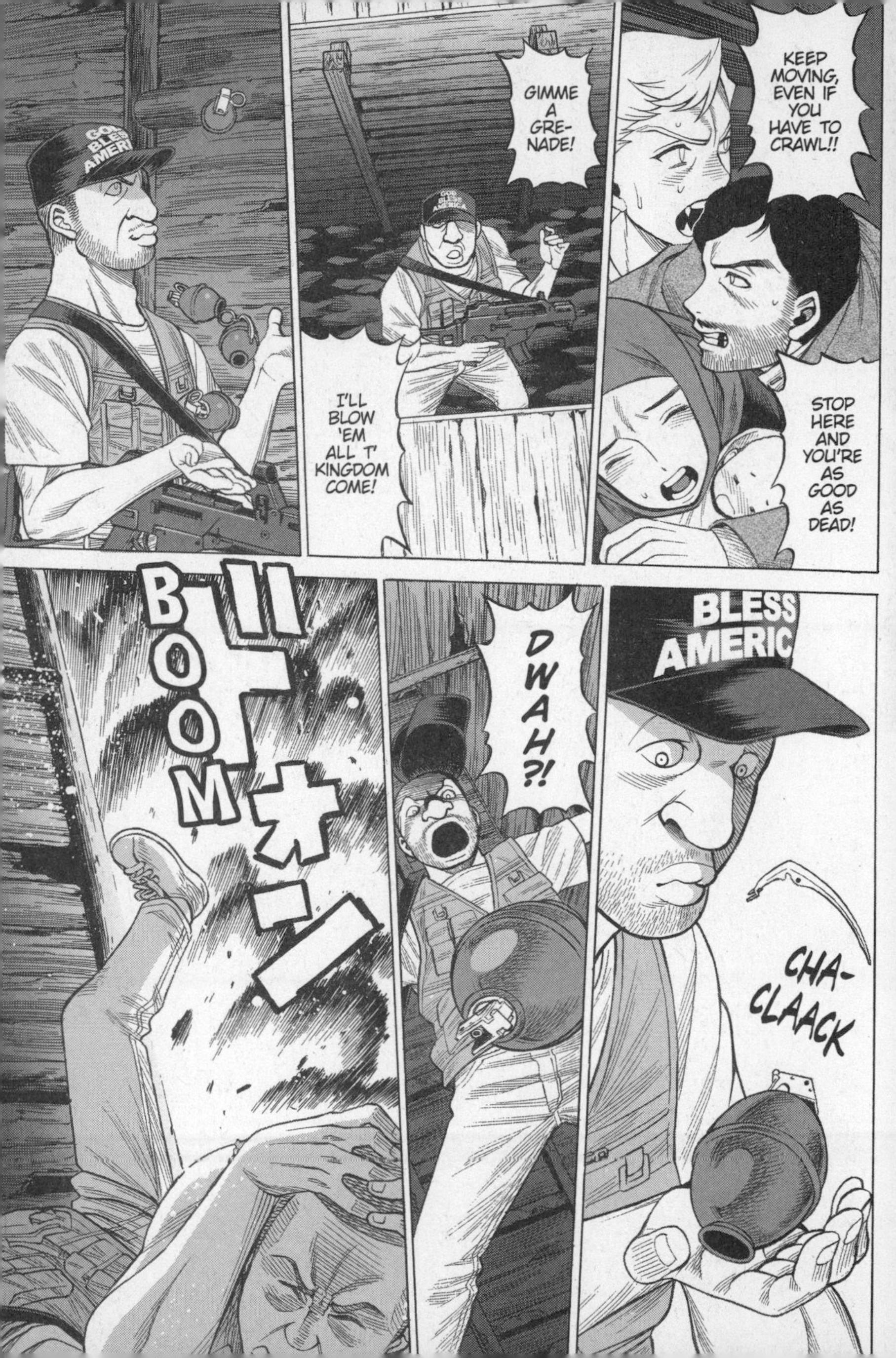
KEEP MOVING, EVEN IF YOU HAVE TO CRAWL!!
STOP HERE AND YOU'RE AS GOOD AS DEAD!
GIMME A GRE-NADE!
I'LL BLOW 'EM ALL T' KINGDOM COME!
BLESS AMERIC
CHA-CLAACK
DWAH?!
BOOM

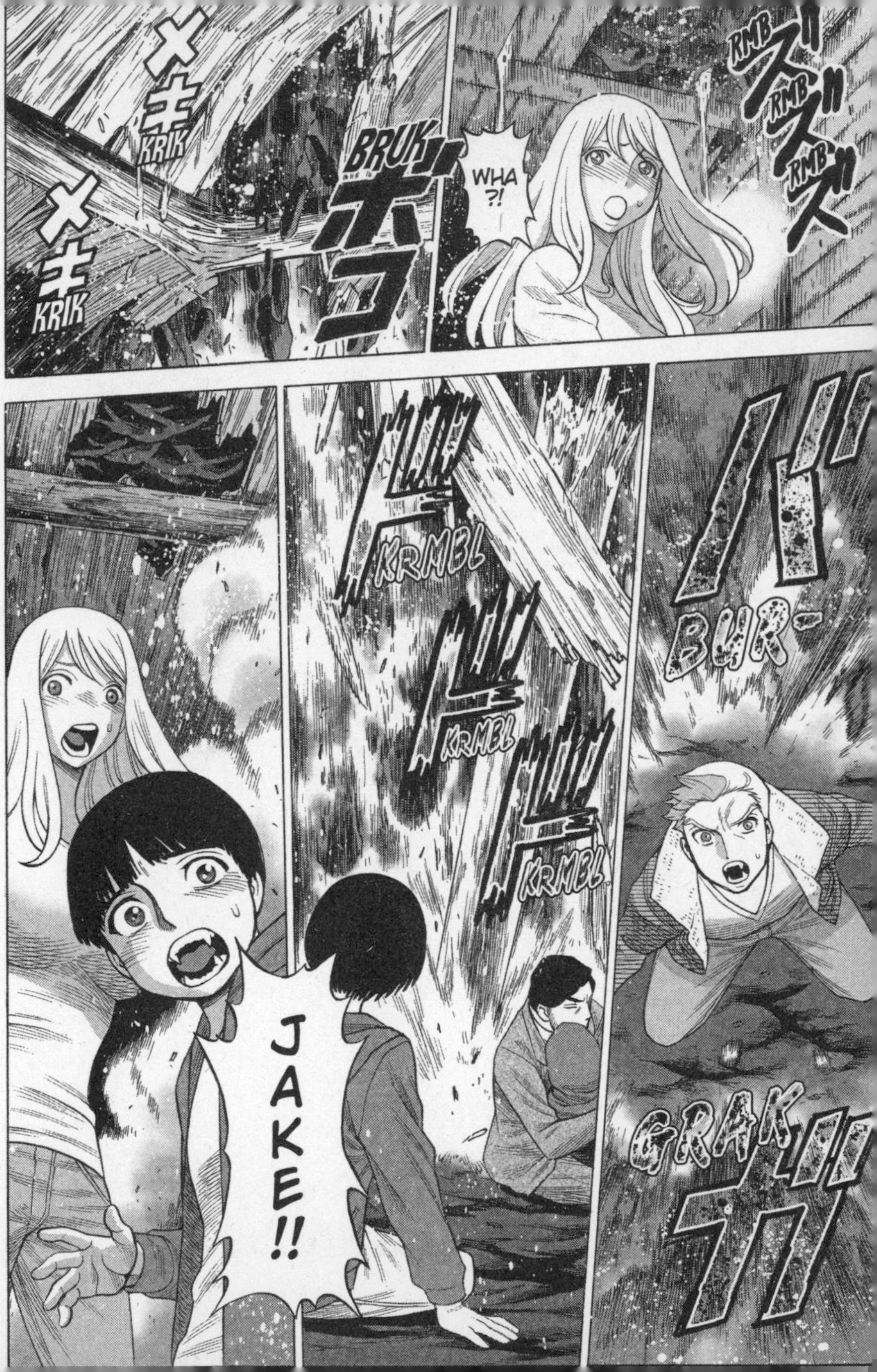
RMB
RMB
RMB
WHA ?!
KRIK
KRIK
BRUK
BUR-
GRAK
KRMBL
KRMBL
KRMBL
JAKE!!

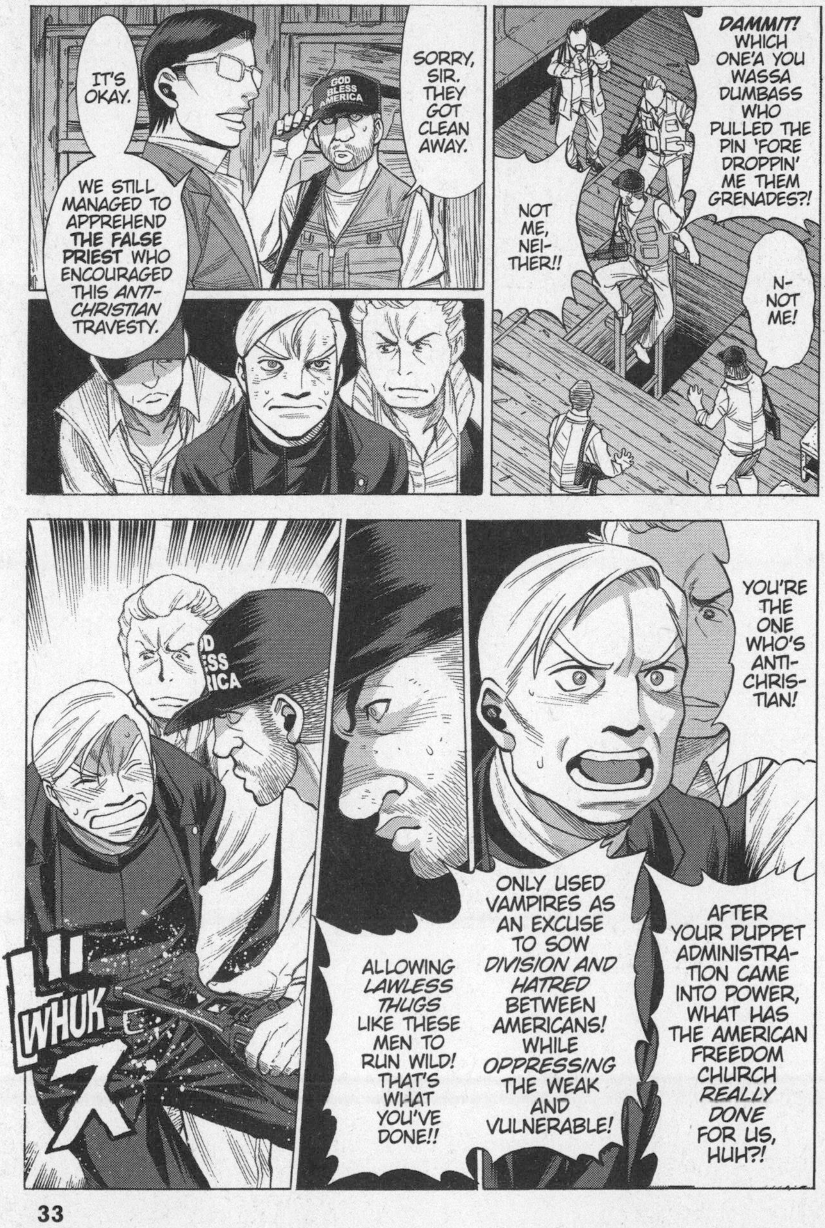
DAMMIT! WHICH ONE'A YOU WASSA DUMBASS WHO PULLED THE PIN 'FORE DROPPIN' ME THEM GRENADES?!
NOT ME, NEITHER!!
N-NOT ME!
SORRY, SIR. THEY GOT CLEAN AWAY.
GOD BLESS AMERICA
IT'S OKAY.
WE STILL MANAGED TO APPREHEND THE FALSE PRIEST WHO ENCOURAGED THIS ANTI-CHRISTIAN TRAVESTY.
YOU'RE THE ONE WHO'S ANTI-CHRISTIAN!
AFTER YOUR PUPPET ADMINISTRATION CAME INTO POWER, WHAT HAS THE AMERICAN FREEDOM CHURCH REALLY DONE FOR US, HUH?!
ONLY USED VAMPIRES AS AN EXCUSE TO SOW DIVISION AND HATRED BETWEEN AMERICANS! WHILE OPPRESSING THE WEAK AND VULNERABLE!
ALLOWING LAWLESS THUGS LIKE THESE MEN TO RUN WILD! THAT'S WHAT YOU'VE DONE!!
WHUK

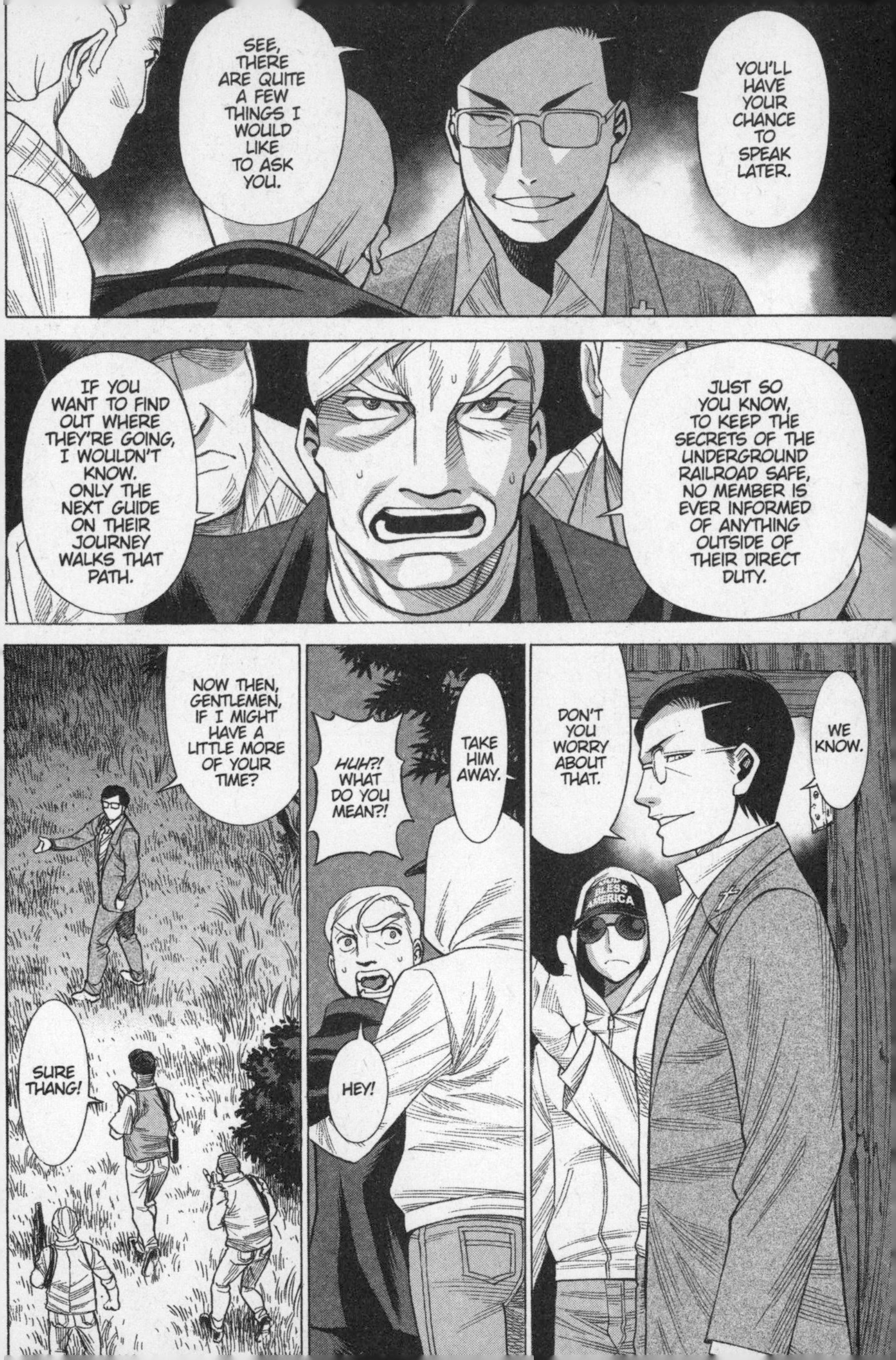
YOU'LL HAVE YOUR CHANCE TO SPEAK LATER.
SEE, THERE ARE QUITE A FEW THINGS I WOULD LIKE TO ASK YOU.
JUST SO YOU KNOW, TO KEEP THE SECRETS OF THE UNDERGROUND RAILROAD SAFE, NO MEMBER IS EVER INFORMED OF ANYTHING OUTSIDE OF THEIR DIRECT DUTY.
IF YOU WANT TO FIND OUT WHERE THEY'RE GOING, I WOULDN'T KNOW. ONLY THE NEXT GUIDE ON THEIR JOURNEY WALKS THAT PATH.
WE KNOW.
DON'T YOU WORRY ABOUT THAT.
GOD BLESS AMERICA
TAKE HIM AWAY.
HUH?! WHAT DO YOU MEAN?!
HEY!
NOW THEN, GENTLEMEN, IF I MIGHT HAVE A LITTLE MORE OF YOUR TIME?
SURE THANG!

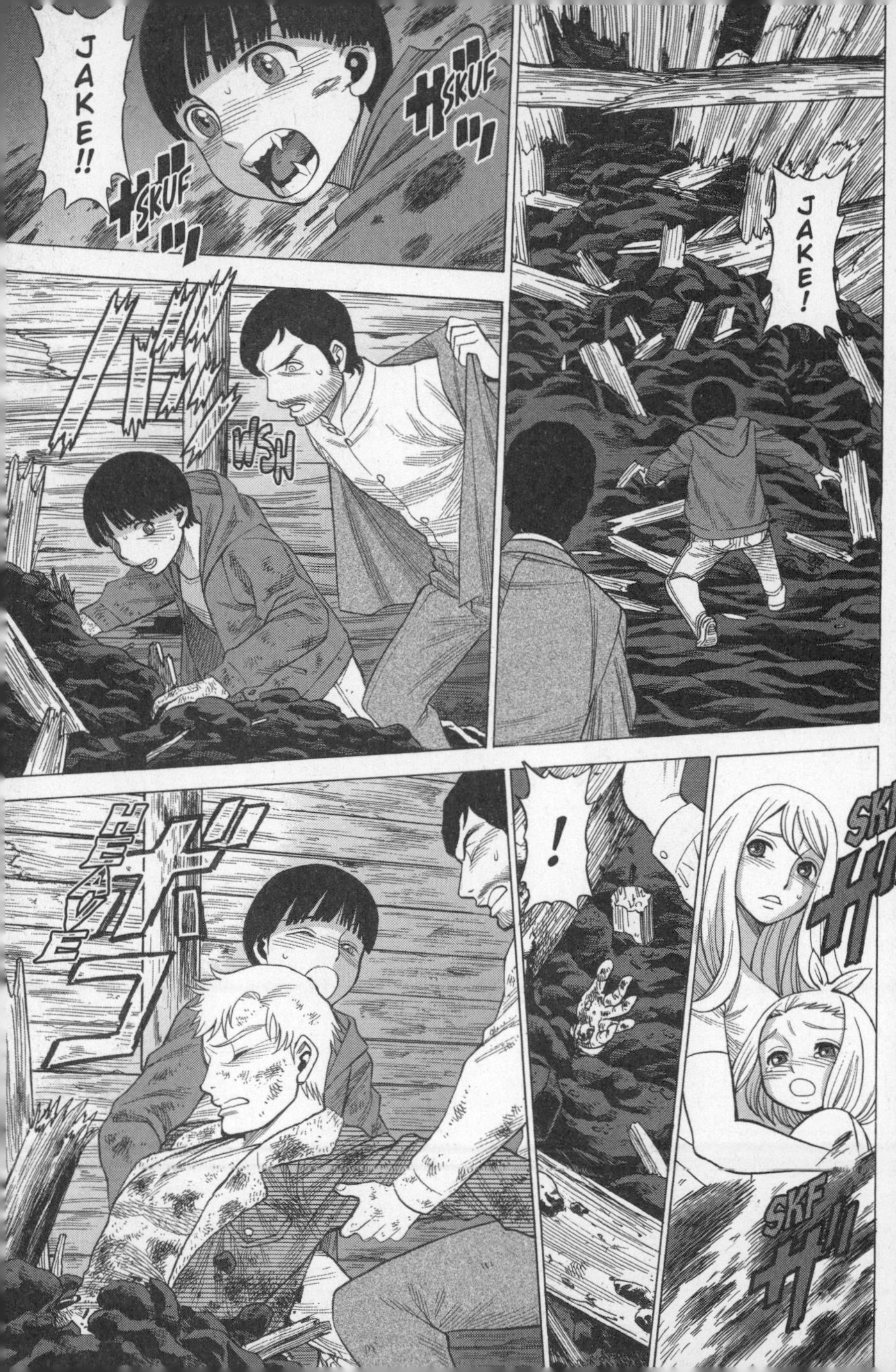
JAKE!
JAKE!!
SKUF
SKUF
WSH
SKF
SKF
!
HEAVE

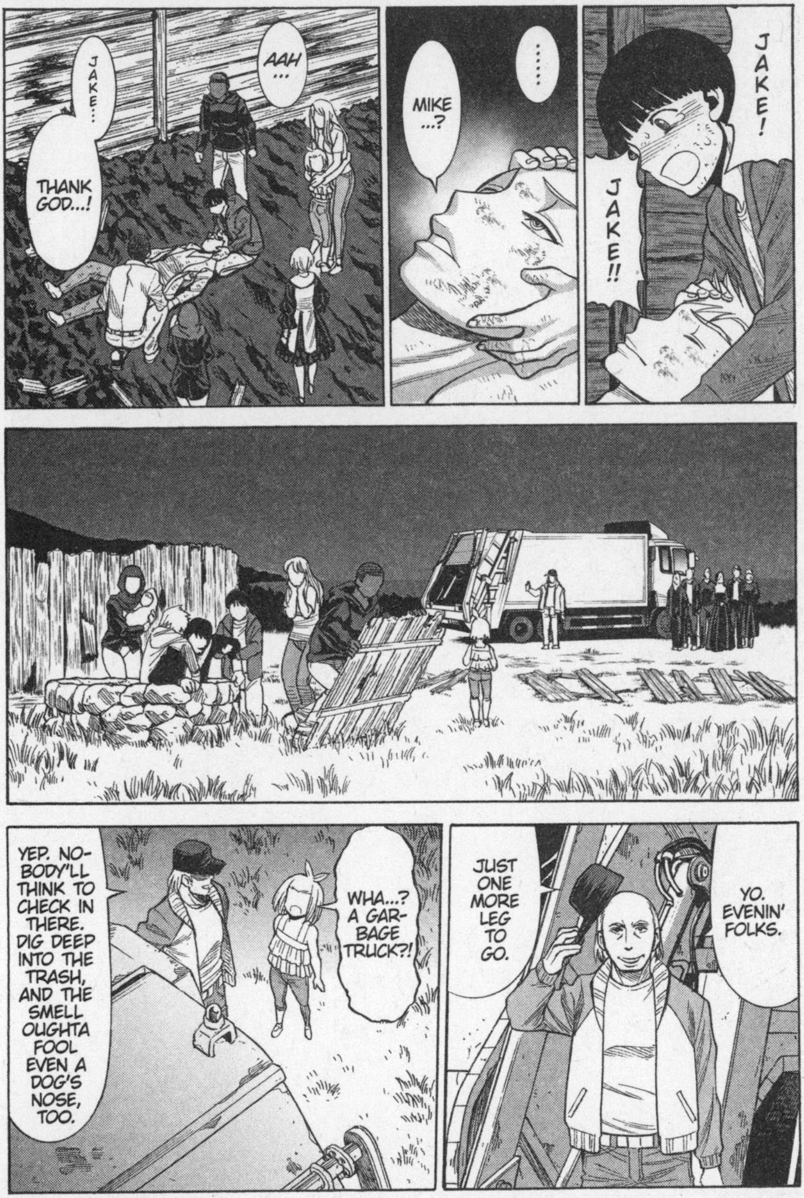
JAKE! JAKE!!
......
MIKE...?
AAH...
JAKE...
THANK GOD...!
YO. EVENIN' FOLKS.
JUST ONE MORE LEG TO GO.
WHA...? A GAR-BAGE TRUCK?!
YEP. NO-BODY'LL THINK TO CHECK IN THERE. DIG DEEP INTO THE TRASH, AND THE SMELL OUGHTA FOOL EVEN A DOG'S NOSE, TOO.

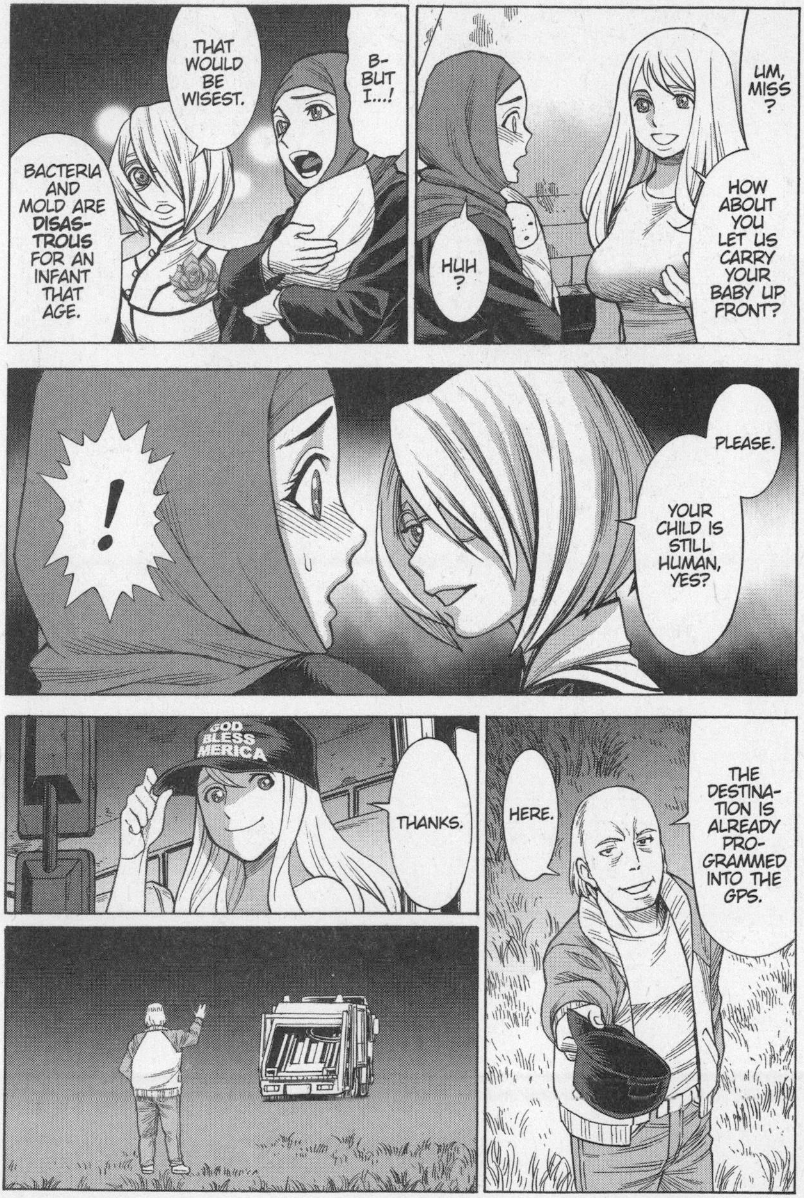
UM, MISS?
HOW ABOUT YOU LET US CARRY YOUR BABY UP FRONT?
HUH?
B-BUT I...!
THAT WOULD BE WISEST.
BACTERIA AND MOLD ARE DISASTROUS FOR AN INFANT THAT AGE.
PLEASE.
YOUR CHILD IS STILL HUMAN, YES?
!
THE DESTINATION IS ALREADY PROGRAMMED INTO THE GPS.
HERE.
GOD BLESS MERICA
THANKS.

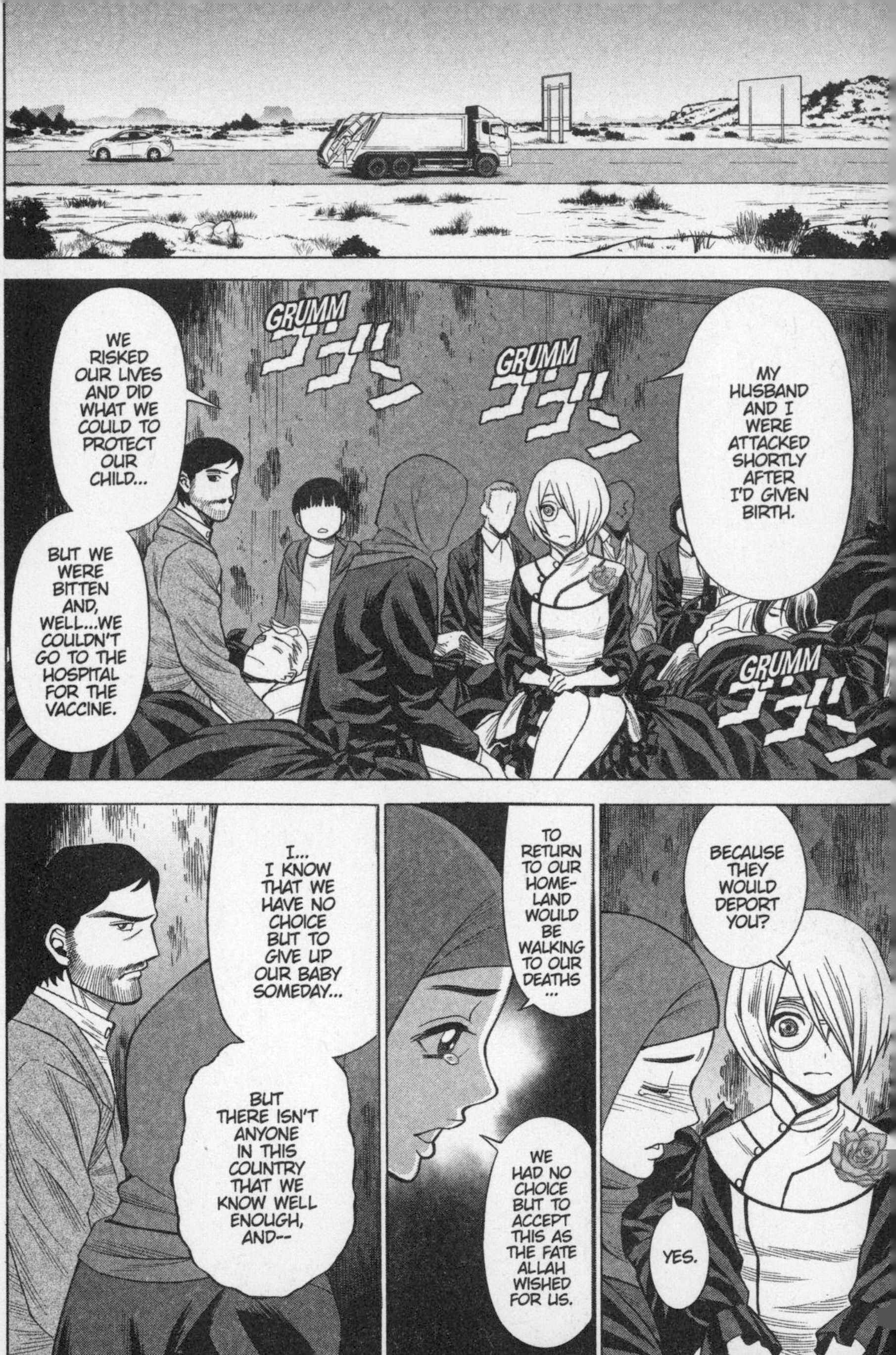
MY HUSBAND AND I WERE ATTACKED SHORTLY AFTER I'D GIVEN BIRTH.
GRUMM ゴゴン
GRUMM ゴゴン
GRUMM ゴゴン
WE RISKED OUR LIVES AND DID WHAT WE COULD TO PROTECT OUR CHILD...
BUT WE WERE BITTEN AND, WELL...WE COULDN'T GO TO THE HOSPITAL FOR THE VACCINE.
BECAUSE THEY WOULD DEPORT YOU?
YES.
TO RETURN TO OUR HOME-LAND WOULD BE WALKING TO OUR DEATHS...
WE HAD NO CHOICE BUT TO ACCEPT THIS AS THE FATE ALLAH WISHED FOR US.
I... I KNOW THAT WE HAVE NO CHOICE BUT TO GIVE UP OUR BABY SOMEDAY...
BUT THERE ISN'T ANYONE IN THIS COUNTRY THAT WE KNOW WELL ENOUGH, AND--

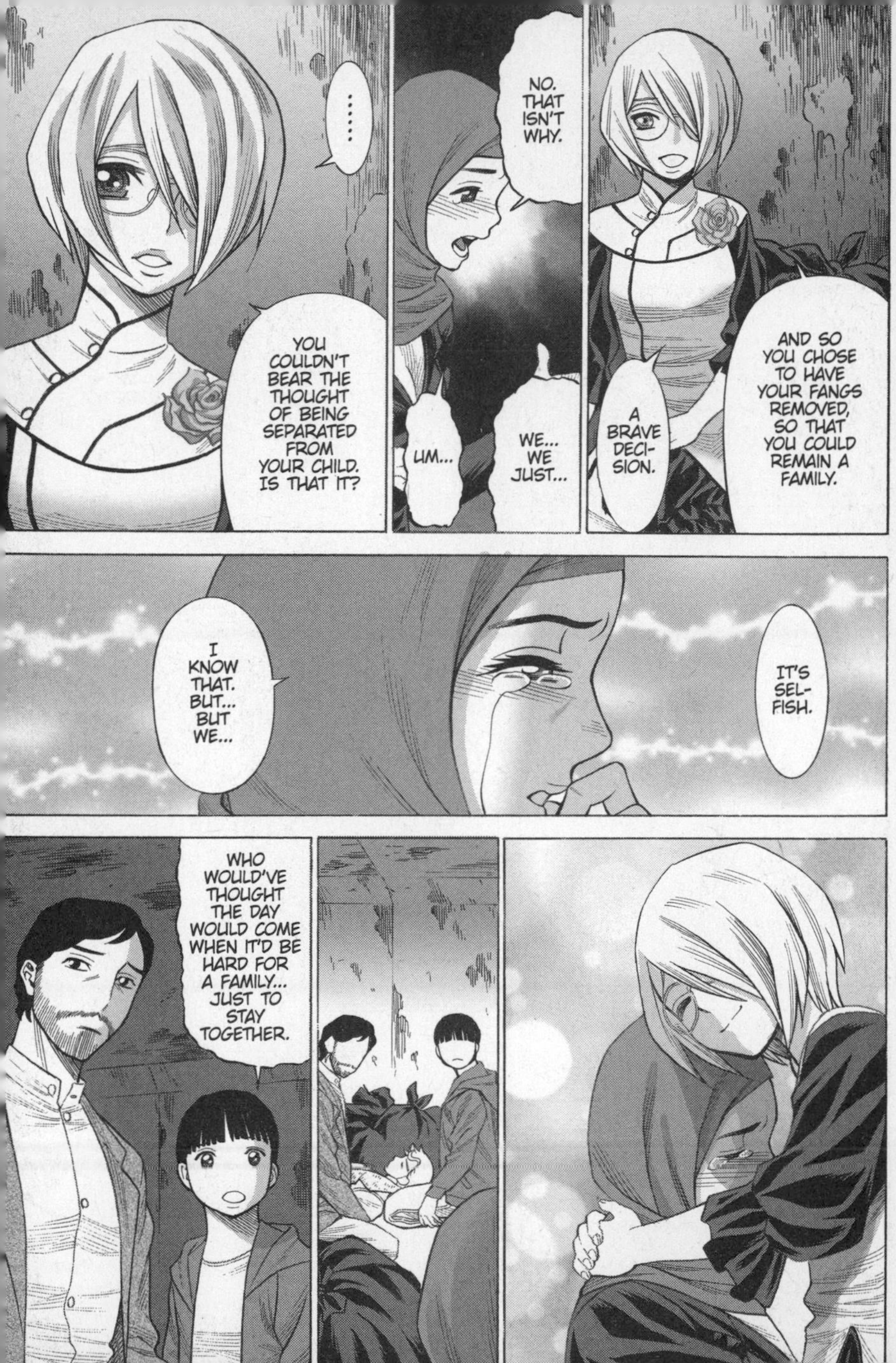
AND SO YOU CHOSE TO HAVE YOUR FANGS REMOVED, SO THAT YOU COULD REMAIN A FAMILY.
A BRAVE DECI-SION.
NO. THAT ISN'T WHY.
WE... WE JUST...
UM...
......
YOU COULDN'T BEAR THE THOUGHT OF BEING SEPARATED FROM YOUR CHILD. IS THAT IT?
IT'S SEL-FISH.
I KNOW THAT. BUT... BUT WE...
WHO WOULD'VE THOUGHT THE DAY WOULD COME WHEN IT'D BE HARD FOR A FAMILY... JUST TO STAY TOGETHER.

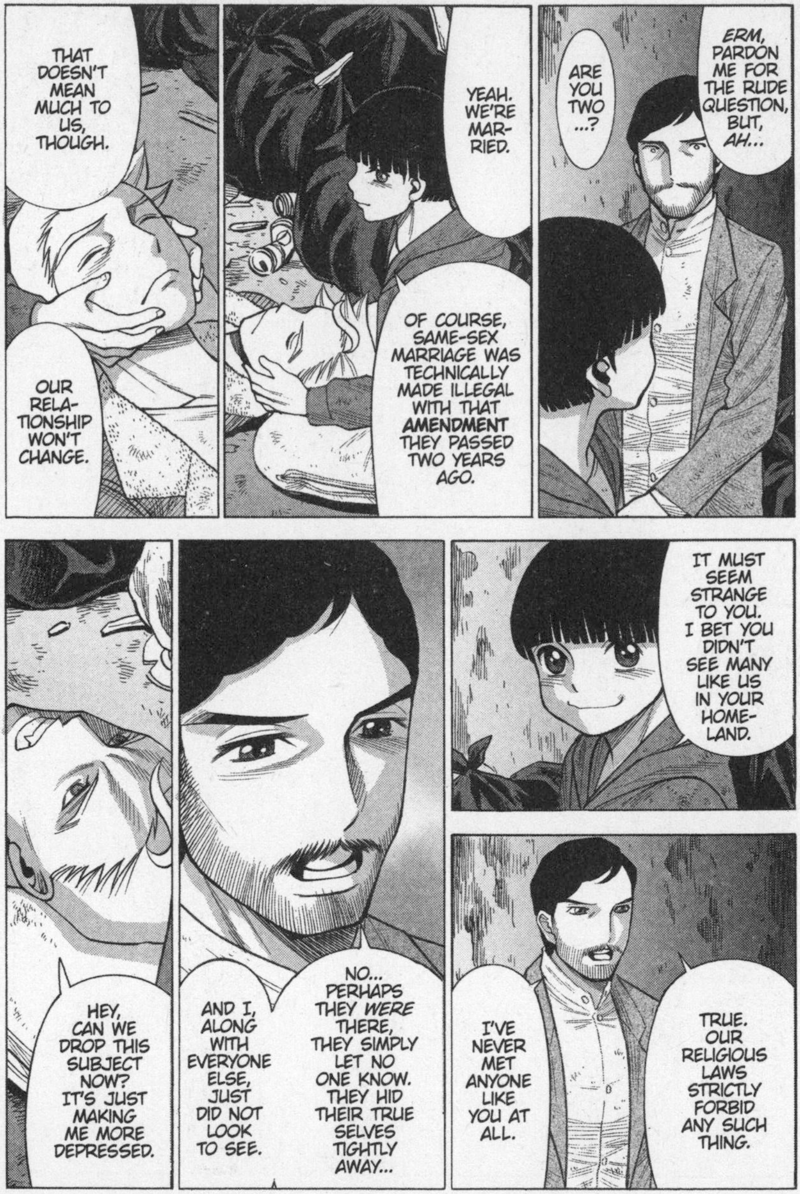
ERM, PARDON ME FOR THE RUDE QUESTION, BUT, AH...
ARE YOU TWO ...?
YEAH. WE'RE MARRIED.
OF COURSE, SAME-SEX MARRIAGE WAS TECHNICALLY MADE ILLEGAL WITH THAT **AMENDMENT** THEY PASSED TWO YEARS AGO.
THAT DOESN'T MEAN MUCH TO US, THOUGH.
OUR RELATIONSHIP WON'T CHANGE.
IT MUST SEEM STRANGE TO YOU. I BET YOU DIDN'T SEE MANY LIKE US IN YOUR HOMELAND.
TRUE. OUR RELIGIOUS LAWS STRICTLY FORBID ANY SUCH THING.
I'VE NEVER MET ANYONE LIKE YOU AT ALL.
NO... PERHAPS THEY *WERE* THERE, THEY SIMPLY LET NO ONE KNOW. THEY HID THEIR TRUE SELVES TIGHTLY AWAY...
AND I, ALONG WITH EVERYONE ELSE, JUST DID NOT LOOK TO SEE.
HEY, CAN WE DROP THIS SUBJECT NOW? IT'S JUST MAKING ME MORE DEPRESSED.

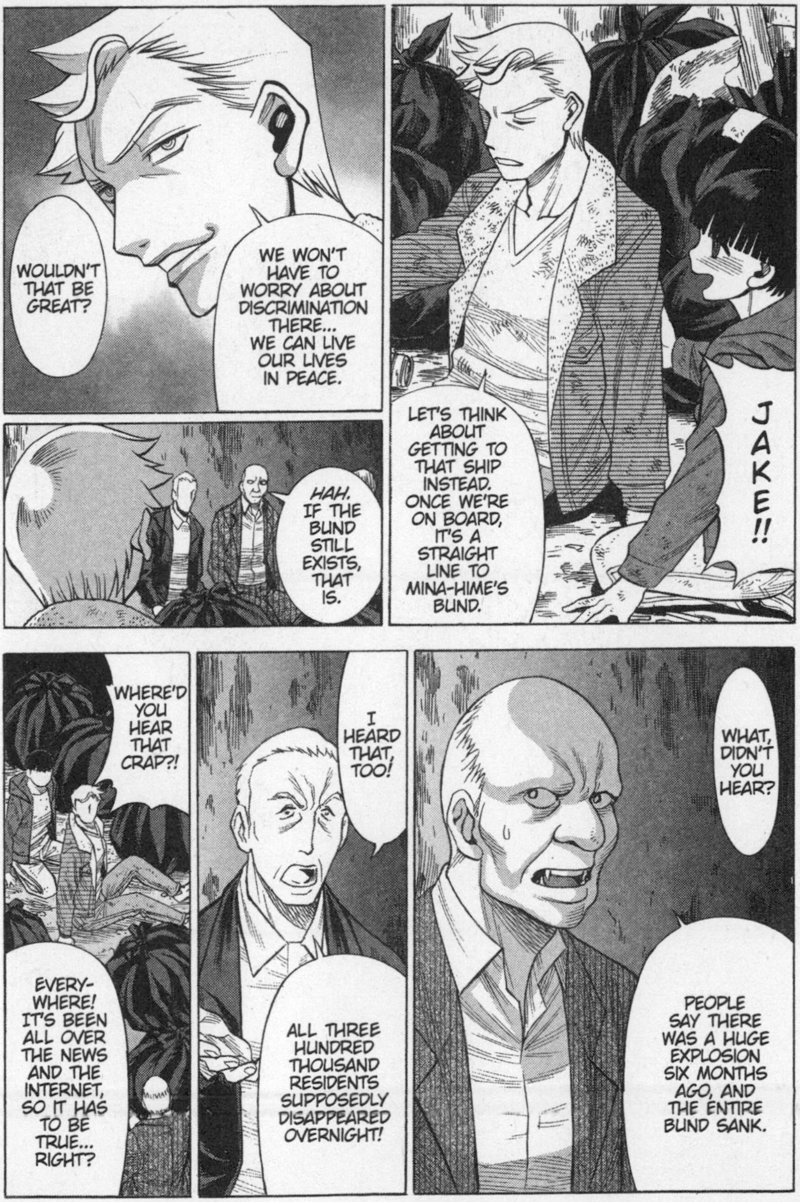
JAKE!!
LET'S THINK ABOUT GETTING TO THAT SHIP INSTEAD. ONCE WE'RE ON BOARD, IT'S A STRAIGHT LINE TO MINA-HIME'S BUND.
WE WON'T HAVE TO WORRY ABOUT DISCRIMINATION THERE... WE CAN LIVE OUR LIVES IN PEACE.
WOULDN'T THAT BE GREAT?
HAH. IF THE BUND STILL EXISTS, THAT IS.
WHAT, DIDN'T YOU HEAR?
PEOPLE SAY THERE WAS A HUGE EXPLOSION SIX MONTHS AGO, AND THE ENTIRE BUND SANK.
I HEARD THAT, TOO!
ALL THREE HUNDRED THOUSAND RESIDENTS SUPPOSEDLY DISAPPEARED OVERNIGHT!
WHERE'D YOU HEAR THAT CRAP?!
EVERY-WHERE! IT'S BEEN ALL OVER THE NEWS AND THE INTERNET, SO IT HAS TO BE TRUE... RIGHT?

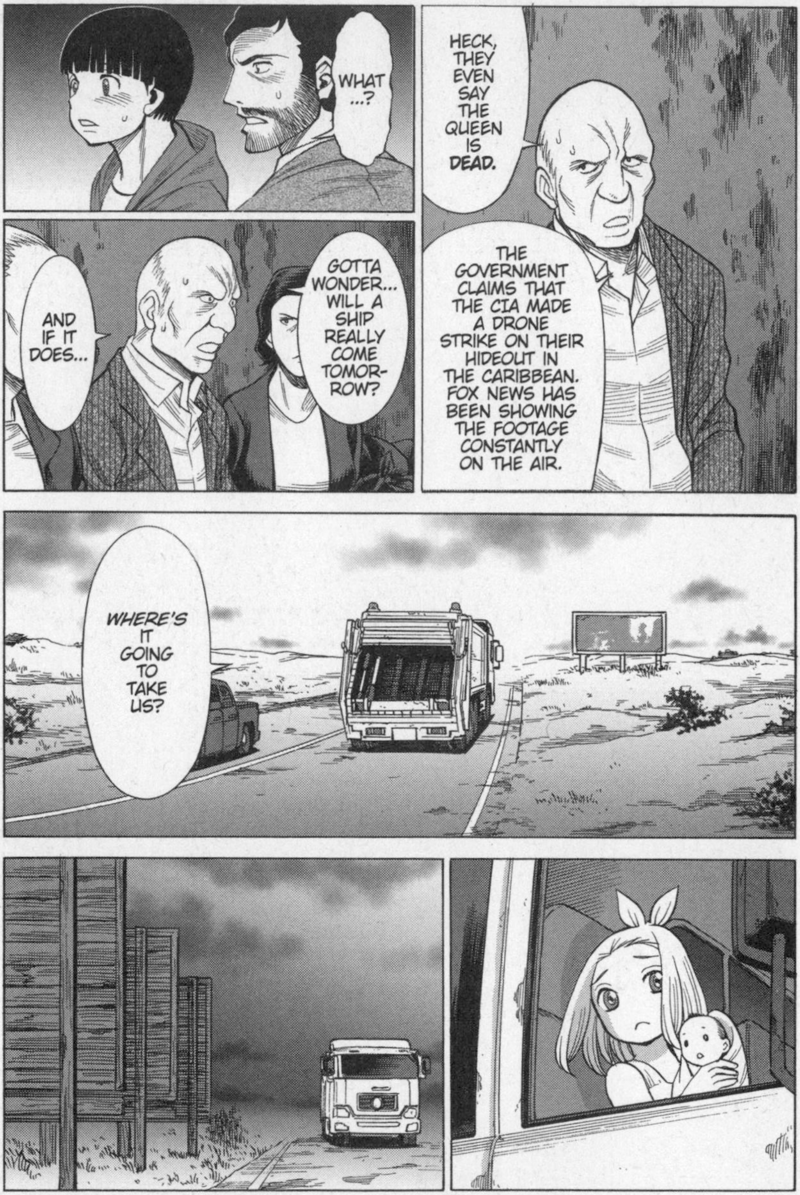
HECK, THEY EVEN SAY THE QUEEN IS DEAD.
THE GOVERNMENT CLAIMS THAT THE CIA MADE A DRONE STRIKE ON THEIR HIDEOUT IN THE CARIBBEAN. FOX NEWS HAS BEEN SHOWING THE FOOTAGE CONSTANTLY ON THE AIR.
WHAT ...?
GOTTA WONDER... WILL A SHIP REALLY COME TOMORROW?
AND IF IT DOES...
WHERE'S IT GOING TO TAKE US?

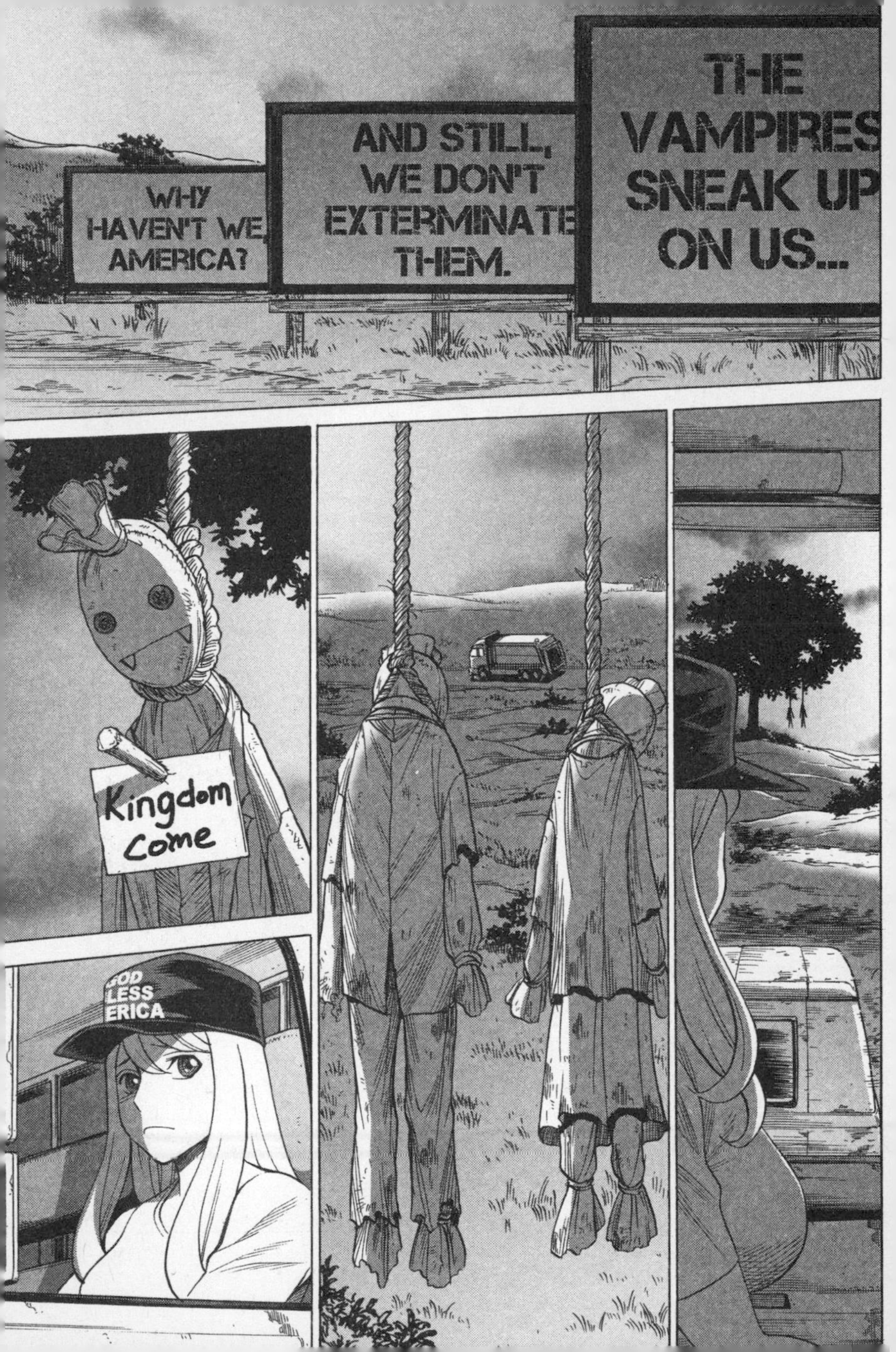
THE VAMPIRES SNEAK UP ON US...
AND STILL, WE DON'T EXTERMINATE THEM.
WHY HAVEN'T WE, AMERICA?
Kingdom Come
GOD LESS ERICA

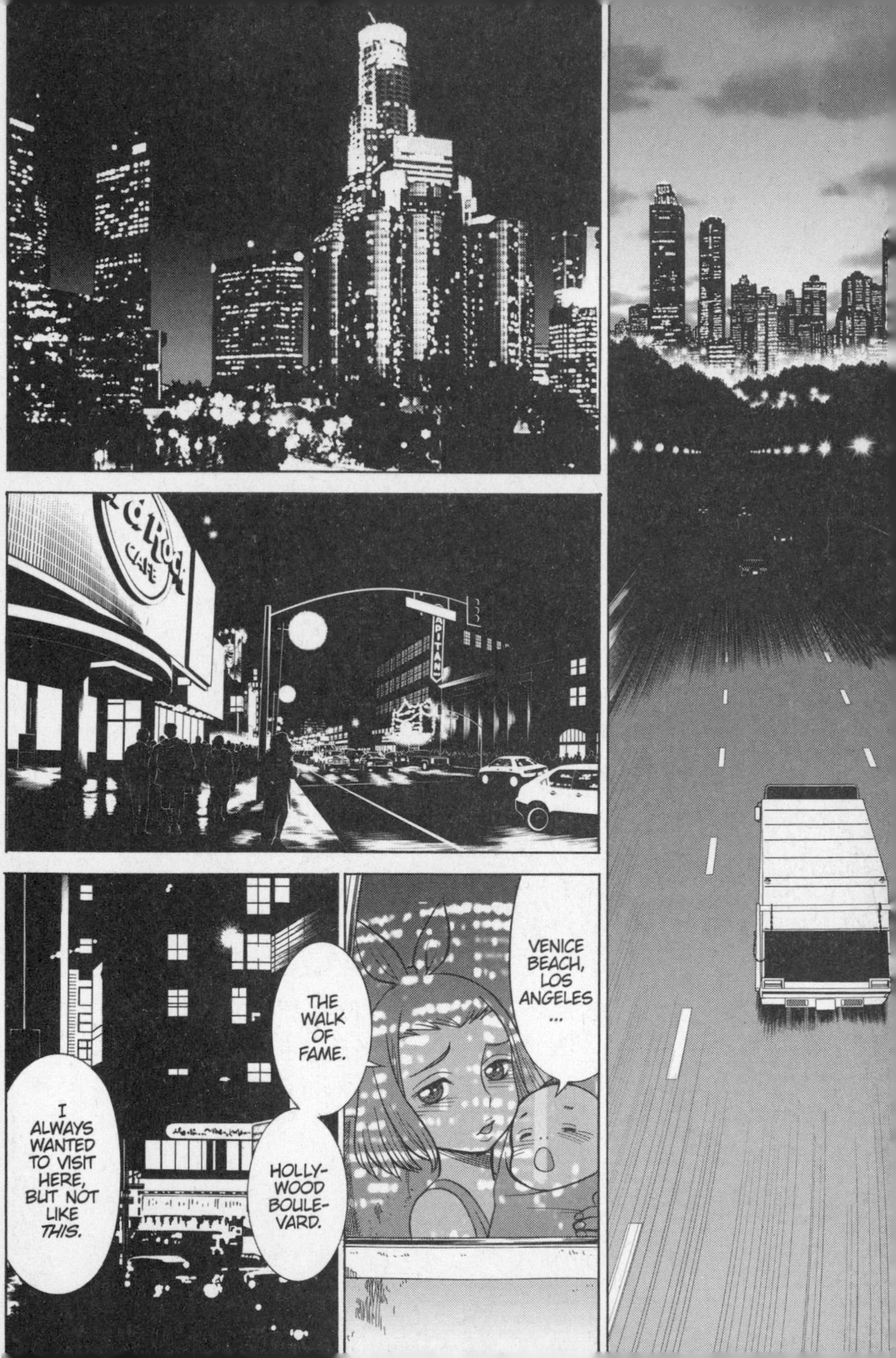
VENICE BEACH, LOS ANGELES ...
THE WALK OF FAME.
HOLLY-WOOD BOULE-VARD.
I ALWAYS WANTED TO VISIT HERE, BUT NOT LIKE *THIS*.

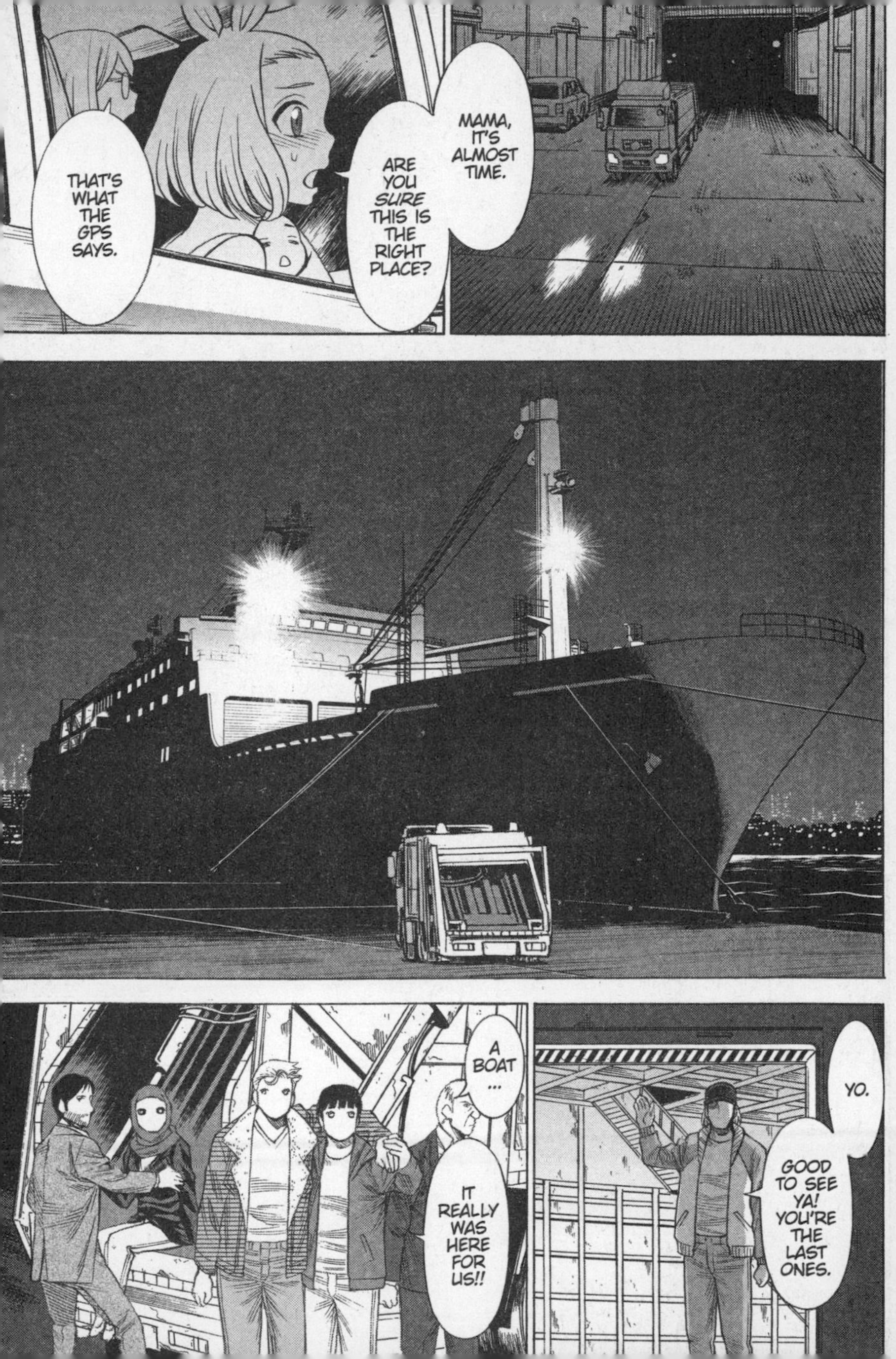
MAMA, IT'S ALMOST TIME.
ARE YOU *SURE* THIS IS THE RIGHT PLACE?
THAT'S WHAT THE GPS SAYS.
YO.
GOOD TO SEE YA! YOU'RE THE LAST ONES.
A BOAT...
IT REALLY WAS HERE FOR US!!

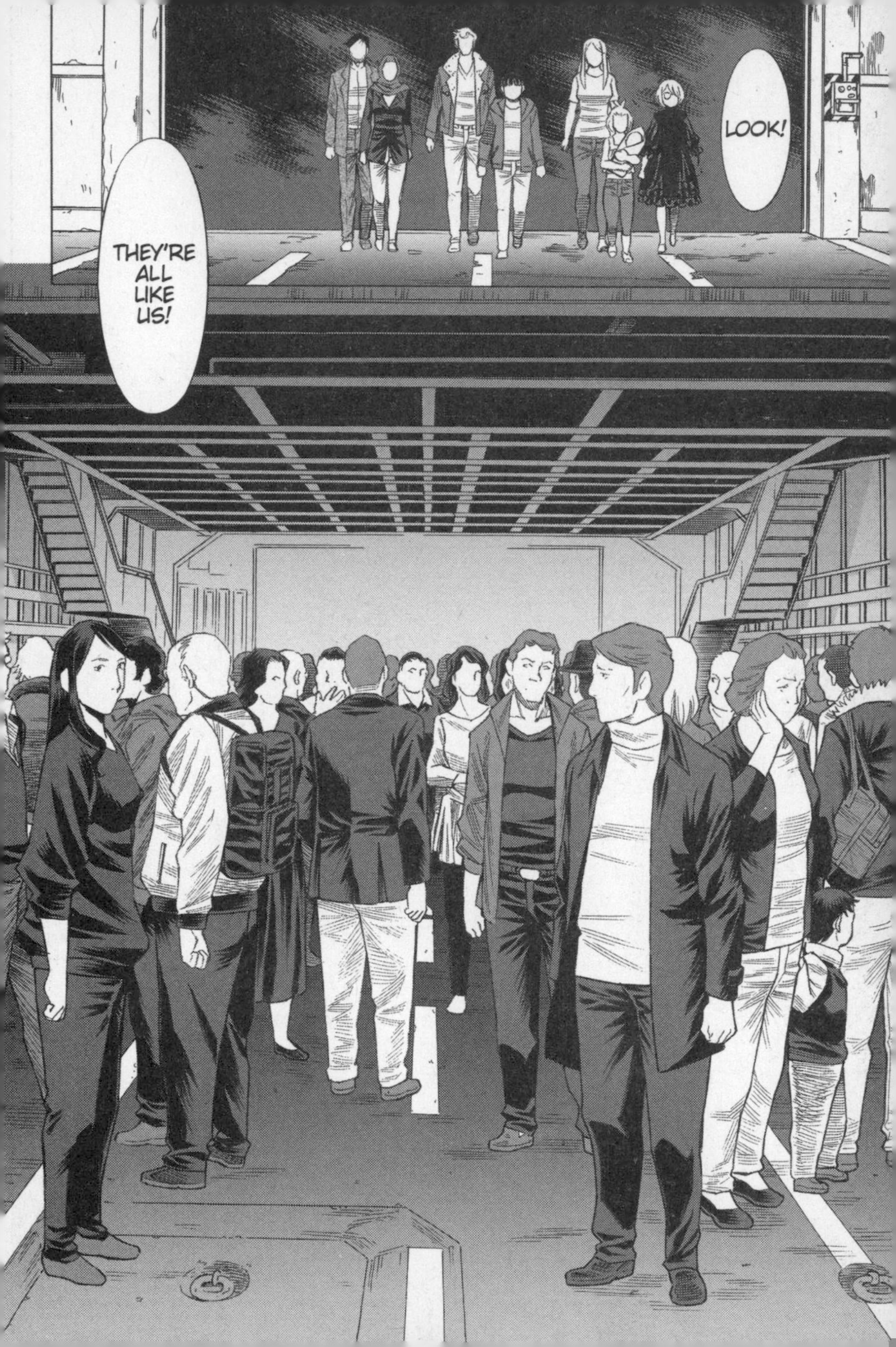
LOOK!
THEY'RE ALL LIKE US!

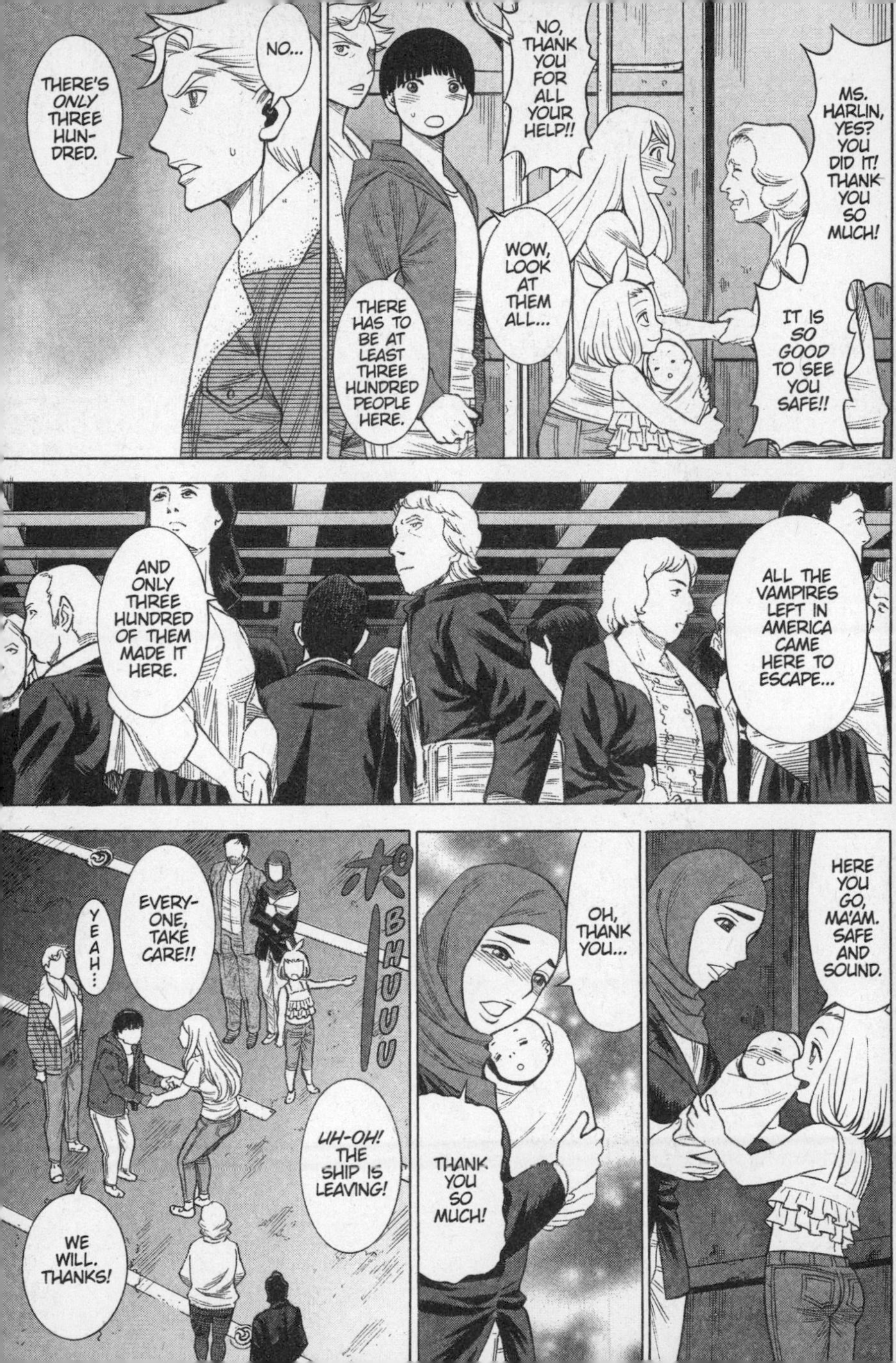
MS. HARLIN, YES? YOU DID IT! THANK YOU SO MUCH!
IT IS SO GOOD TO SEE YOU SAFE!!
NO, THANK YOU FOR ALL YOUR HELP!!
WOW, LOOK AT THEM ALL...
THERE HAS TO BE AT LEAST THREE HUNDRED PEOPLE HERE.
NO...
THERE'S ONLY THREE HUN-DRED.
ALL THE VAMPIRES LEFT IN AMERICA CAME HERE TO ESCAPE...
AND ONLY THREE HUNDRED OF THEM MADE IT HERE.
HERE YOU GO, MA'AM. SAFE AND SOUND.
OH, THANK YOU...
THANK YOU SO MUCH!
BHUUUU
UH-OH! THE SHIP IS LEAVING!
EVERY-ONE, TAKE CARE!!
YEAH...
WE WILL. THANKS!

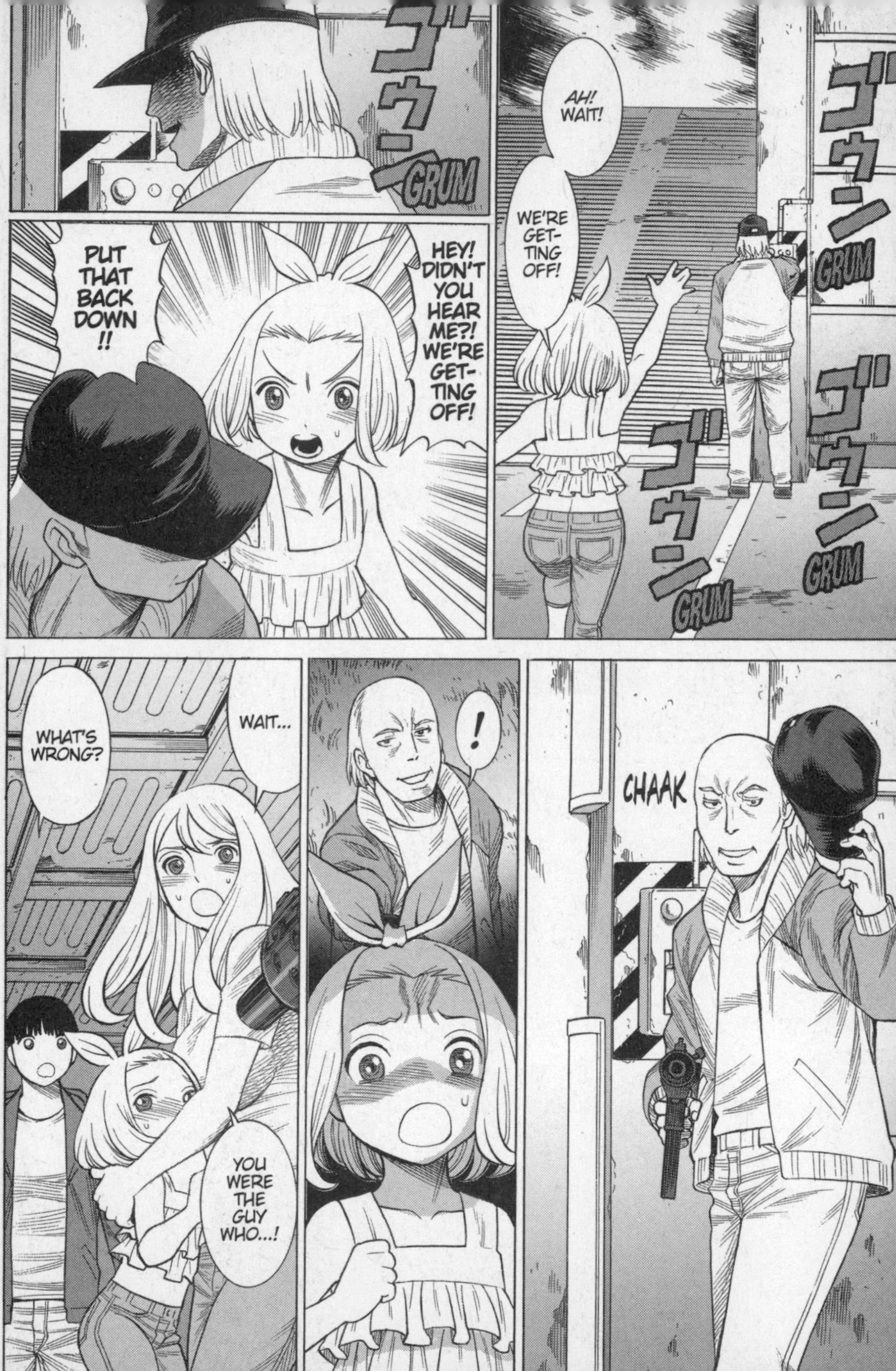
AH! WAIT!
WE'RE GET-TING OFF!
ゴウン
GRUM
ゴウン
GRUM
ゴウン
GRUM
ゴウー
GRUM
HEY! DIDN'T YOU HEAR ME?! WE'RE GET-TING OFF!
PUT THAT BACK DOWN!!
CHAAK
!
WAIT...
WHAT'S WRONG?
YOU WERE THE GUY WHO...!

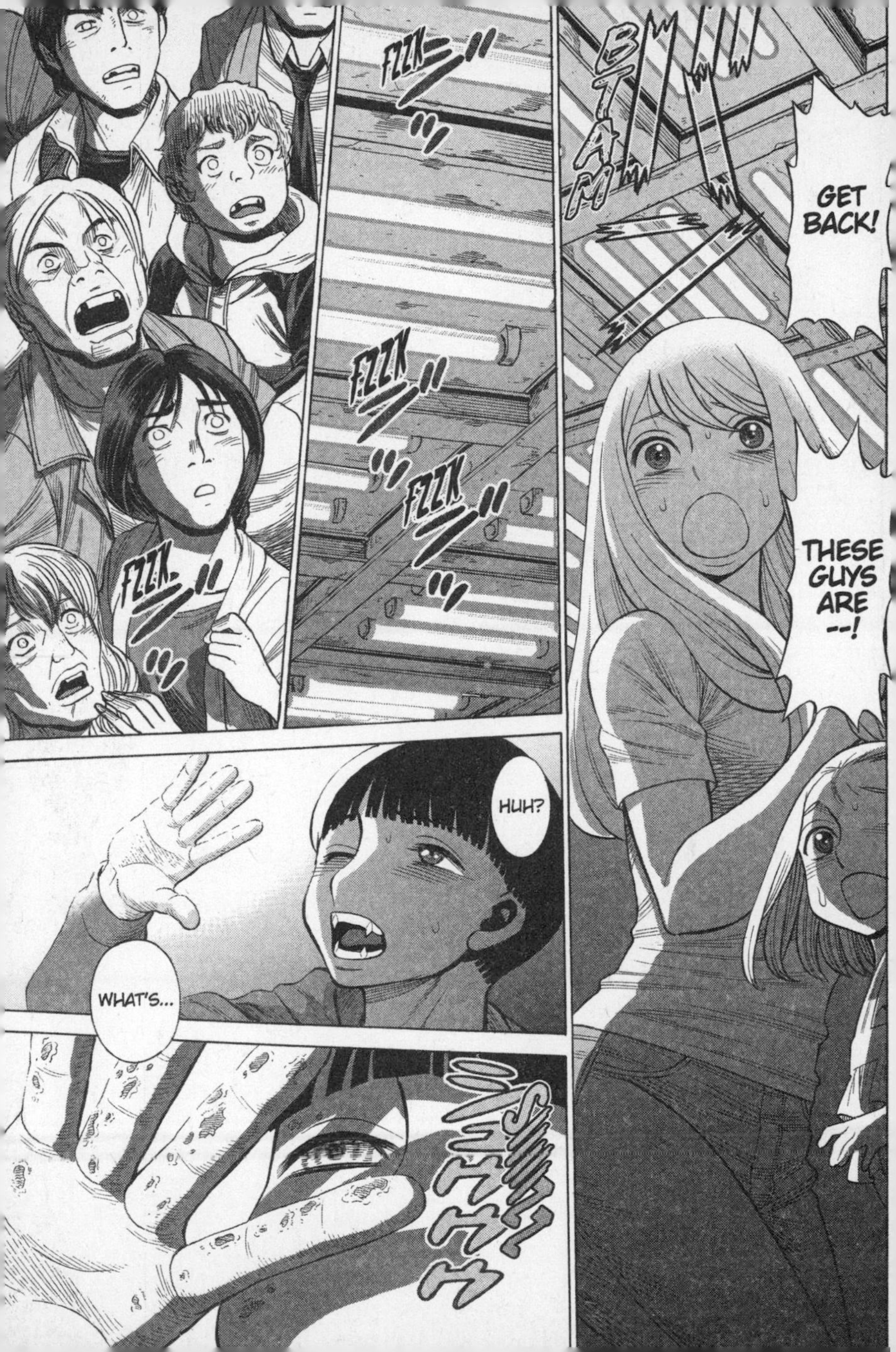
BLAM
GET BACK!
THESE GUYS ARE --!
FZZK
FZZK
FZZK
FZZK
HUH?
WHAT'S...

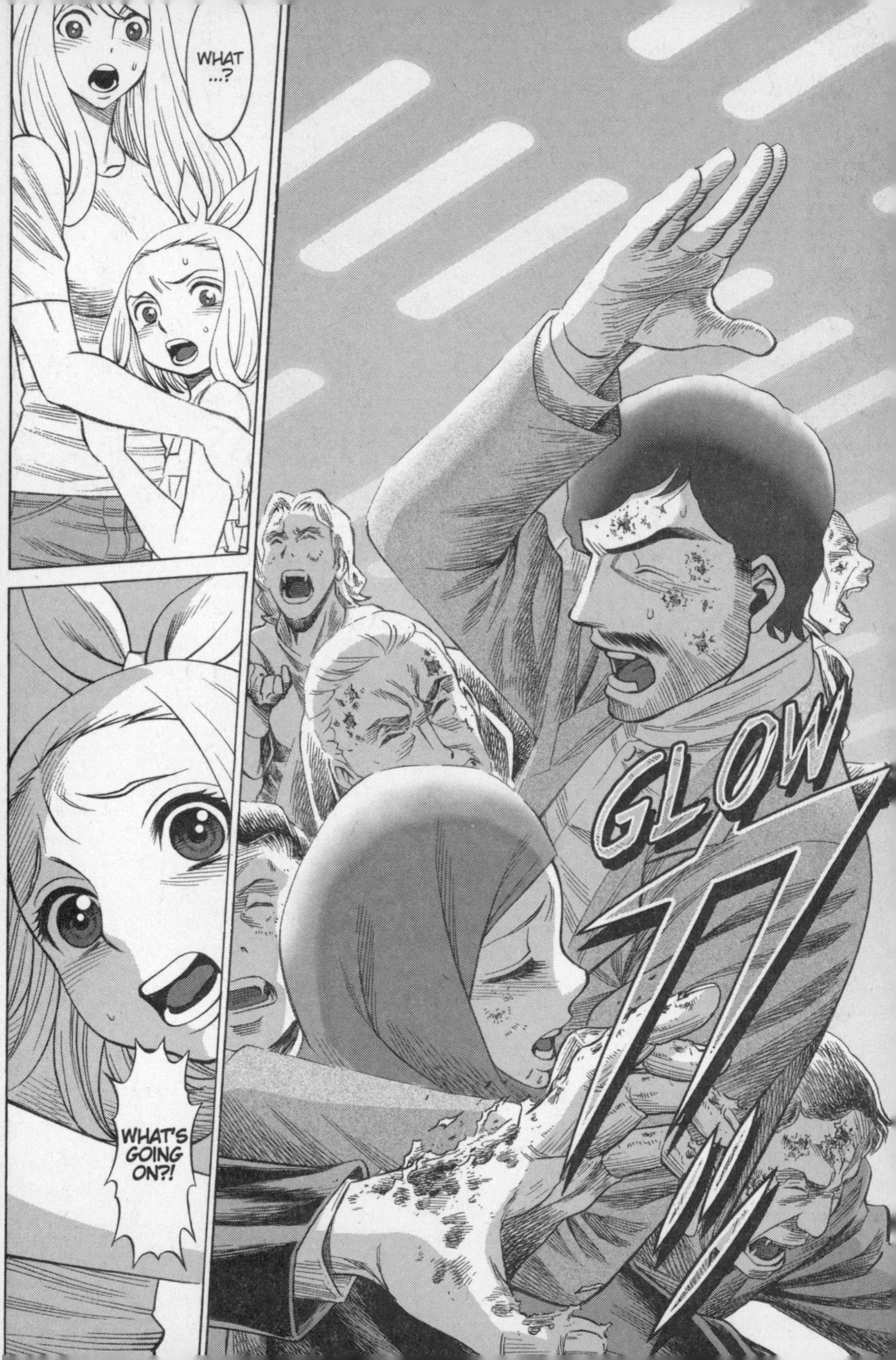
GLOW
WHAT ...?
WHAT'S GOING ON?!

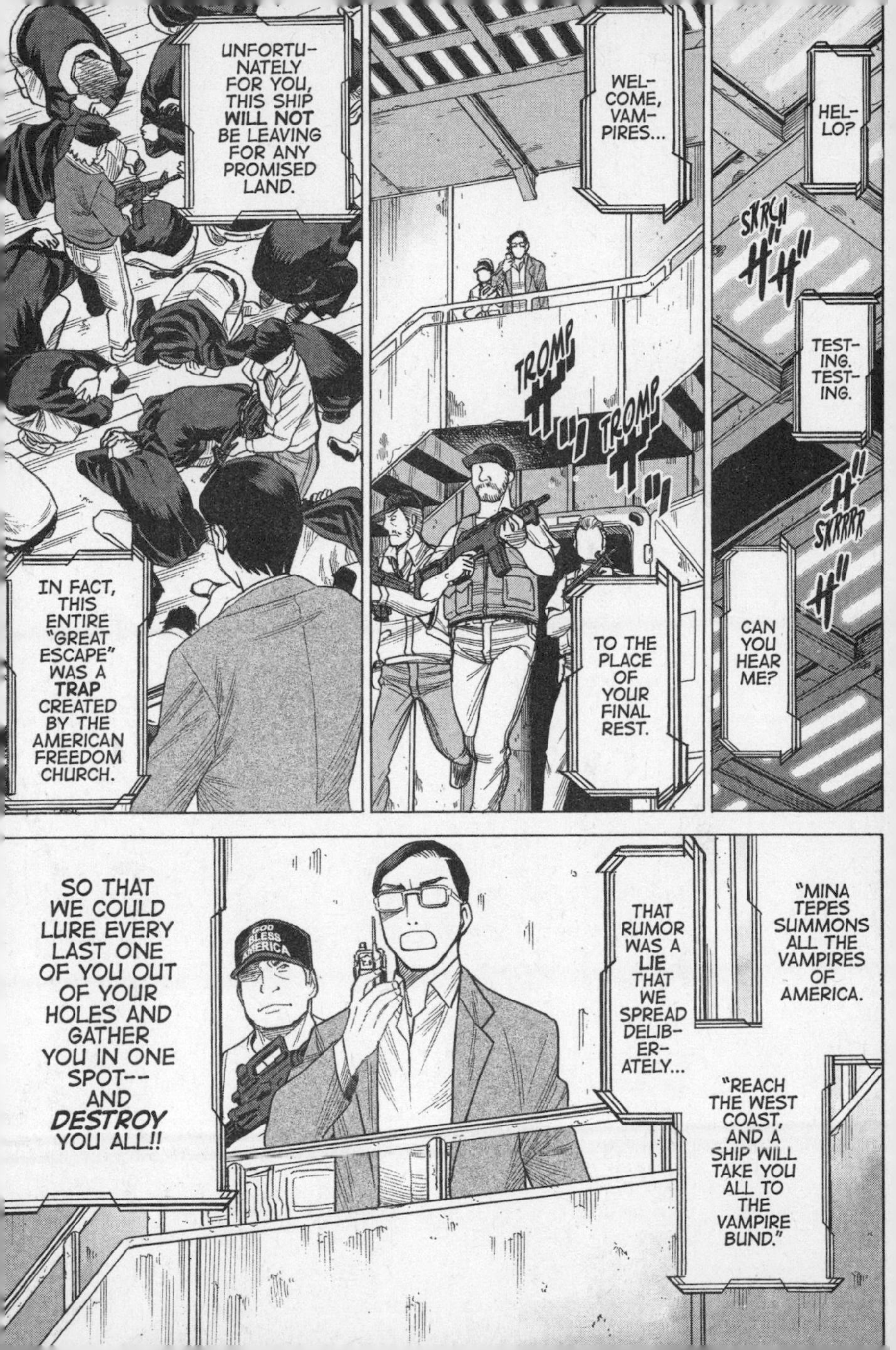
HEL-LO?
SKRCH
TESTING. TESTING.
SKRRRR
CAN YOU HEAR ME?
WELCOME, VAMPIRES...
TROMP
TROMP
TO THE PLACE OF YOUR FINAL REST.
UNFORTUNATELY FOR YOU, THIS SHIP **WILL NOT** BE LEAVING FOR ANY PROMISED LAND.
IN FACT, THIS ENTIRE "GREAT ESCAPE" WAS A **TRAP** CREATED BY THE AMERICAN FREEDOM CHURCH.
"MINA TEPES SUMMONS ALL THE VAMPIRES OF AMERICA.
"REACH THE WEST COAST, AND A SHIP WILL TAKE YOU ALL TO THE VAMPIRE BUND."
THAT RUMOR WAS A **LIE** THAT WE SPREAD DELIBERATELY...
GOD BLESS AMERICA
SO THAT WE COULD LURE EVERY LAST ONE OF YOU OUT OF YOUR HOLES AND GATHER YOU IN ONE SPOT-- AND ***DESTROY*** YOU ALL!!

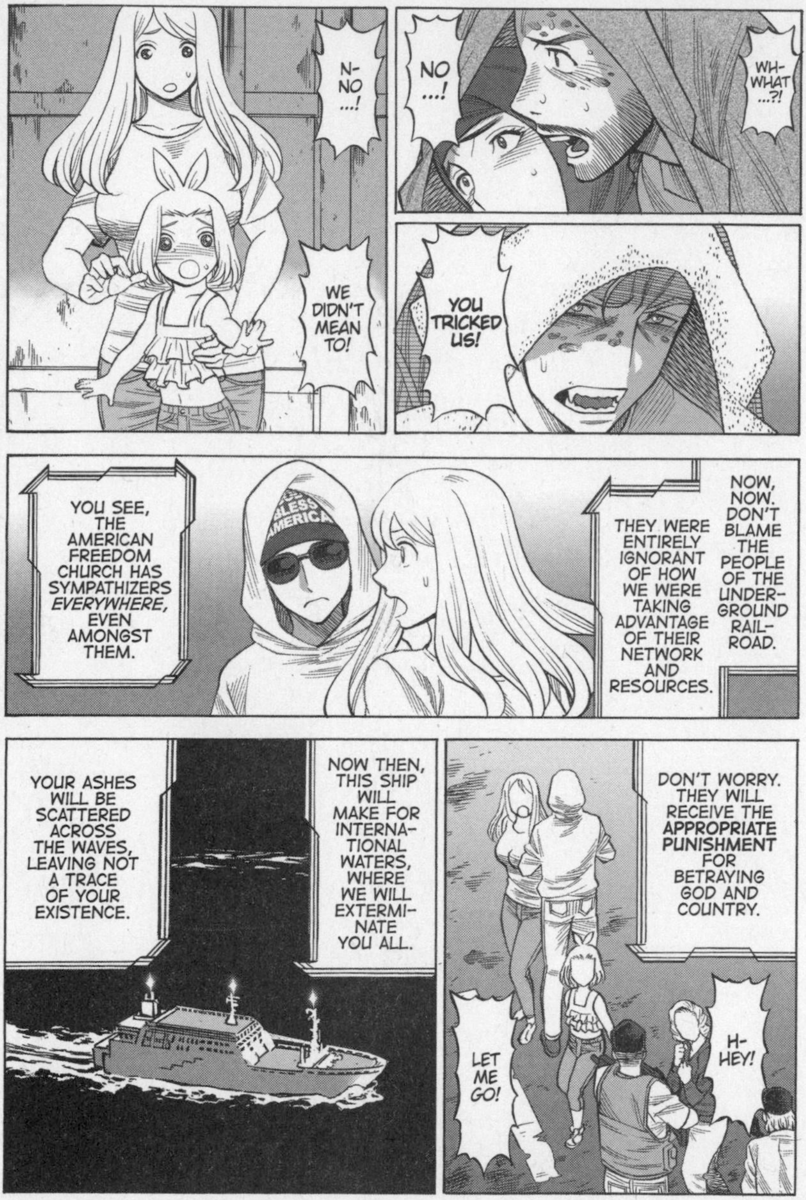
WH-WHAT ...?!
NO ...!
YOU TRICKED US!
N-NO ...!
WE DIDN'T MEAN TO!
NOW, NOW. DON'T BLAME THE PEOPLE OF THE UNDERGROUND RAILROAD.
THEY WERE ENTIRELY IGNORANT OF HOW WE WERE TAKING ADVANTAGE OF THEIR NETWORK AND RESOURCES.
YOU SEE, THE AMERICAN FREEDOM CHURCH HAS SYMPATHIZERS *EVERYWHERE*, EVEN AMONGST THEM.
GOD BLESS AMERICA
DON'T WORRY. THEY WILL RECEIVE THE **APPROPRIATE PUNISHMENT** FOR BETRAYING GOD AND COUNTRY.
H-HEY!
LET ME GO!
NOW THEN, THIS SHIP WILL MAKE FOR INTERNATIONAL WATERS, WHERE WE WILL EXTERMINATE YOU ALL.
YOUR ASHES WILL BE SCATTERED ACROSS THE WAVES, LEAVING NOT A TRACE OF YOUR EXISTENCE.

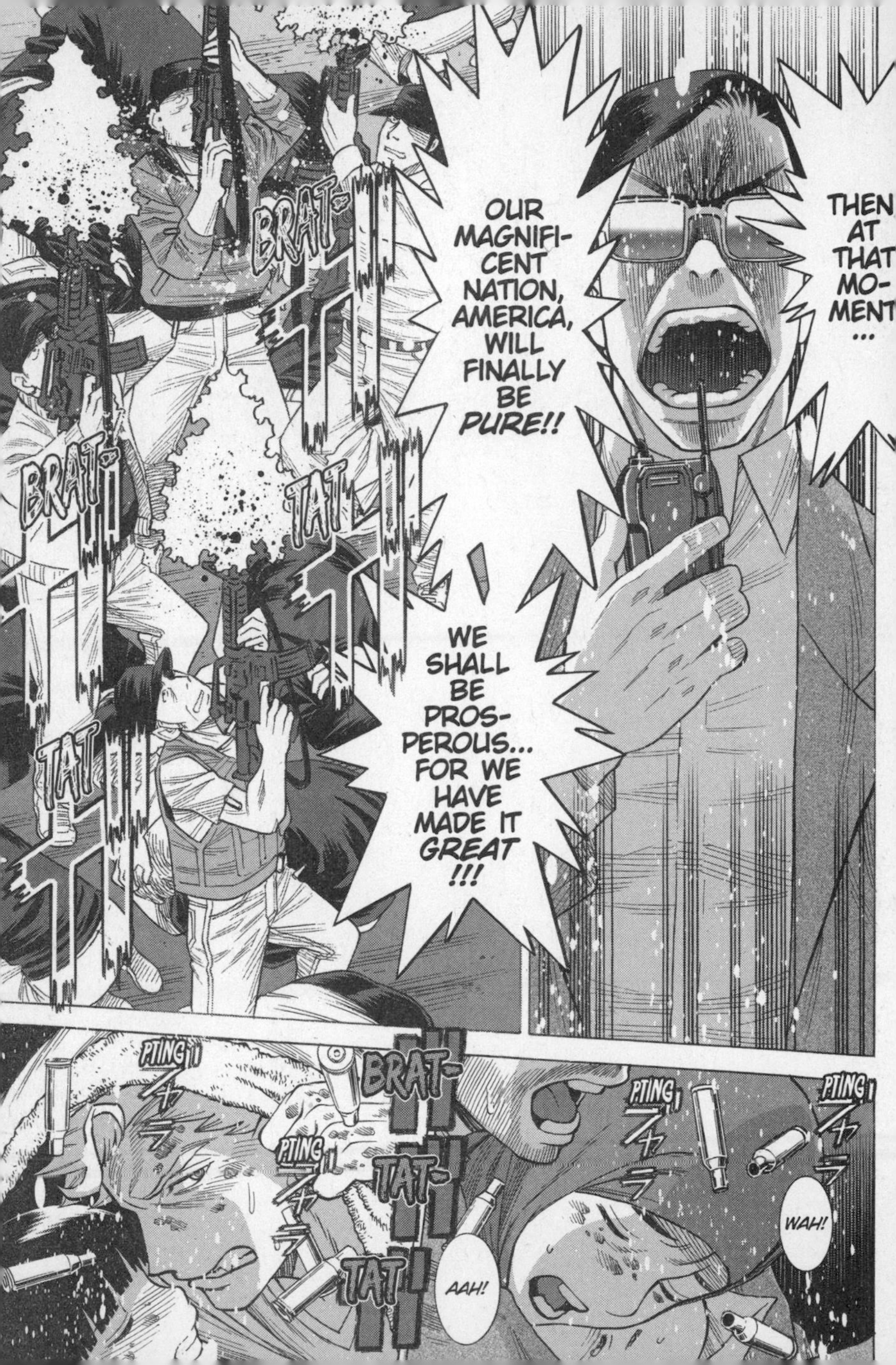
THEN AT THAT MOMENT...
OUR MAGNIFICENT NATION, AMERICA, WILL FINALLY BE PURE!!
WE SHALL BE PROSPEROUS... FOR WE HAVE MADE IT GREAT!!!
BRAT-
TAT
BRAT-
TAT
PTING
PTING
WAH!
BRAT-
TAT-
TAT
AAH!
PTING
PTING

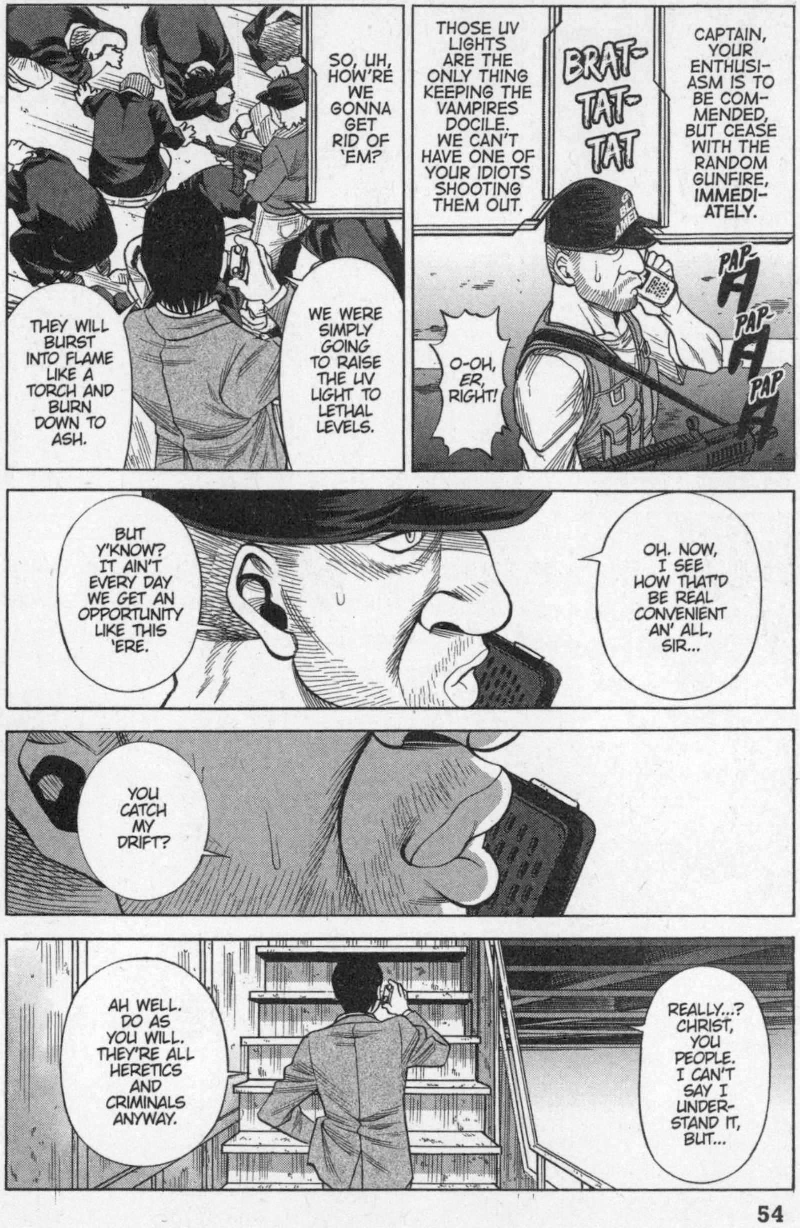
CAPTAIN, YOUR ENTHUSIASM IS TO BE COMMENDED, BUT CEASE WITH THE RANDOM GUNFIRE, IMMEDIATELY.
BRAT-TAT-TAT
THOSE UV LIGHTS ARE THE ONLY THING KEEPING THE VAMPIRES DOCILE. WE CAN'T HAVE ONE OF YOUR IDIOTS SHOOTING THEM OUT.
PAP-A PAP-A PAP-A
O-OH, ER, RIGHT!
SO, UH, HOW'RE WE GONNA GET RID OF 'EM?
WE WERE SIMPLY GOING TO RAISE THE UV LIGHT TO LETHAL LEVELS.
THEY WILL BURST INTO FLAME LIKE A TORCH AND BURN DOWN TO ASH.
OH. NOW, I SEE HOW THAT'D BE REAL CONVENIENT AN' ALL, SIR...
BUT Y'KNOW? IT AIN'T EVERY DAY WE GET AN OPPORTUNITY LIKE THIS 'ERE.
YOU CATCH MY DRIFT?
REALLY...? CHRIST, YOU PEOPLE. I CAN'T SAY I UNDERSTAND IT, BUT...
AH WELL. DO AS YOU WILL. THEY'RE ALL HERETICS AND CRIMINALS ANYWAY.

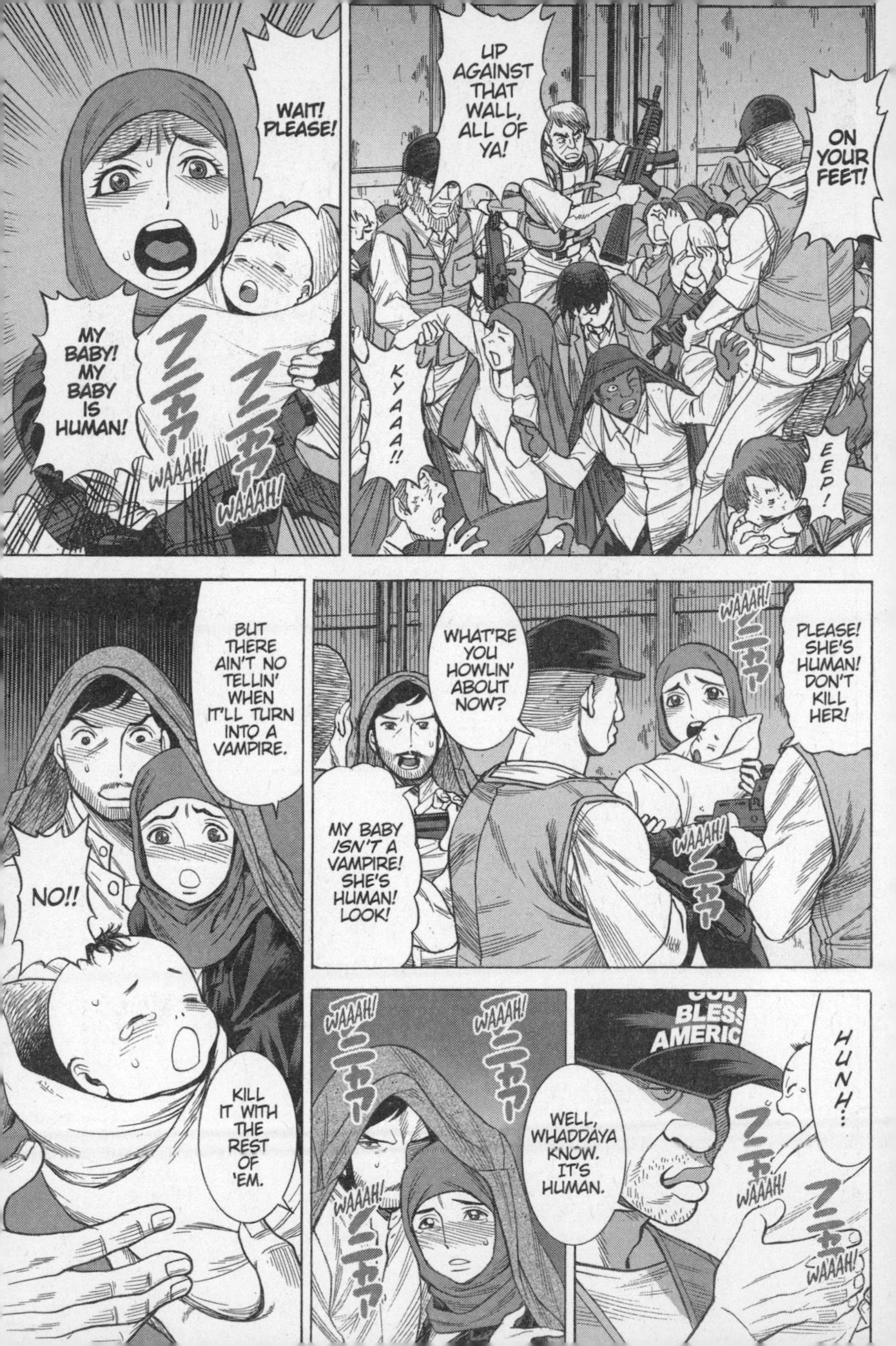
ON YOUR FEET!
UP AGAINST THAT WALL, ALL OF YA!
EEP!
KYAAAA!!
WAIT! PLEASE!
MY BABY! MY BABY IS HUMAN!
WAAAH!
WAAAH!
WAAAH!
PLEASE! SHE'S HUMAN! DON'T KILL HER!
WHAT'RE YOU HOWLIN' ABOUT NOW?
WAAAH!
MY BABY ISN'T A VAMPIRE! SHE'S HUMAN! LOOK!
BLESS AMERIC
HUNH...
WELL, WHADDAYA KNOW. IT'S HUMAN.
WAAAH!
WAAAH!
WAAAH!
WAAAH!
WAAAH!
BUT THERE AIN'T NO TELLIN' WHEN IT'LL TURN INTO A VAMPIRE.
NO!!
KILL IT WITH THE REST OF 'EM.

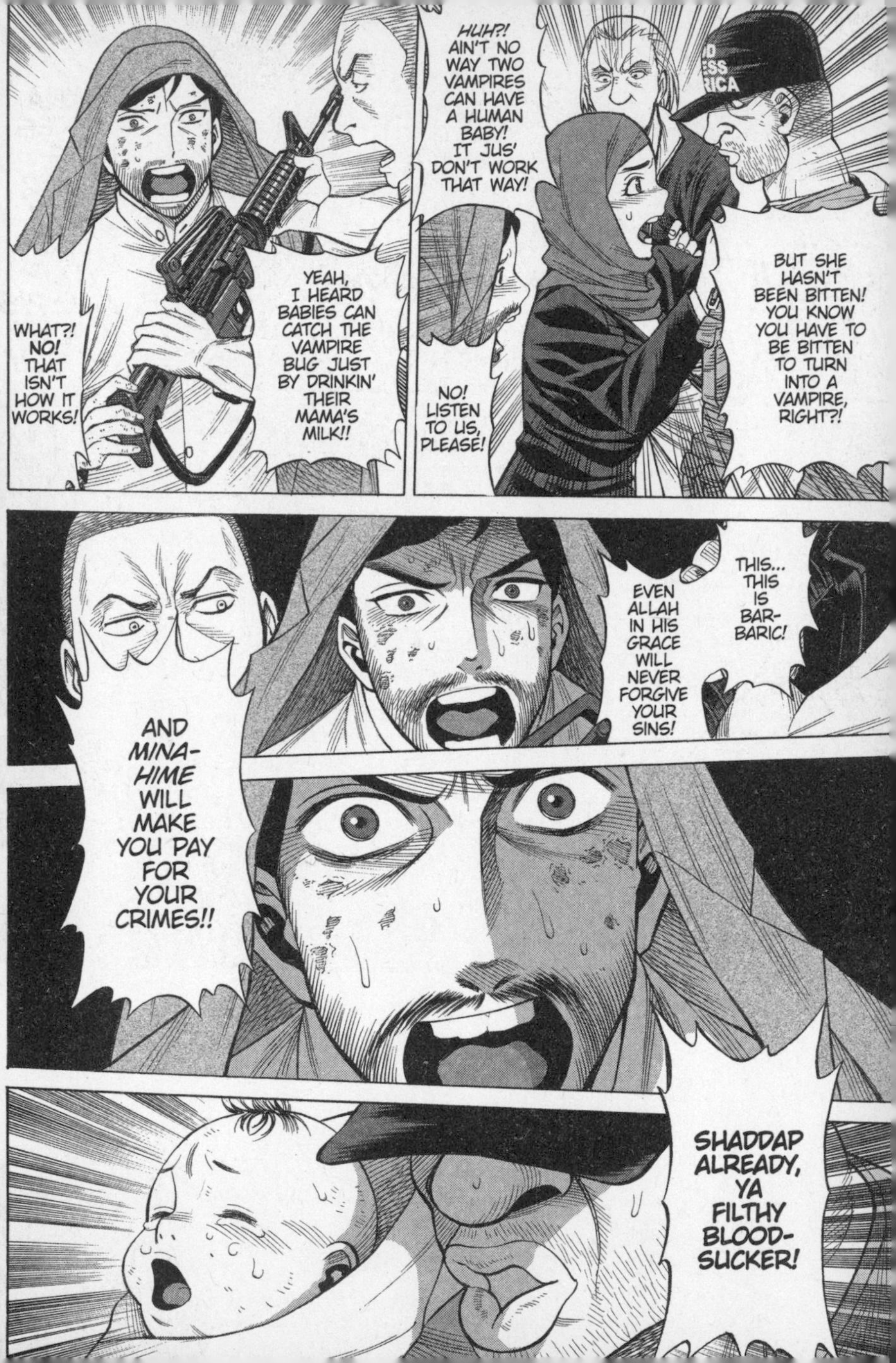
HUH?! AIN'T NO WAY TWO VAMPIRES CAN HAVE A HUMAN BABY! IT JUS' DON'T WORK THAT WAY!
BUT SHE HASN'T BEEN BITTEN! YOU KNOW YOU HAVE TO BE BITTEN TO TURN INTO A VAMPIRE, RIGHT?!
NO! LISTEN TO US, PLEASE!
YEAH, I HEARD BABIES CAN CATCH THE VAMPIRE BUG JUST BY DRINKIN' THEIR MAMA'S MILK!!
WHAT?! NO! THAT ISN'T HOW IT WORKS!
THIS... THIS IS BAR-BARIC!
EVEN ALLAH IN HIS GRACE WILL NEVER FORGIVE YOUR SINS!
AND *MINA-HIME* WILL MAKE YOU PAY FOR YOUR CRIMES!!
SHADDAP ALREADY, YA FILTHY BLOOD-SUCKER!

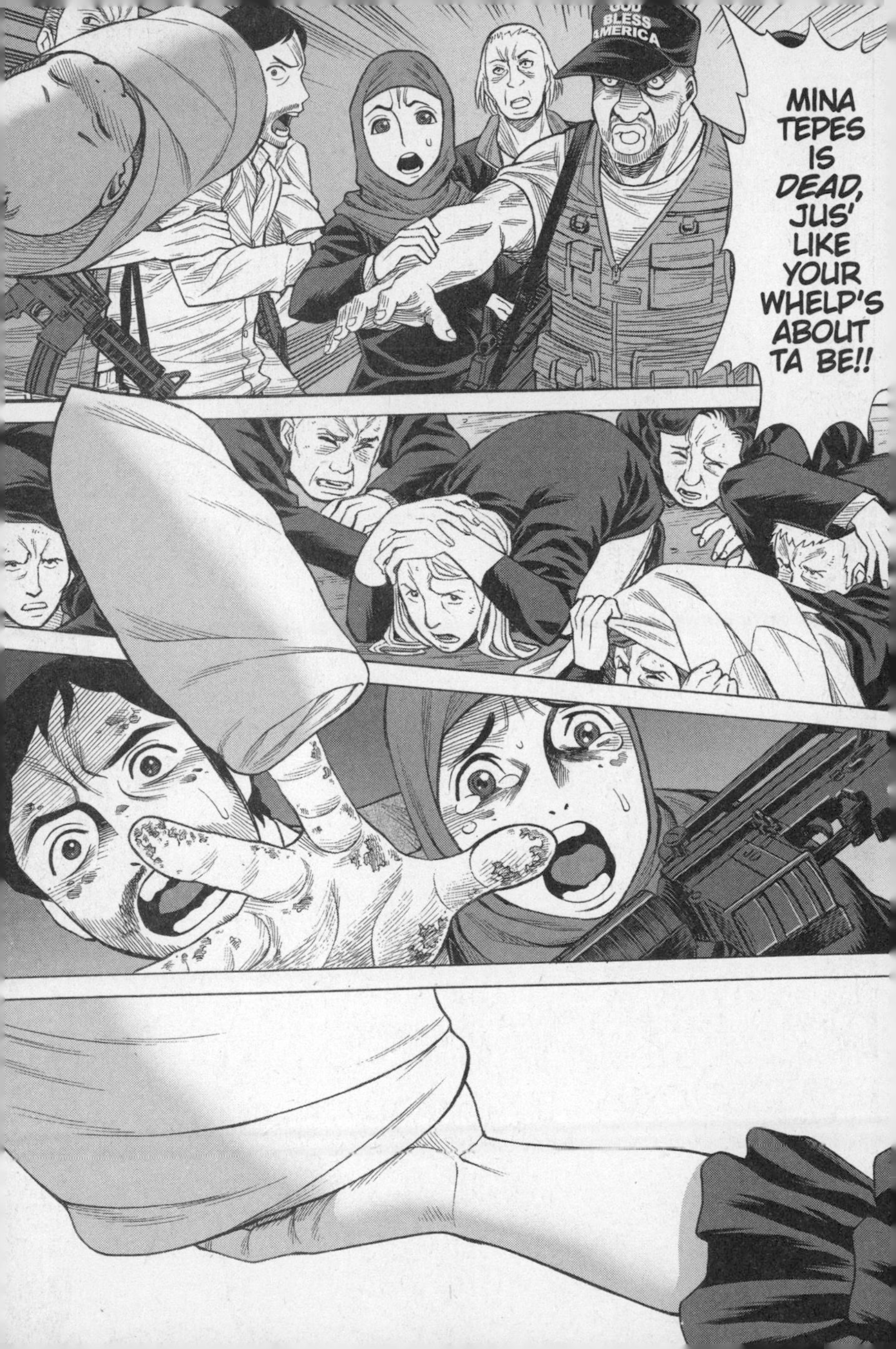
MINA TEPES IS *DEAD,* JUS' LIKE YOUR WHELP'S ABOUT TA BE!!

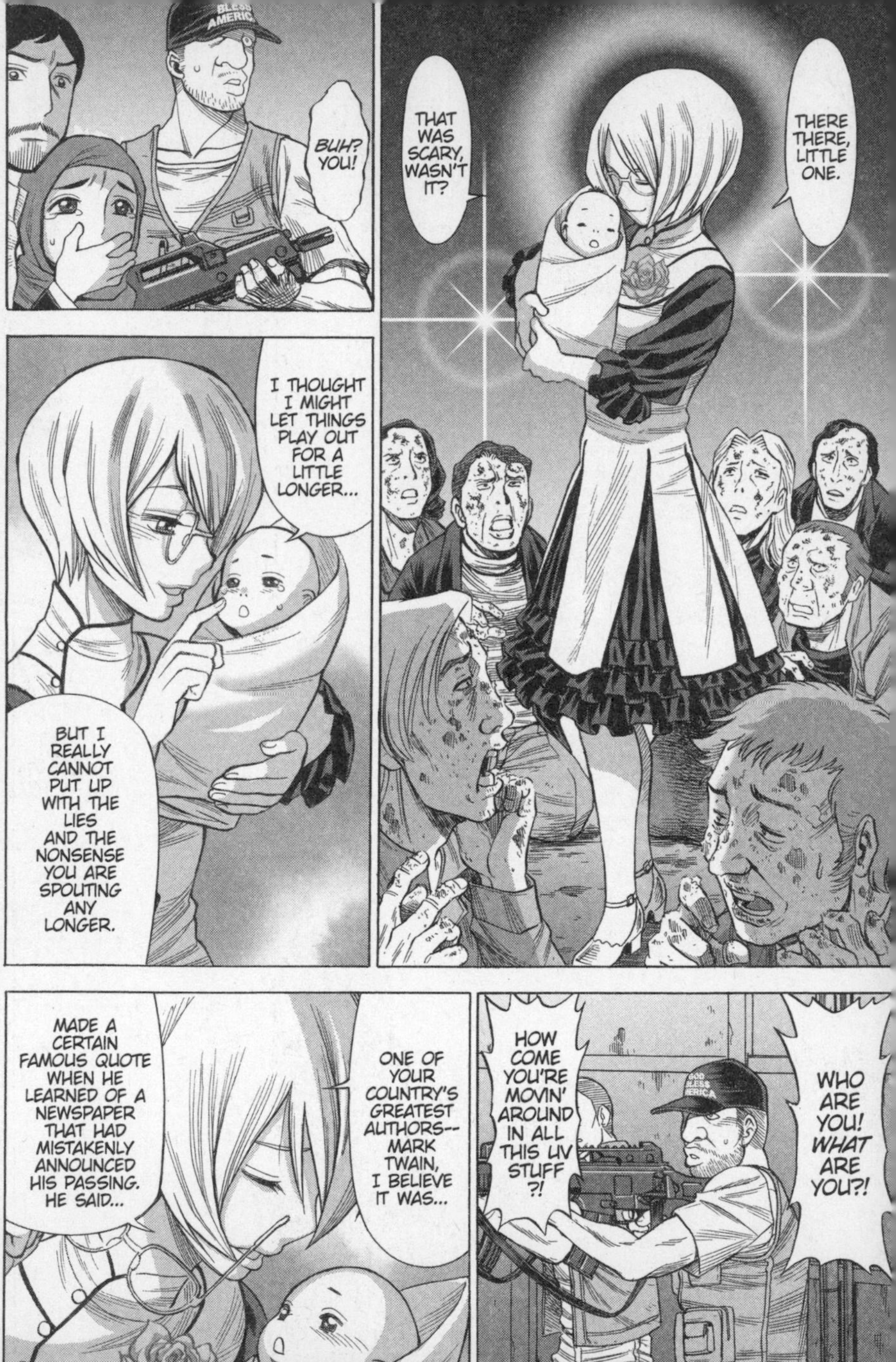

THERE THERE, LITTLE ONE.
THAT WAS SCARY, WASN'T IT?
BUH? YOU!
I THOUGHT I MIGHT LET THINGS PLAY OUT FOR A LITTLE LONGER...
BUT I REALLY CANNOT PUT UP WITH THE LIES AND THE NONSENSE YOU ARE SPOUTING ANY LONGER.
WHO ARE YOU! WHAT ARE YOU?!
HOW COME YOU'RE MOVIN' AROUND IN ALL THIS UV STUFF ?!
ONE OF YOUR COUNTRY'S GREATEST AUTHORS-- MARK TWAIN, I BELIEVE IT WAS...
MADE A CERTAIN FAMOUS QUOTE WHEN HE LEARNED OF A NEWSPAPER THAT HAD MISTAKENLY ANNOUNCED HIS PASSING. HE SAID...

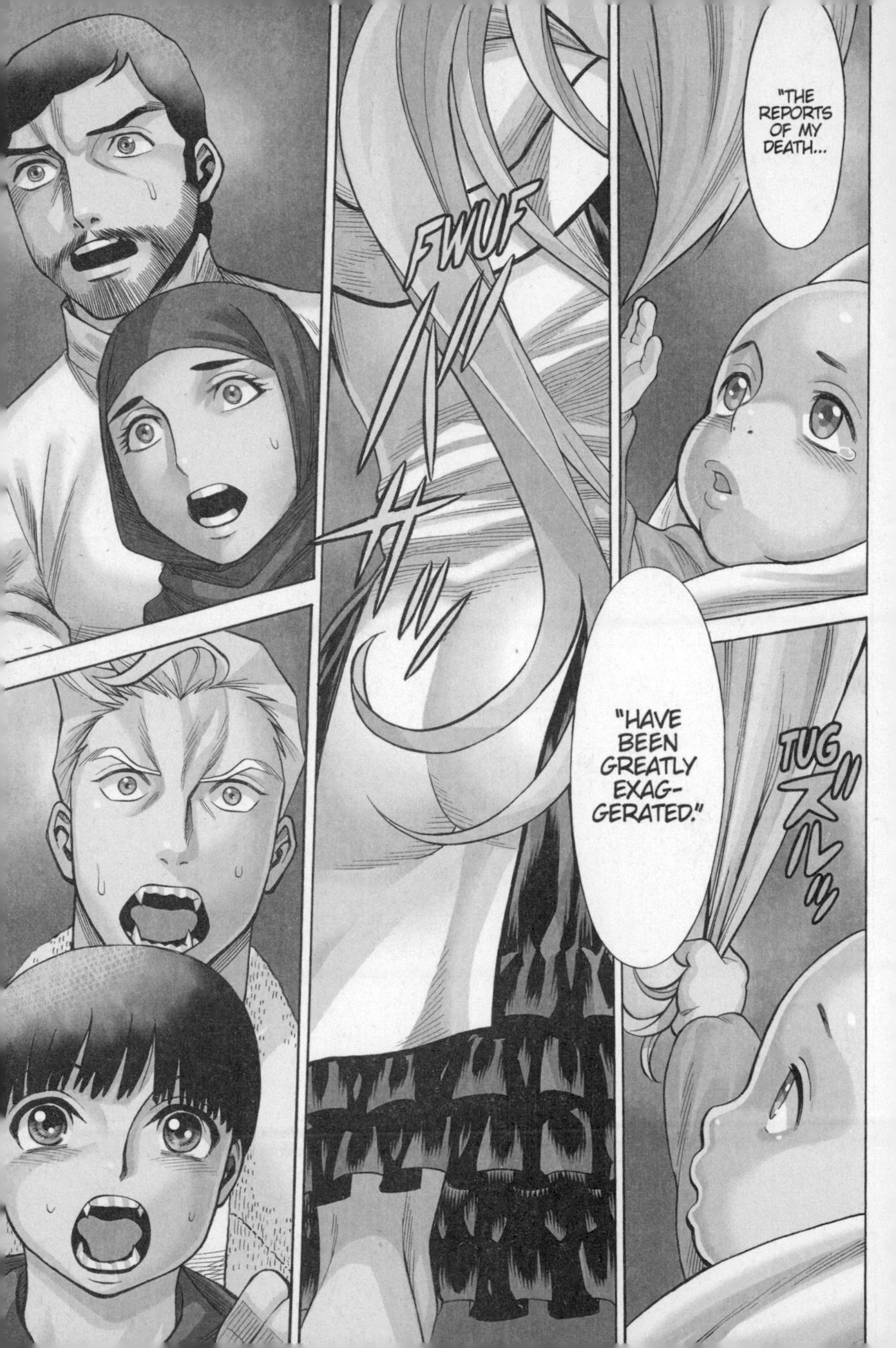
"THE REPORTS OF MY DEATH...
"HAVE BEEN GREATLY EXAG-GERATED."
TUG
FWUF

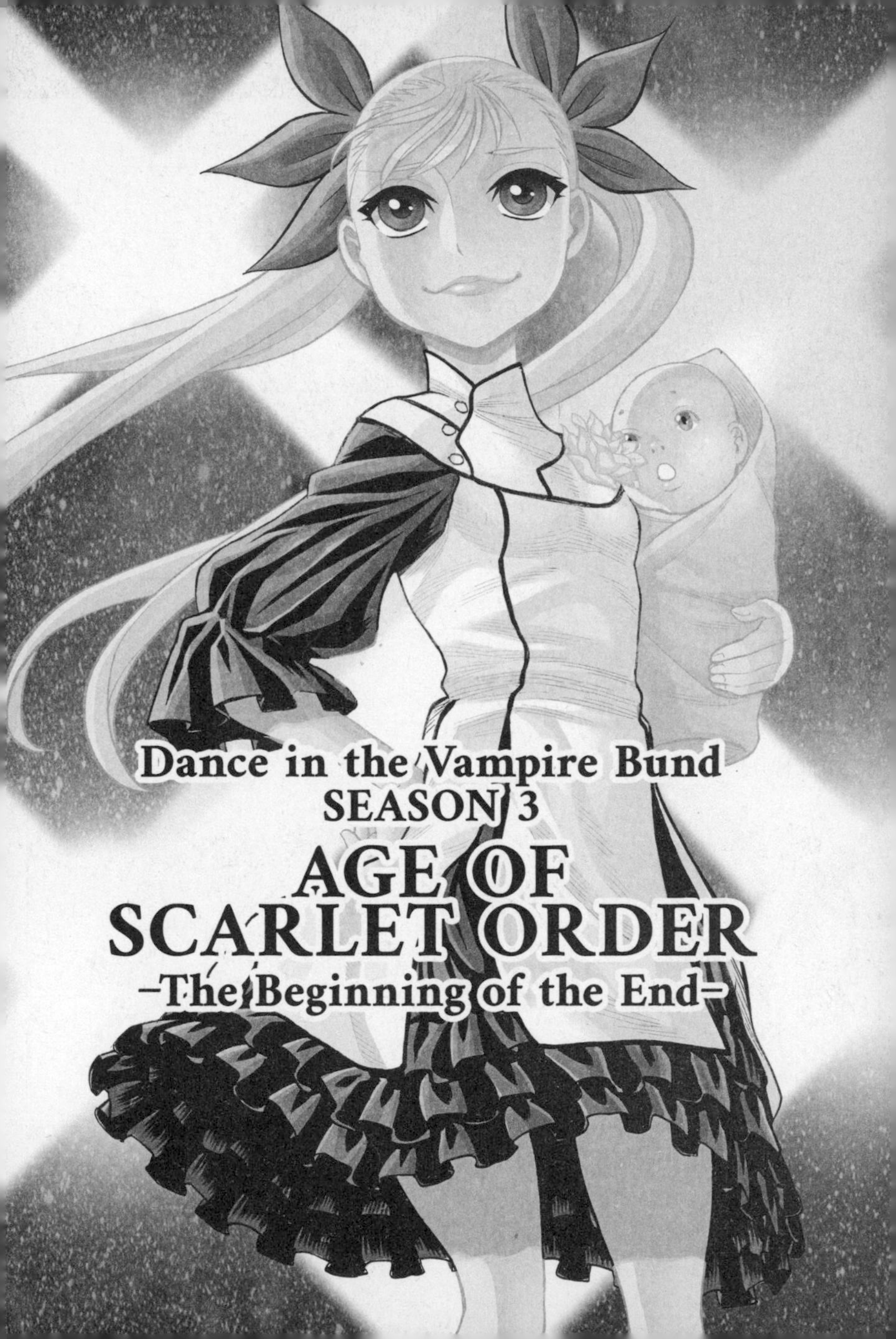
Dance in the Vampire Bund
SEASON 3
AGE OF
SCARLET ORDER
–The Beginning of the End–

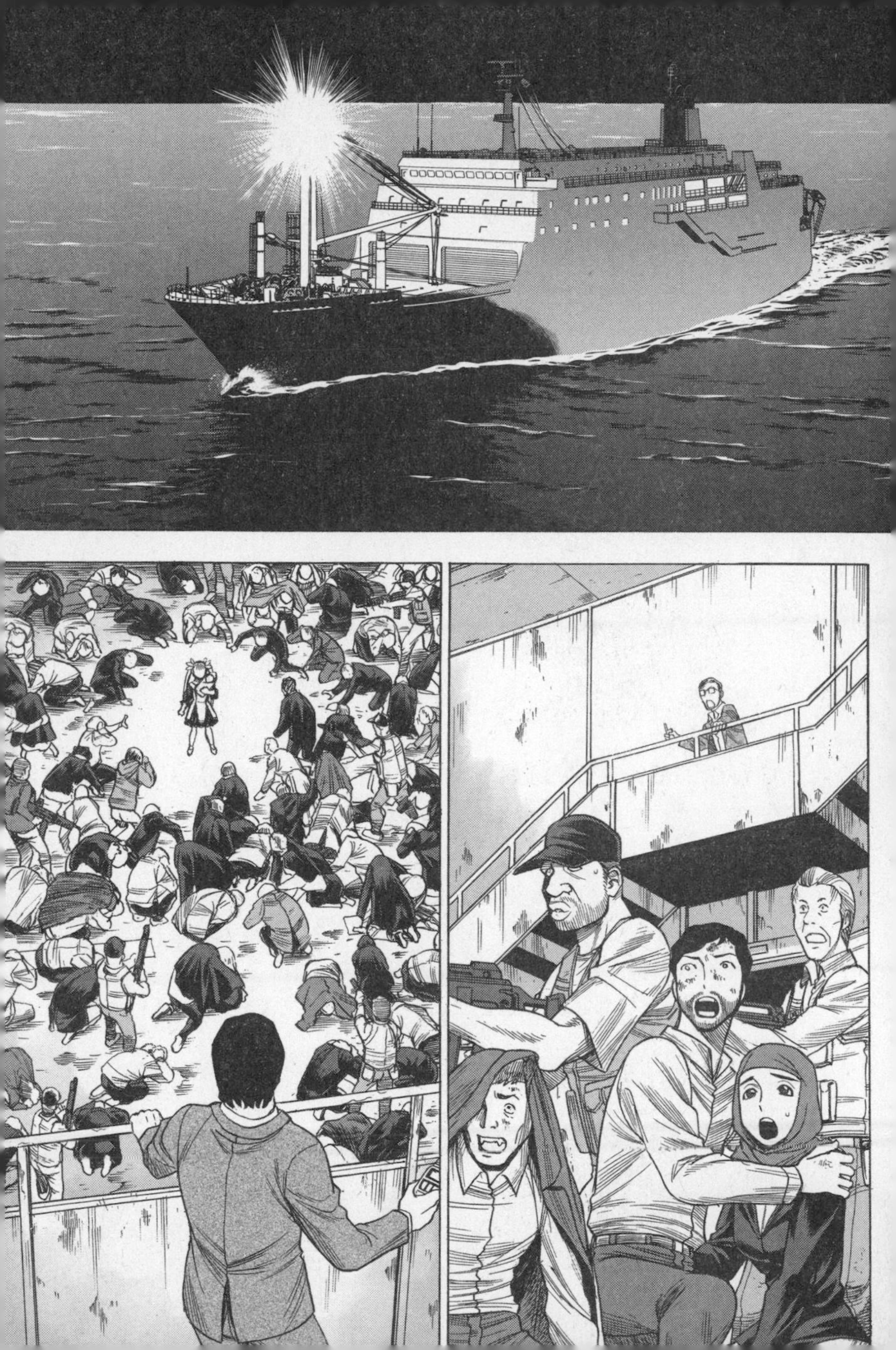

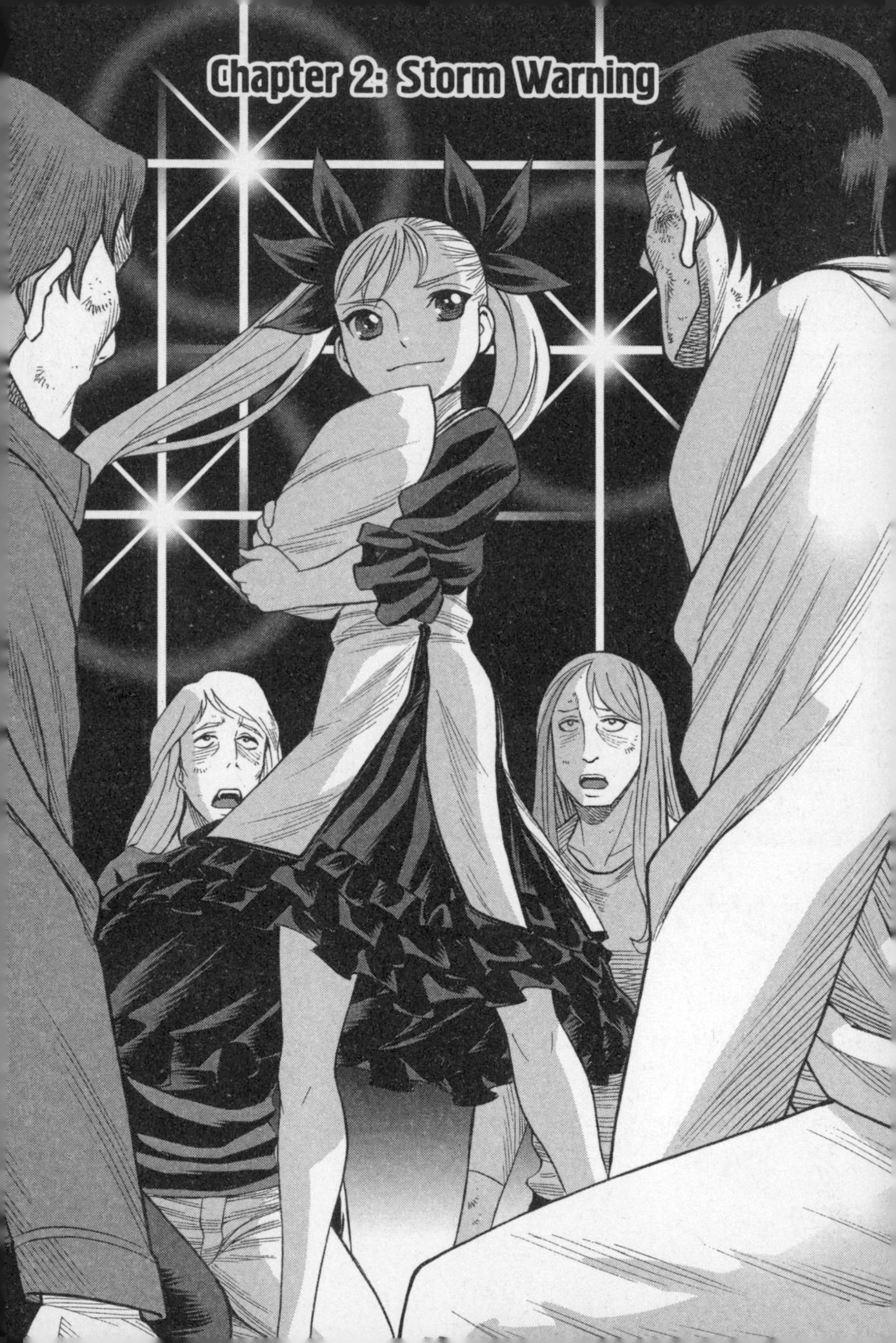
Chapter 2: Storm Warning

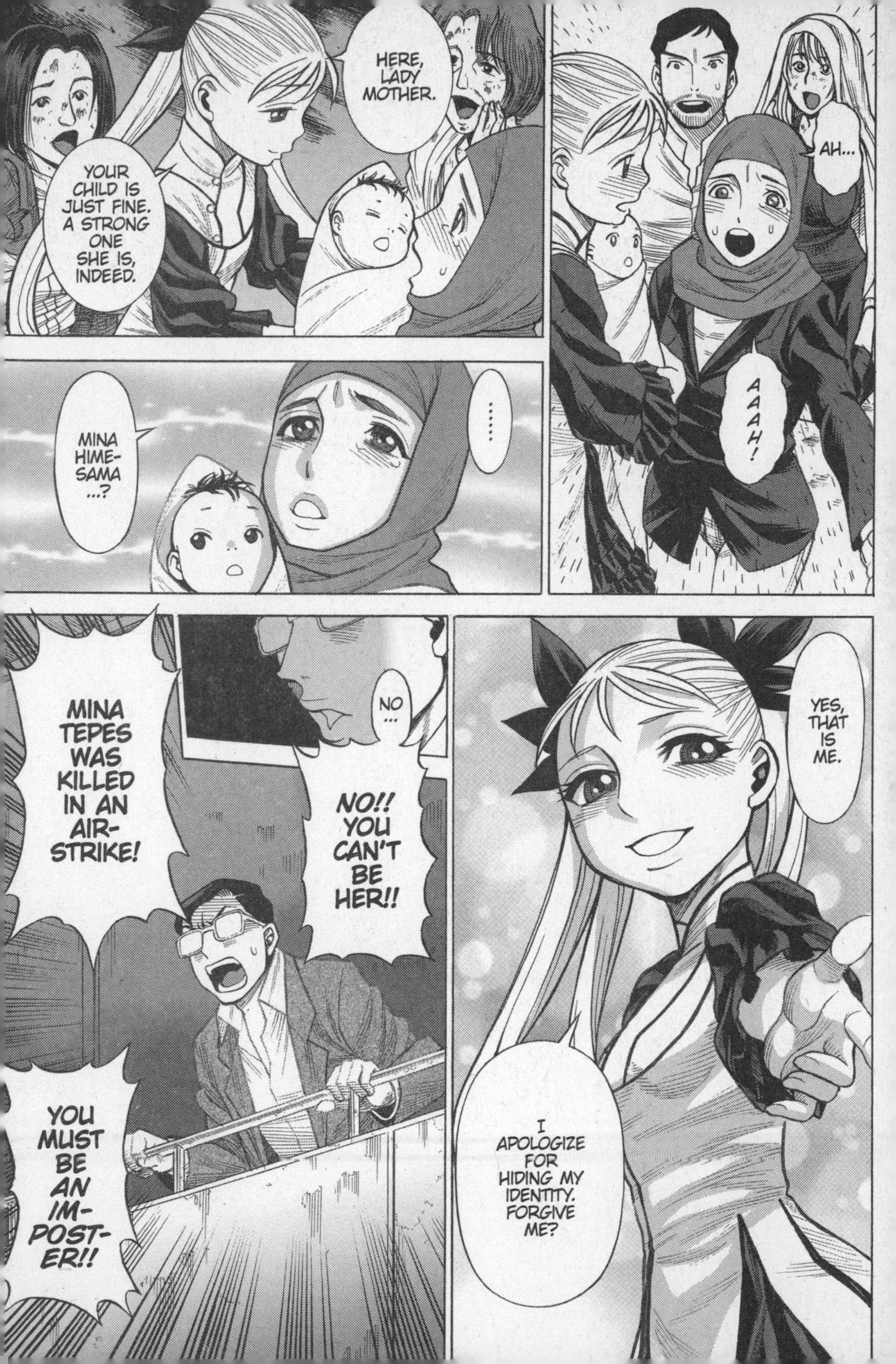
AH...
AAAH!
HERE, LADY MOTHER.
YOUR CHILD IS JUST FINE. A STRONG ONE SHE IS, INDEED.
......
MINA HIME-SAMA ...?
YES, THAT IS ME.
I APOLOGIZE FOR HIDING MY IDENTITY. FORGIVE ME?
NO ...
MINA TEPES WAS KILLED IN AN AIR-STRIKE!
NO!! YOU CAN'T BE HER!!
YOU MUST BE AN IM-POSTER-ER!!

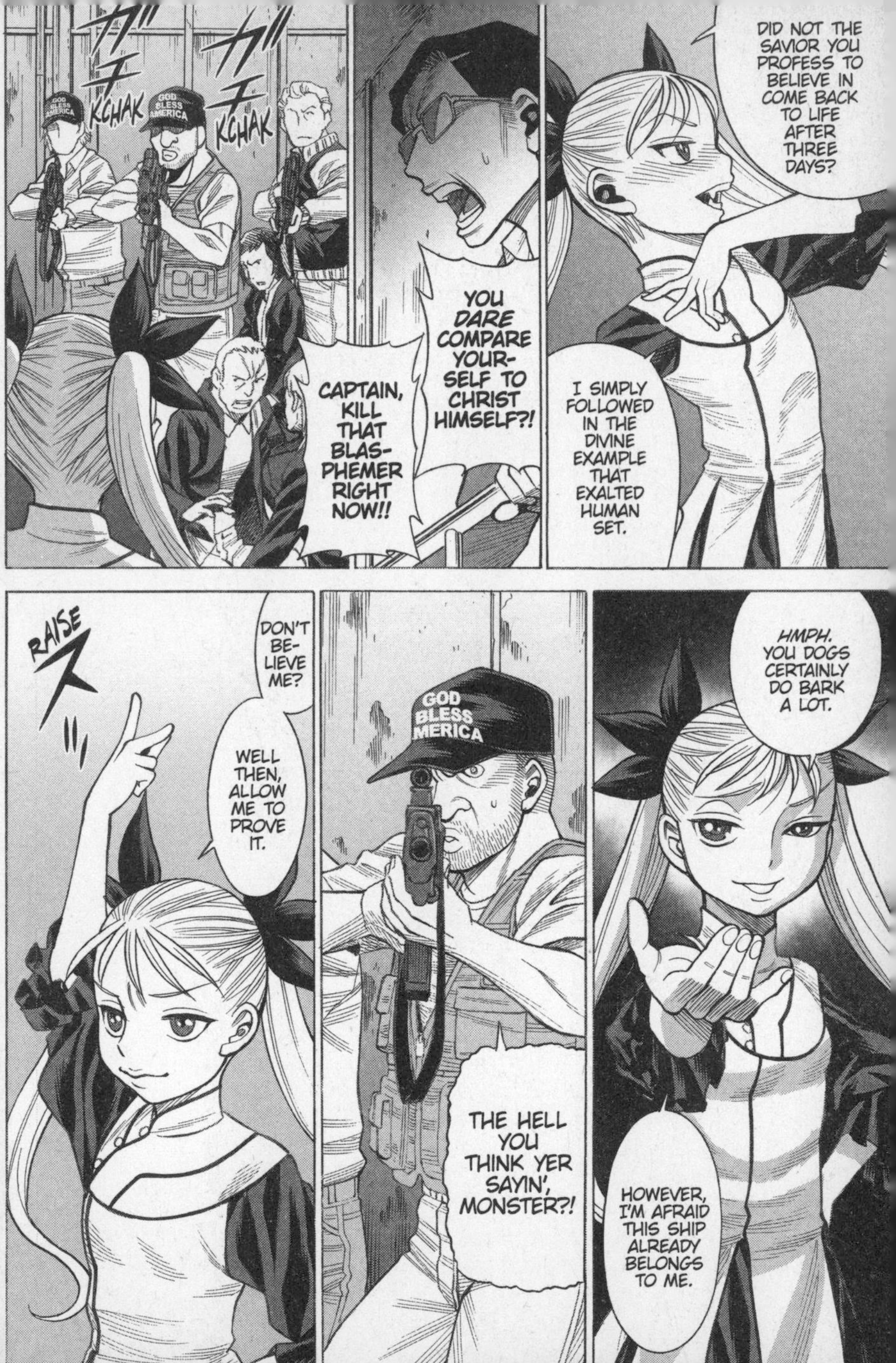
DID NOT THE SAVIOR YOU PROFESS TO BELIEVE IN COME BACK TO LIFE AFTER THREE DAYS?
I SIMPLY FOLLOWED IN THE DIVINE EXAMPLE THAT EXALTED HUMAN SET.
YOU DARE COMPARE YOURSELF TO CHRIST HIMSELF?!
KCHAK
KCHAK
CAPTAIN, KILL THAT BLASPHEMER RIGHT NOW!!
HMPH. YOU DOGS CERTAINLY DO BARK A LOT.
HOWEVER, I'M AFRAID THIS SHIP ALREADY BELONGS TO ME.
THE HELL YOU THINK YER SAYIN', MONSTER?!
RAISE
DON'T BELIEVE ME?
WELL THEN, ALLOW ME TO PROVE IT.

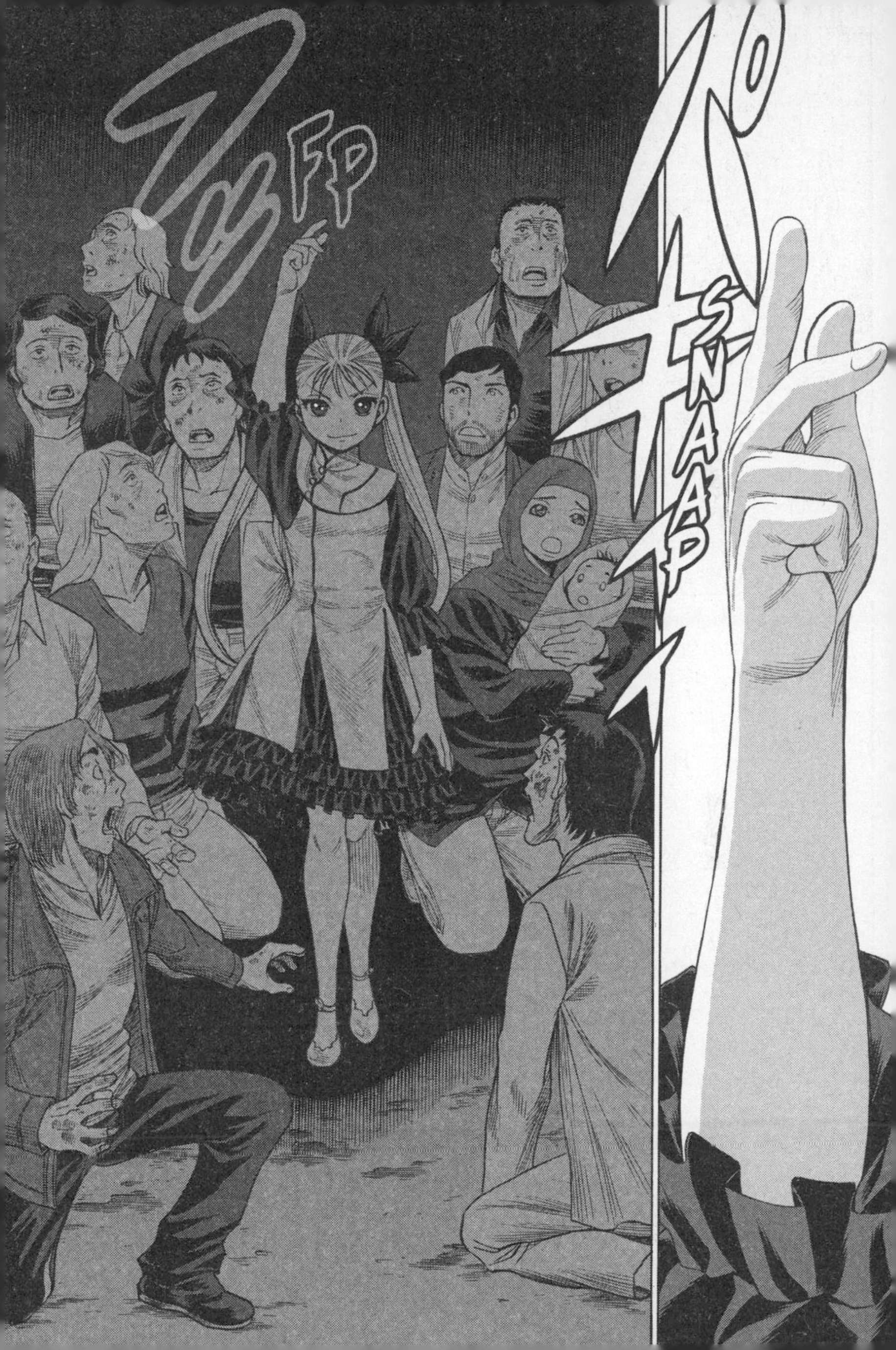
SNAAP
FP

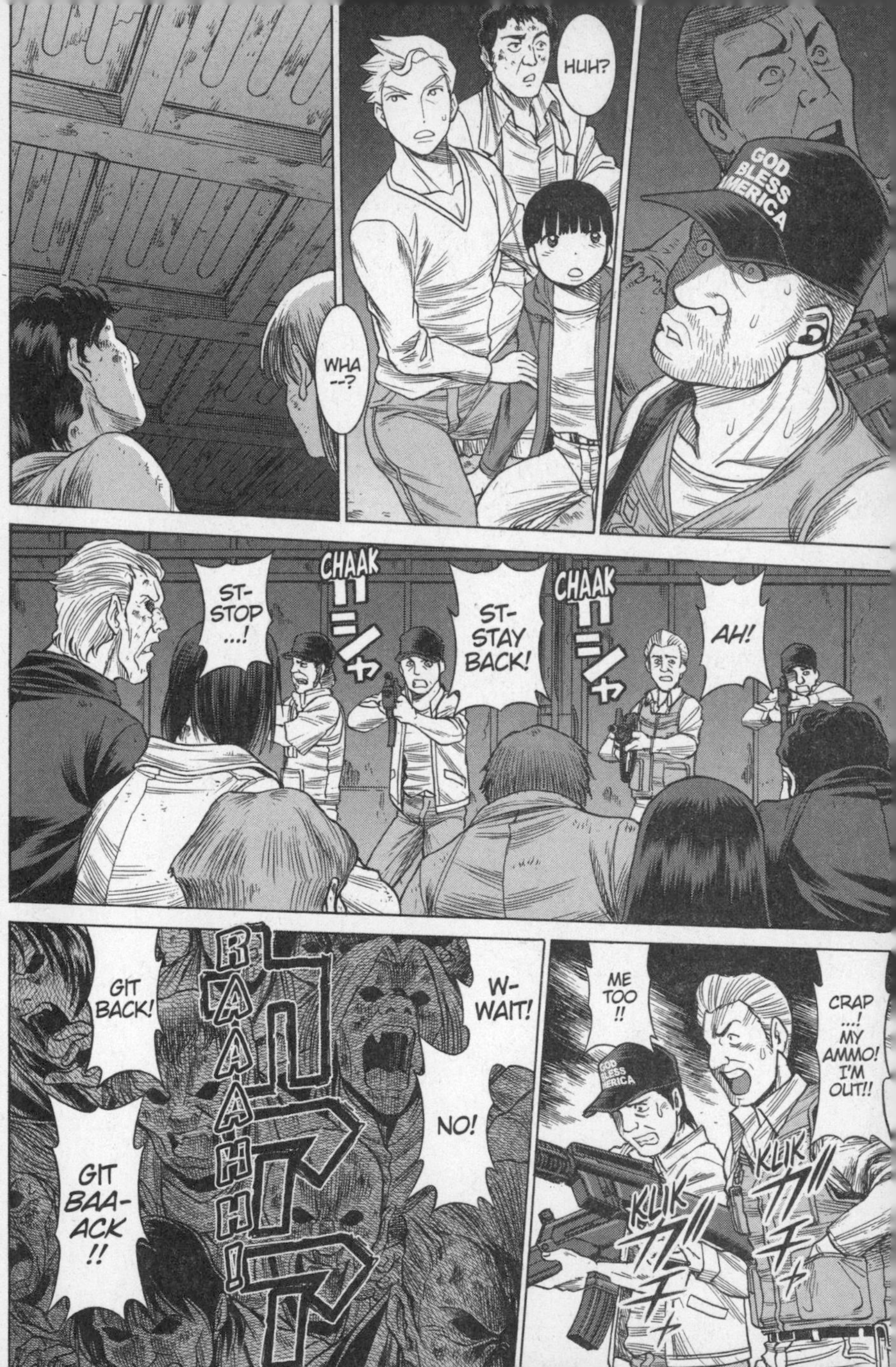
HUH?
WHA--?
AH!
CHAAK
ST-STAY BACK!
CHAAK
ST-STOP...!
CRAP...! MY AMMO! I'M OUT!!
ME TOO!!
KLIK
KLIK
W-WAIT!
NO!
RAAAAHH!
GIT BACK!
GIT BAAACK!!

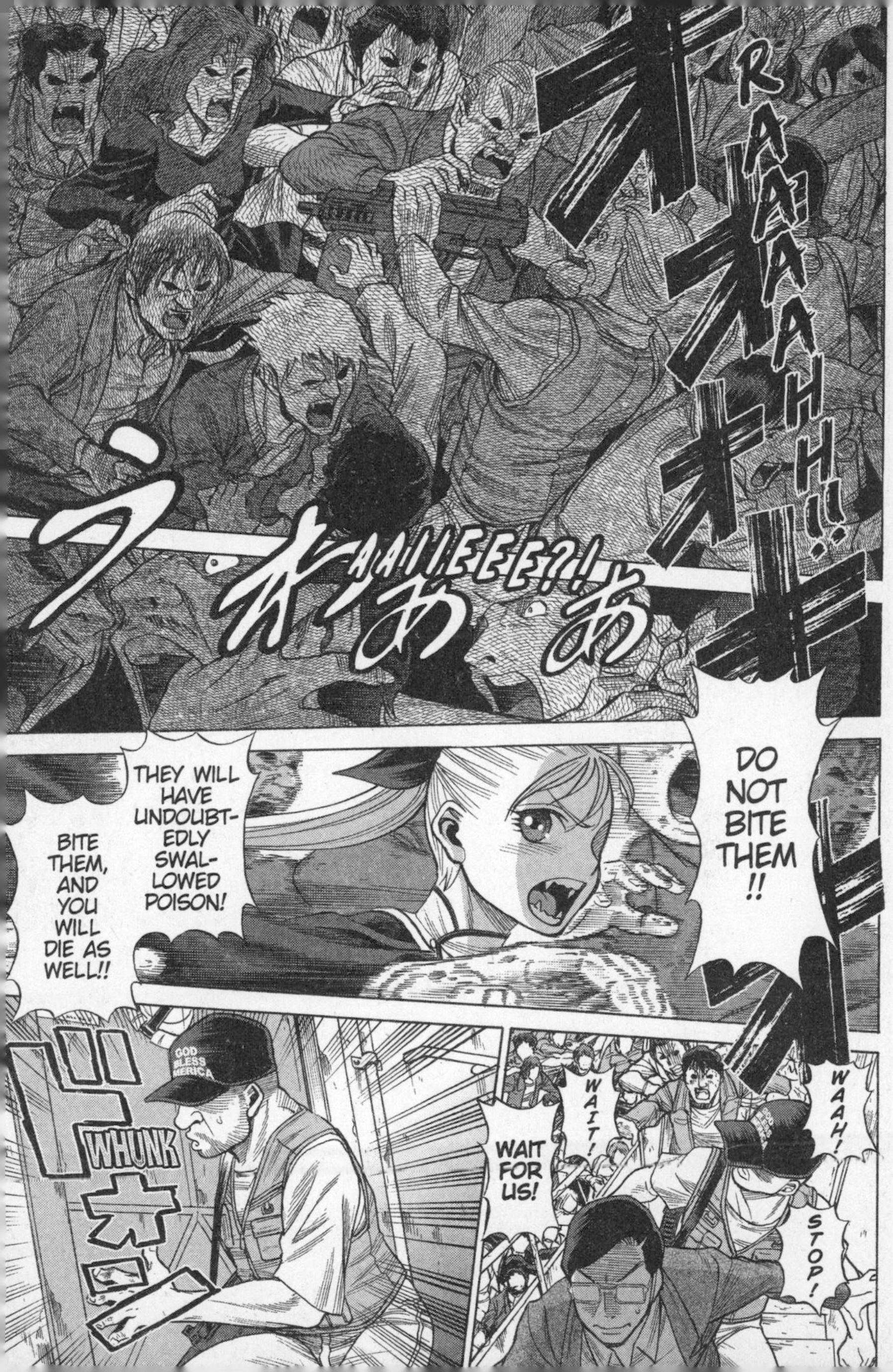
RAAAAHH!!
AAIEEEE?!
DO NOT BITE THEM!!
THEY WILL HAVE UNDOUBTEDLY SWALLOWED POISON!
BITE THEM, AND YOU WILL DIE AS WELL!!
WAAH!
WAIT!
WAIT FOR US!
STOP!
GOD BLESS AMERICA
WHUNK

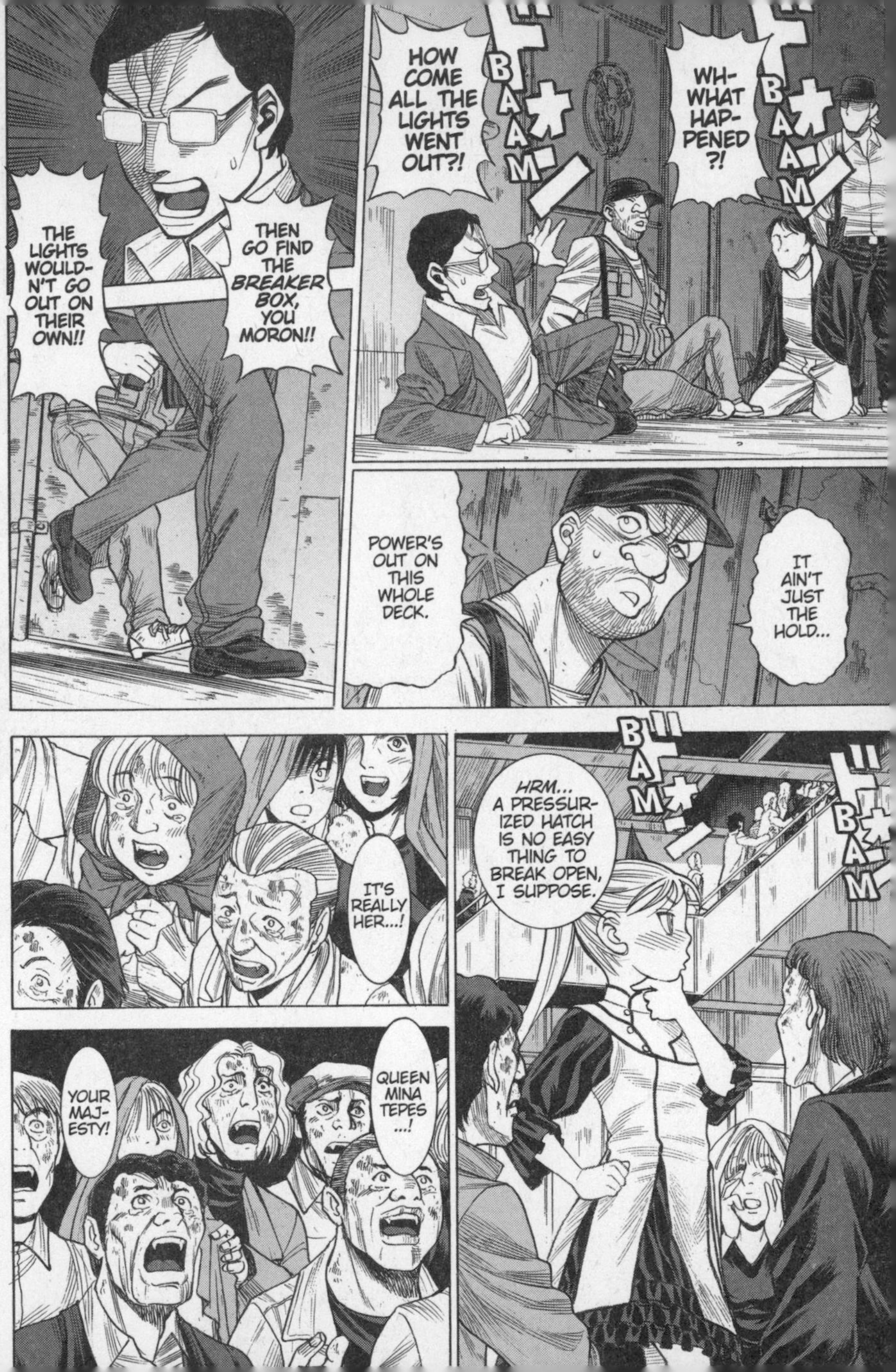
BAAM-
WH-WHAT HAPPENED?!
BAAM-
HOW COME ALL THE LIGHTS WENT OUT?!
IT AIN'T JUST THE HOLD...
POWER'S OUT ON THIS WHOLE DECK.
THEN GO FIND THE BREAKER BOX, YOU MORON!!
THE LIGHTS WOULDN'T GO OUT ON THEIR OWN!!
BAM-
BAM-
HRM... A PRESSURIZED HATCH IS NO EASY THING TO BREAK OPEN, I SUPPOSE.
IT'S REALLY HER...!
QUEEN MINA TEPES...!
YOUR MAJESTY!

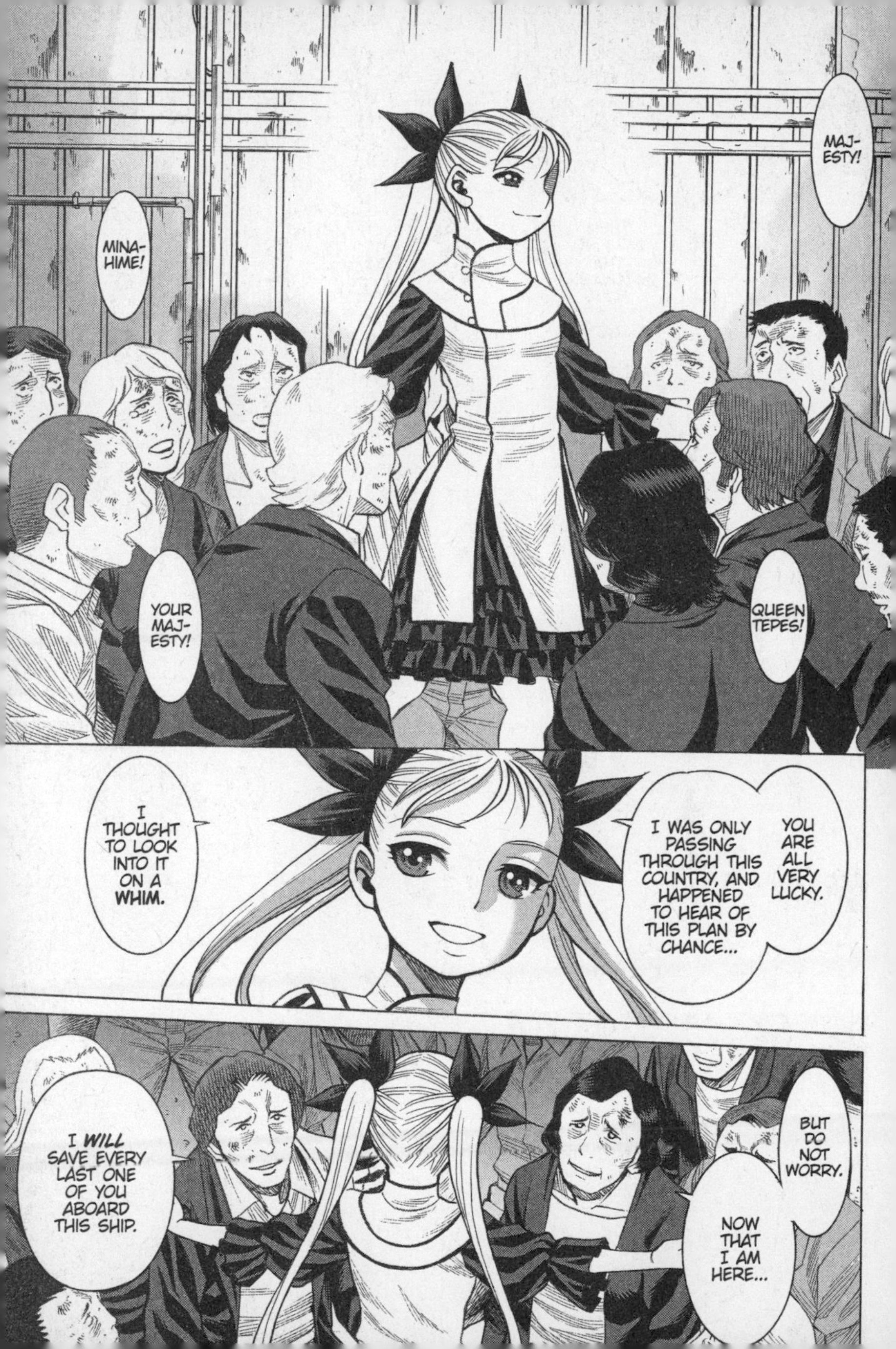
MAJ-ESTY!
QUEEN TEPES!
MINA-HIME!
YOUR MAJ-ESTY!
YOU ARE ALL VERY LUCKY.
I WAS ONLY PASSING THROUGH THIS COUNTRY, AND HAPPENED TO HEAR OF THIS PLAN BY CHANCE...
I THOUGHT TO LOOK INTO IT ON A WHIM.
BUT DO NOT WORRY.
NOW THAT I AM HERE...
I WILL SAVE EVERY LAST ONE OF YOU ABOARD THIS SHIP.

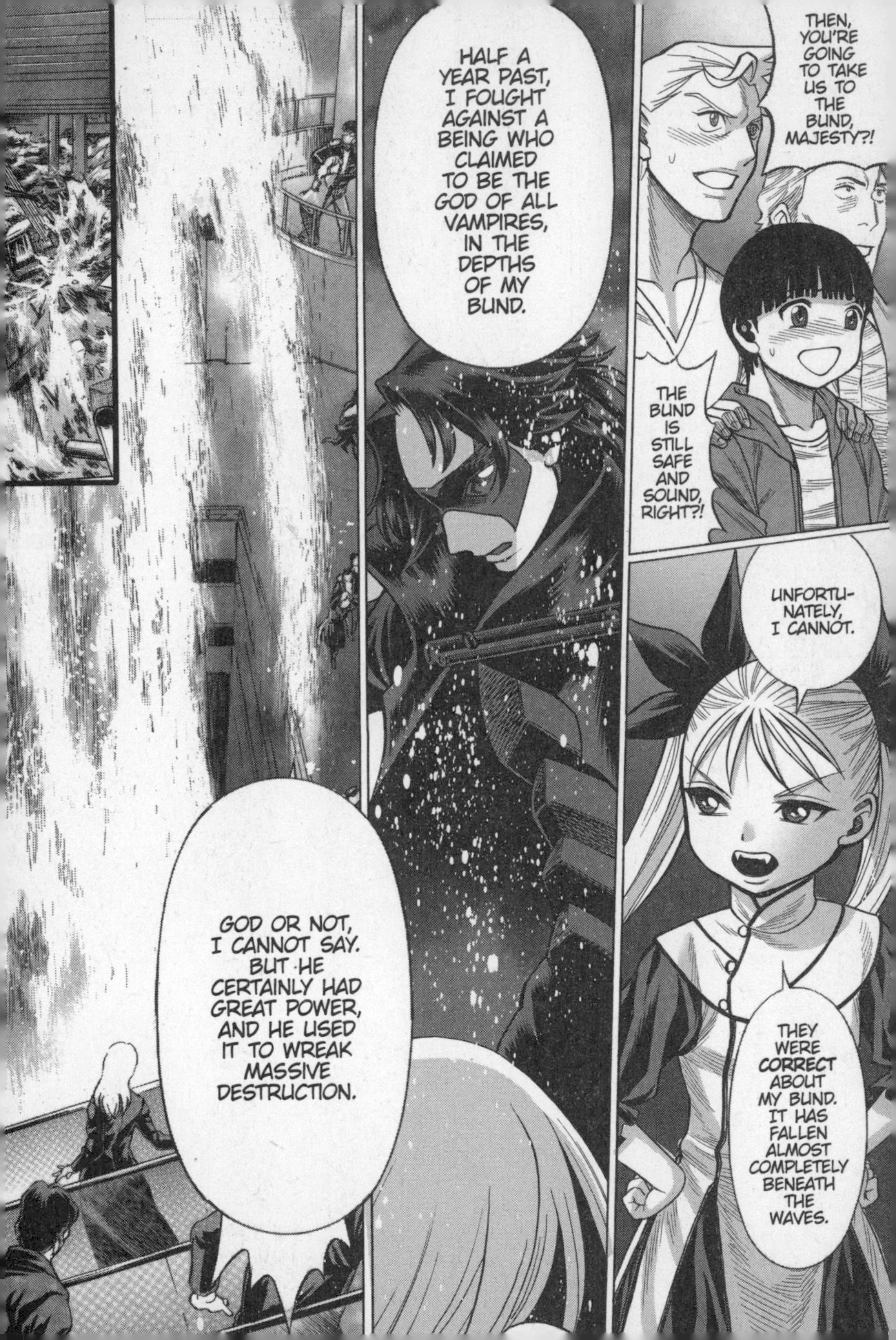
THEN, YOU'RE GOING TO TAKE US TO THE BUND, MAJESTY?!
THE BUND IS STILL SAFE AND SOUND, RIGHT?!
UNFORTU-NATELY, I CANNOT.
THEY WERE CORRECT ABOUT MY BUND. IT HAS FALLEN ALMOST COMPLETELY BENEATH THE WAVES.
HALF A YEAR PAST, I FOUGHT AGAINST A BEING WHO CLAIMED TO BE THE GOD OF ALL VAMPIRES, IN THE DEPTHS OF MY BUND.
GOD OR NOT, I CANNOT SAY. BUT HE CERTAINLY HAD GREAT POWER, AND HE USED IT TO WREAK MASSIVE DESTRUCTION.

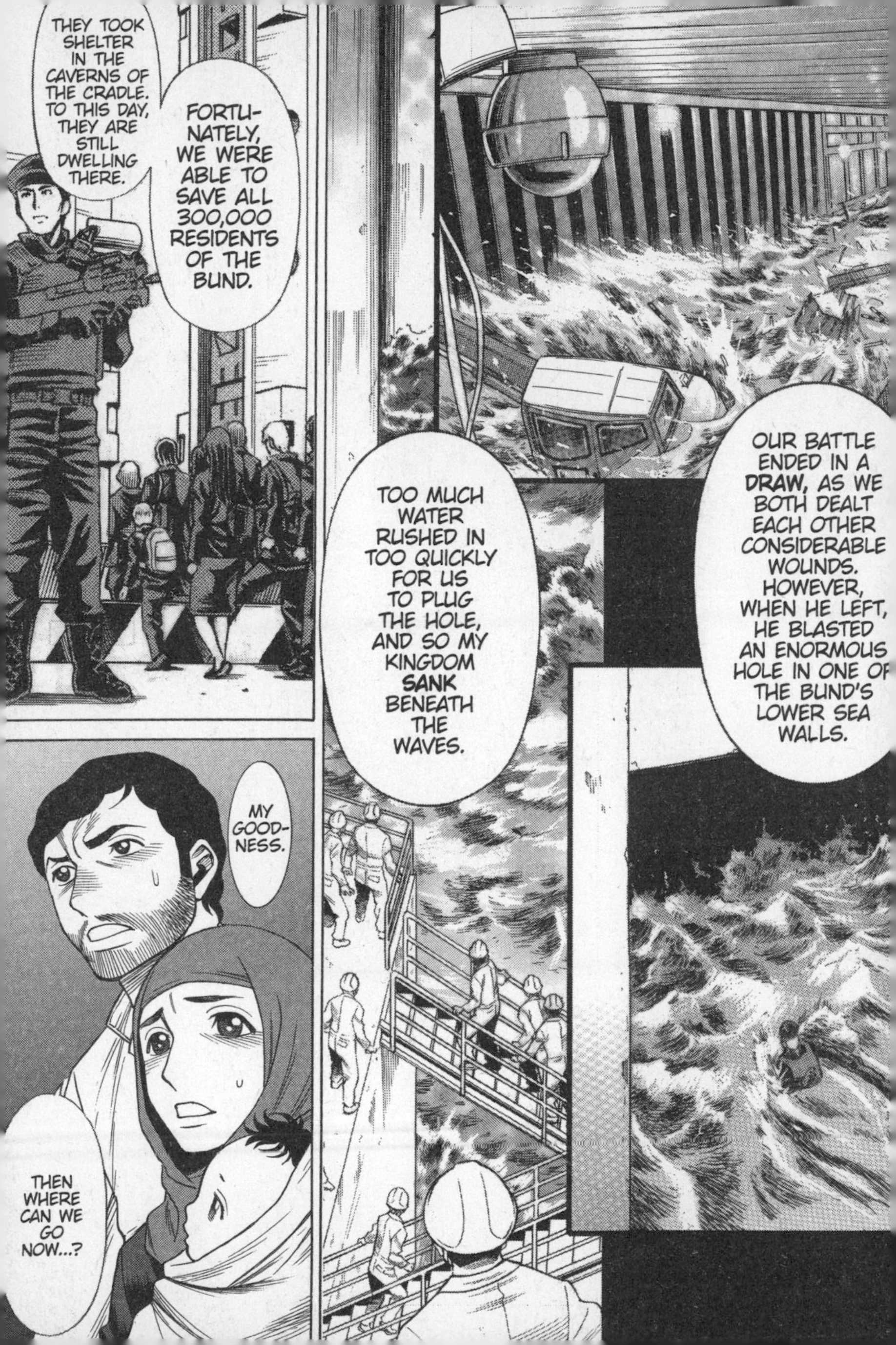
OUR BATTLE ENDED IN A **DRAW,** AS WE BOTH DEALT EACH OTHER CONSIDERABLE WOUNDS. HOWEVER, WHEN HE LEFT, HE BLASTED AN ENORMOUS HOLE IN ONE OF THE BUND'S LOWER SEA WALLS.
TOO MUCH WATER RUSHED IN TOO QUICKLY FOR US TO PLUG THE HOLE, AND SO MY KINGDOM **SANK** BENEATH THE WAVES.
FORTU-NATELY, WE WERE ABLE TO SAVE ALL 300,000 RESIDENTS OF THE BUND.
THEY TOOK SHELTER IN THE CAVERNS OF THE CRADLE. TO THIS DAY, THEY ARE STILL DWELLING THERE.
MY GOOD-NESS.
THEN WHERE CAN WE GO NOW...?

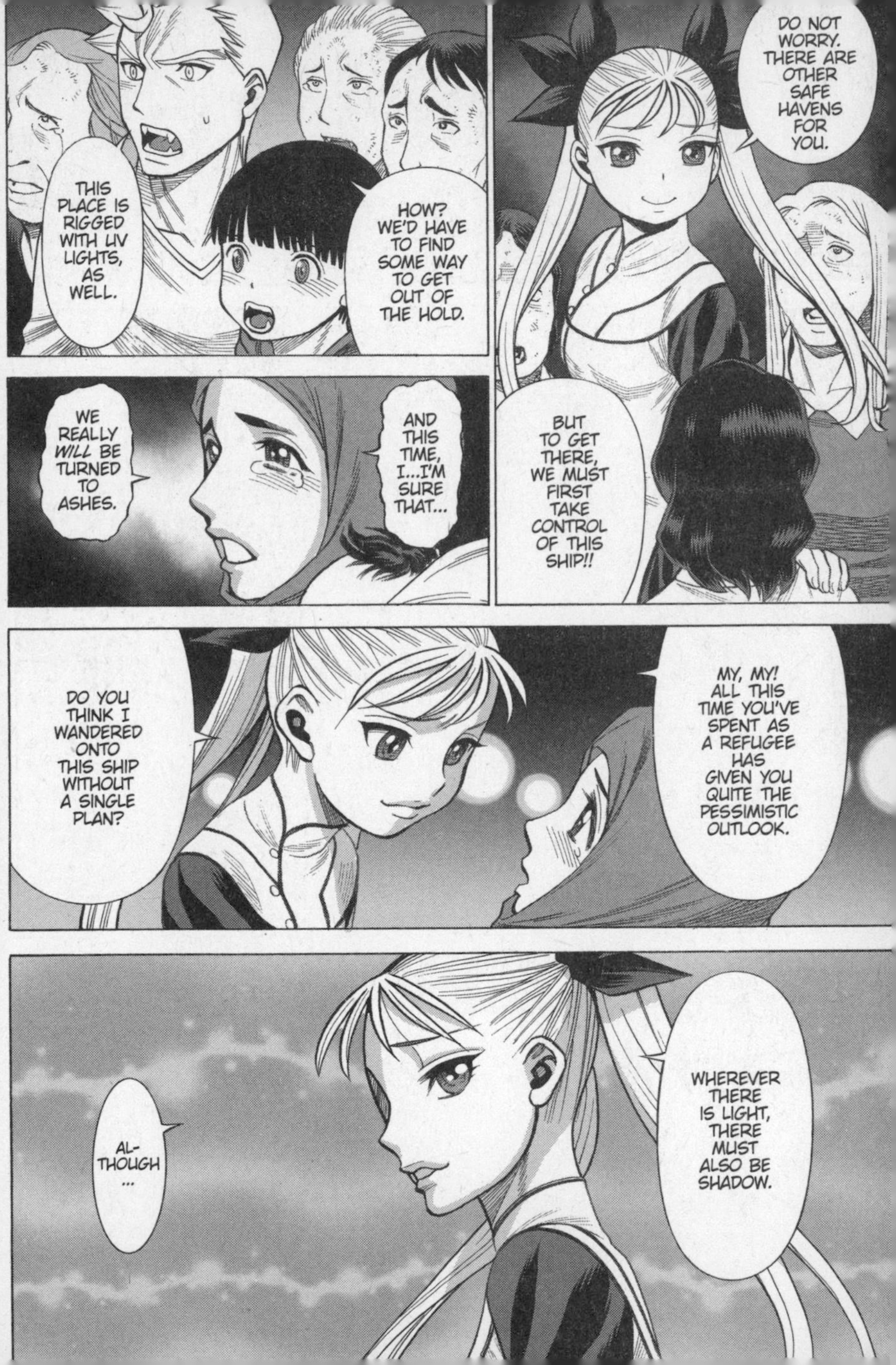
DO NOT WORRY. THERE ARE OTHER SAFE HAVENS FOR YOU.
BUT TO GET THERE, WE MUST FIRST TAKE CONTROL OF THIS SHIP!!
HOW? WE'D HAVE TO FIND SOME WAY TO GET OUT OF THE HOLD.
THIS PLACE IS RIGGED WITH UV LIGHTS, AS WELL.
AND THIS TIME, I...I'M SURE THAT...
WE REALLY *WILL* BE TURNED TO ASHES.
MY, MY! ALL THIS TIME YOU'VE SPENT AS A REFUGEE HAS GIVEN YOU QUITE THE PESSIMISTIC OUTLOOK.
DO YOU THINK I WANDERED ONTO THIS SHIP WITHOUT A SINGLE PLAN?
WHEREVER THERE IS LIGHT, THERE MUST ALSO BE SHADOW.
AL-THOUGH ...

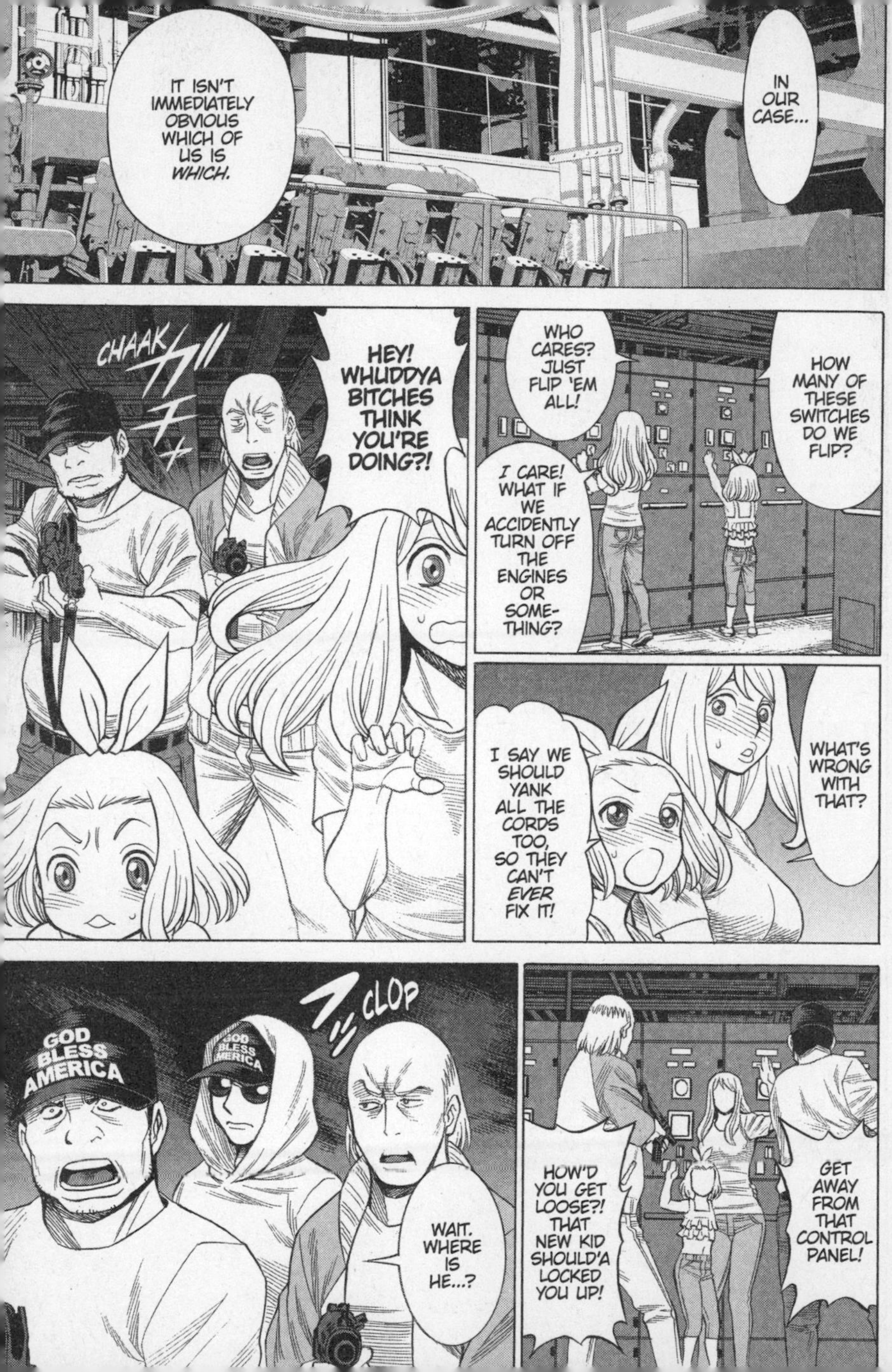
IN OUR CASE...
IT ISN'T IMMEDIATELY OBVIOUS WHICH OF US IS *WHICH.*
HOW MANY OF THESE SWITCHES DO WE FLIP?
WHO CARES? JUST FLIP 'EM ALL!
I CARE! WHAT IF WE ACCIDENTLY TURN OFF THE ENGINES OR SOME-THING?
WHAT'S WRONG WITH THAT?
I SAY WE SHOULD YANK ALL THE CORDS TOO, SO THEY CAN'T *EVER* FIX IT!
CHAAK
HEY! WHUDDYA BITCHES THINK YOU'RE DOING?!
GET AWAY FROM THAT CONTROL PANEL!
HOW'D YOU GET LOOSE?! THAT NEW KID SHOULD'A LOCKED YOU UP!
CLOP
GOD BLESS AMERICA
GOD BLESS AMERICA
WAIT. WHERE IS HE...?

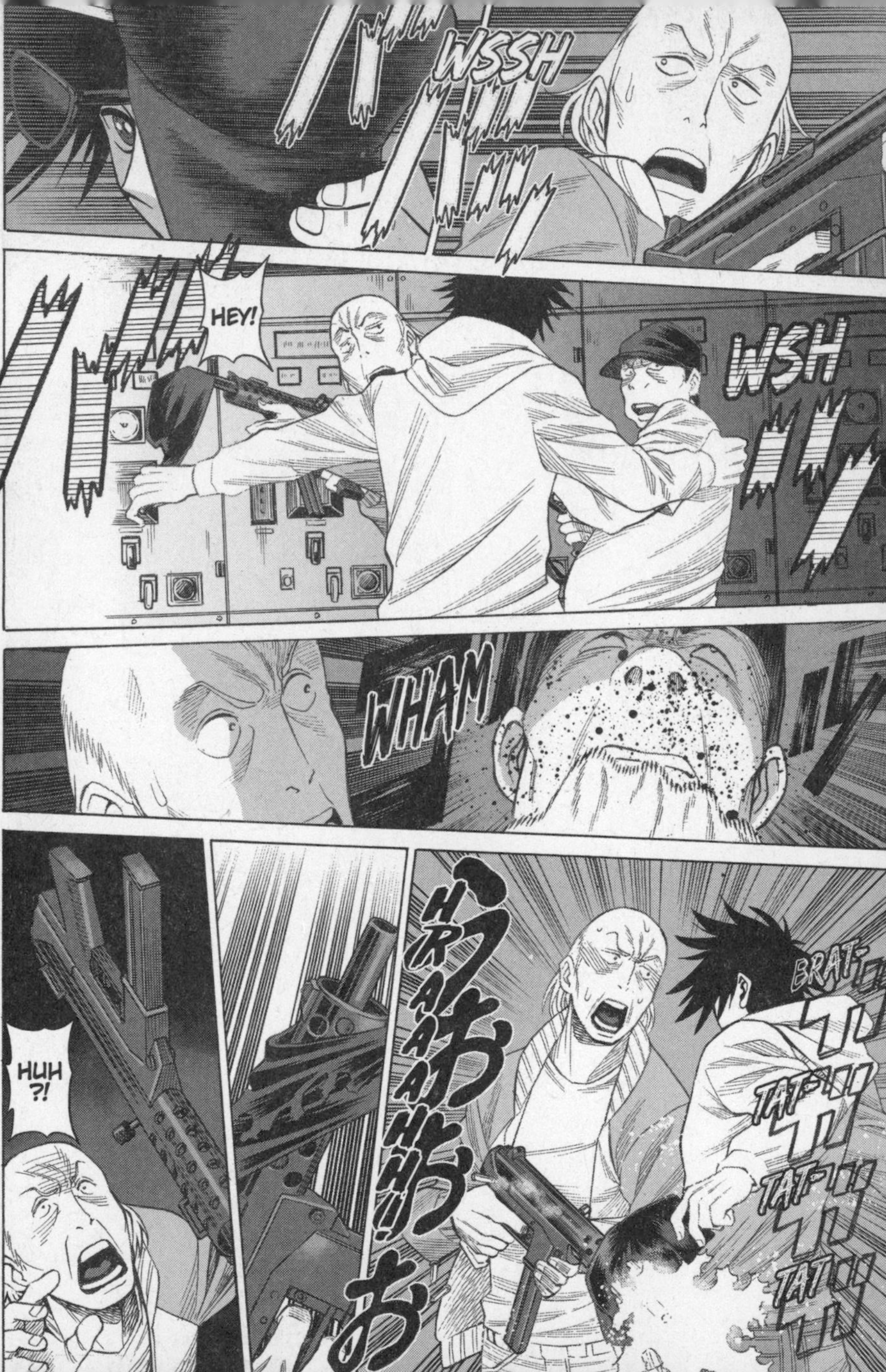
WSSH
WSH
HEY!
WHAM
BRAT-
HRAAAAAHH!!
TAT-
TAT-
TAT
HUH?!

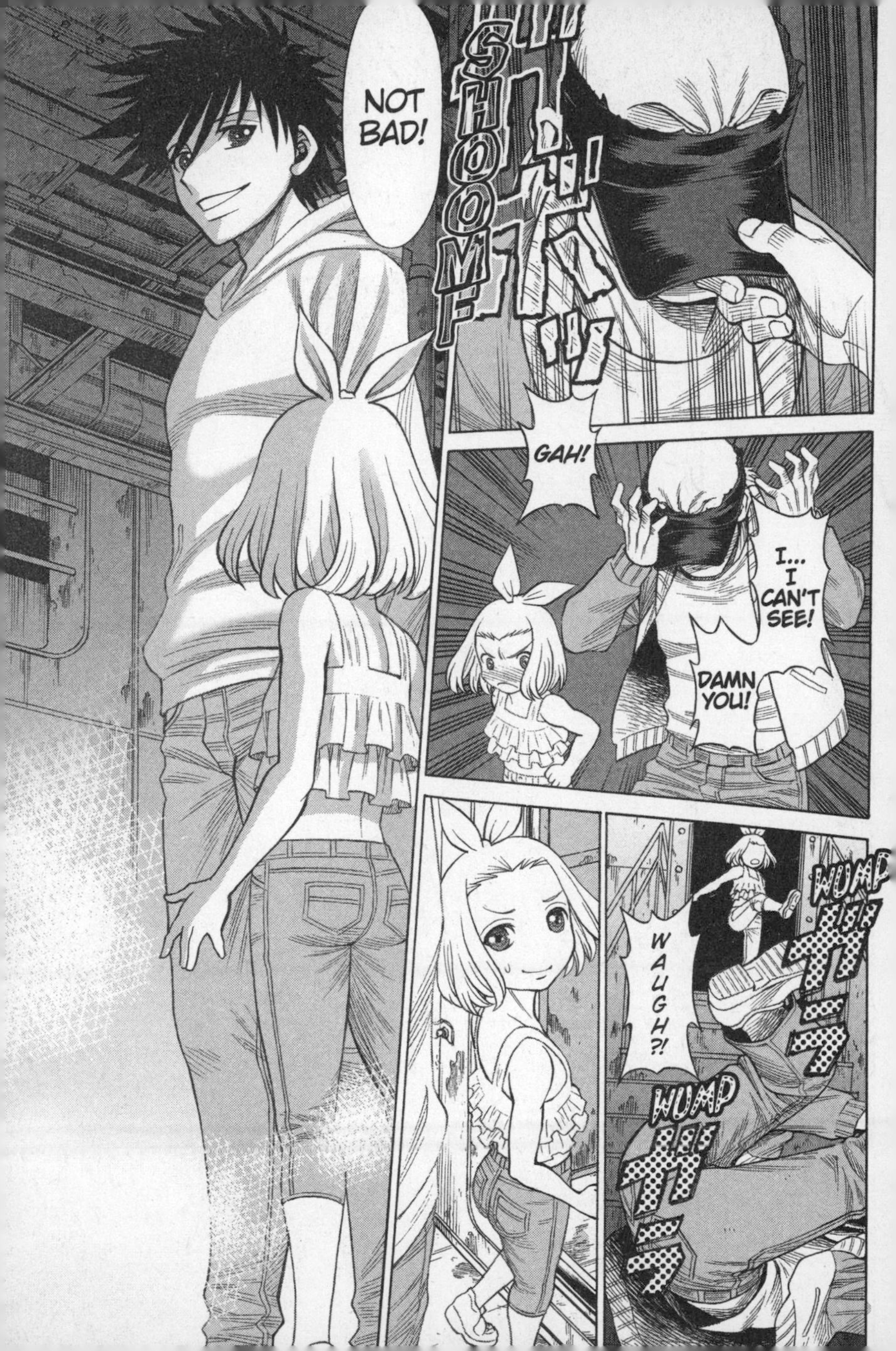
SHOOOMF
GAH!
I... I CAN'T SEE!
DAMN YOU!
WUMP
WAUGH?!
WUMP
NOT BAD!

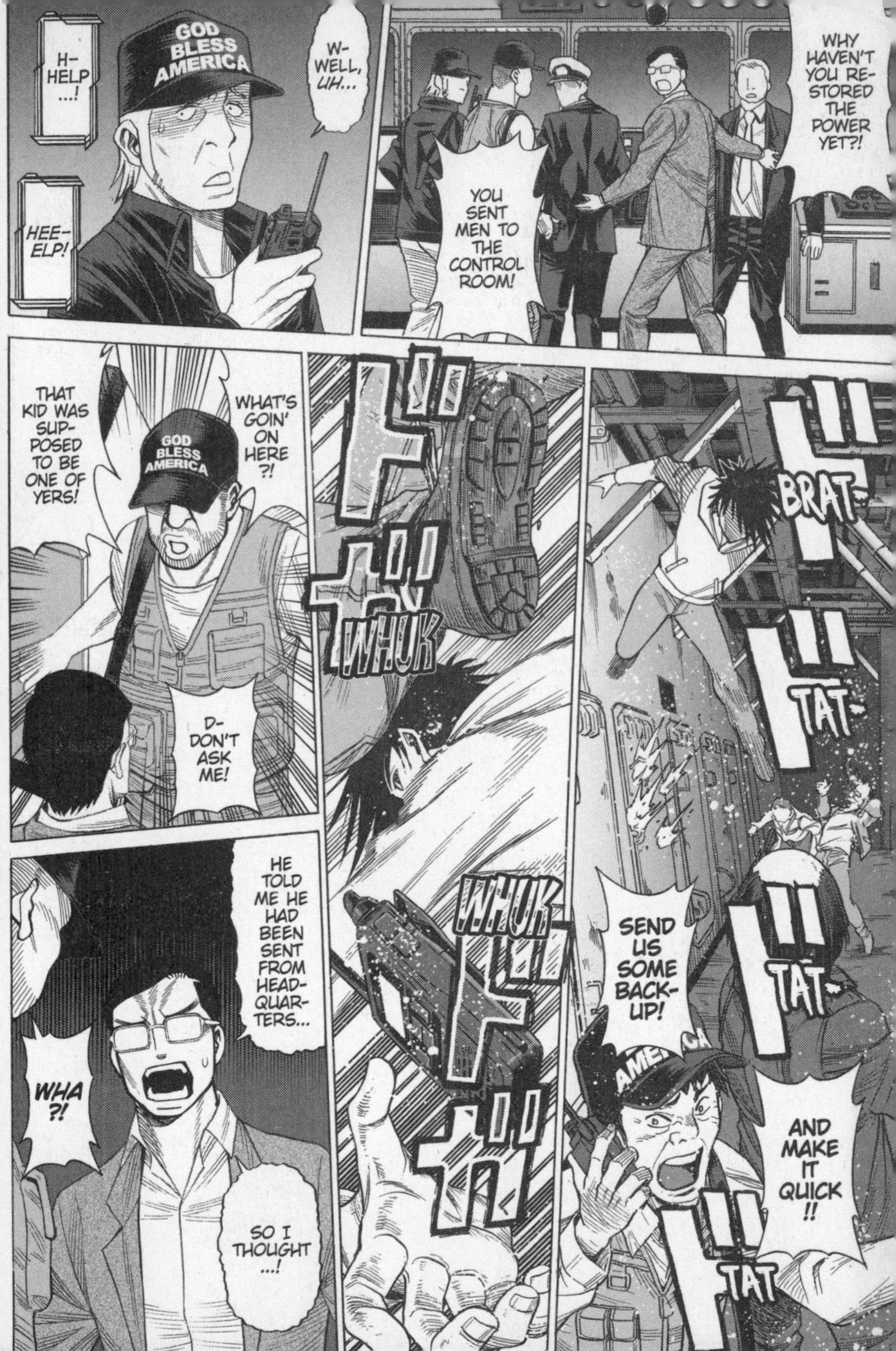
WHY HAVEN'T YOU RESTORED THE POWER YET?!
YOU SENT MEN TO THE CONTROL ROOM!
W-WELL, UH...
H-HELP...!
HEE-ELP!
BRAT
TAT
TAT
SEND US SOME BACK-UP!
AND MAKE IT QUICK!!
TAT
WHUK
WHUK
WHAT'S GOIN' ON HERE?!
THAT KID WAS SUPPOSED TO BE ONE OF YERS!
D-DON'T ASK ME!
HE TOLD ME HE HAD BEEN SENT FROM HEADQUARTERS...
WHA?!
SO I THOUGHT...!

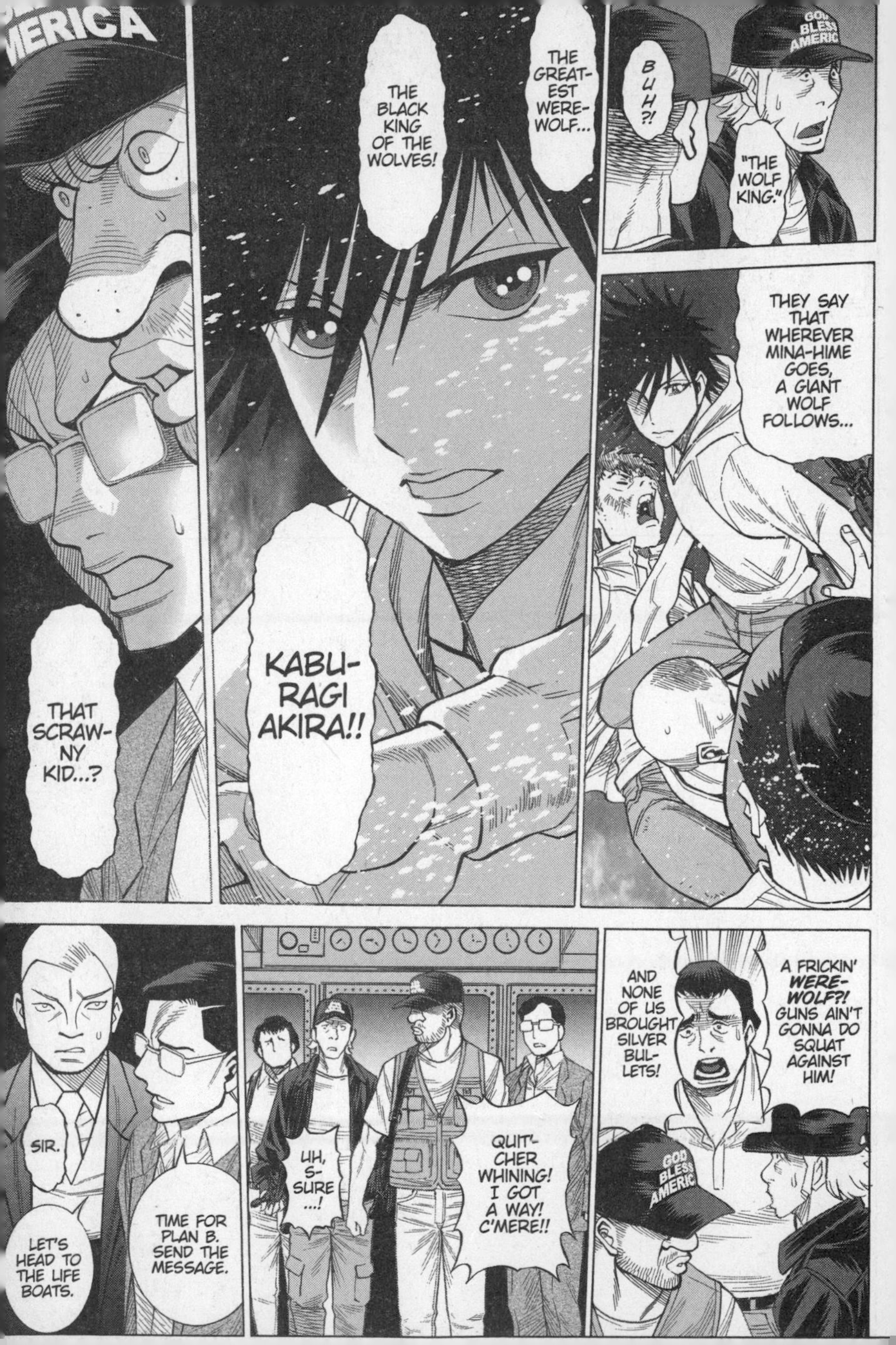
BUH?!
"THE WOLF KING."
THEY SAY THAT WHEREVER MINA-HIME GOES, A GIANT WOLF FOLLOWS...
THE GREAT-EST WERE-WOLF...
THE BLACK KING OF THE WOLVES!
KABU-RAGI AKIRA!!
THAT SCRAW-NY KID...?
A FRICKIN' *WERE-WOLF?!* GUNS AIN'T GONNA DO SQUAT AGAINST HIM!
AND NONE OF US BROUGHT SILVER BUL-LETS!
QUIT'-CHER WHINING! I GOT A WAY! C'MERE!!
UH, S-SURE ...!
SIR.
TIME FOR PLAN B. SEND THE MESSAGE.
LET'S HEAD TO THE LIFE BOATS.

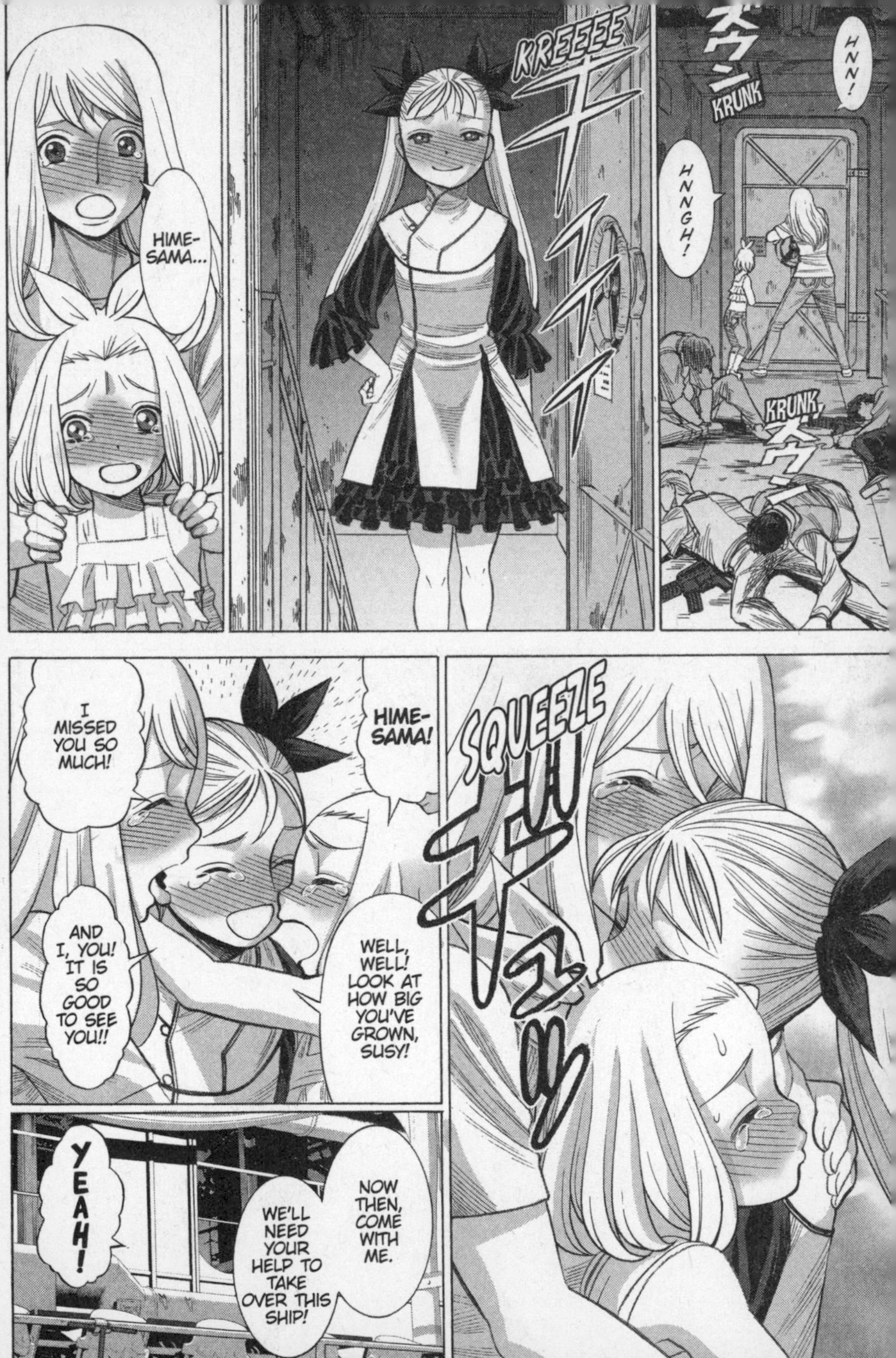

HNN!
KRUNK
HNNGH!
KRUNK
KREEEE
HIME-SAMA...
SQUEEZE
HIME-SAMA!
I MISSED YOU SO MUCH!
WELL, WELL! LOOK AT HOW BIG YOU'VE GROWN, SUSY!
AND I, YOU! IT IS SO GOOD TO SEE YOU!!
NOW THEN, COME WITH ME.
WE'LL NEED YOUR HELP TO TAKE OVER THIS SHIP!
YEAH!

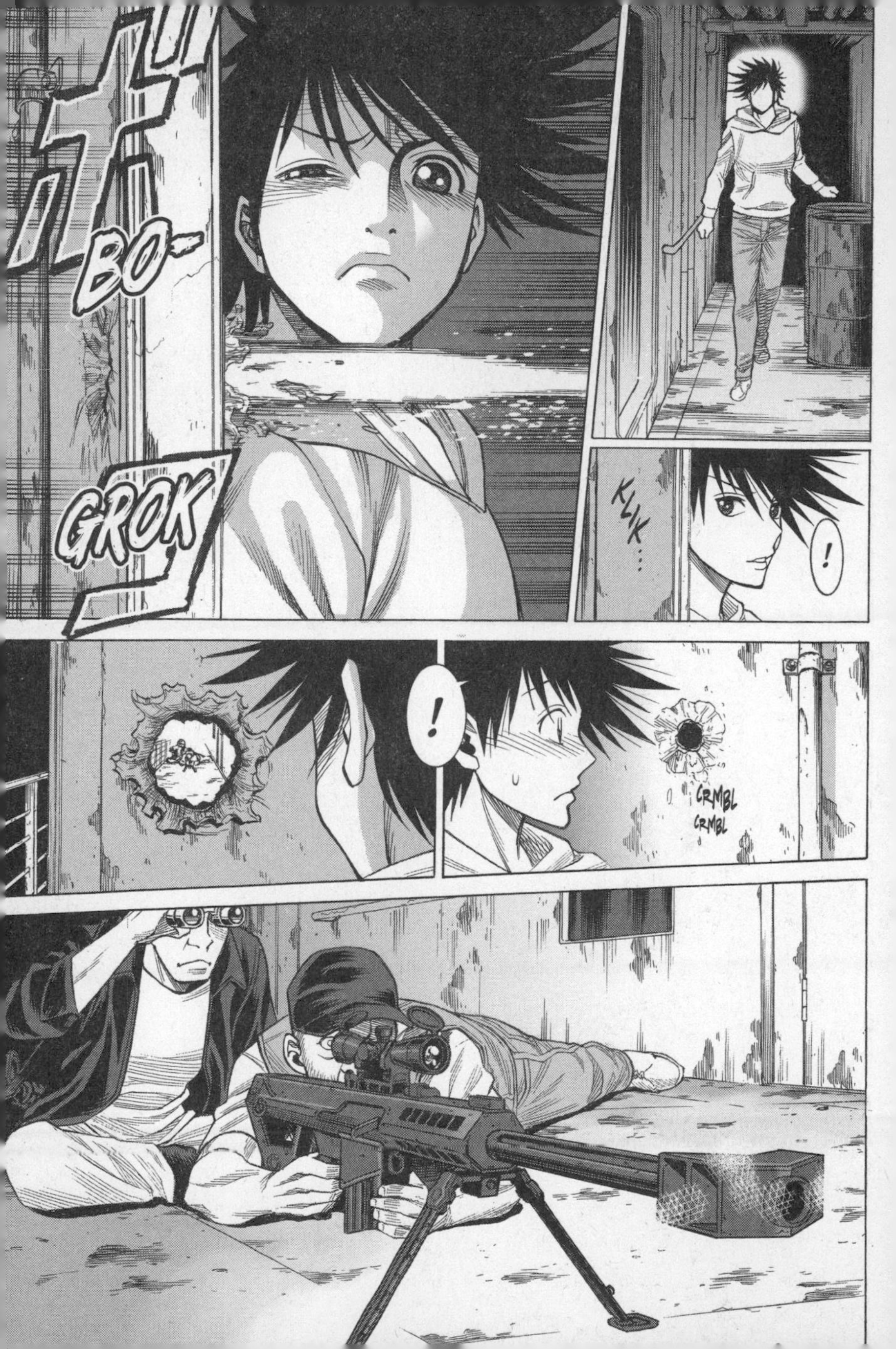
KLIK...
!
BO-
GROK
!
CRMBL
CRMBL

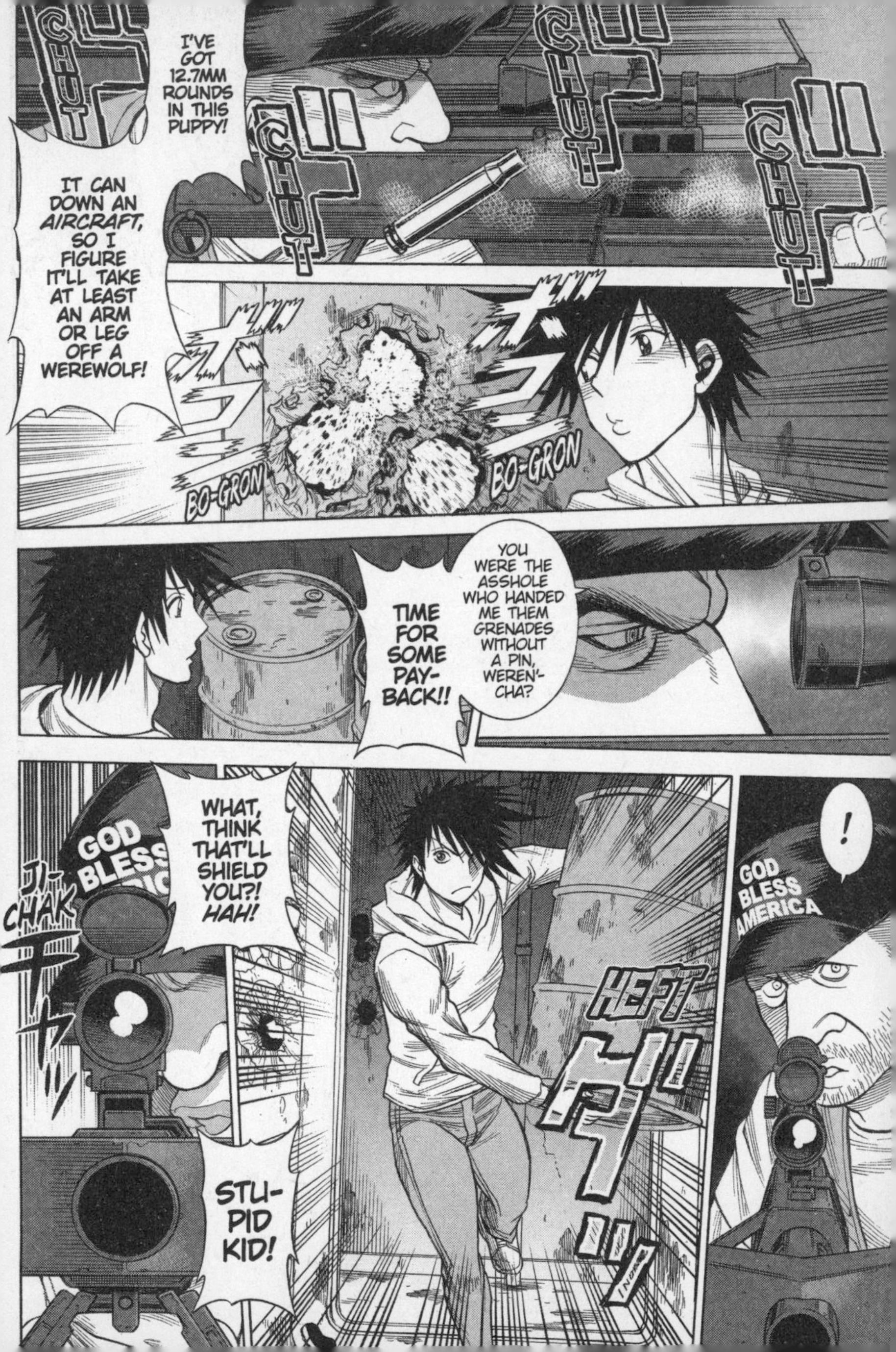
CHUT
CHUT
CHUT
CHUT
I'VE GOT 12.7MM ROUNDS IN THIS PUPPY!
BO-GRON
BO-GRON
IT CAN DOWN AN AIRCRAFT, SO I FIGURE IT'LL TAKE AT LEAST AN ARM OR LEG OFF A WEREWOLF!
YOU WERE THE ASSHOLE WHO HANDED ME THEM GRENADES WITHOUT A PIN, WEREN'-CHA?
TIME FOR SOME PAY-BACK!!
!
GOD BLESS AMERICA
HEFT
WHAT, THINK THAT'LL SHIELD YOU?! HAH!
JI-CHAK
STU-PID KID!

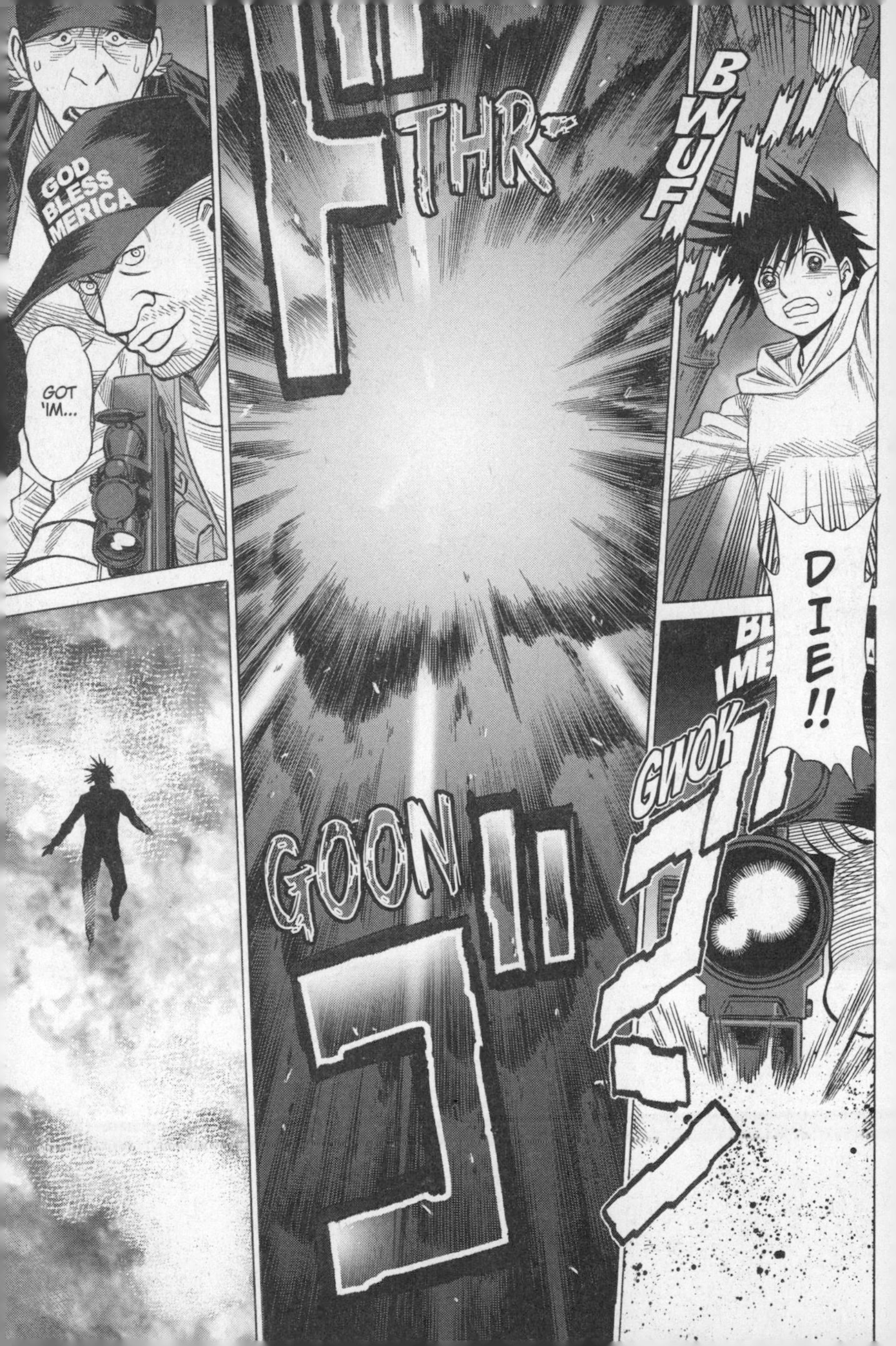
BWUF
DIE!!
GWOK
THR
GOON
GOD BLESS MERICA
GOT 'IM...

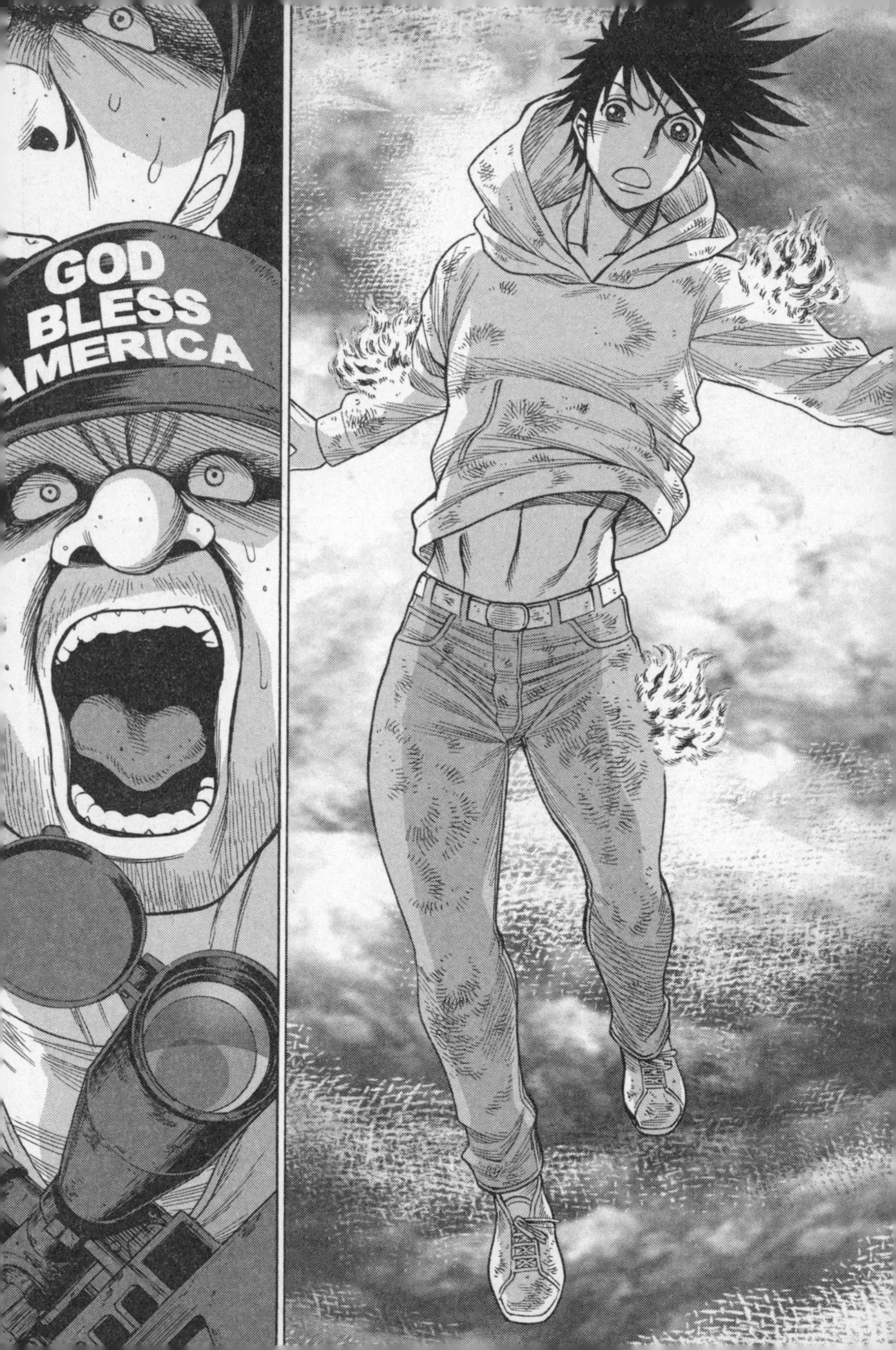
GOD
BLESS
AMERICA

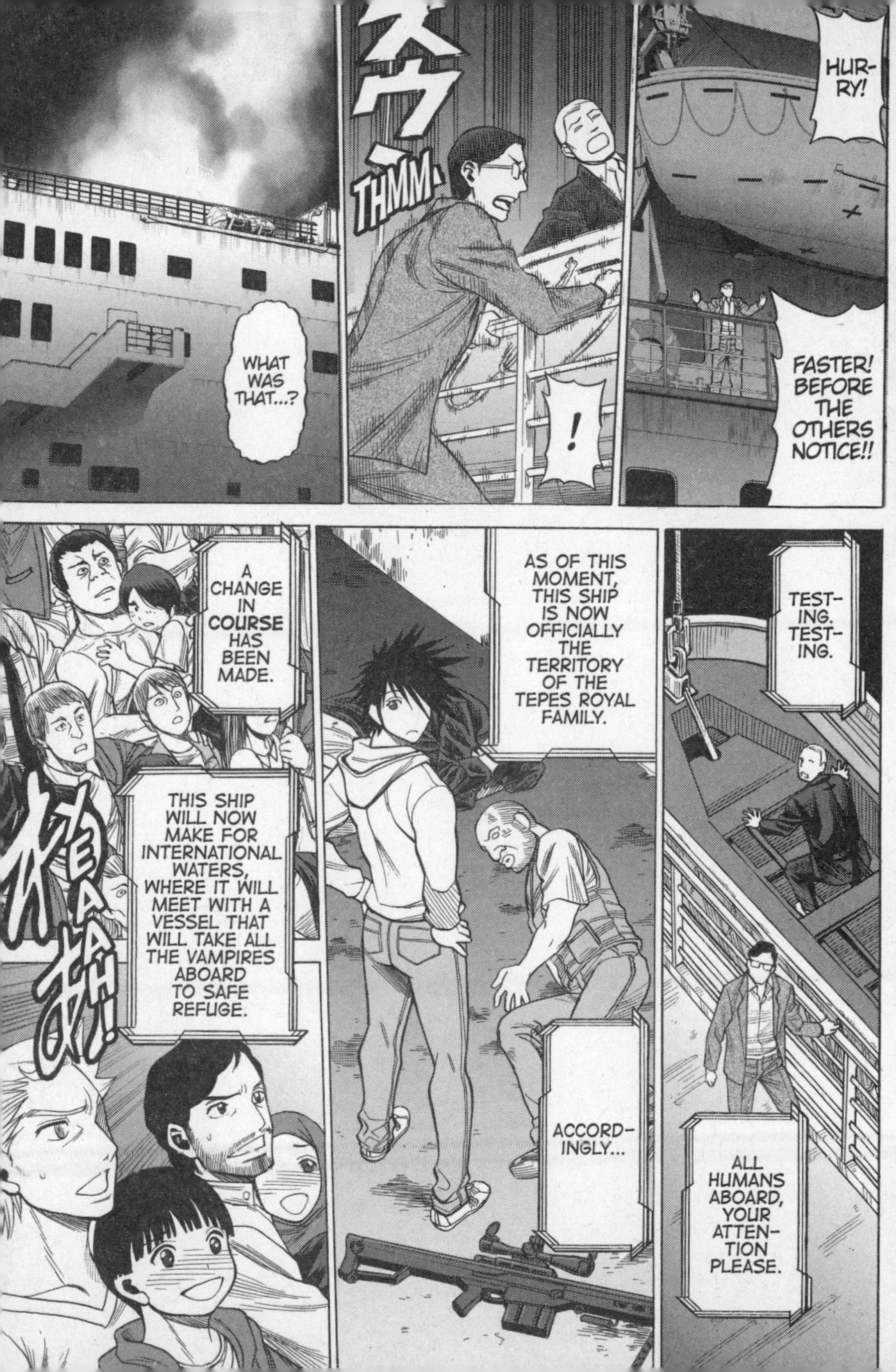

HUR-RY!
FASTER! BEFORE THE OTHERS NOTICE!!
THMM
!
WHAT WAS THAT...?
TEST-ING. TEST-ING.
ALL HUMANS ABOARD, YOUR ATTEN-TION PLEASE.
AS OF THIS MOMENT, THIS SHIP IS NOW OFFICIALLY THE TERRITORY OF THE TEPES ROYAL FAMILY.
ACCORD-INGLY...
A CHANGE IN COURSE HAS BEEN MADE.
THIS SHIP WILL NOW MAKE FOR INTERNATIONAL WATERS, WHERE IT WILL MEET WITH A VESSEL THAT WILL TAKE ALL THE VAMPIRES ABOARD TO SAFE REFUGE.
YEAAH!

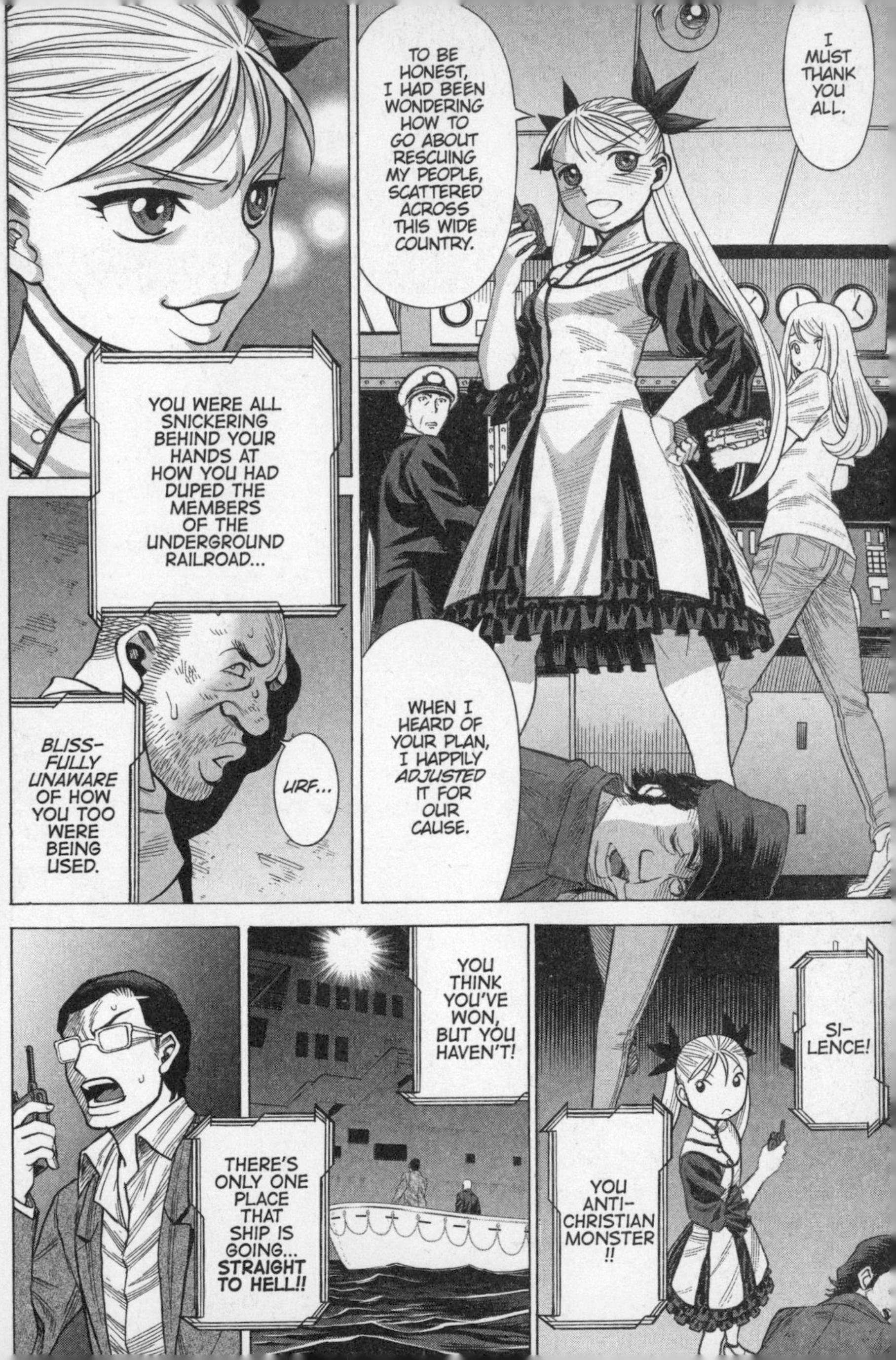
I MUST THANK YOU ALL.
TO BE HONEST, I HAD BEEN WONDERING HOW TO GO ABOUT RESCUING MY PEOPLE, SCATTERED ACROSS THIS WIDE COUNTRY.
WHEN I HEARD OF YOUR PLAN, I HAPPILY *ADJUSTED* IT FOR OUR CAUSE.
YOU WERE ALL SNICKERING BEHIND YOUR HANDS AT HOW YOU HAD DUPED THE MEMBERS OF THE UNDERGROUND RAILROAD...
URF...
BLISS-FULLY UNAWARE OF HOW YOU TOO WERE BEING USED.
SI-LENCE!
YOU ANTI-CHRISTIAN MONSTER!!
YOU THINK YOU'VE WON, BUT YOU HAVEN'T!
THERE'S ONLY ONE PLACE THAT SHIP IS GOING... **STRAIGHT TO HELL!!**

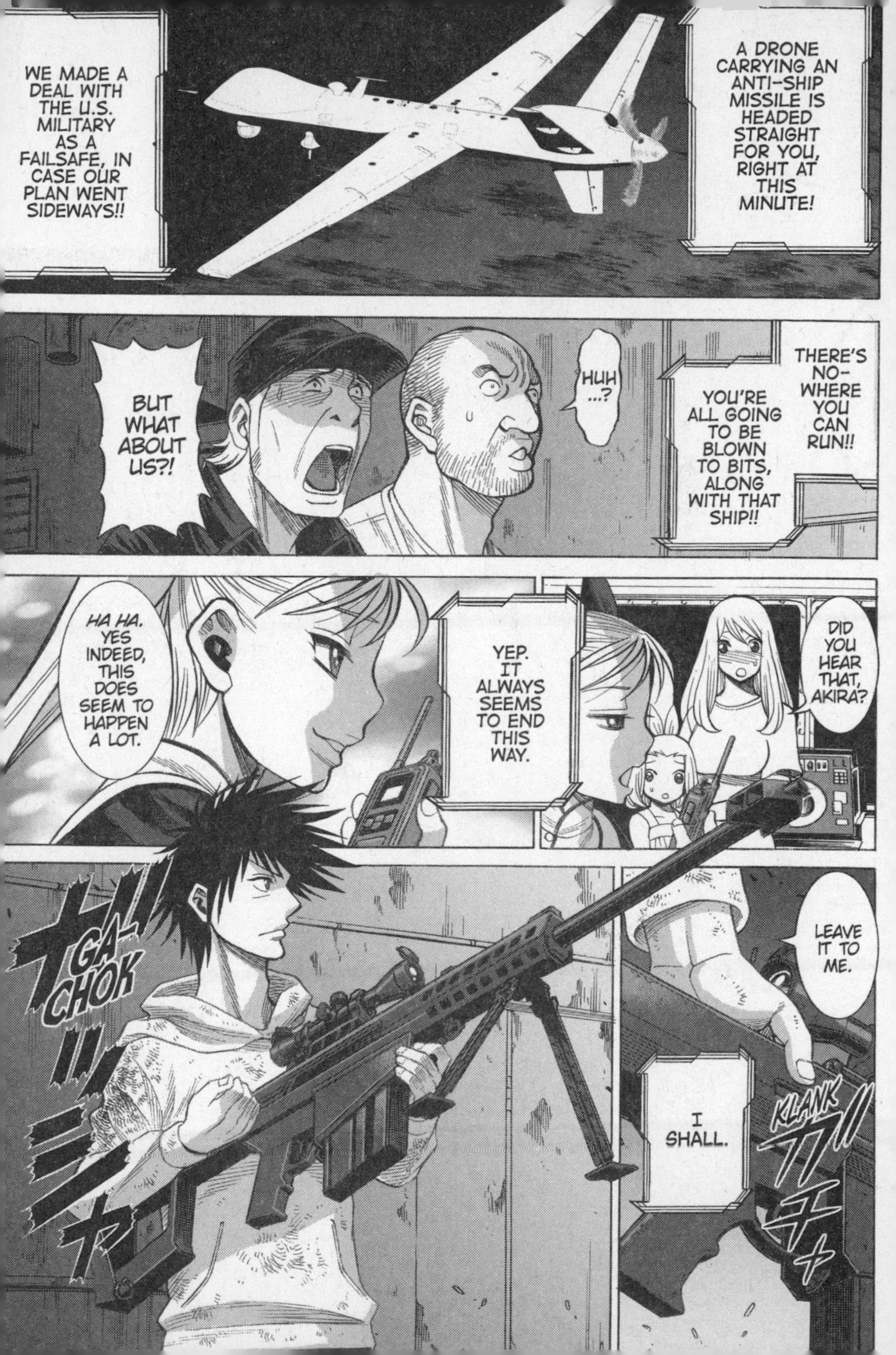

A DRONE CARRYING AN ANTI-SHIP MISSILE IS HEADED STRAIGHT FOR YOU, RIGHT AT THIS MINUTE!
WE MADE A DEAL WITH THE U.S. MILITARY AS A FAILSAFE, IN CASE OUR PLAN WENT SIDEWAYS!!
THERE'S NO-WHERE YOU CAN RUN!!
YOU'RE ALL GOING TO BE BLOWN TO BITS, ALONG WITH THAT SHIP!!
HUH ...?
BUT WHAT ABOUT US?!
DID YOU HEAR THAT, AKIRA?
YEP. IT ALWAYS SEEMS TO END THIS WAY.
HA HA. YES INDEED, THIS DOES SEEM TO HAPPEN A LOT.
LEAVE IT TO ME.
I SHALL.
KLANK
GA-CHOK

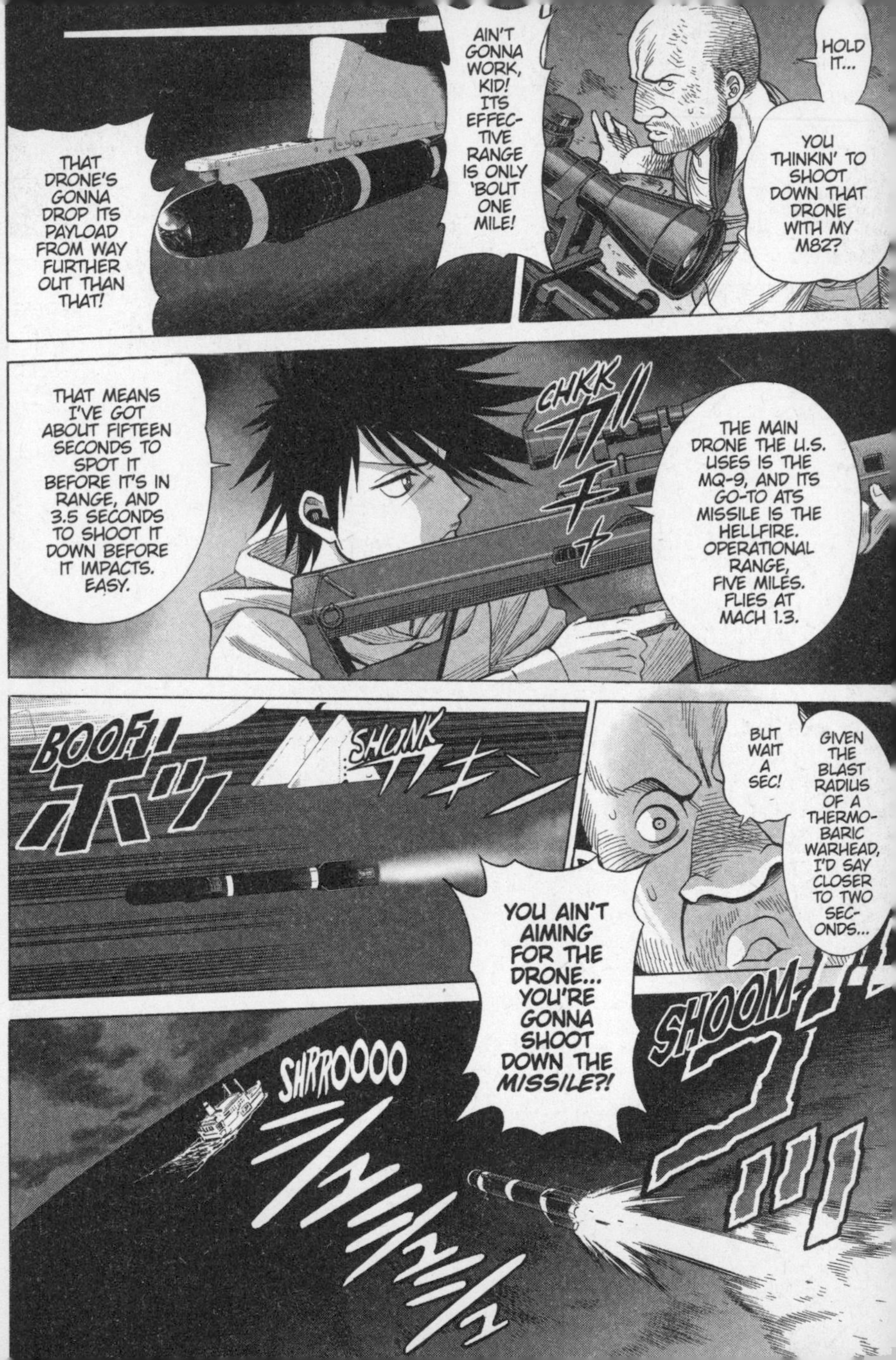
HOLD IT...
YOU THINKIN' TO SHOOT DOWN THAT DRONE WITH MY M82?
AIN'T GONNA WORK, KID! ITS EFFECTIVE RANGE IS ONLY 'BOUT ONE MILE!
THAT DRONE'S GONNA DROP ITS PAYLOAD FROM WAY FURTHER OUT THAN THAT!
THE MAIN DRONE THE U.S. USES IS THE MQ-9, AND ITS GO-TO ATS MISSILE IS THE HELLFIRE. OPERATIONAL RANGE, FIVE MILES. FLIES AT MACH 1.3.
CHKK
THAT MEANS I'VE GOT ABOUT FIFTEEN SECONDS TO SPOT IT BEFORE IT'S IN RANGE, AND 3.5 SECONDS TO SHOOT IT DOWN BEFORE IT IMPACTS. EASY.
GIVEN THE BLAST RADIUS OF A THERMOBARIC WARHEAD, I'D SAY CLOSER TO TWO SECONDS...
BUT WAIT A SEC!
YOU AIN'T AIMING FOR THE DRONE... YOU'RE GONNA SHOOT DOWN THE *MISSILE*?!
SHUNK
BOOF!!
SHOOM
SHRROOOO

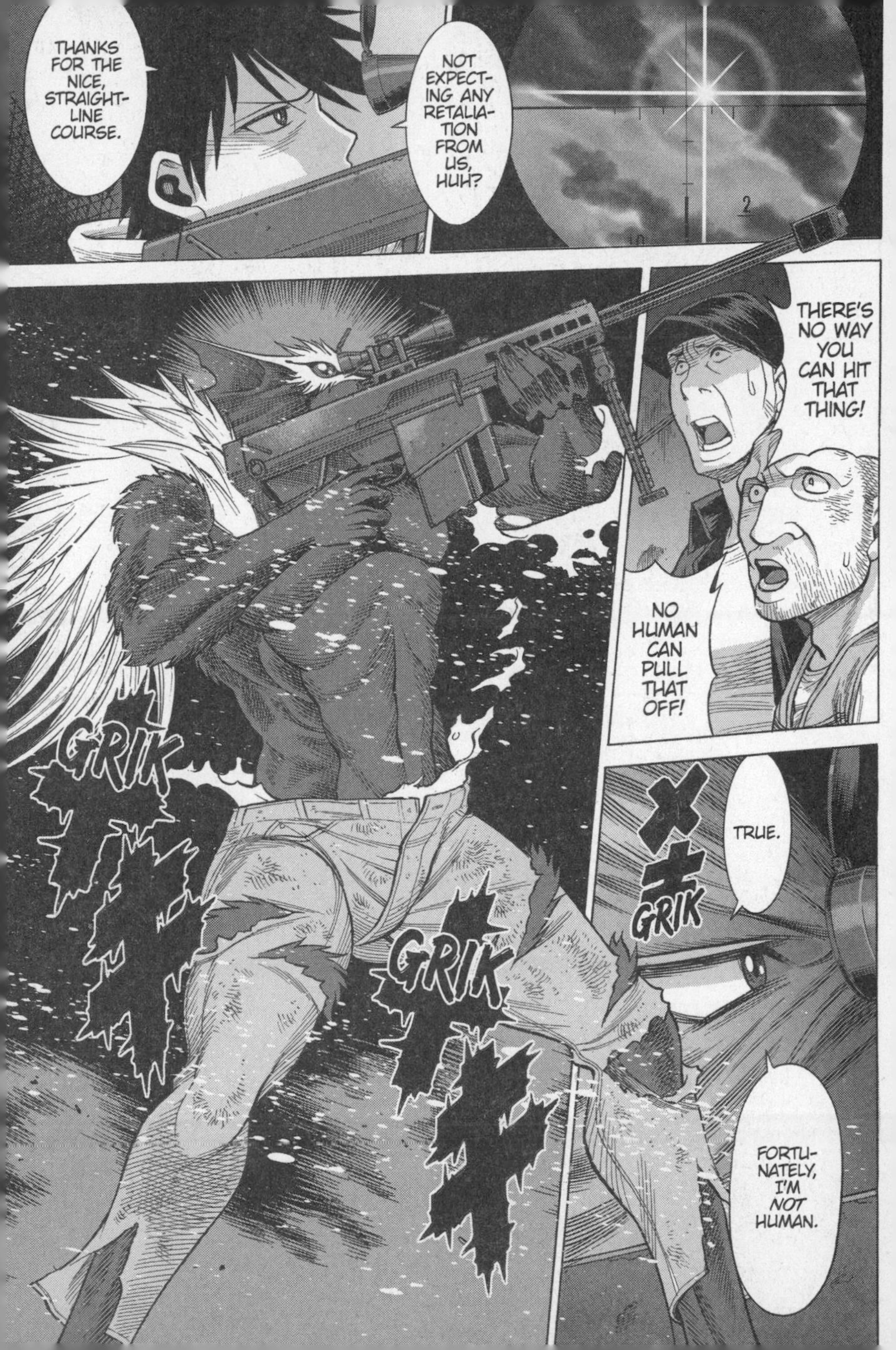
NOT EXPECTING ANY RETALIATION FROM US, HUH?
THANKS FOR THE NICE, STRAIGHT-LINE COURSE.
THERE'S NO WAY YOU CAN HIT THAT THING!
NO HUMAN CAN PULL THAT OFF!
TRUE.
GRIK
FORTUNATELY, I'M *NOT* HUMAN.
GRIK
GRIK

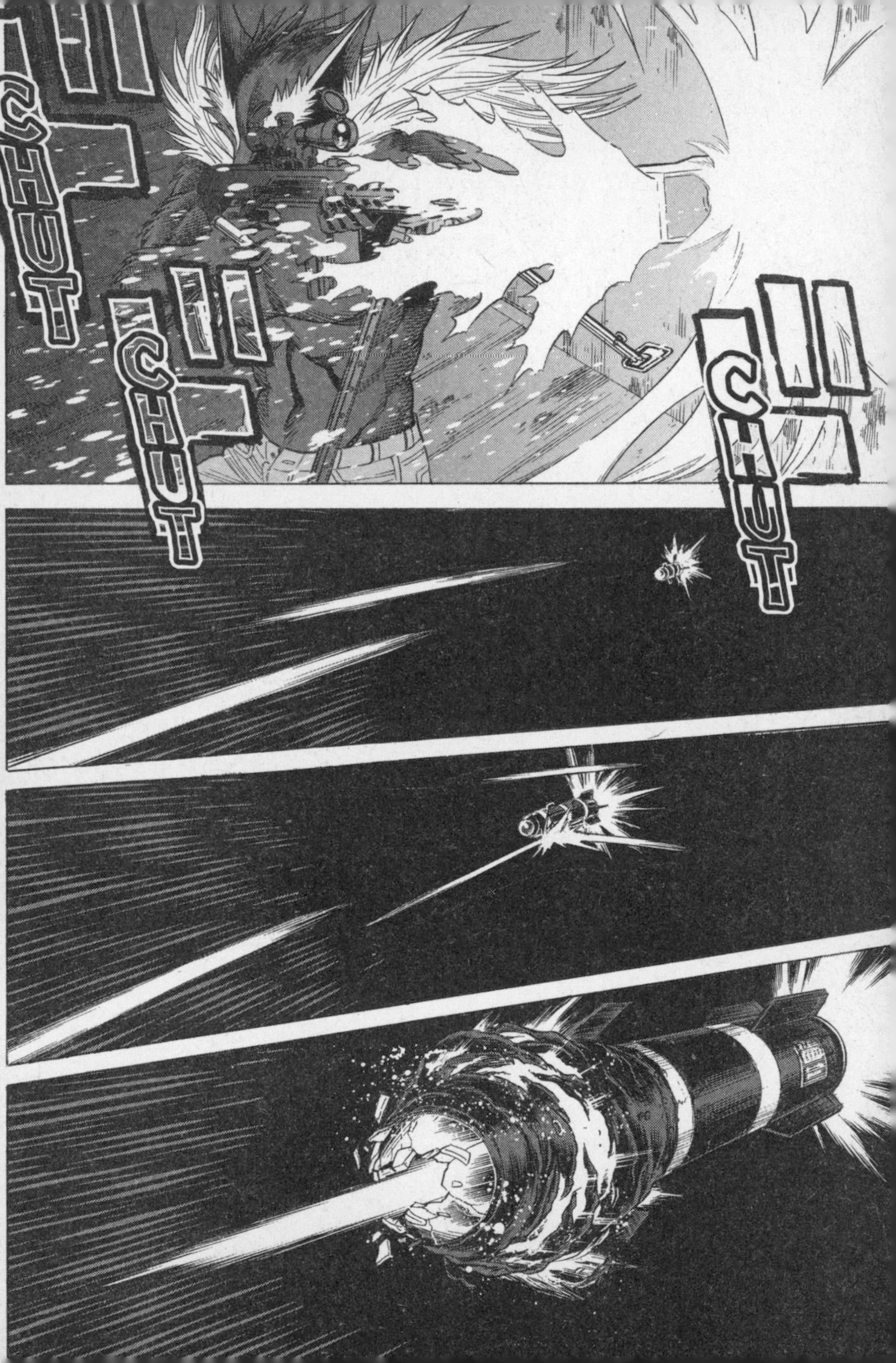
CHUT!!
CHUT!!
CHUT!!

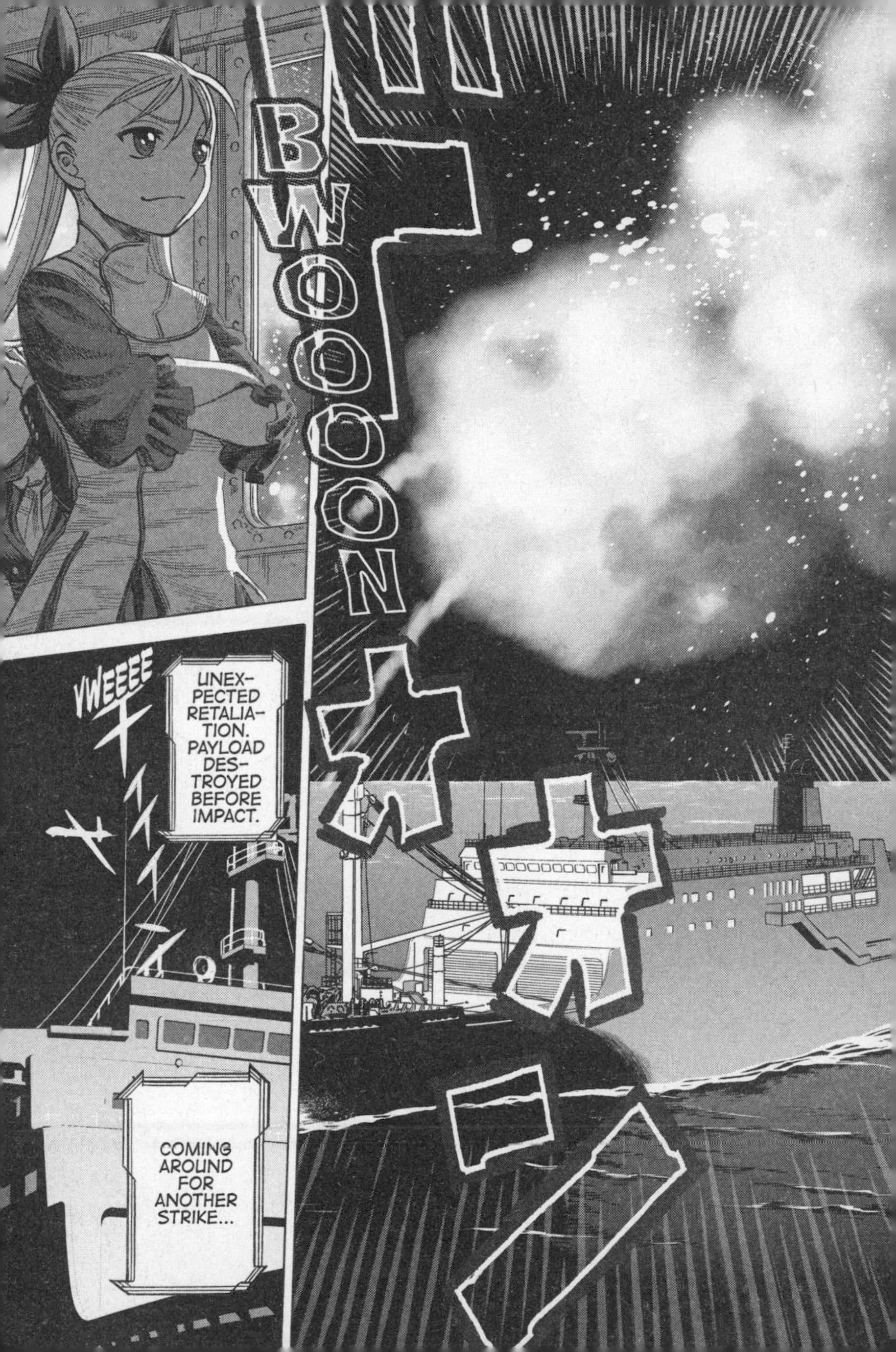
BWOOOON
VWEEEE
UNEX-PECTED RETALIA-TION. PAYLOAD DES-TROYED BEFORE IMPACT.
COMING AROUND FOR ANOTHER STRIKE...

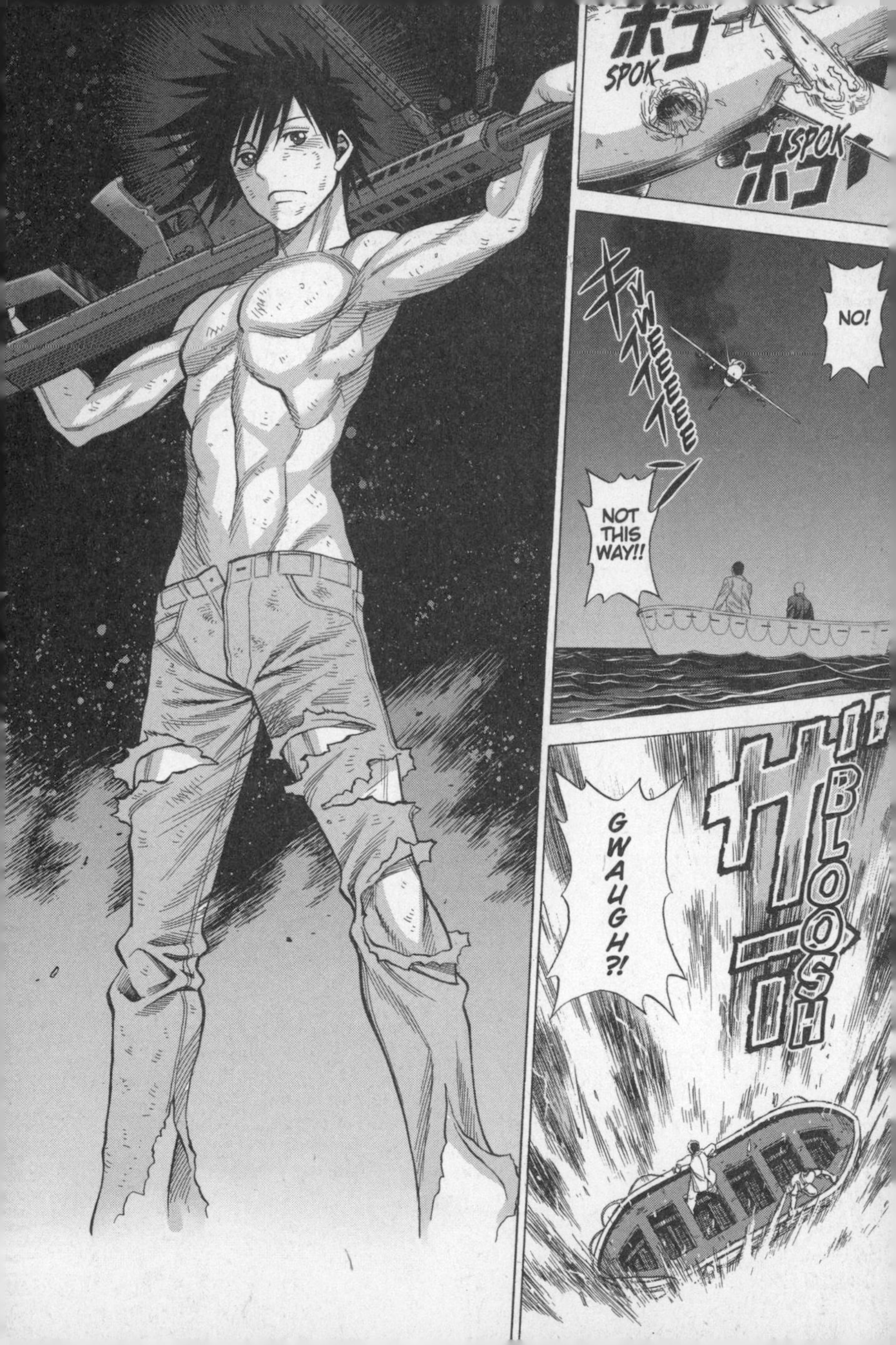

ボコ
SPOK
SPOK
ボコ
YWEEEEEE
NO!
NOT THIS WAY!!
BLOOSH
GWAUGH?!

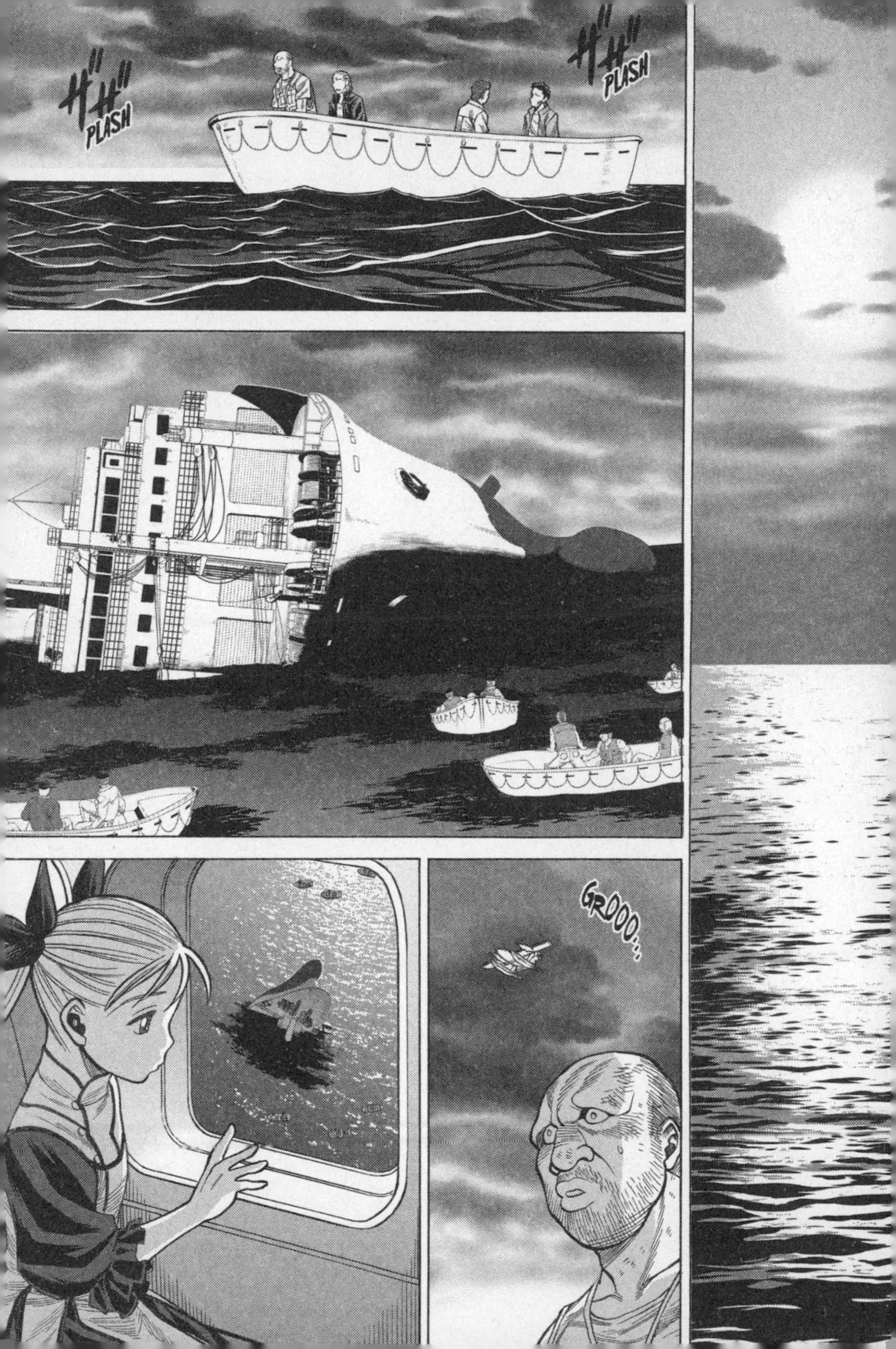
PLASH
PLASH
GROOO...

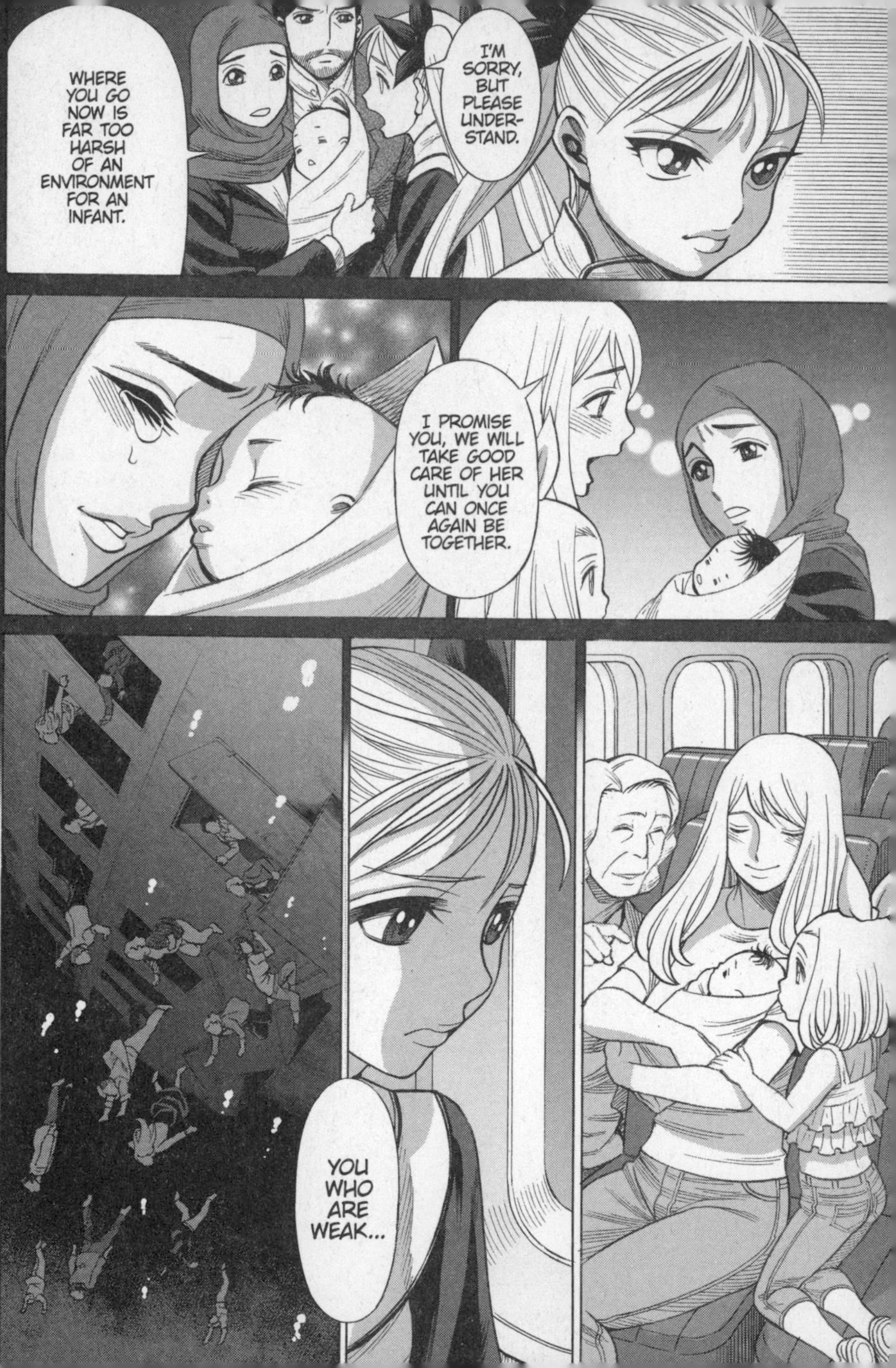
I'M SORRY, BUT PLEASE UNDER-STAND.
WHERE YOU GO NOW IS FAR TOO HARSH OF AN ENVIRONMENT FOR AN INFANT.
I PROMISE YOU, WE WILL TAKE GOOD CARE OF HER UNTIL YOU CAN ONCE AGAIN BE TOGETHER.
YOU WHO ARE WEAK...

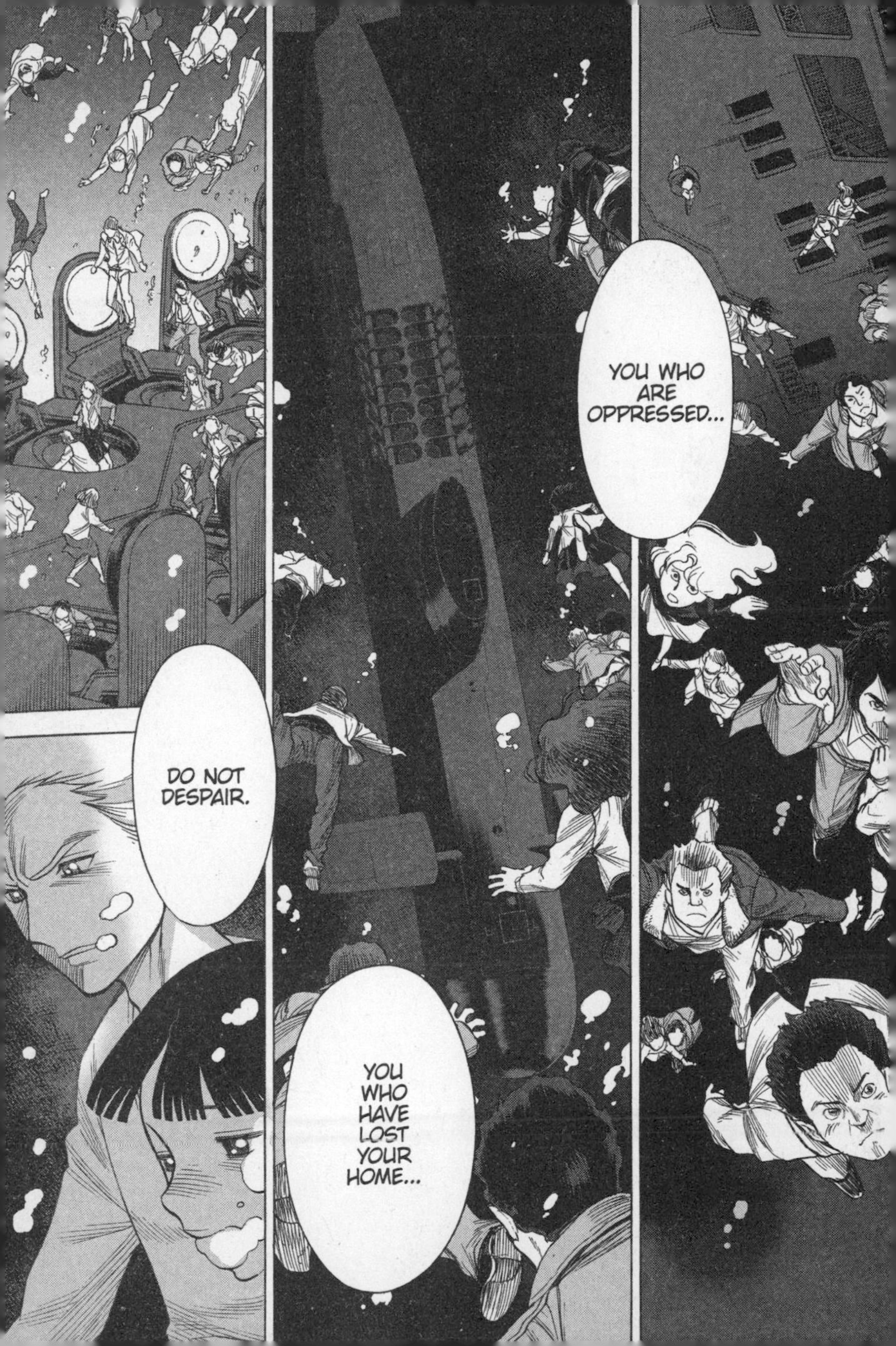
YOU WHO ARE OPPRESSED...
YOU WHO HAVE LOST YOUR HOME...
DO NOT DESPAIR.

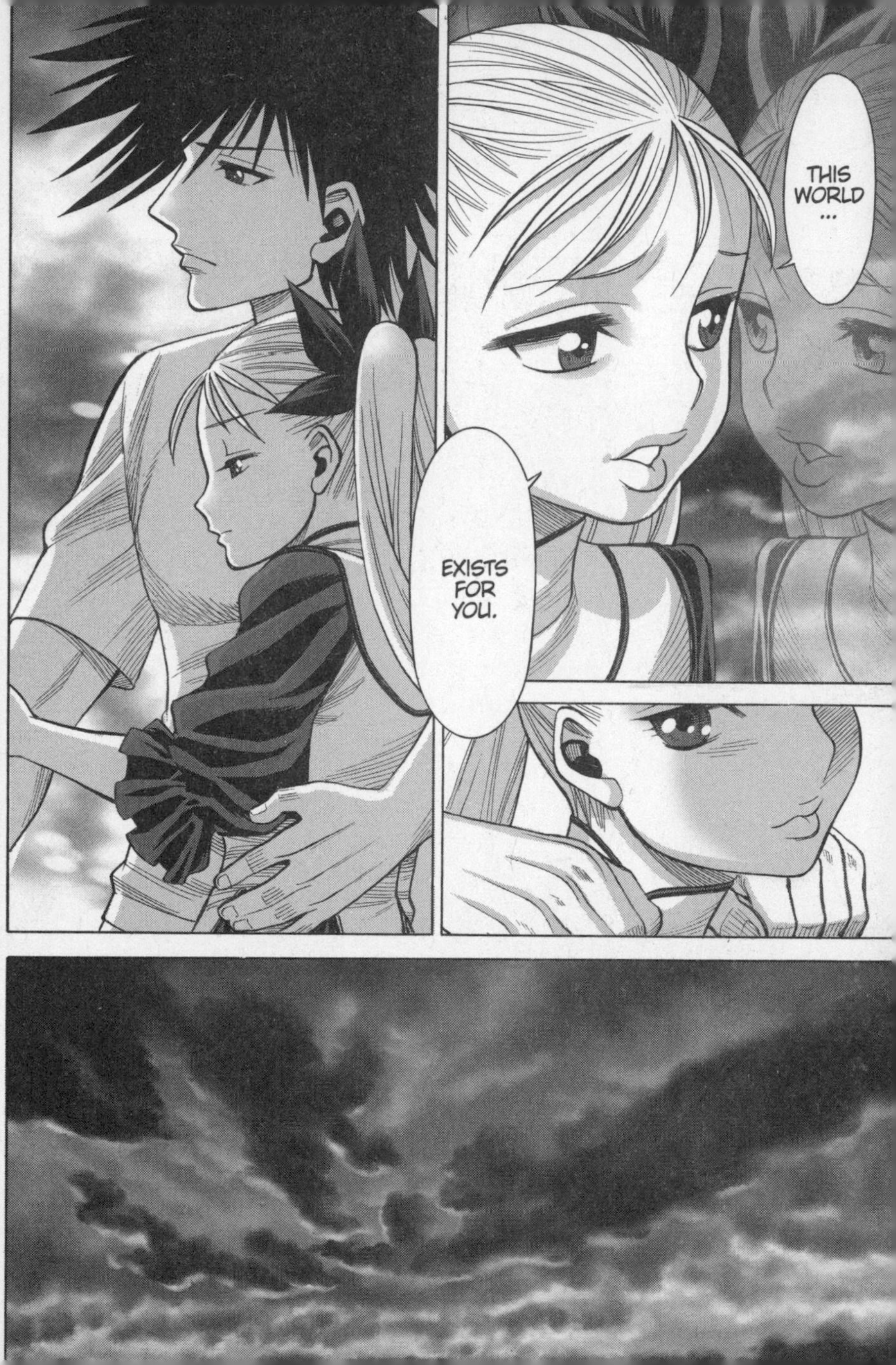
THIS WORLD ...
EXISTS FOR YOU.

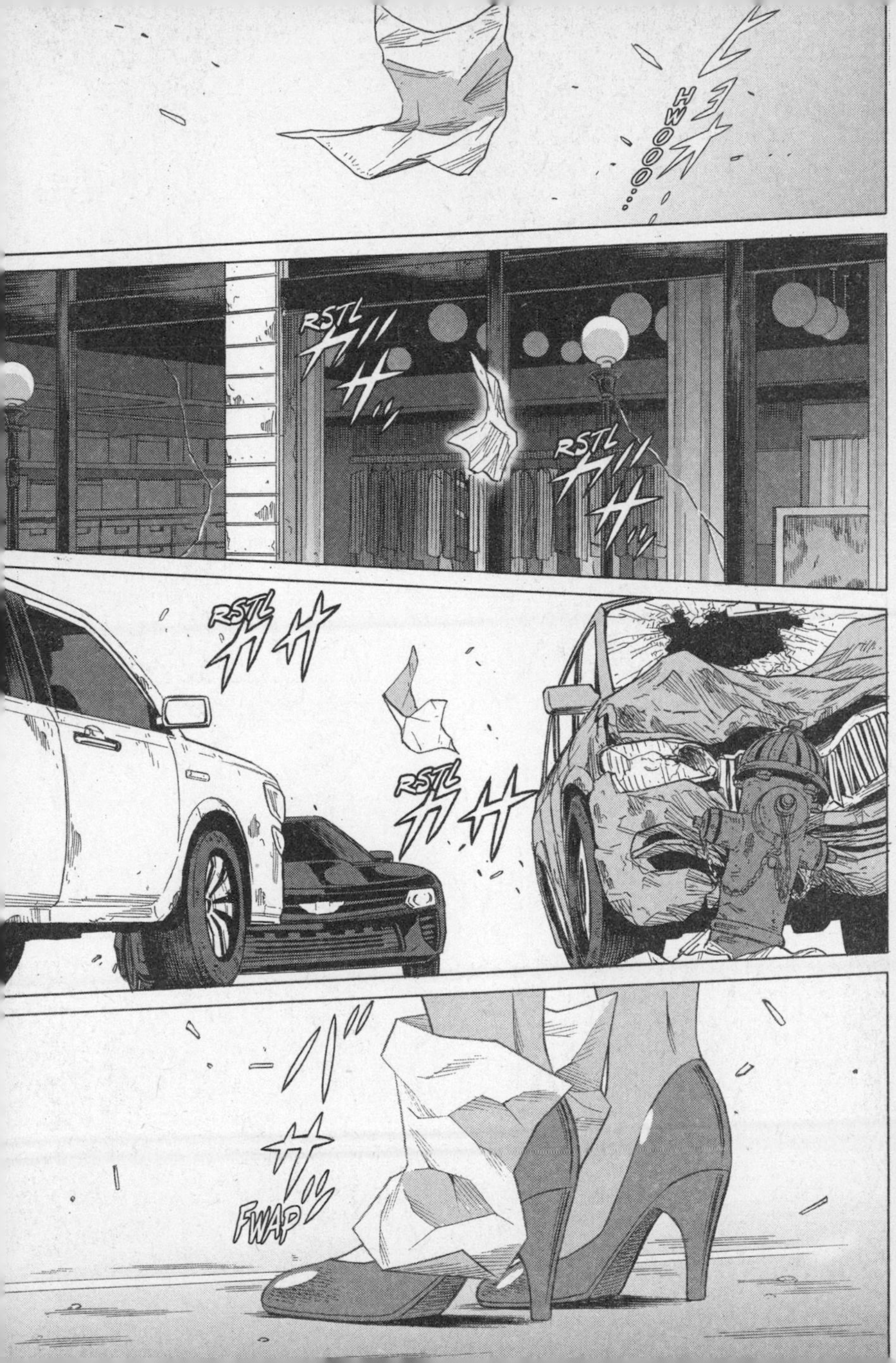
HWOOO...
RSTL
RSTL
RSTL
RSTL
FWAP

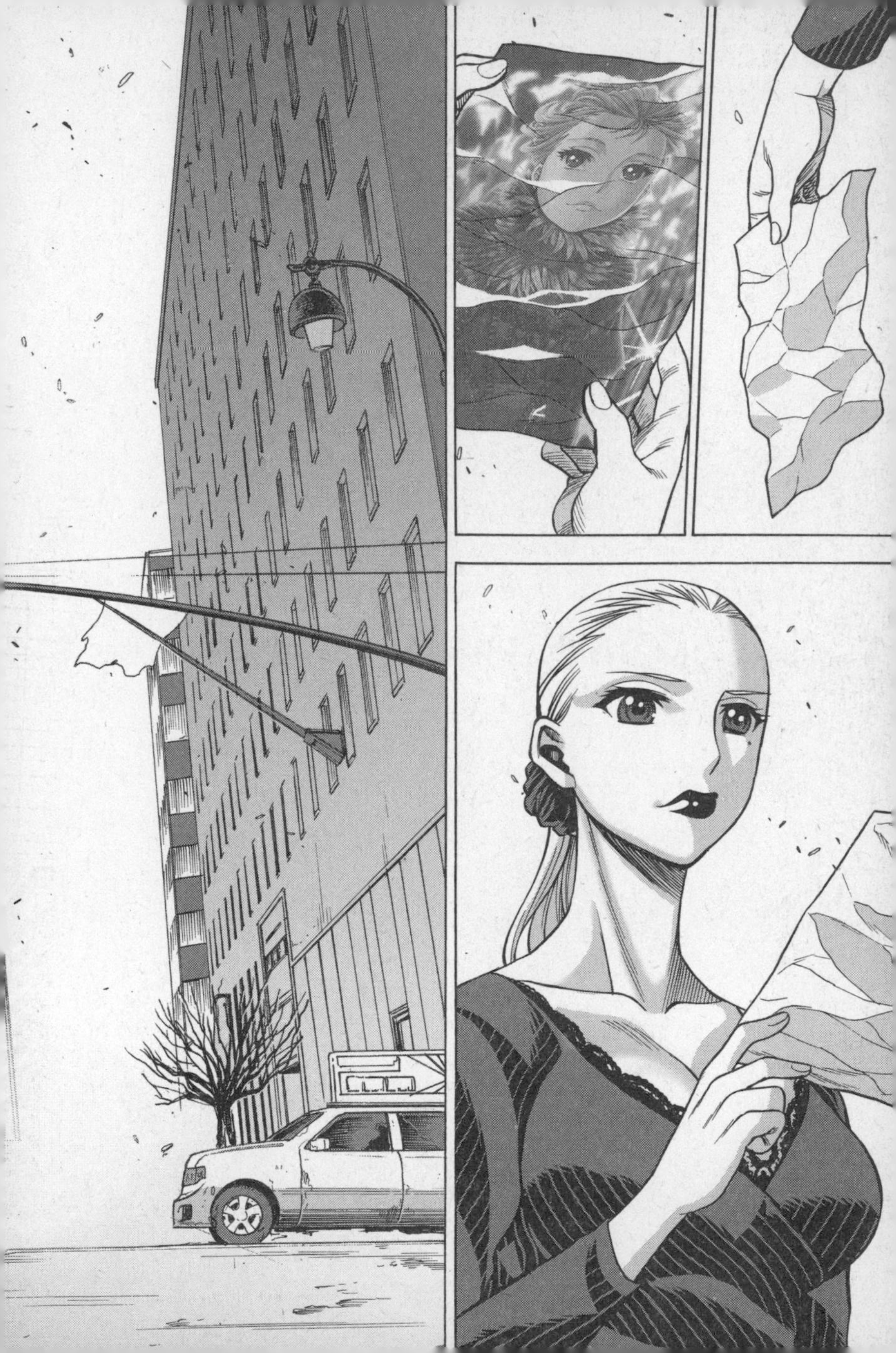

Chapter 3: Handsome Women

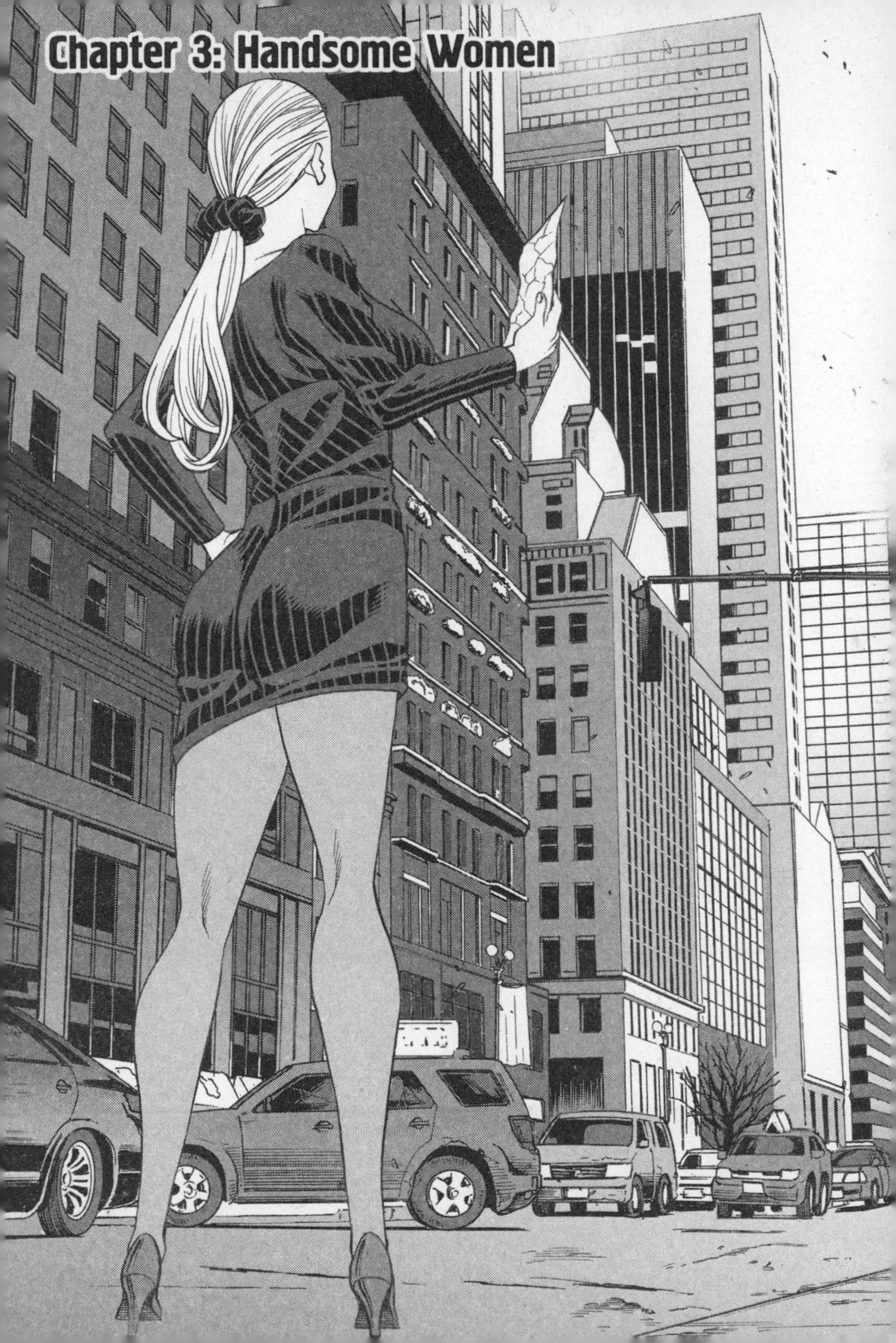

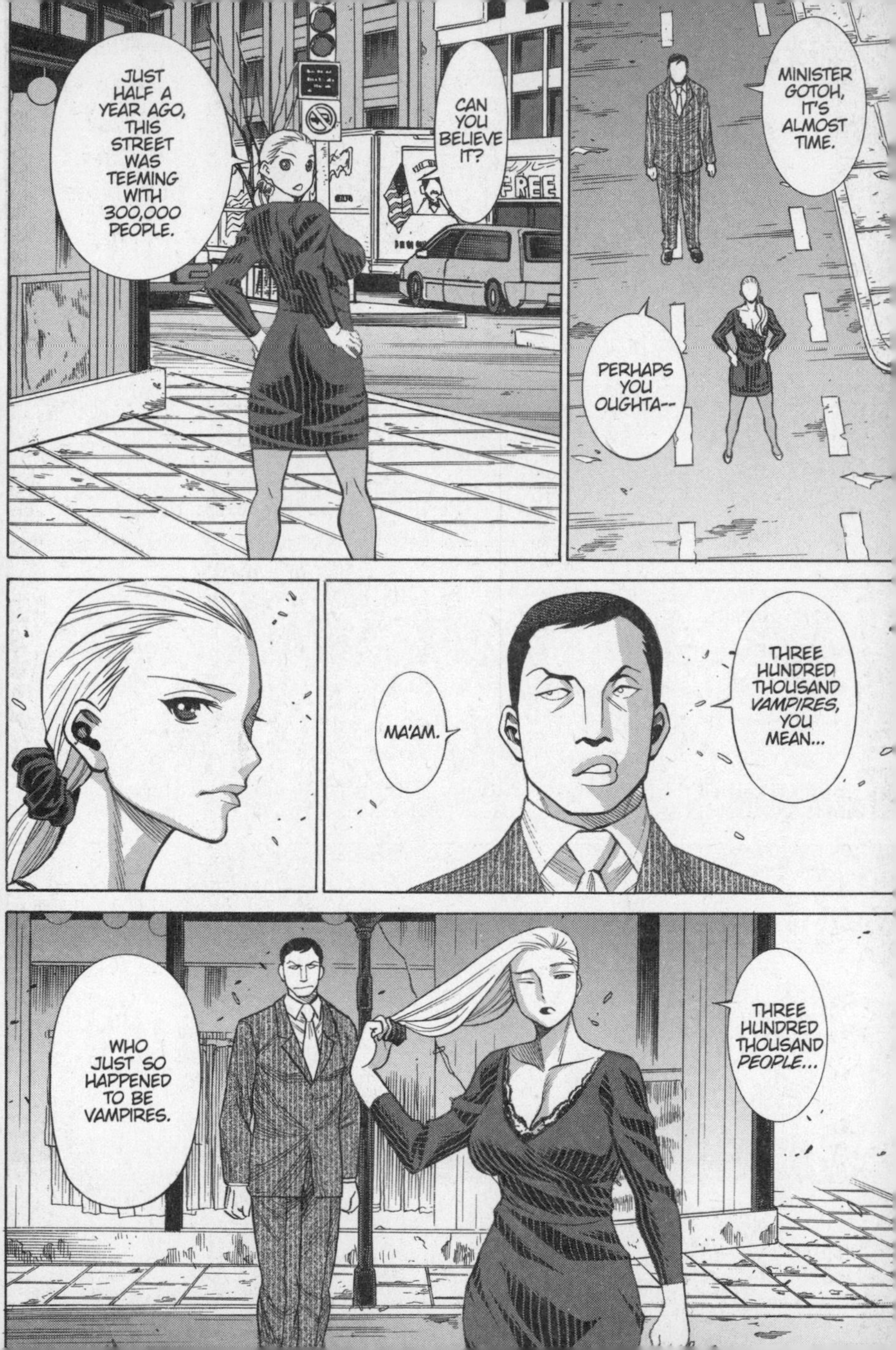
MINISTER GOTOH, IT'S ALMOST TIME.
PERHAPS YOU OUGHTA--
JUST HALF A YEAR AGO, THIS STREET WAS TEEMING WITH 300,000 PEOPLE.
CAN YOU BELIEVE IT?
FREE
THREE HUNDRED THOUSAND *VAMPIRES*, YOU MEAN...
MA'AM.
THREE HUNDRED THOUSAND *PEOPLE*...
WHO JUST SO HAPPENED TO BE VAMPIRES.

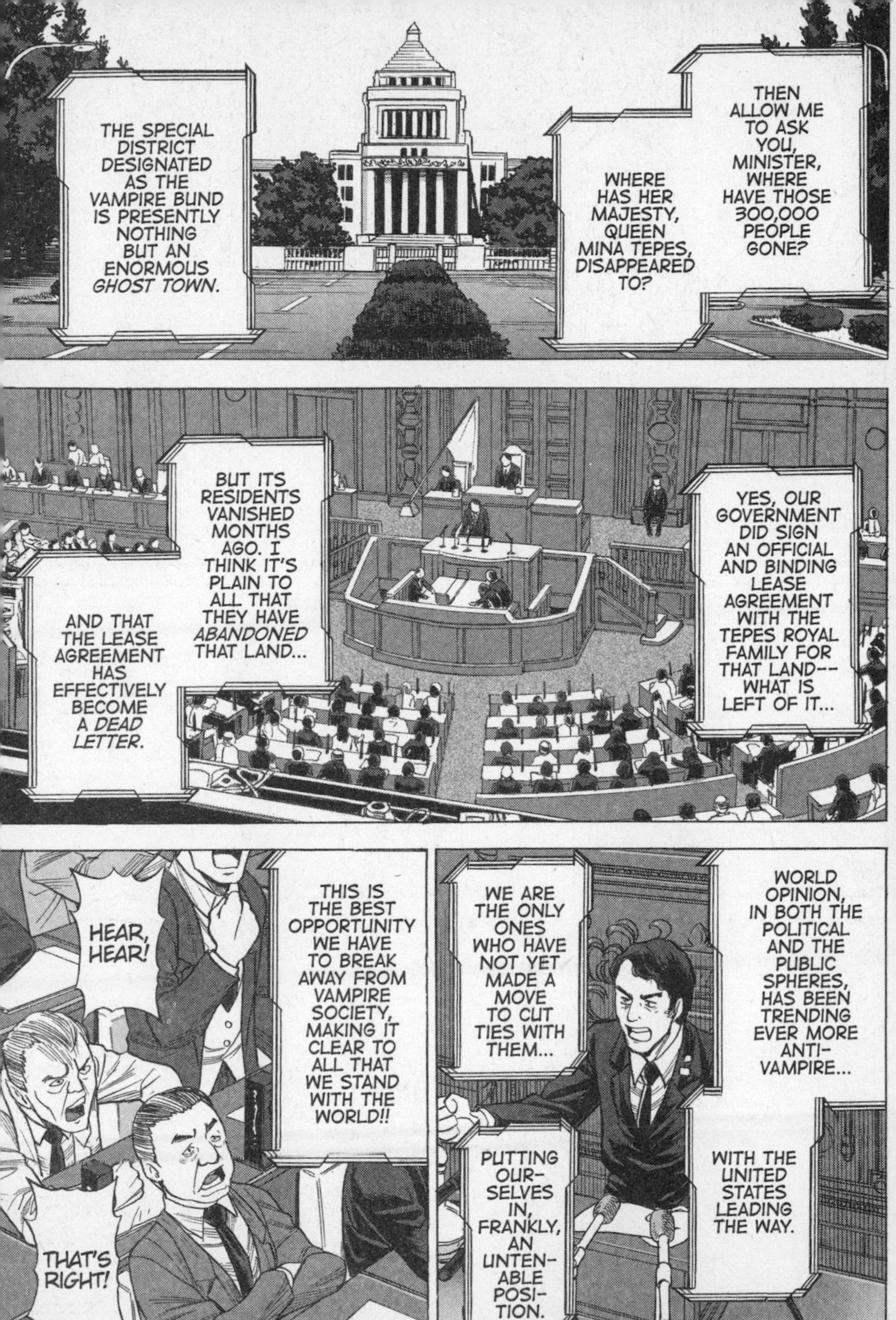

THEN ALLOW ME TO ASK YOU, MINISTER, WHERE HAVE THOSE 300,000 PEOPLE GONE?
WHERE HAS HER MAJESTY, QUEEN MINA TEPES, DISAPPEARED TO?
THE SPECIAL DISTRICT DESIGNATED AS THE VAMPIRE BUND IS PRESENTLY NOTHING BUT AN ENORMOUS *GHOST TOWN*.
YES, OUR GOVERNMENT DID SIGN AN OFFICIAL AND BINDING LEASE AGREEMENT WITH THE TEPES ROYAL FAMILY FOR THAT LAND-- WHAT IS LEFT OF IT...
BUT ITS RESIDENTS VANISHED MONTHS AGO. I THINK IT'S PLAIN TO ALL THAT THEY HAVE *ABANDONED* THAT LAND...
AND THAT THE LEASE AGREEMENT HAS EFFECTIVELY BECOME A *DEAD LETTER*.
WORLD OPINION, IN BOTH THE POLITICAL AND THE PUBLIC SPHERES, HAS BEEN TRENDING EVER MORE ANTI-VAMPIRE...
WITH THE UNITED STATES LEADING THE WAY.
WE ARE THE ONLY ONES WHO HAVE NOT YET MADE A MOVE TO CUT TIES WITH THEM...
PUTTING OUR-SELVES IN, FRANKLY, AN UNTEN-ABLE POSI-TION.
THIS IS THE BEST OPPORTUNITY WE HAVE TO BREAK AWAY FROM VAMPIRE SOCIETY, MAKING IT CLEAR TO ALL THAT WE STAND WITH THE WORLD!!
HEAR, HEAR!
THAT'S RIGHT!

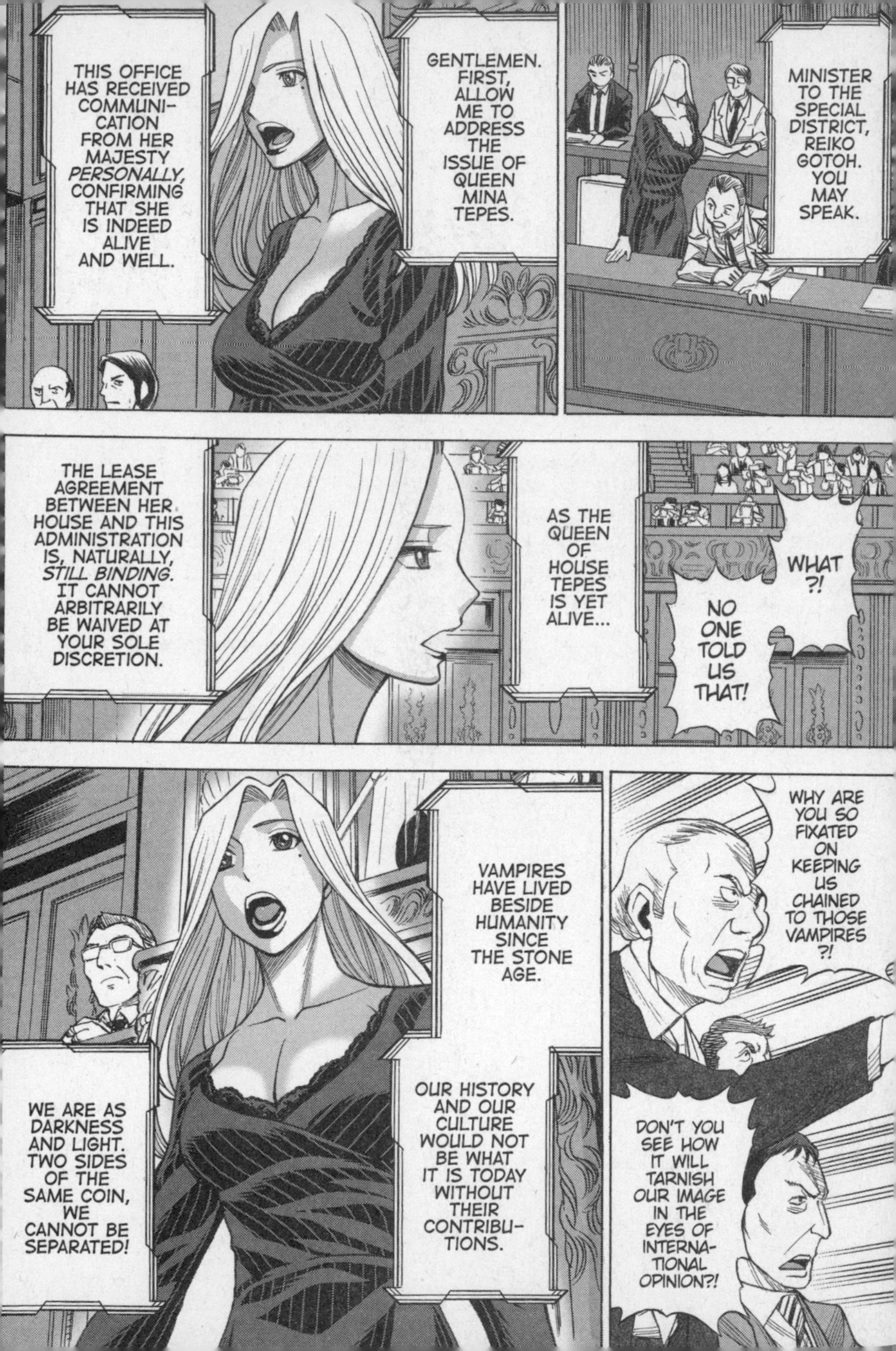
MINISTER TO THE SPECIAL DISTRICT, REIKO GOTOH. YOU MAY SPEAK.
GENTLEMEN. FIRST, ALLOW ME TO ADDRESS THE ISSUE OF QUEEN MINA TEPES.
THIS OFFICE HAS RECEIVED COMMUNI-CATION FROM HER MAJESTY *PERSONALLY*, CONFIRMING THAT SHE IS INDEED ALIVE AND WELL.
WHAT?!
NO ONE TOLD US THAT!
AS THE QUEEN OF HOUSE TEPES IS YET ALIVE...
THE LEASE AGREEMENT BETWEEN HER HOUSE AND THIS ADMINISTRATION IS, NATURALLY, *STILL BINDING*. IT CANNOT ARBITRARILY BE WAIVED AT YOUR SOLE DISCRETION.
WHY ARE YOU SO FIXATED ON KEEPING US CHAINED TO THOSE VAMPIRES?!
DON'T YOU SEE HOW IT WILL TARNISH OUR IMAGE IN THE EYES OF INTERNA-TIONAL OPINION?!
VAMPIRES HAVE LIVED BESIDE HUMANITY SINCE THE STONE AGE.
OUR HISTORY AND OUR CULTURE WOULD NOT BE WHAT IT IS TODAY WITHOUT THEIR CONTRIBU-TIONS.
WE ARE AS DARKNESS AND LIGHT. TWO SIDES OF THE SAME COIN, WE CANNOT BE SEPARATED!

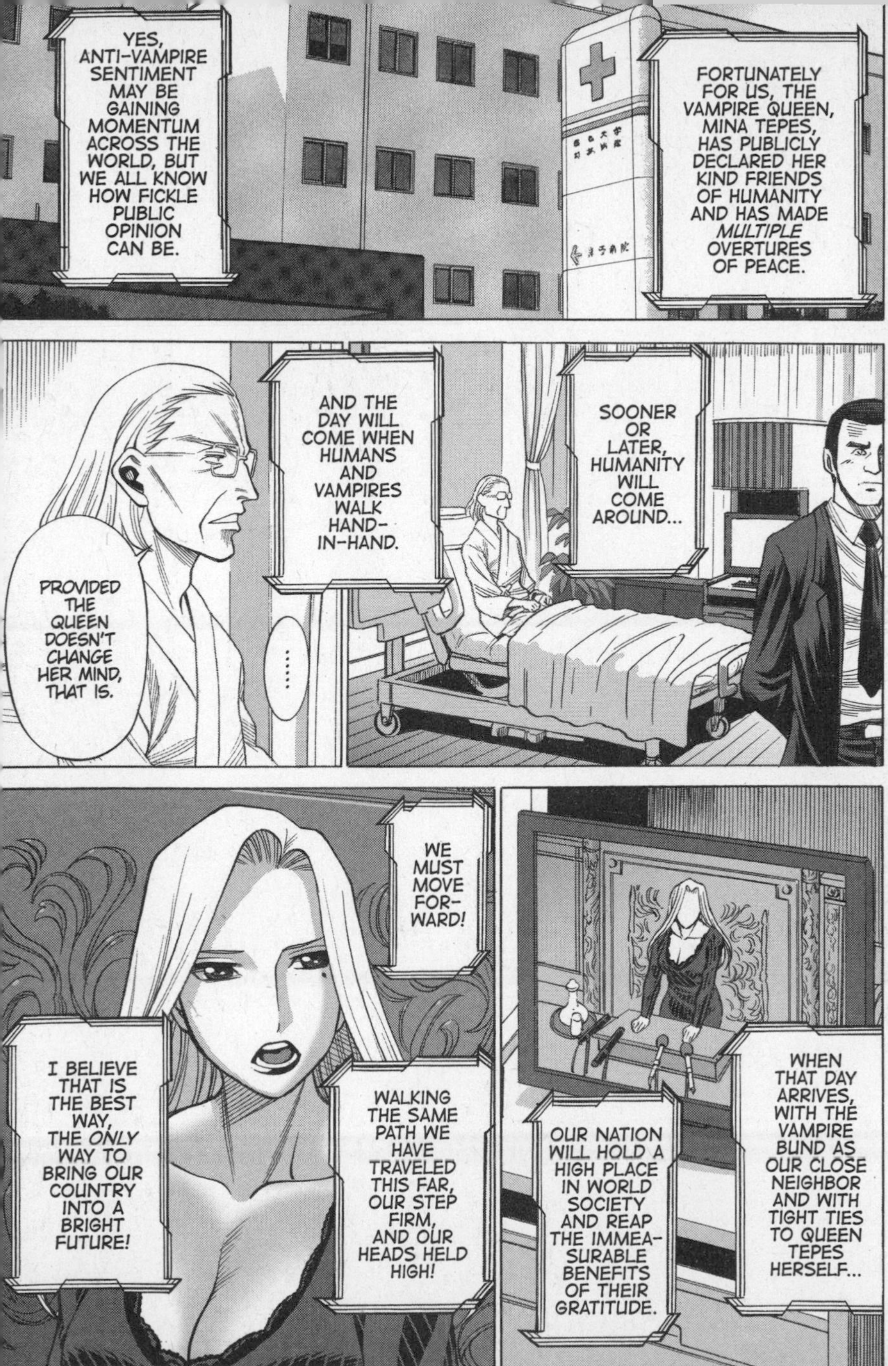
FORTUNATELY FOR US, THE VAMPIRE QUEEN, MINA TEPES, HAS PUBLICLY DECLARED HER KIND FRIENDS OF HUMANITY AND HAS MADE *MULTIPLE* OVERTURES OF PEACE.
YES, ANTI-VAMPIRE SENTIMENT MAY BE GAINING MOMENTUM ACROSS THE WORLD, BUT WE ALL KNOW HOW FICKLE PUBLIC OPINION CAN BE.
SOONER OR LATER, HUMANITY WILL COME AROUND...
AND THE DAY WILL COME WHEN HUMANS AND VAMPIRES WALK HAND-IN-HAND.
PROVIDED THE QUEEN DOESN'T CHANGE HER MIND, THAT IS.
......
WHEN THAT DAY ARRIVES, WITH THE VAMPIRE BUND AS OUR CLOSE NEIGHBOR AND WITH TIGHT TIES TO QUEEN TEPES HERSELF...
OUR NATION WILL HOLD A HIGH PLACE IN WORLD SOCIETY AND REAP THE IMMEA-SURABLE BENEFITS OF THEIR GRATITUDE.
WE MUST MOVE FOR-WARD!
WALKING THE SAME PATH WE HAVE TRAVELED THIS FAR, OUR STEP FIRM, AND OUR HEADS HELD HIGH!
I BELIEVE THAT IS THE BEST WAY, THE *ONLY* WAY TO BRING OUR COUNTRY INTO A BRIGHT FUTURE!

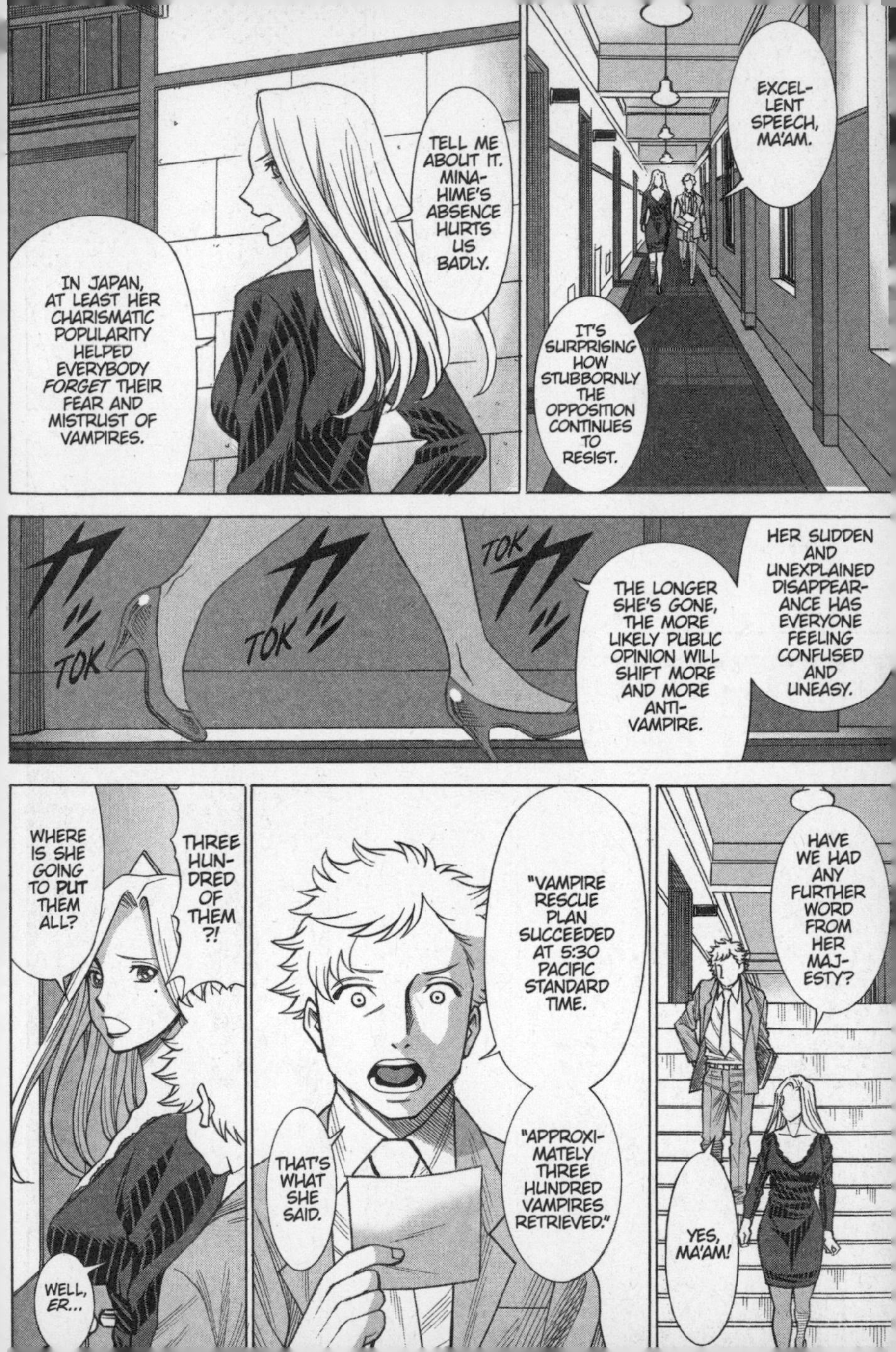
EXCELLENT SPEECH, MA'AM.
IT'S SURPRISING HOW STUBBORNLY THE OPPOSITION CONTINUES TO RESIST.
TELL ME ABOUT IT. MINA-HIME'S ABSENCE HURTS US BADLY.
IN JAPAN, AT LEAST HER CHARISMATIC POPULARITY HELPED EVERYBODY *FORGET* THEIR FEAR AND MISTRUST OF VAMPIRES.
HER SUDDEN AND UNEXPLAINED DISAPPEARANCE HAS EVERYONE FEELING CONFUSED AND UNEASY.
THE LONGER SHE'S GONE, THE MORE LIKELY PUBLIC OPINION WILL SHIFT MORE AND MORE ANTI-VAMPIRE.
TOK
TOK
TOK
HAVE WE HAD ANY FURTHER WORD FROM HER MAJESTY?
YES, MA'AM!
"VAMPIRE RESCUE PLAN SUCCEEDED AT 5:30 PACIFIC STANDARD TIME.
"APPROXIMATELY THREE HUNDRED VAMPIRES RETRIEVED."
THAT'S WHAT SHE SAID.
THREE HUNDRED OF THEM?!
WHERE IS SHE GOING TO **PUT** THEM ALL?
WELL, ER...

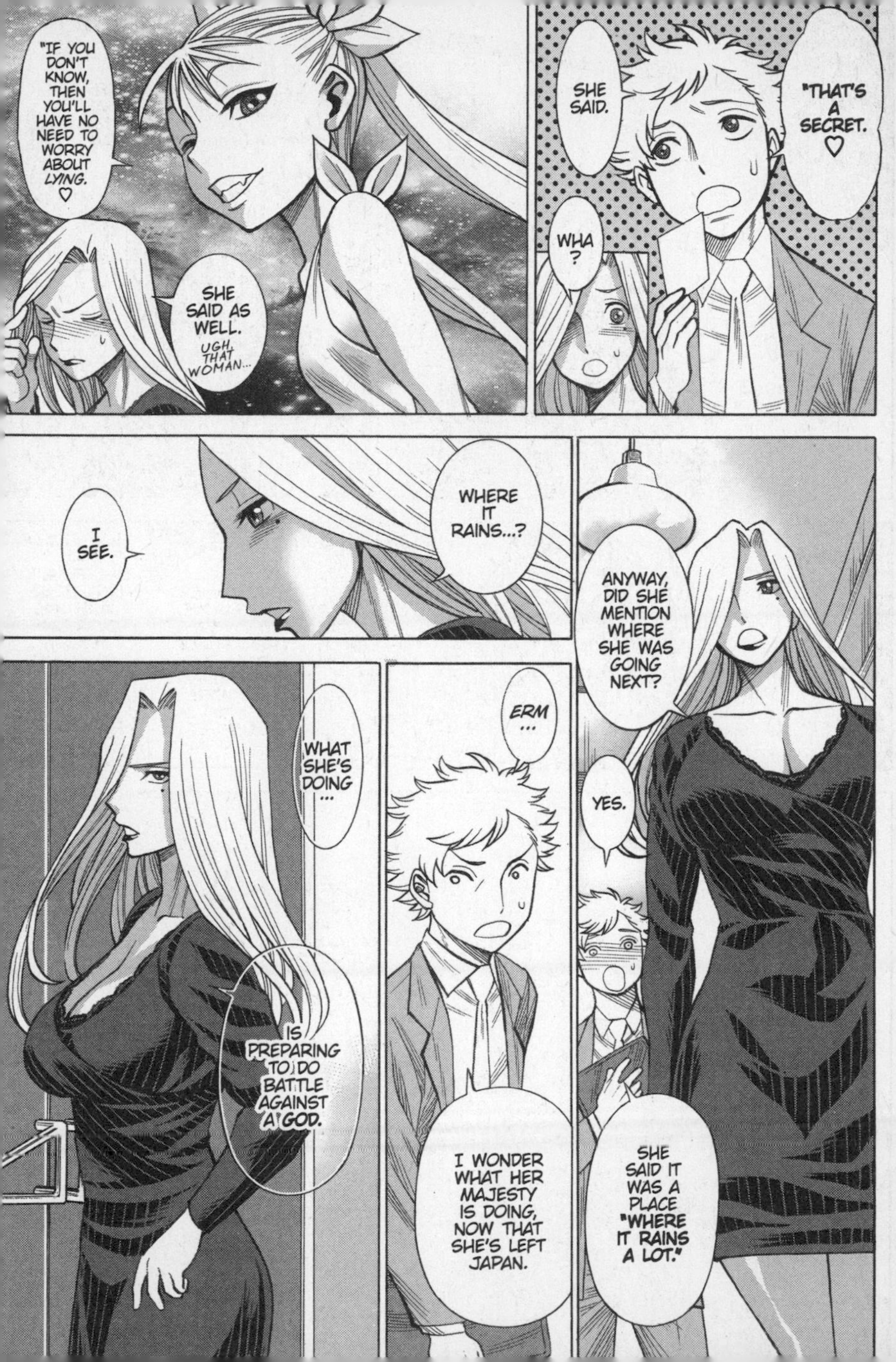
"THAT'S A SECRET. ♡
SHE SAID.
WHA?
"IF YOU DON'T KNOW, THEN YOU'LL HAVE NO NEED TO WORRY ABOUT *LYING*. ♡
SHE SAID AS WELL.
UGH THAT WOMAN...
ANYWAY, DID SHE MENTION WHERE SHE WAS GOING NEXT?
YES.
SHE SAID IT WAS A PLACE "WHERE IT RAINS A LOT."
WHERE IT RAINS...?
I SEE.
ERM...
I WONDER WHAT HER MAJESTY IS DOING, NOW THAT SHE'S LEFT JAPAN.
WHAT SHE'S DOING...
IS PREPARING TO DO BATTLE AGAINST A GOD.

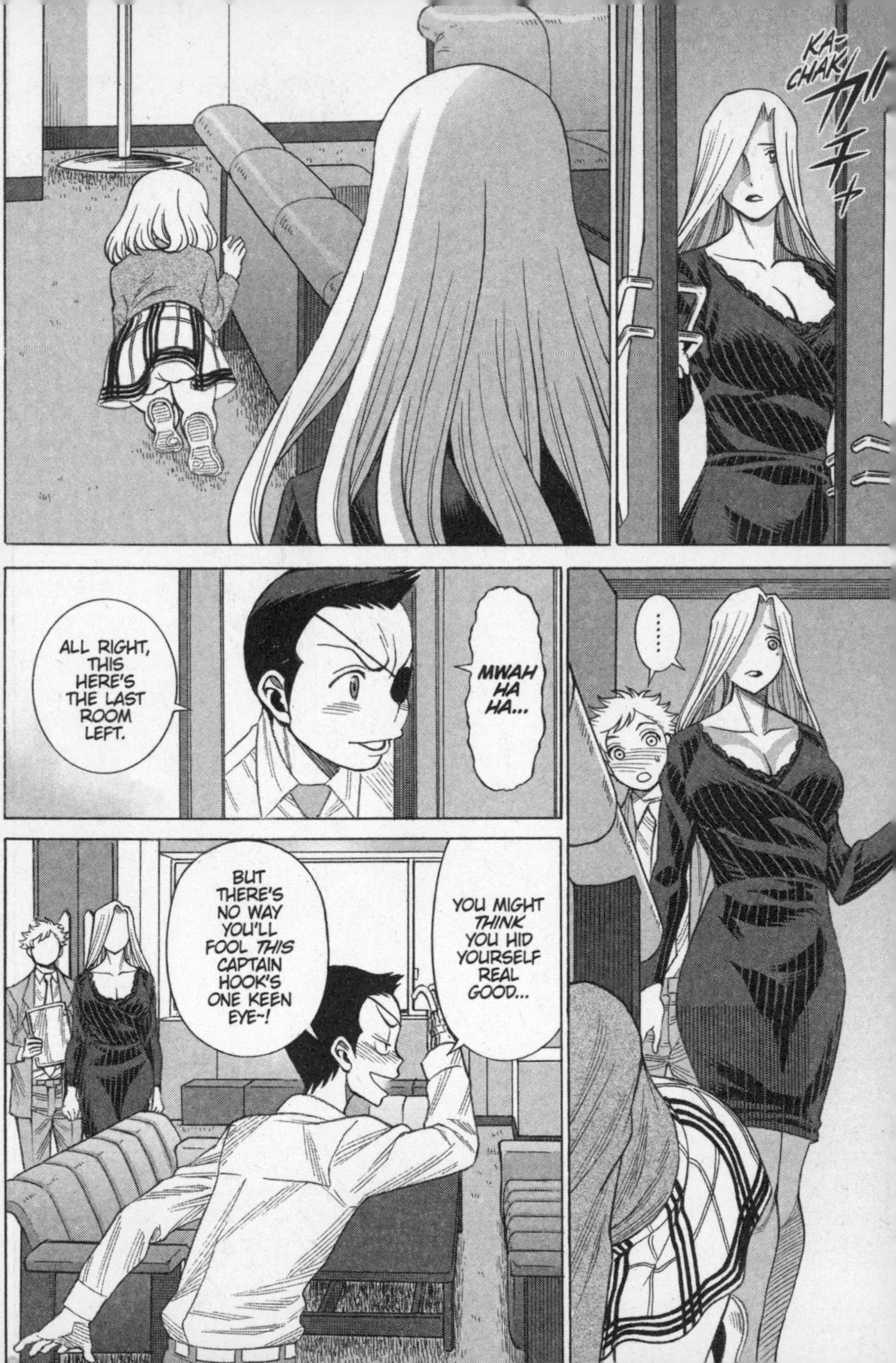

KA-CHAK
......
MWAH HA HA...
ALL RIGHT, THIS HERE'S THE LAST ROOM LEFT.
YOU MIGHT *THINK* YOU HID YOURSELF REAL GOOD...
BUT THERE'S NO WAY YOU'LL FOOL *THIS* CAPTAIN HOOK'S ONE KEEN EYE~!

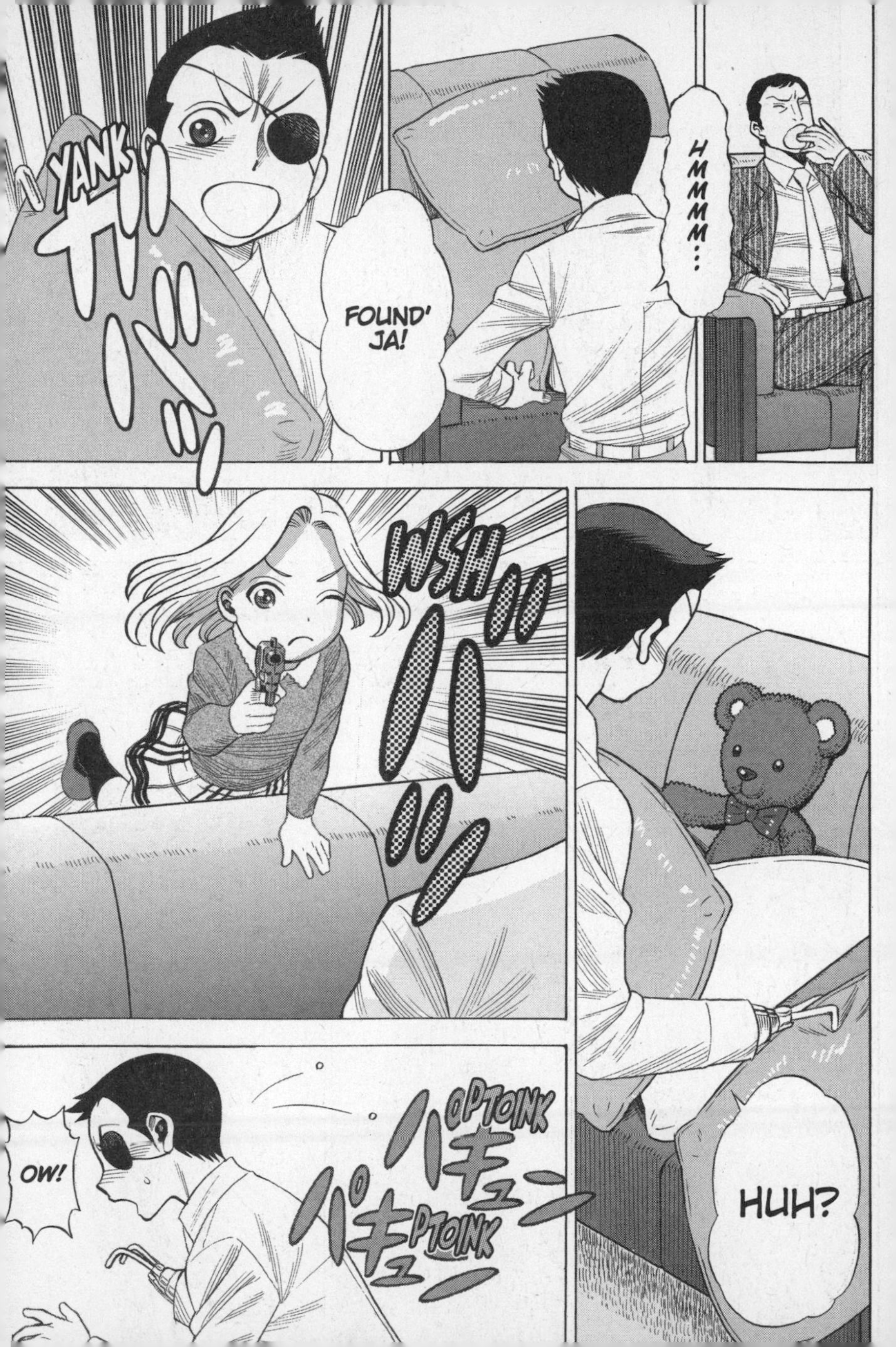

HMMMM...
FOUND' JA!
YANK
HUH?
WSH
PTOINK
PTOINK
OW!

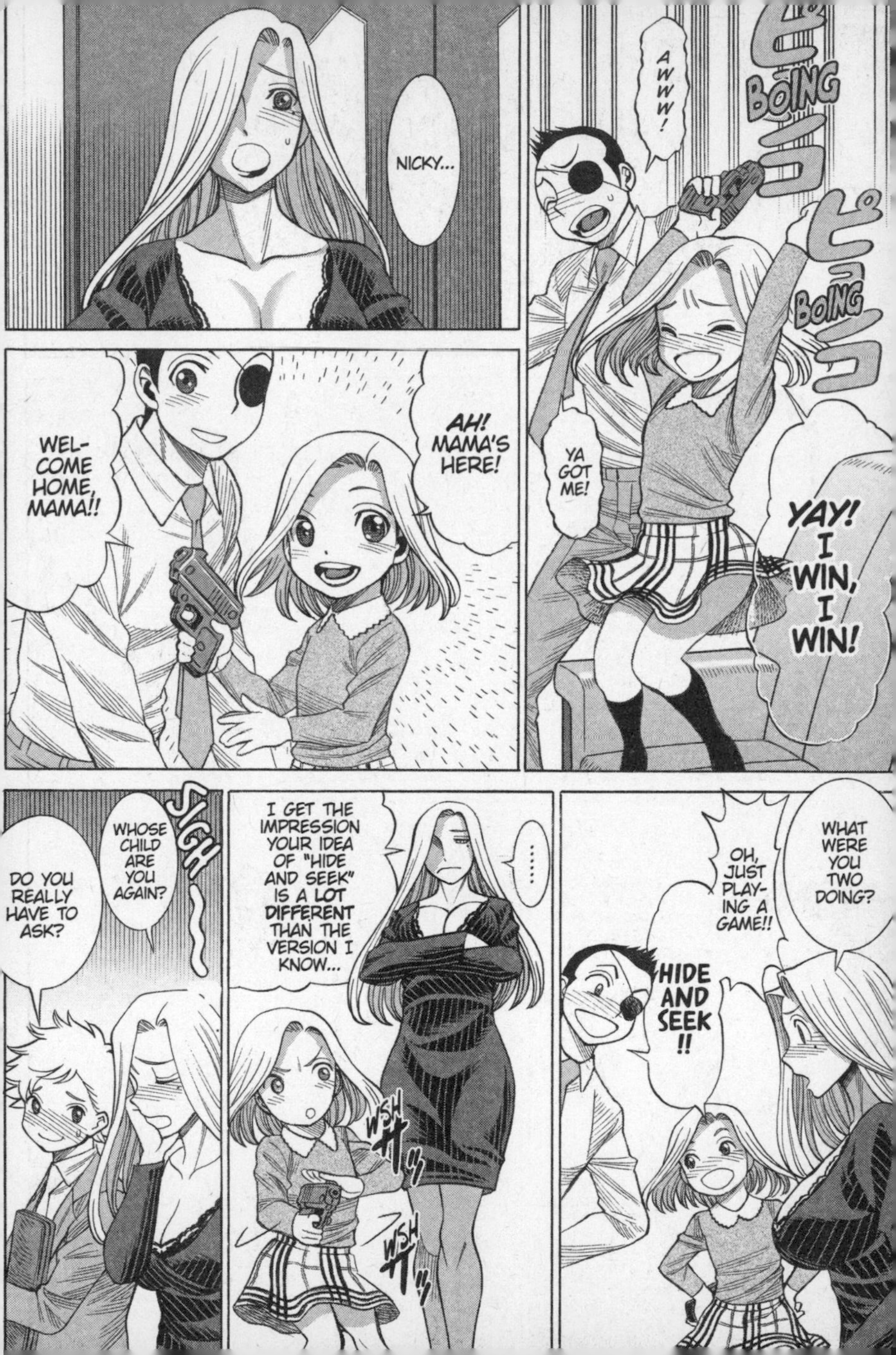

AWWW!
BOING
BOING
YA GOT ME!
YAY! I WIN, I WIN!
NICKY...
AH! MAMA'S HERE!
WEL-COME HOME, MAMA!!
WHAT WERE YOU TWO DOING?
OH, JUST PLAY-ING A GAME!!
HIDE AND SEEK!!
......
I GET THE IMPRESSION YOUR IDEA OF "HIDE AND SEEK" IS A LOT DIFFERENT THAN THE VERSION I KNOW...
WSH
WSH
SIGH
WHOSE CHILD ARE YOU AGAIN?
DO YOU REALLY HAVE TO ASK?

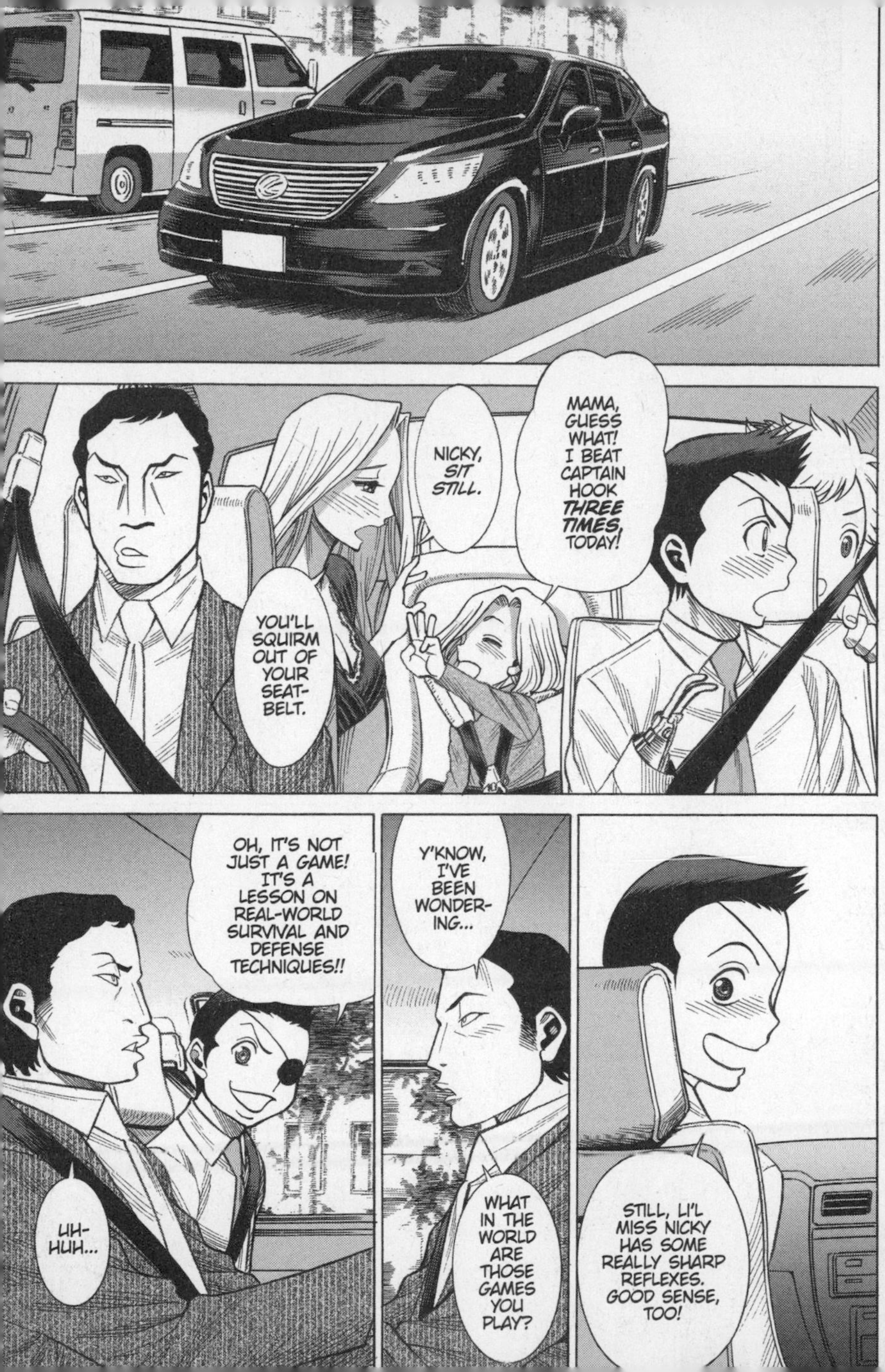
MAMA, GUESS WHAT! I BEAT CAPTAIN HOOK *THREE TIMES*, TODAY!
NICKY, *SIT STILL*.
YOU'LL SQUIRM OUT OF YOUR SEAT-BELT.
STILL, LI'L MISS NICKY HAS SOME REALLY SHARP REFLEXES. GOOD SENSE, TOO!
Y'KNOW, I'VE BEEN WONDER-ING...
WHAT IN THE WORLD ARE THOSE GAMES YOU PLAY?
OH, IT'S NOT JUST A GAME! IT'S A LESSON ON REAL-WORLD SURVIVAL AND DEFENSE TECHNIQUES!!
UH-HUH...

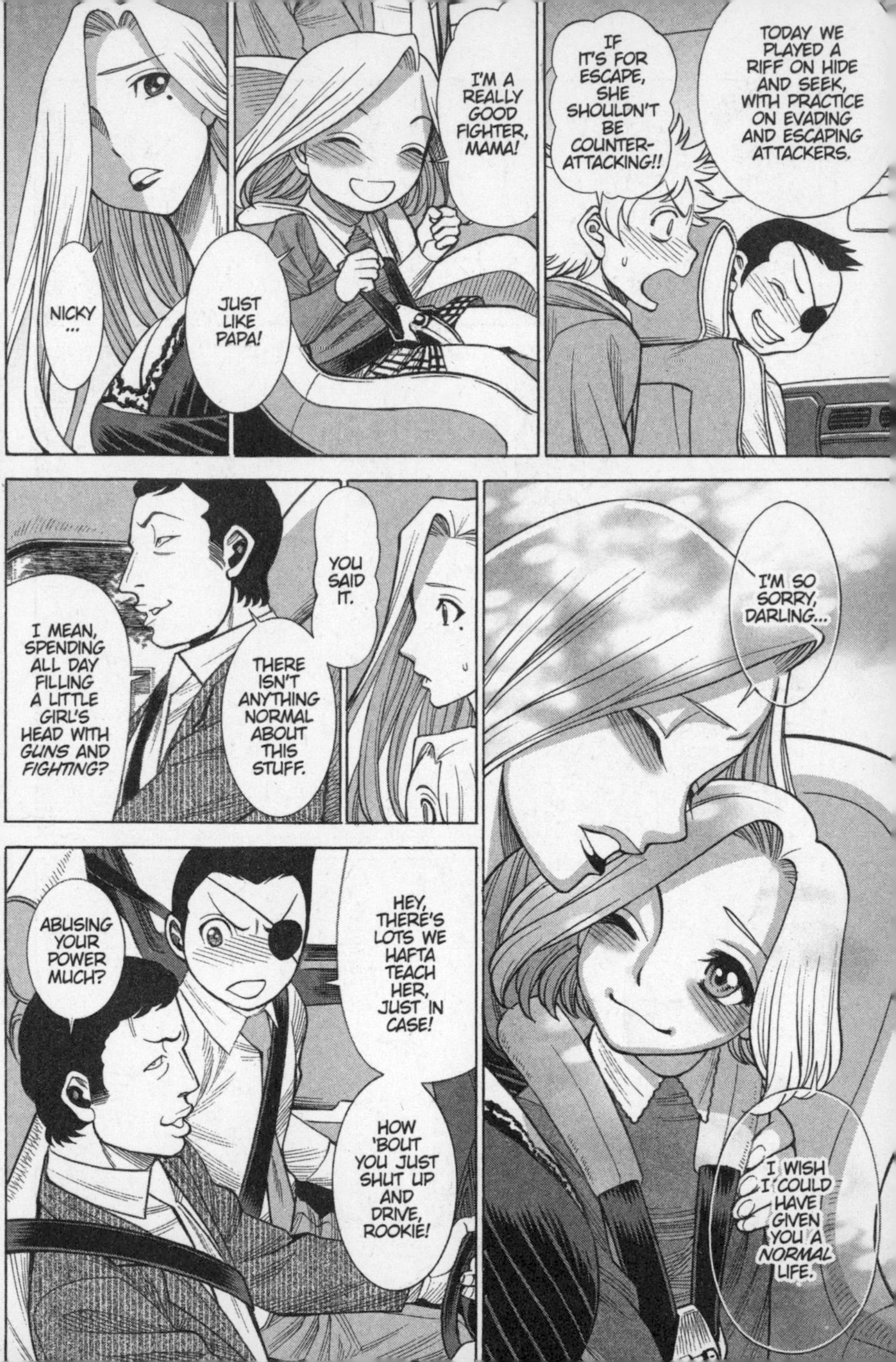
TODAY WE PLAYED A RIFF ON HIDE AND SEEK, WITH PRACTICE ON EVADING AND ESCAPING ATTACKERS.
IF IT'S FOR ESCAPE, SHE SHOULDN'T BE COUNTER-ATTACKING!!
I'M A REALLY GOOD FIGHTER, MAMA!
JUST LIKE PAPA!
NICKY...
I'M SO SORRY, DARLING...
I WISH I COULD HAVE GIVEN YOU A *NORMAL* LIFE.
YOU SAID IT.
THERE ISN'T ANYTHING NORMAL ABOUT THIS STUFF.
I MEAN, SPENDING ALL DAY FILLING A LITTLE GIRL'S HEAD WITH *GUNS AND FIGHTING*?
HEY, THERE'S LOTS WE HAFTA TEACH HER, JUST IN CASE!
ABUSING YOUR POWER MUCH?
HOW 'BOUT YOU JUST SHUT UP AND DRIVE, ROOKIE!

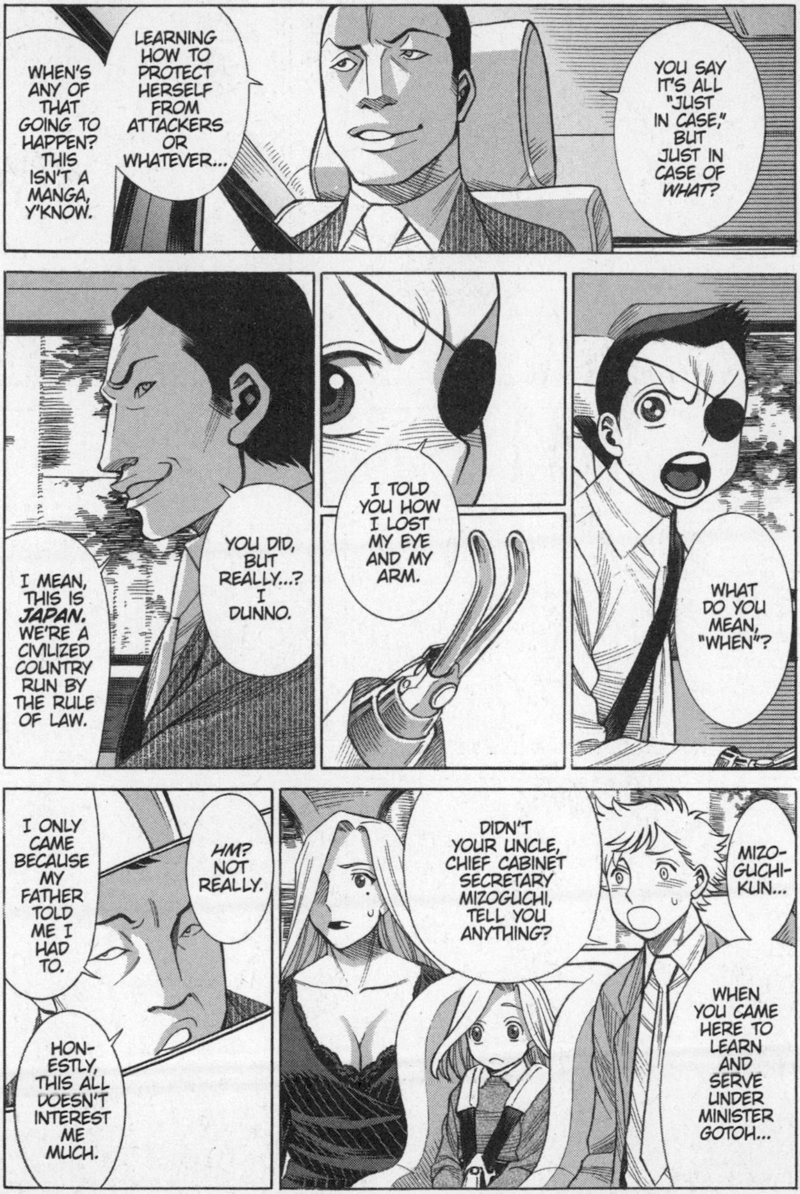
YOU SAY IT'S ALL "JUST IN CASE," BUT JUST IN CASE OF *WHAT?*
LEARNING HOW TO PROTECT HERSELF FROM ATTACKERS OR WHATEVER...
WHEN'S ANY OF THAT GOING TO HAPPEN? THIS ISN'T A MANGA, Y'KNOW.
WHAT DO YOU MEAN, "WHEN"?
I TOLD YOU HOW I LOST MY EYE AND MY ARM.
YOU DID, BUT REALLY...? I DUNNO.
I MEAN, THIS IS ***JAPAN.*** WE'RE A CIVILIZED COUNTRY RUN BY THE RULE OF LAW.
MIZO-GUCHI-KUN...
WHEN YOU CAME HERE TO LEARN AND SERVE UNDER MINISTER GOTOH...
DIDN'T YOUR UNCLE, CHIEF CABINET SECRETARY MIZOGUCHI, TELL YOU ANYTHING?
HM? NOT REALLY.
I ONLY CAME BECAUSE MY FATHER TOLD ME I HAD TO.
HON-ESTLY, THIS ALL DOESN'T INTEREST ME MUCH.

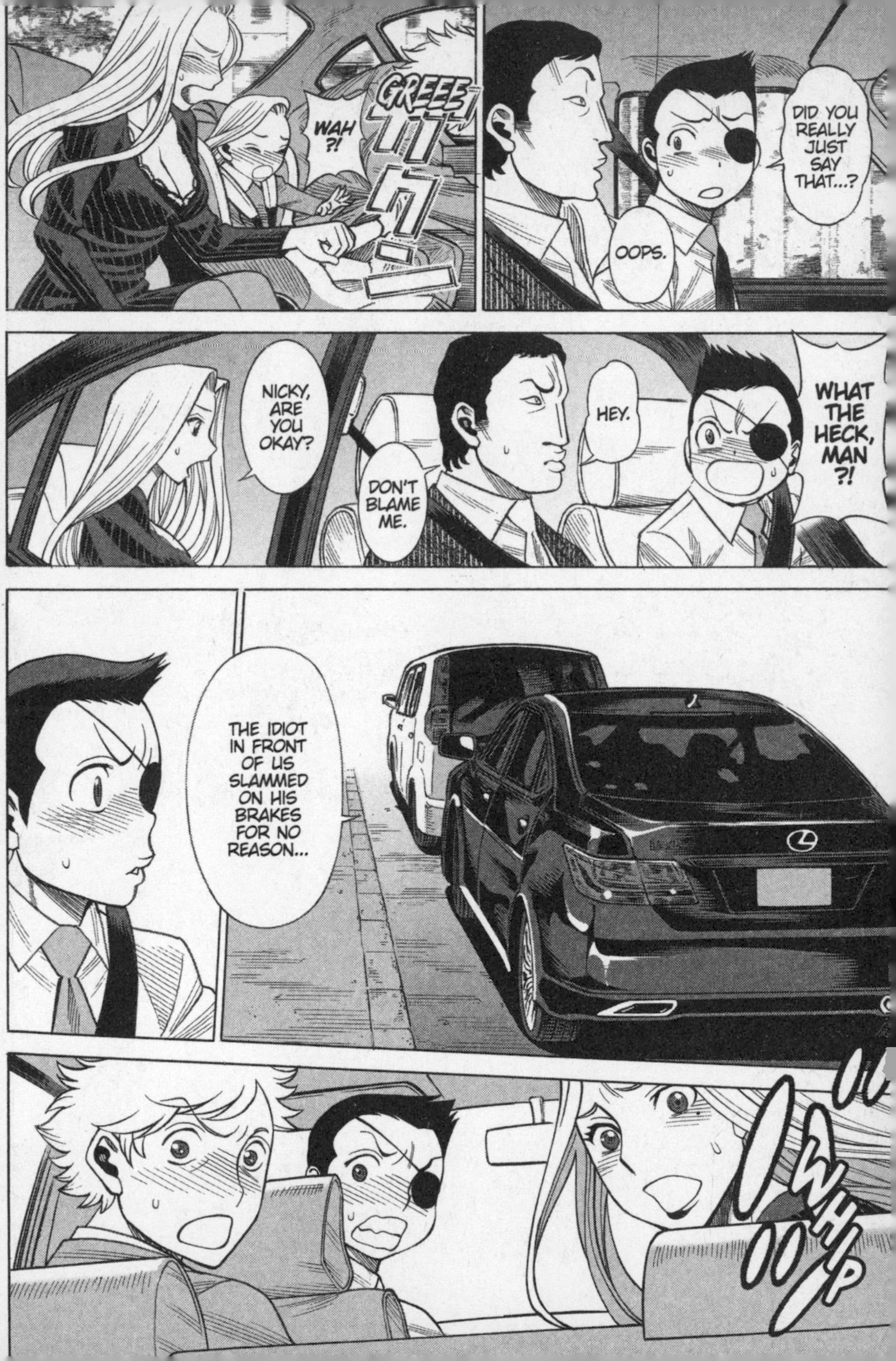
DID YOU REALLY JUST SAY THAT...?
OOPS.
GREEE
WAH ?!
WHAT THE HECK, MAN ?!
HEY.
DON'T BLAME ME.
NICKY, ARE YOU OKAY?
THE IDIOT IN FRONT OF US SLAMMED ON HIS BRAKES FOR NO REASON...
WHIP

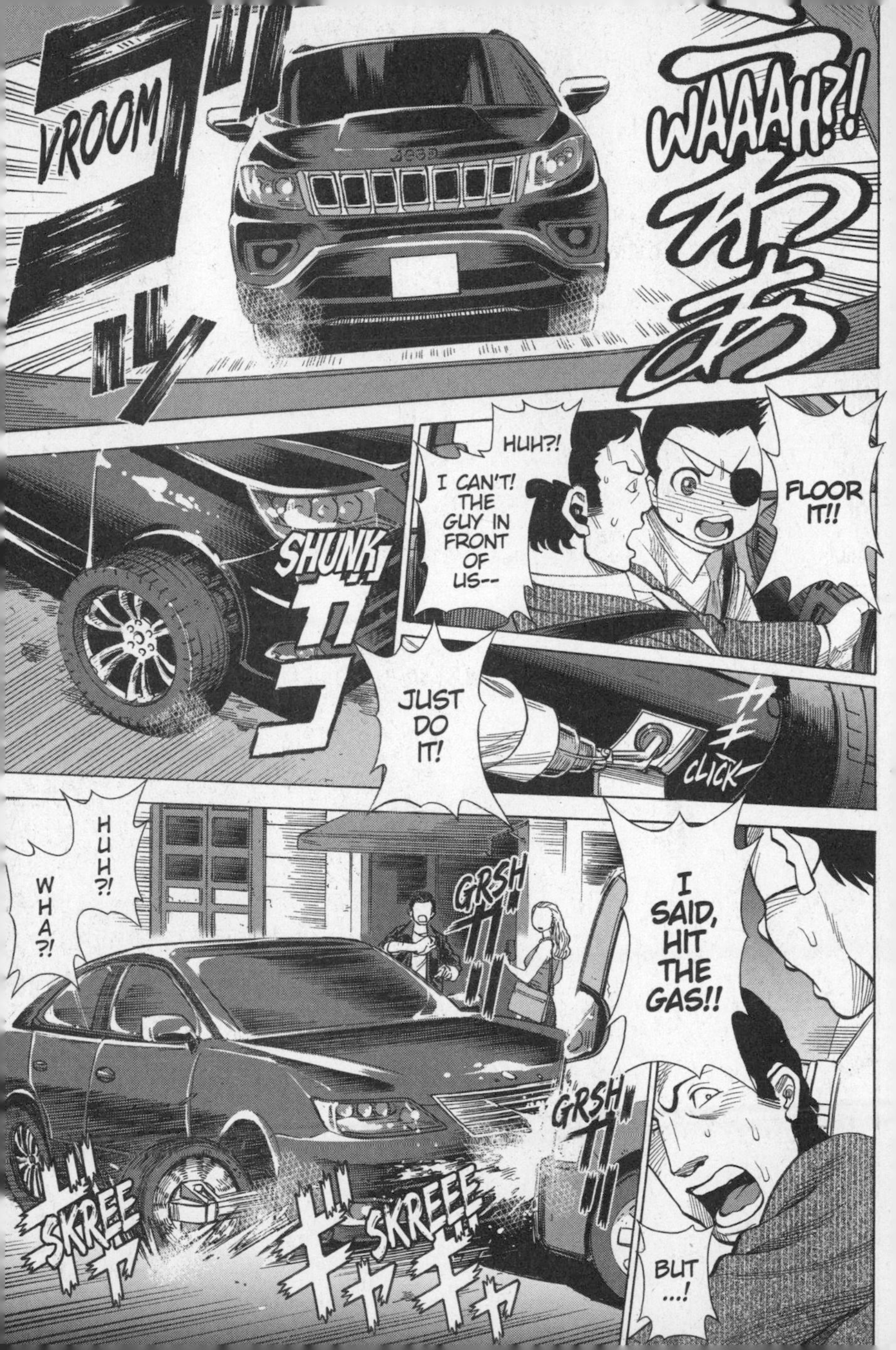

WAAAH?!
VROOM
FLOOR IT!!
HUH?!
I CAN'T! THE GUY IN FRONT OF US--
SHUNK
CLICK
JUST DO IT!
I SAID, HIT THE GAS!!
BUT ...!
GRSH
GRSH
HUH?!
WHA?!
SKREEE
SKREE

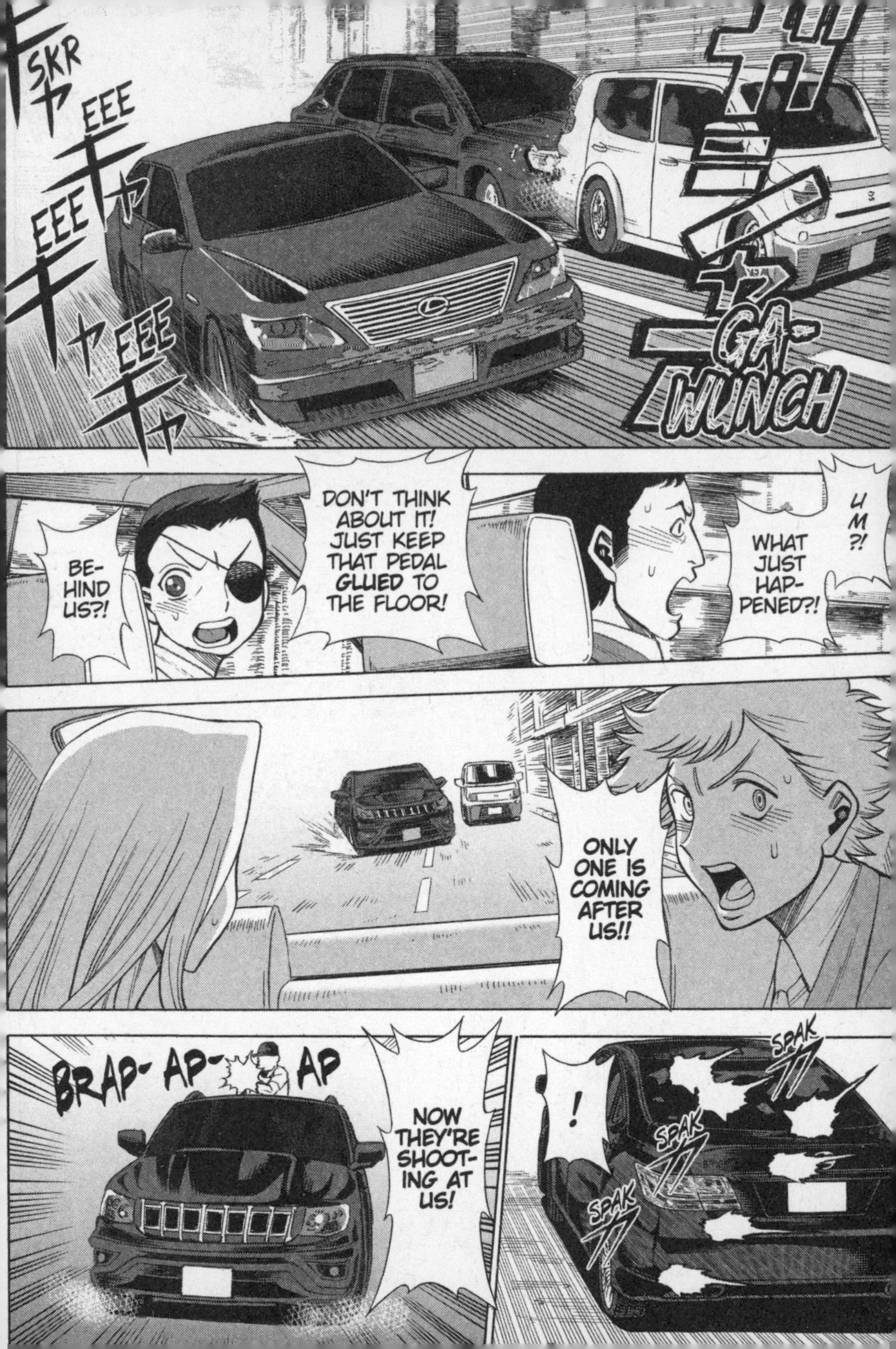
GA-WUNCH
SKREEE
EEE
EEE
UM?!
WHAT JUST HAP-PENED?!
DON'T THINK ABOUT IT! JUST KEEP THAT PEDAL GLUED TO THE FLOOR!
BE-HIND US?!
ONLY ONE IS COMING AFTER US!!
SPAK
SPAK
SPAK
!
NOW THEY'RE SHOOT-ING AT US!
BRAP-AP-AP

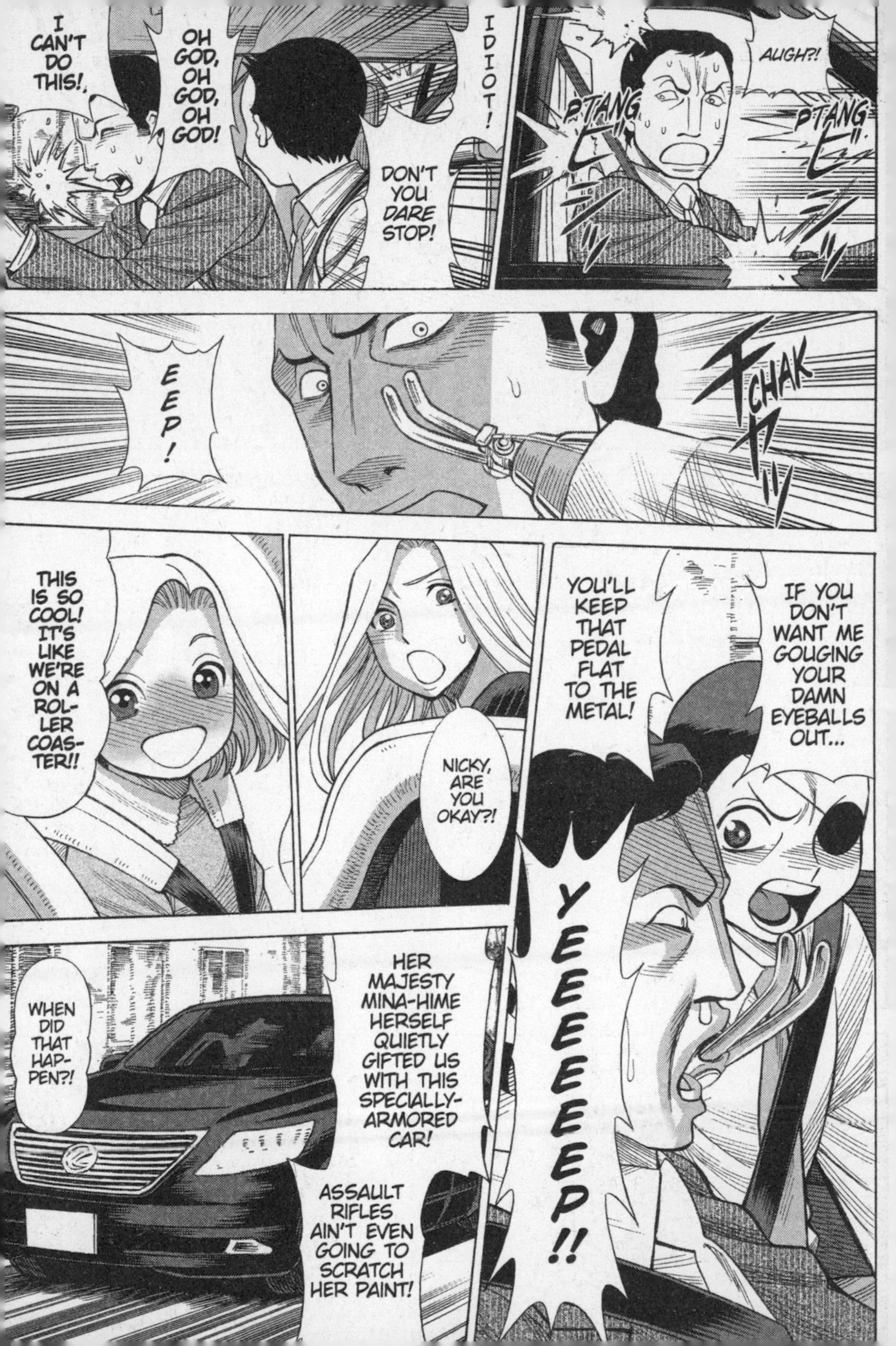
AUGH?!
PTANG
PTANG
IDIOT!
DON'T YOU DARE STOP!
OH GOD, OH GOD, OH GOD!
I CAN'T DO THIS!
CHAK
EEP!
IF YOU DON'T WANT ME GOUGING YOUR DAMN EYEBALLS OUT...
YOU'LL KEEP THAT PEDAL FLAT TO THE METAL!
YEEEEEEEP!!
NICKY, ARE YOU OKAY?!
THIS IS SO COOL! IT'S LIKE WE'RE ON A ROL-LER COAS-TER!!
HER MAJESTY MINA-HIME HERSELF QUIETLY GIFTED US WITH THIS SPECIALLY-ARMORED CAR!
ASSAULT RIFLES AIN'T EVEN GOING TO SCRATCH HER PAINT!
WHEN DID THAT HAP-PEN?!

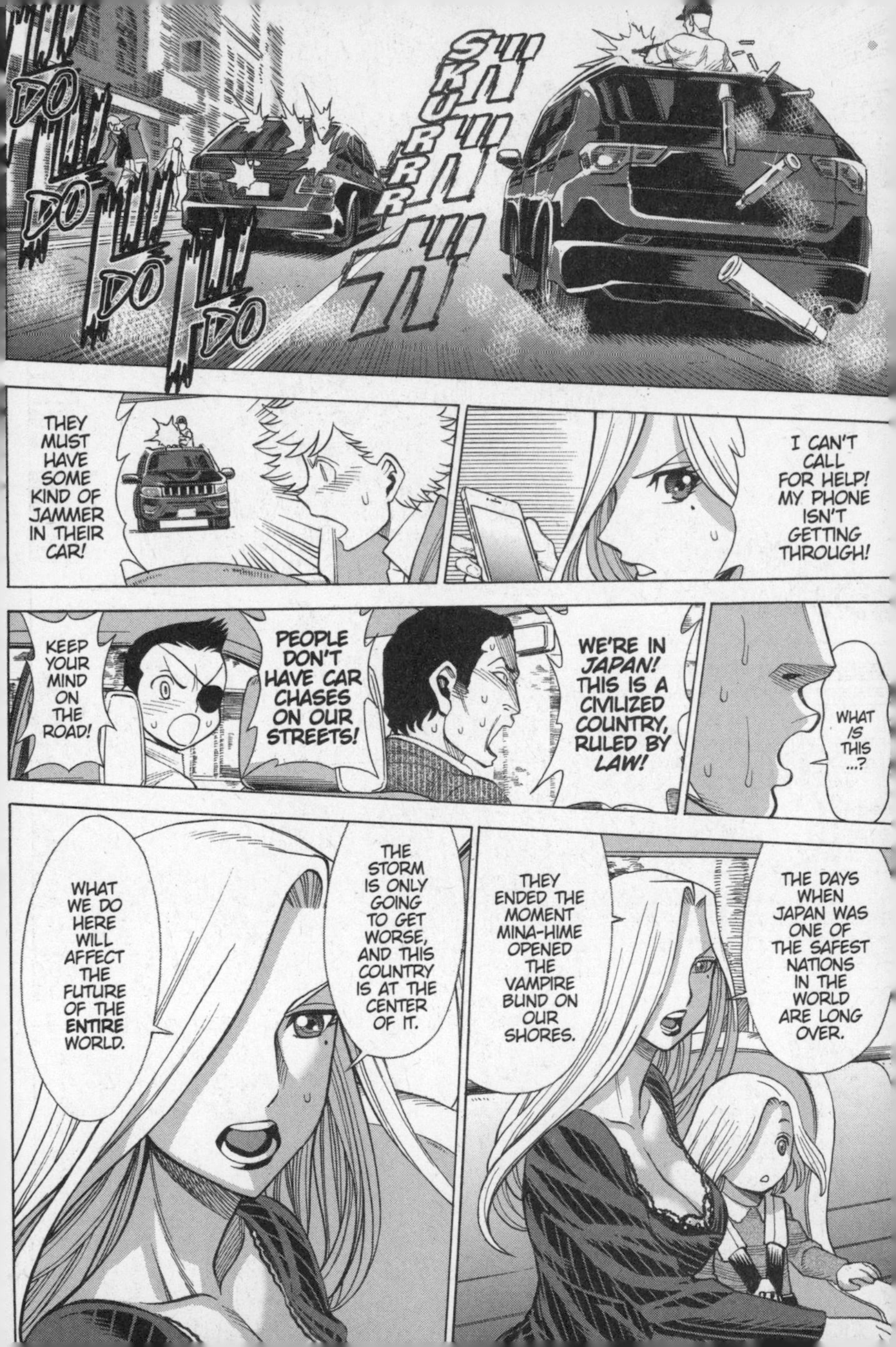
SKURRR
DO DO DO DO
I CAN'T CALL FOR HELP! MY PHONE ISN'T GETTING THROUGH!
THEY MUST HAVE SOME KIND OF JAMMER IN THEIR CAR!
WHAT *IS* THIS ...?
WE'RE IN *JAPAN*! THIS IS A CIVILIZED COUNTRY, RULED BY *LAW*!
PEOPLE DON'T HAVE CAR CHASES ON OUR STREETS!
KEEP YOUR MIND ON THE ROAD!
THE DAYS WHEN JAPAN WAS ONE OF THE SAFEST NATIONS IN THE WORLD ARE LONG OVER.
THEY ENDED THE MOMENT MINA-HIME OPENED THE VAMPIRE BUND ON OUR SHORES.
THE STORM IS ONLY GOING TO GET WORSE, AND THIS COUNTRY IS AT THE CENTER OF IT.
WHAT WE DO HERE WILL AFFECT THE FUTURE OF THE ENTIRE WORLD.

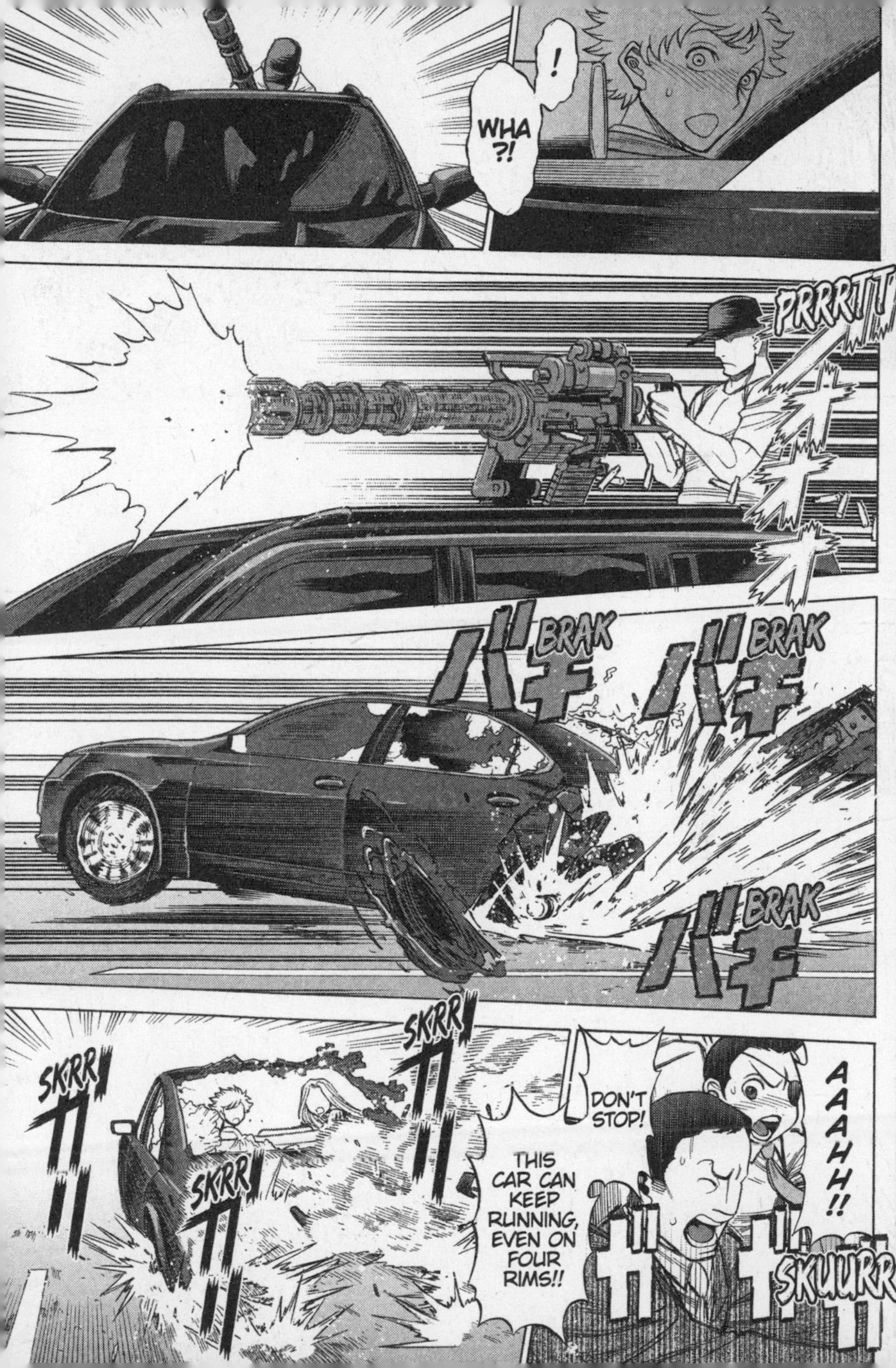
!
WHA?!
PRRRTTT
BRAK
バキ
BRAK
バキ
BRAK
バキ
AAAHH!!
DON'T STOP!
THIS CAR CAN KEEP RUNNING, EVEN ON FOUR RIMS!!
SKUURR
SKRR
SKRR
SKRR

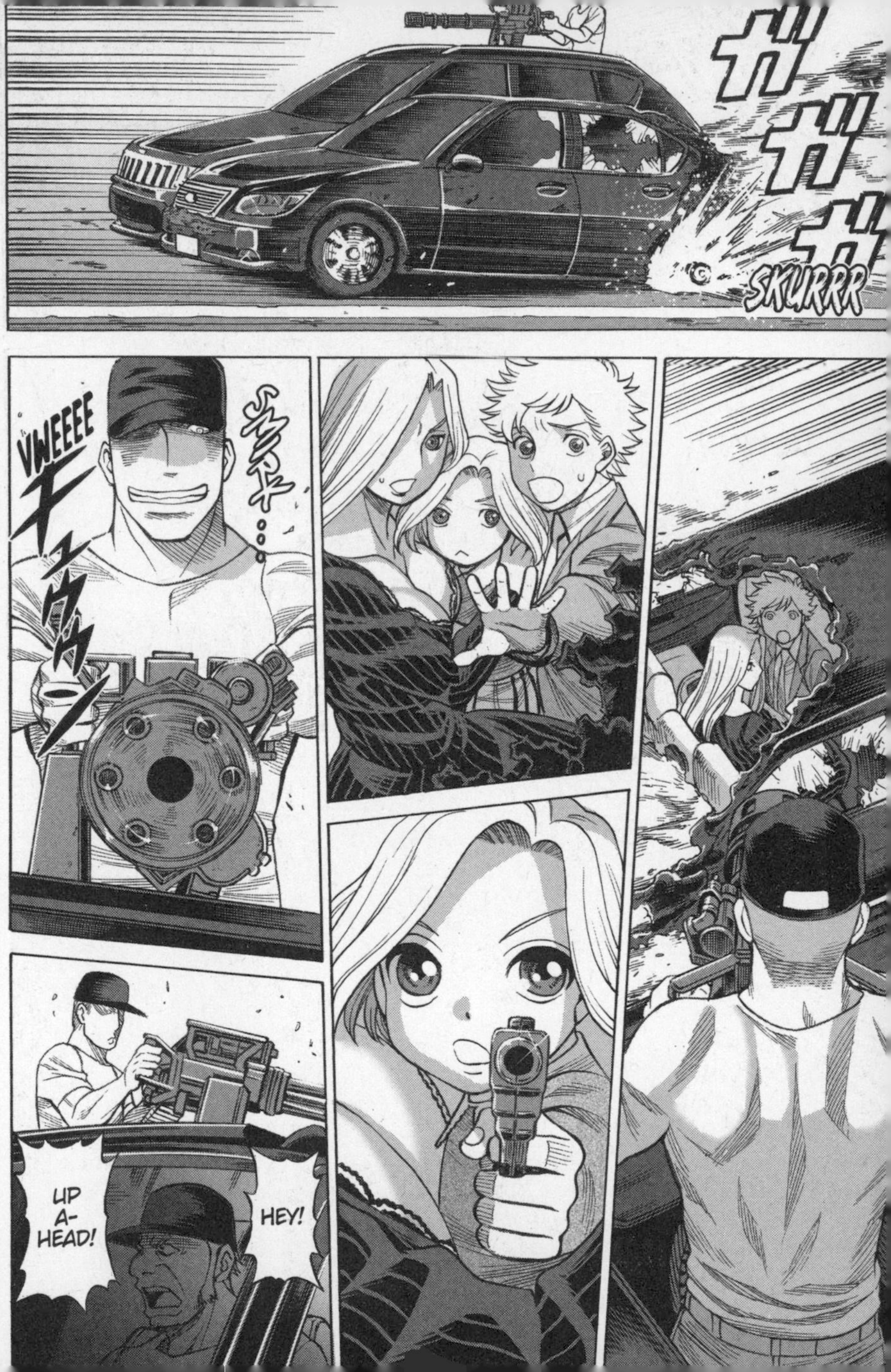
ガガガ
SKURRR
SMIRK...
チュウウン
VWEEEE
HEY!
UP A-HEAD!

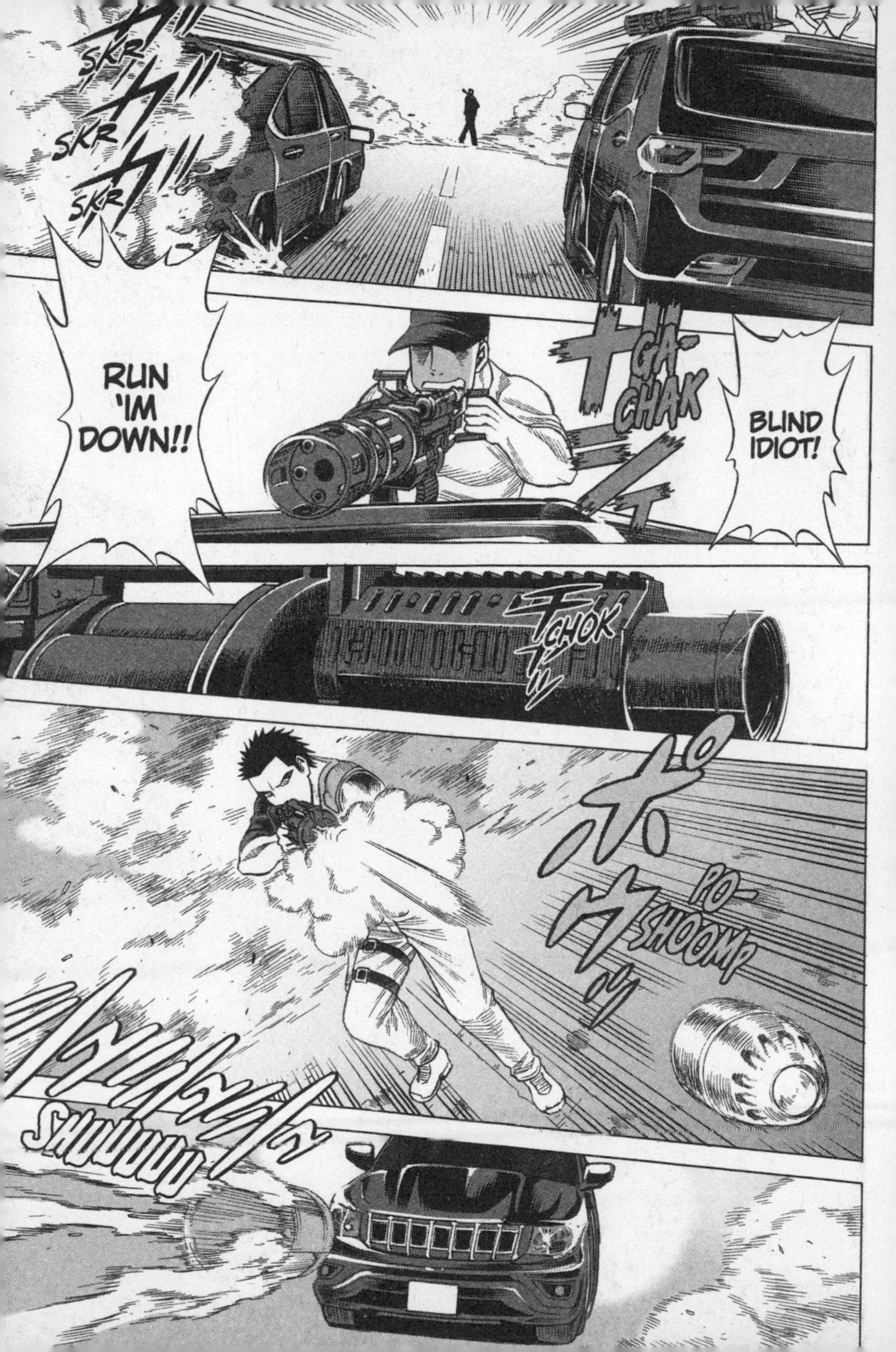
SKR
SKR
SKR
BLIND IDIOT!
GA-CHAK
RUN 'IM DOWN!!
CHOK
PO-SHOOMP
SHUUUU

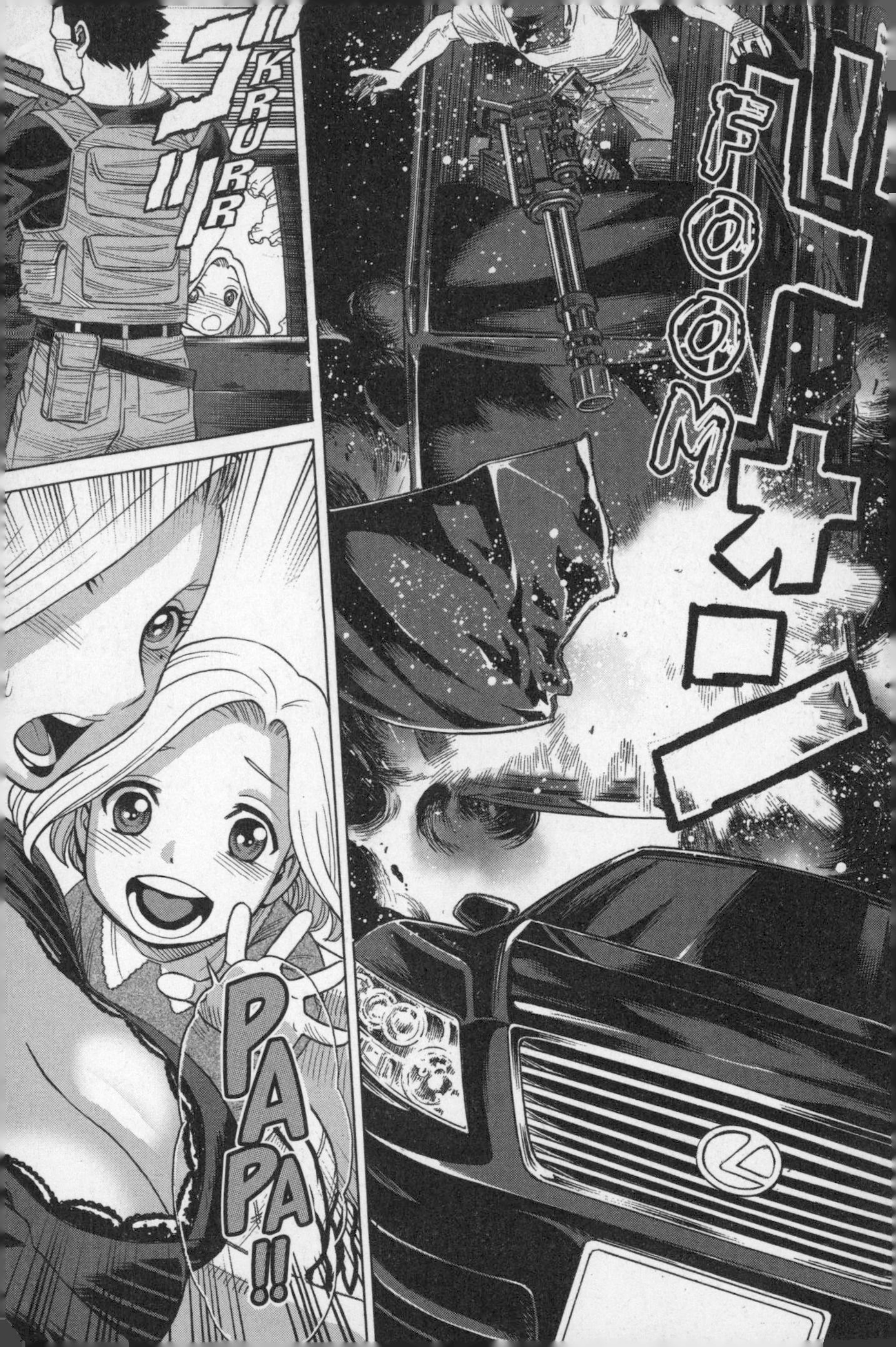
FOOM
KRURRR
PAPA!!

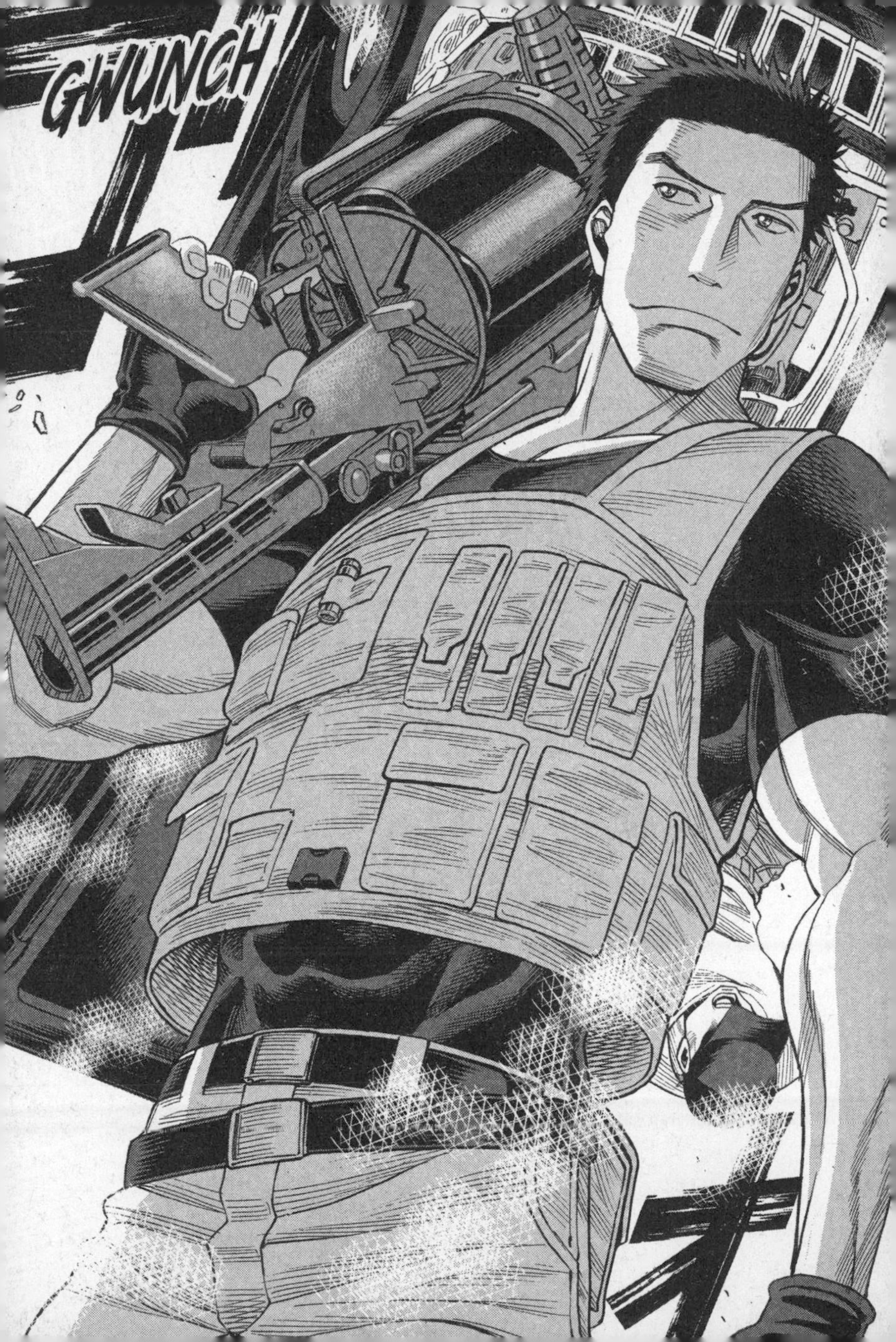
GWUNCH

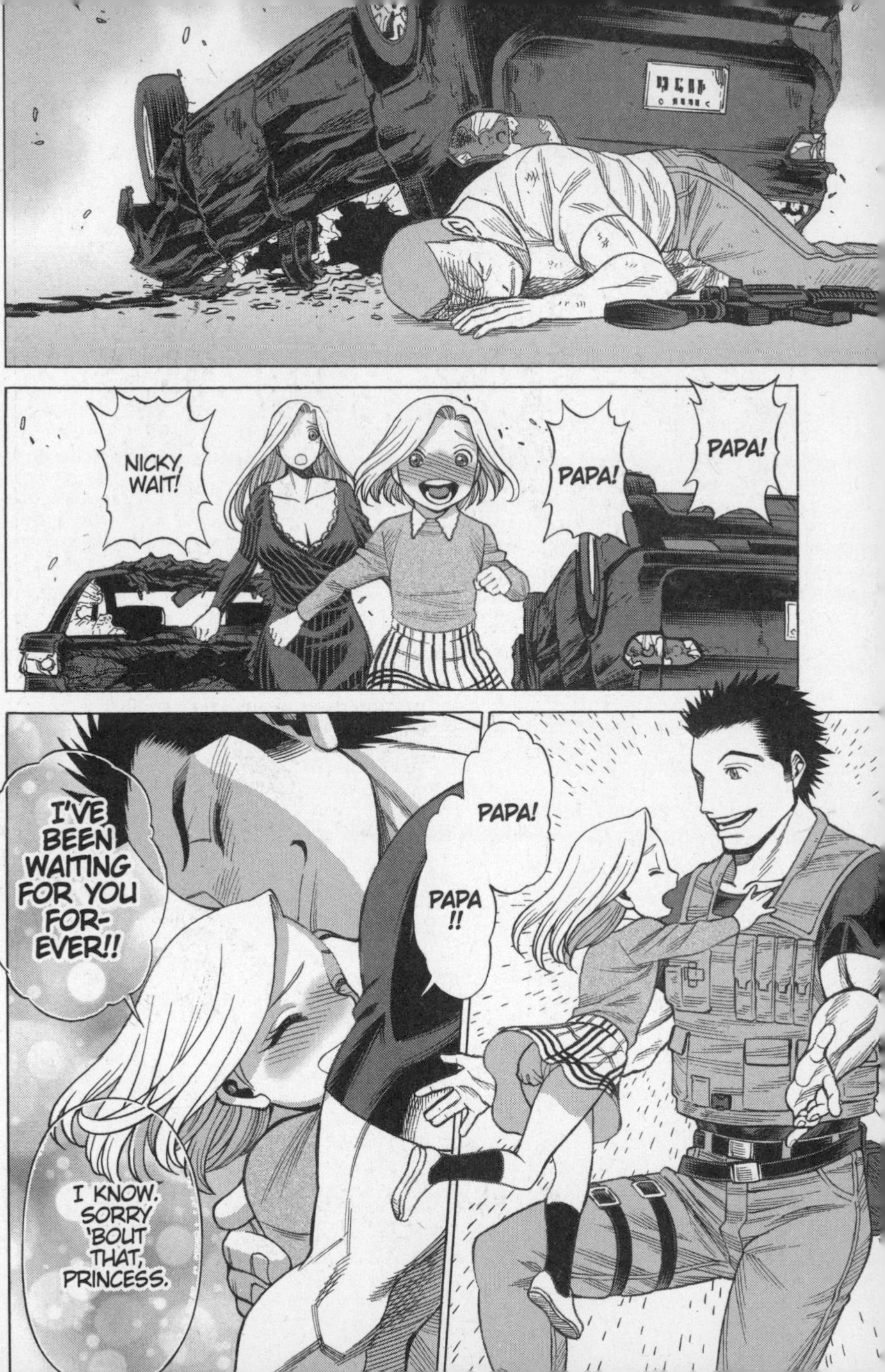
PAPA!
PAPA!
NICKY, WAIT!
PAPA!
PAPA!!
I'VE BEEN WAITING FOR YOU FOR-EVER!!
I KNOW. SORRY 'BOUT THAT, PRINCESS.

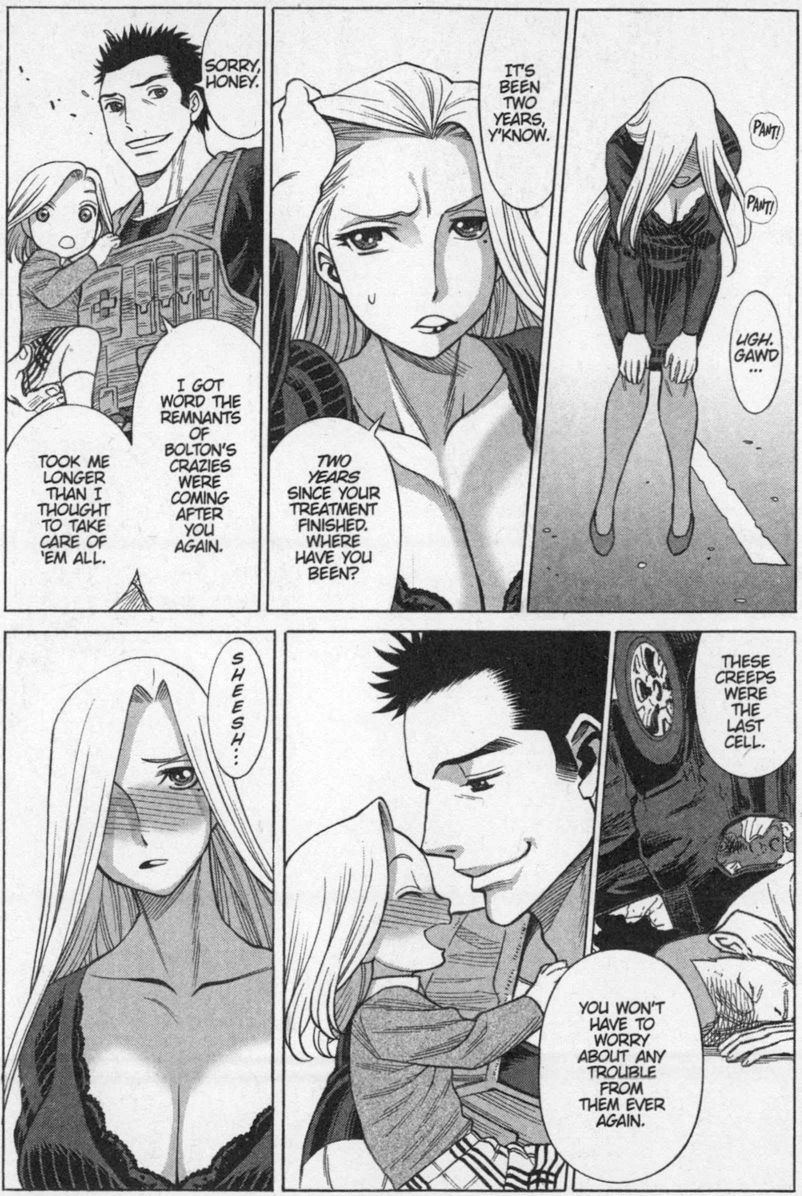
PANT!
PANT!
UGH. GAWD...
IT'S BEEN TWO YEARS, Y'KNOW.
TWO YEARS SINCE YOUR TREATMENT FINISHED. WHERE HAVE YOU BEEN?
SORRY, HONEY.
I GOT WORD THE REMNANTS OF BOLTON'S CRAZIES WERE COMING AFTER YOU AGAIN.
TOOK ME LONGER THAN I THOUGHT TO TAKE CARE OF 'EM ALL.
THESE CREEPS WERE THE LAST CELL.
YOU WON'T HAVE TO WORRY ABOUT ANY TROUBLE FROM THEM EVER AGAIN.
SHEESH...

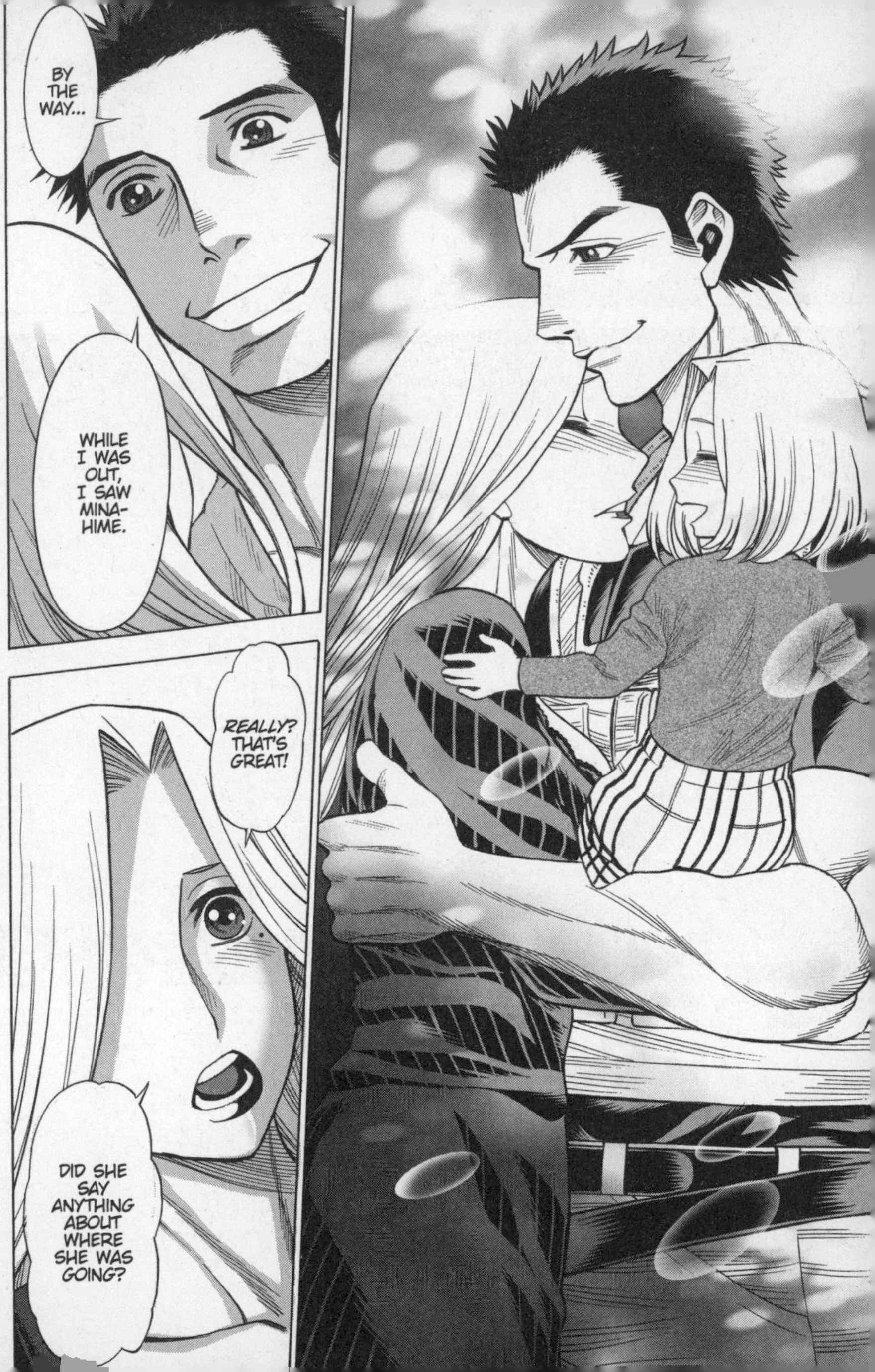
BY THE WAY...
WHILE I WAS OUT, I SAW MINA-HIME.
REALLY? THAT'S GREAT!
DID SHE SAY ANYTHING ABOUT WHERE SHE WAS GOING?

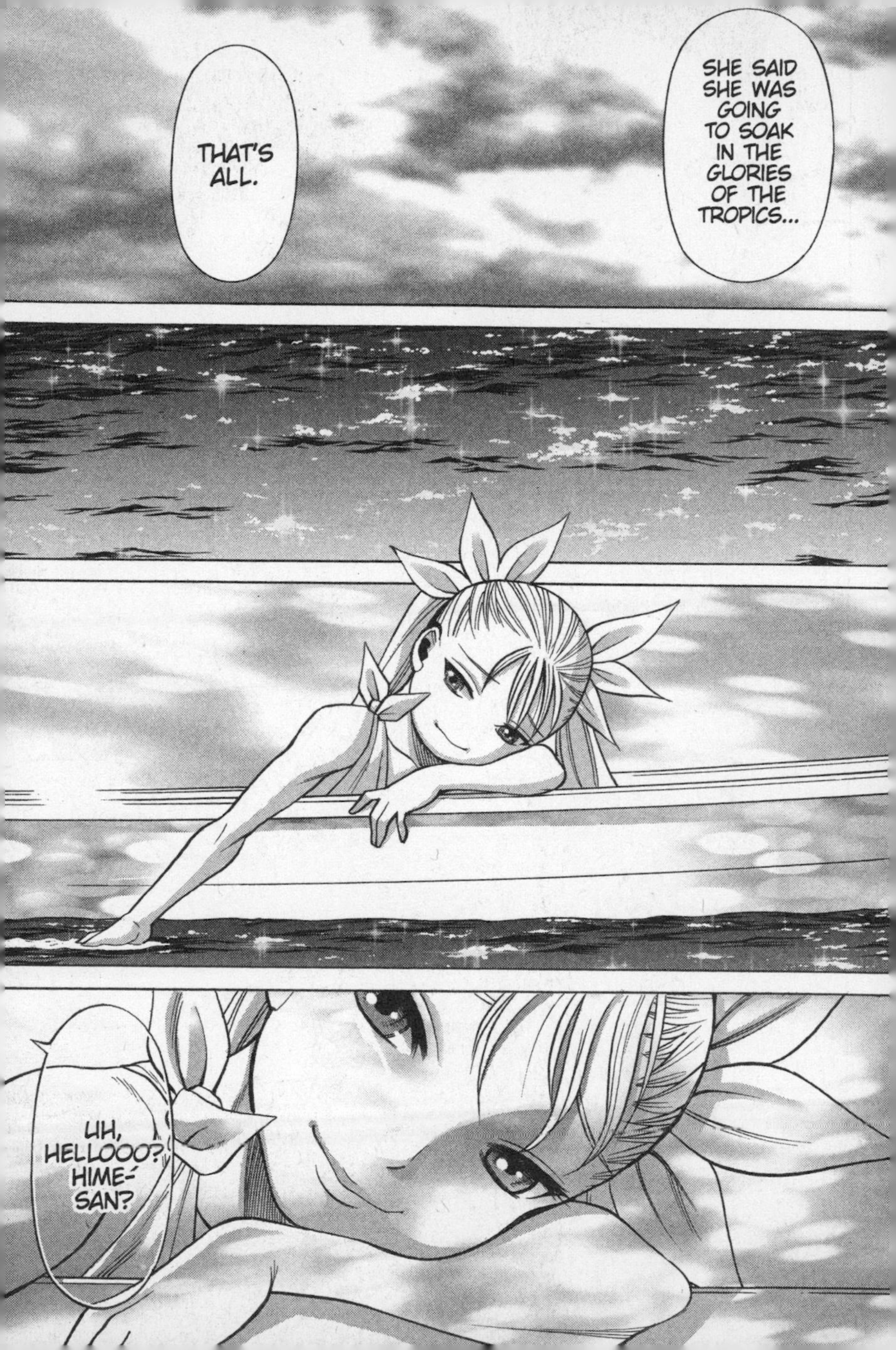
SHE SAID SHE WAS GOING TO SOAK IN THE GLORIES OF THE TROPICS...
THAT'S ALL.
UH, HELLOOO? HIME-SAN?

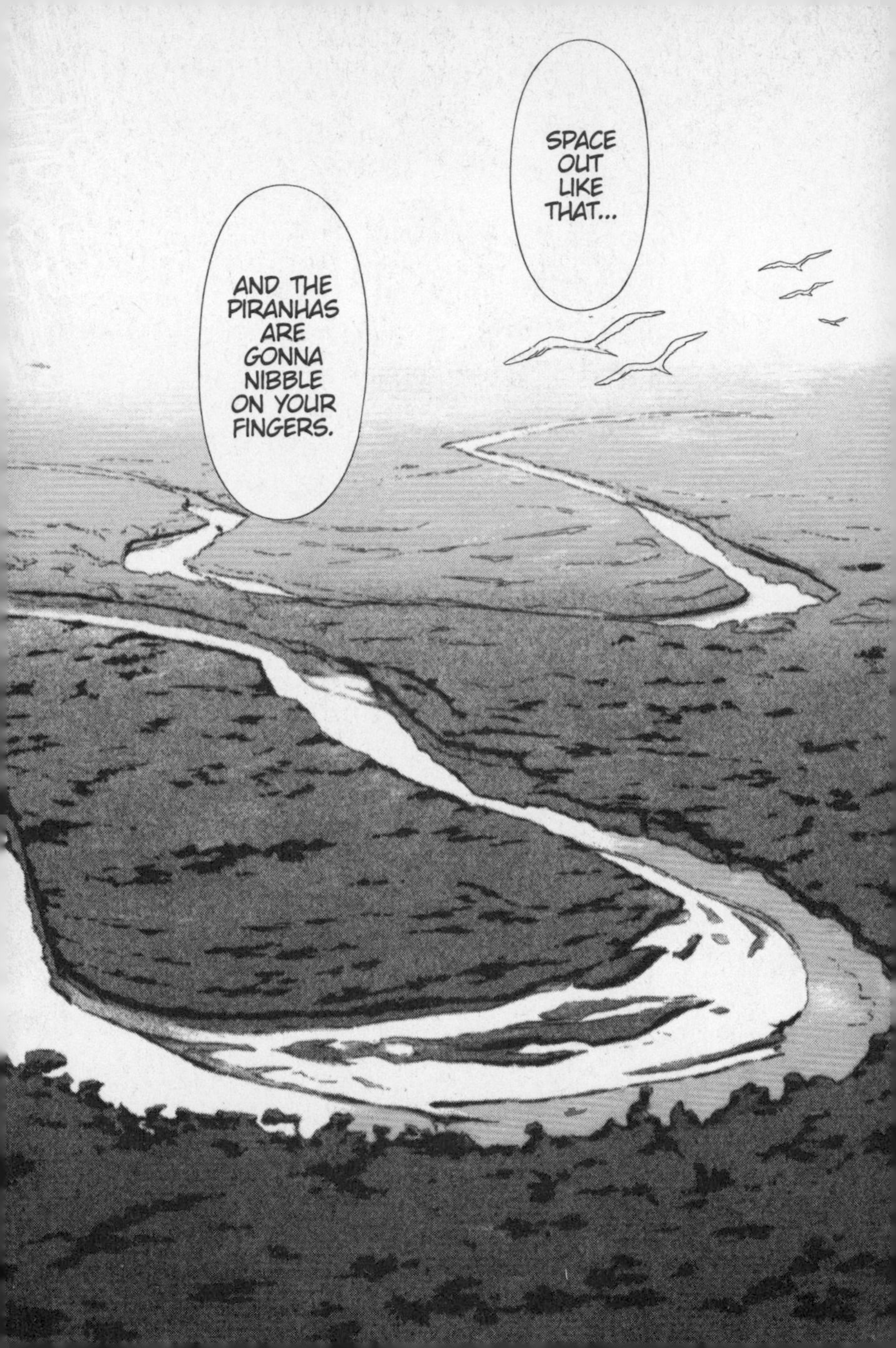
SPACE OUT LIKE THAT...
AND THE PIRANHAS ARE GONNA NIBBLE ON YOUR FINGERS.

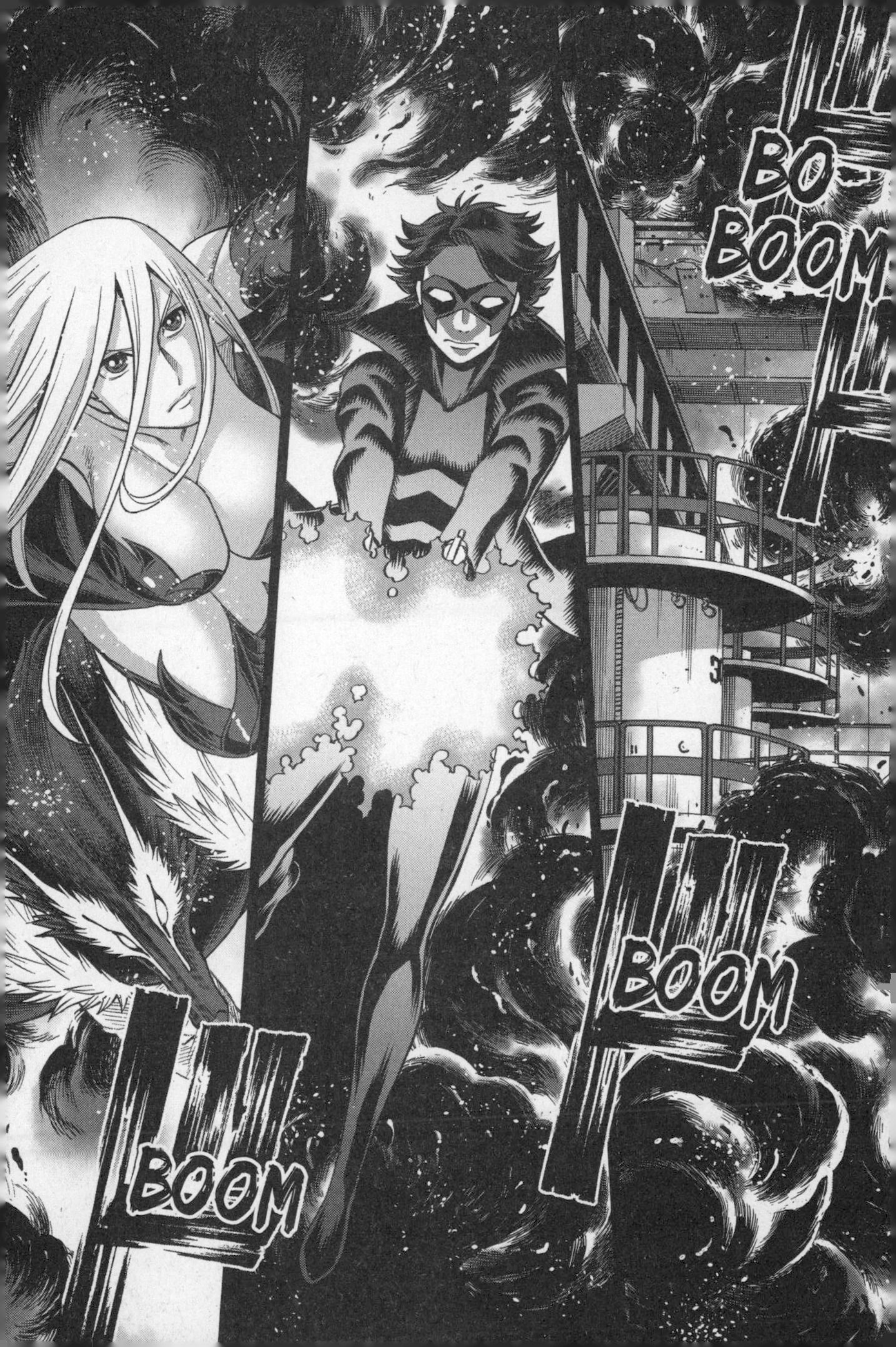
BO-BOOM
BOOM
BOOM

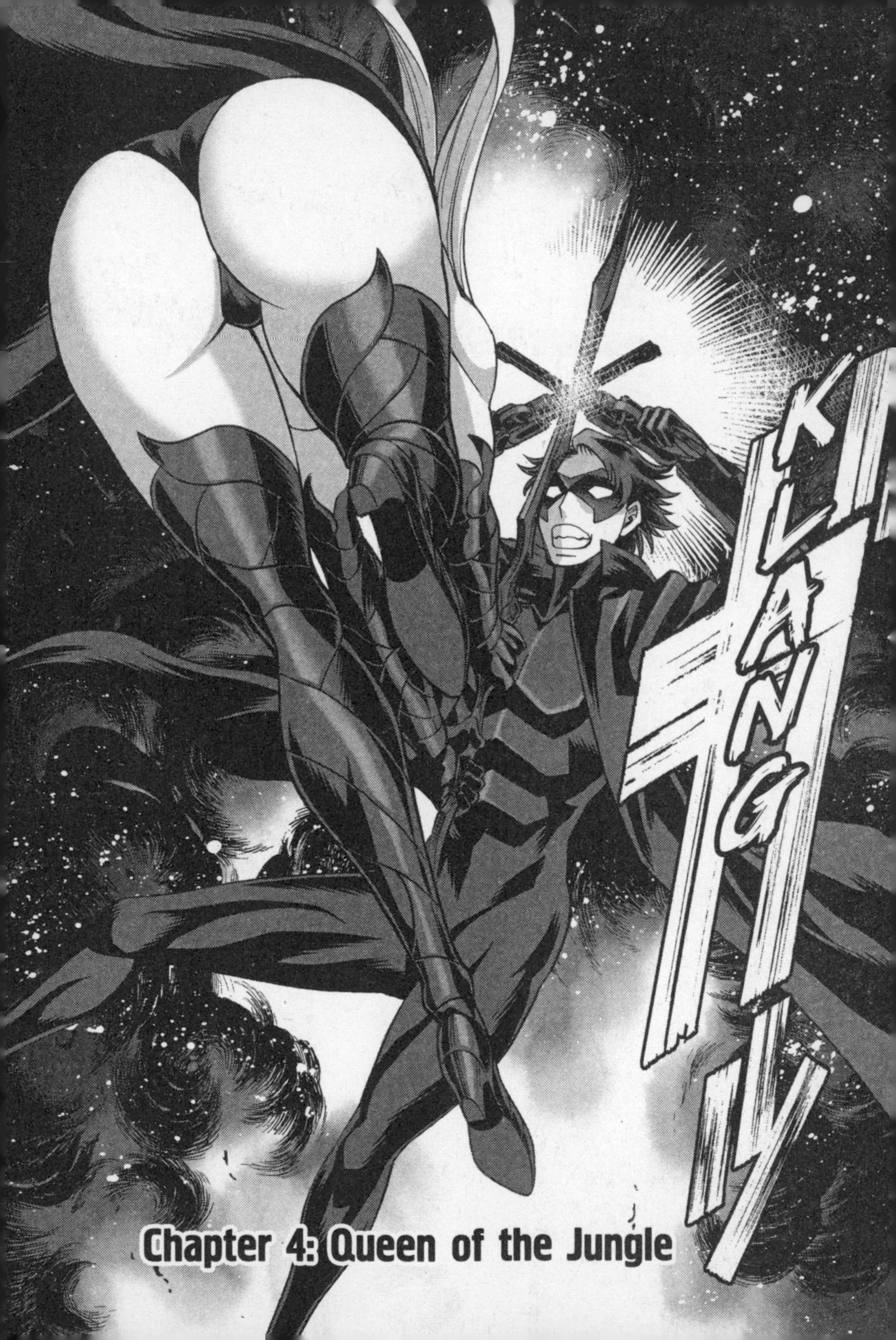
KLANG

Chapter 4: Queen of the Jungle

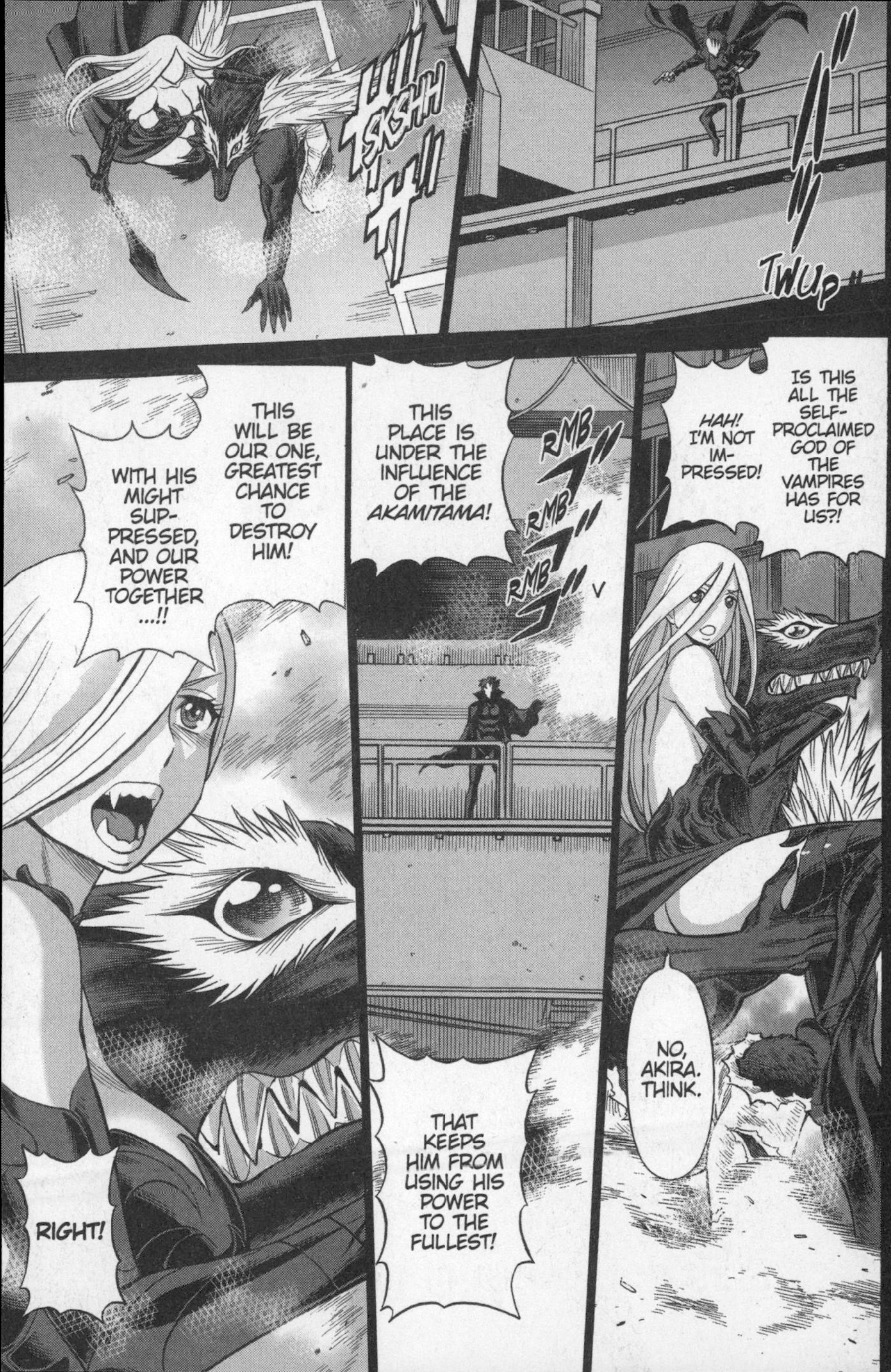

TWUp
SKSHH
IS THIS ALL THE SELF-PROCLAIMED GOD OF THE VAMPIRES HAS FOR US?!
HAH! I'M NOT IM-PRESSED!
NO, AKIRA. THINK.
THIS PLACE IS UNDER THE INFLUENCE OF THE *AKAMITAMA*!
RMB RMB RMB
THAT KEEPS HIM FROM USING HIS POWER TO THE FULLEST!
THIS WILL BE OUR ONE, GREATEST CHANCE TO DESTROY HIM!
WITH HIS MIGHT SUP-PRESSED, AND OUR POWER TOGETHER ...!!
RIGHT!

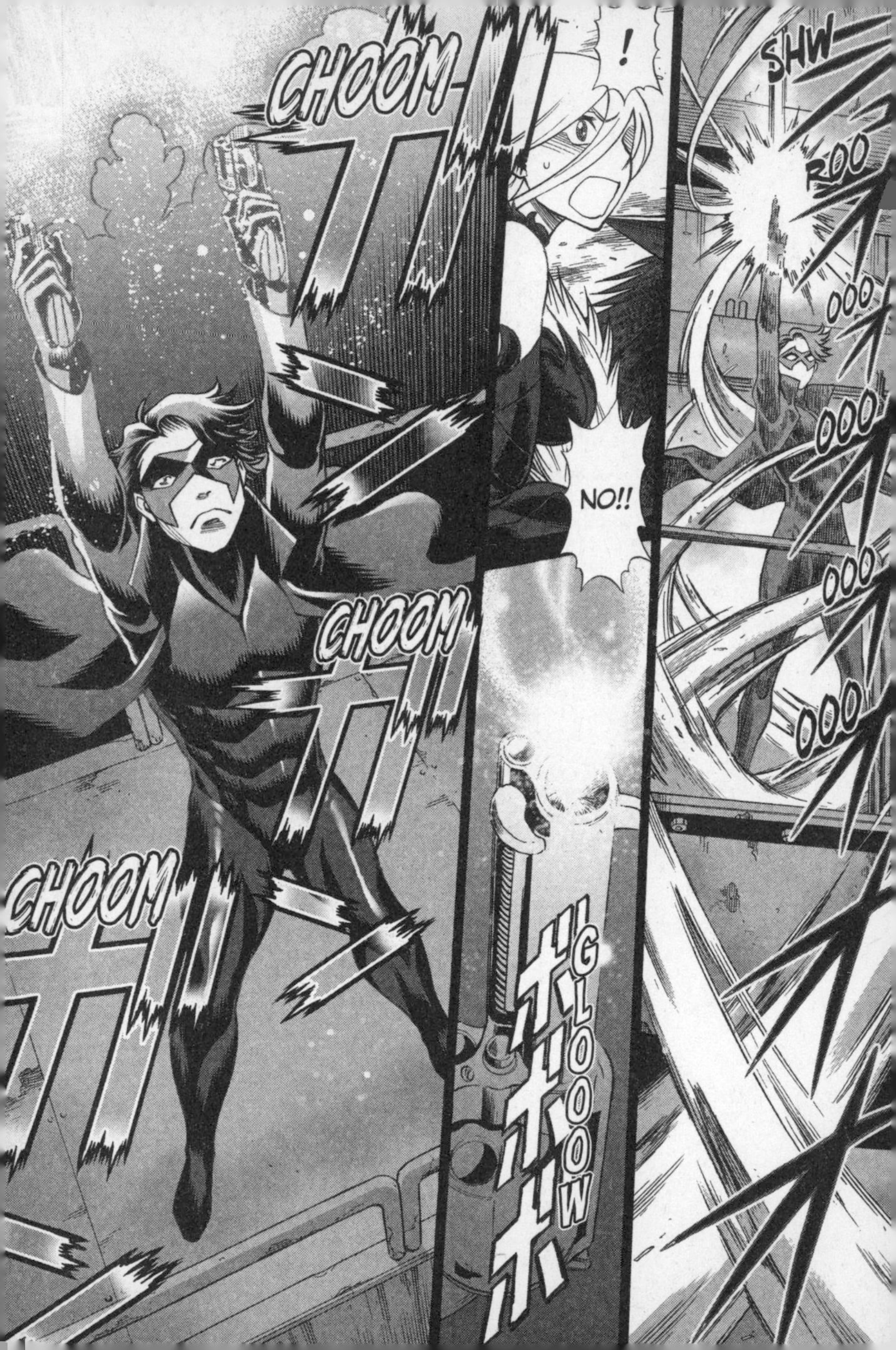
SHW
ROO
OOO
OOO
OOO
OOO
!
NO!!
GLOOOOW
CHOOM
CHOOM
CHOOM

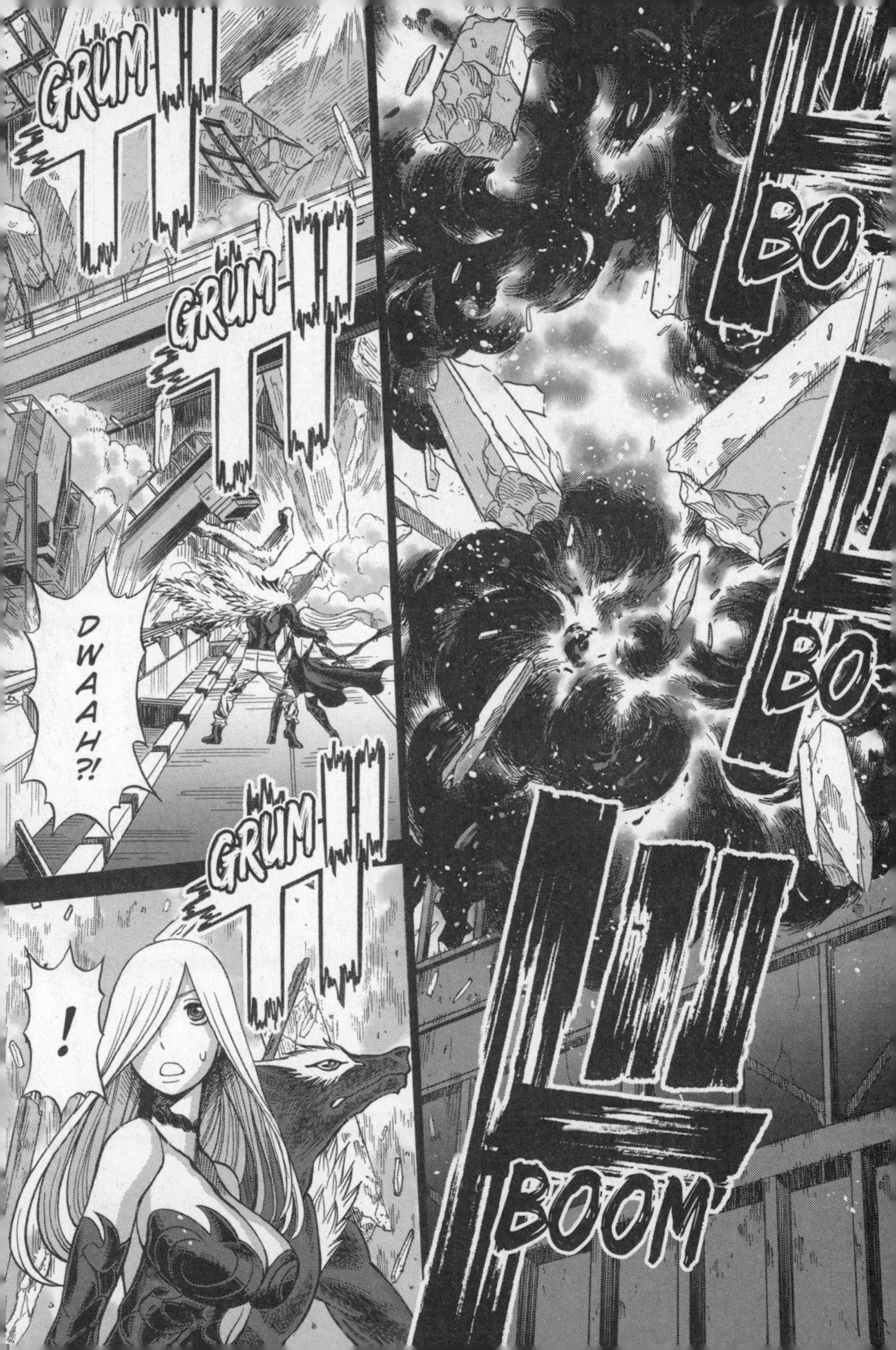
BO-
BO-
BOOM
GRUM
GRUM
DWAAAH?!
GRUM
!

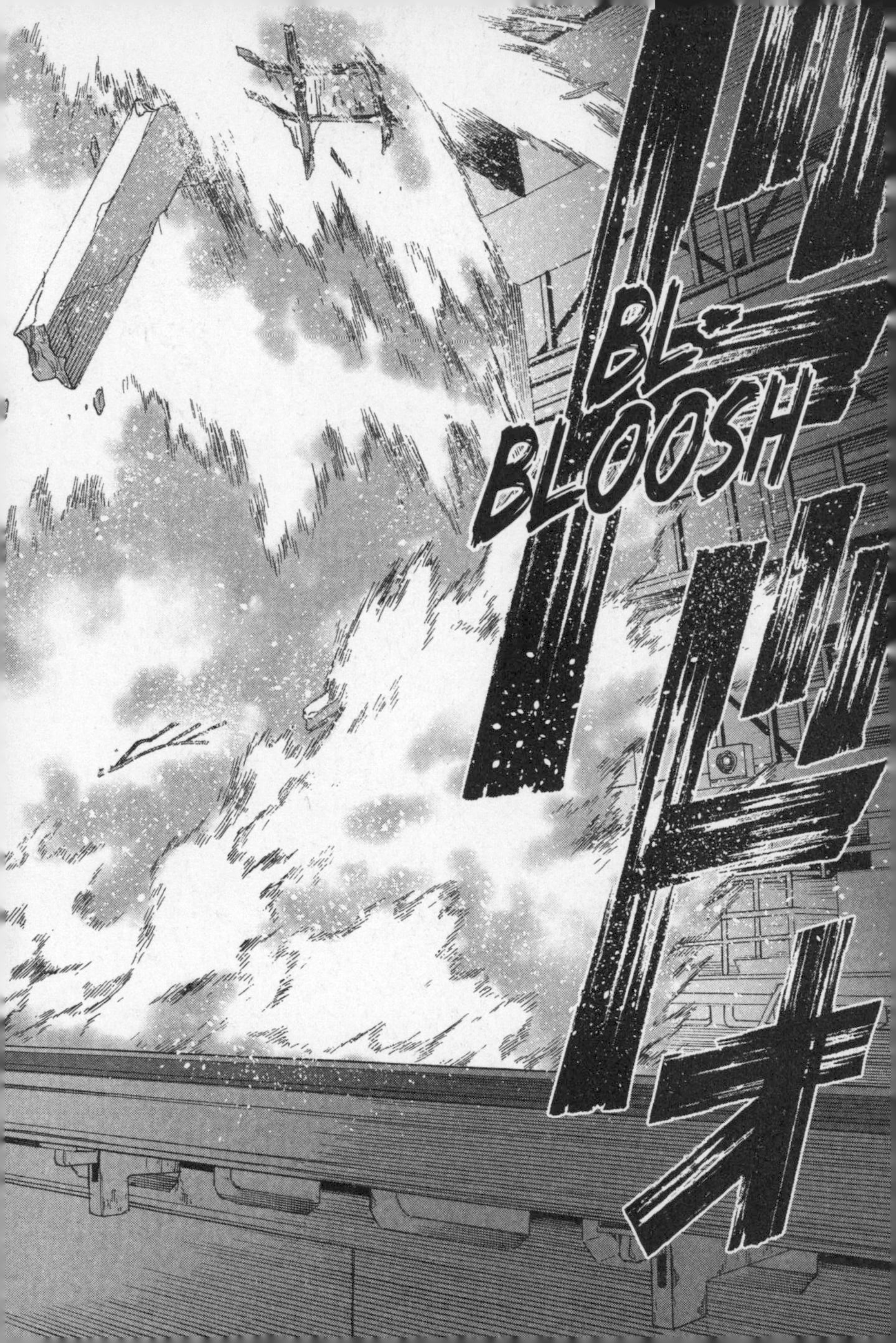
BL-
BLOOSH

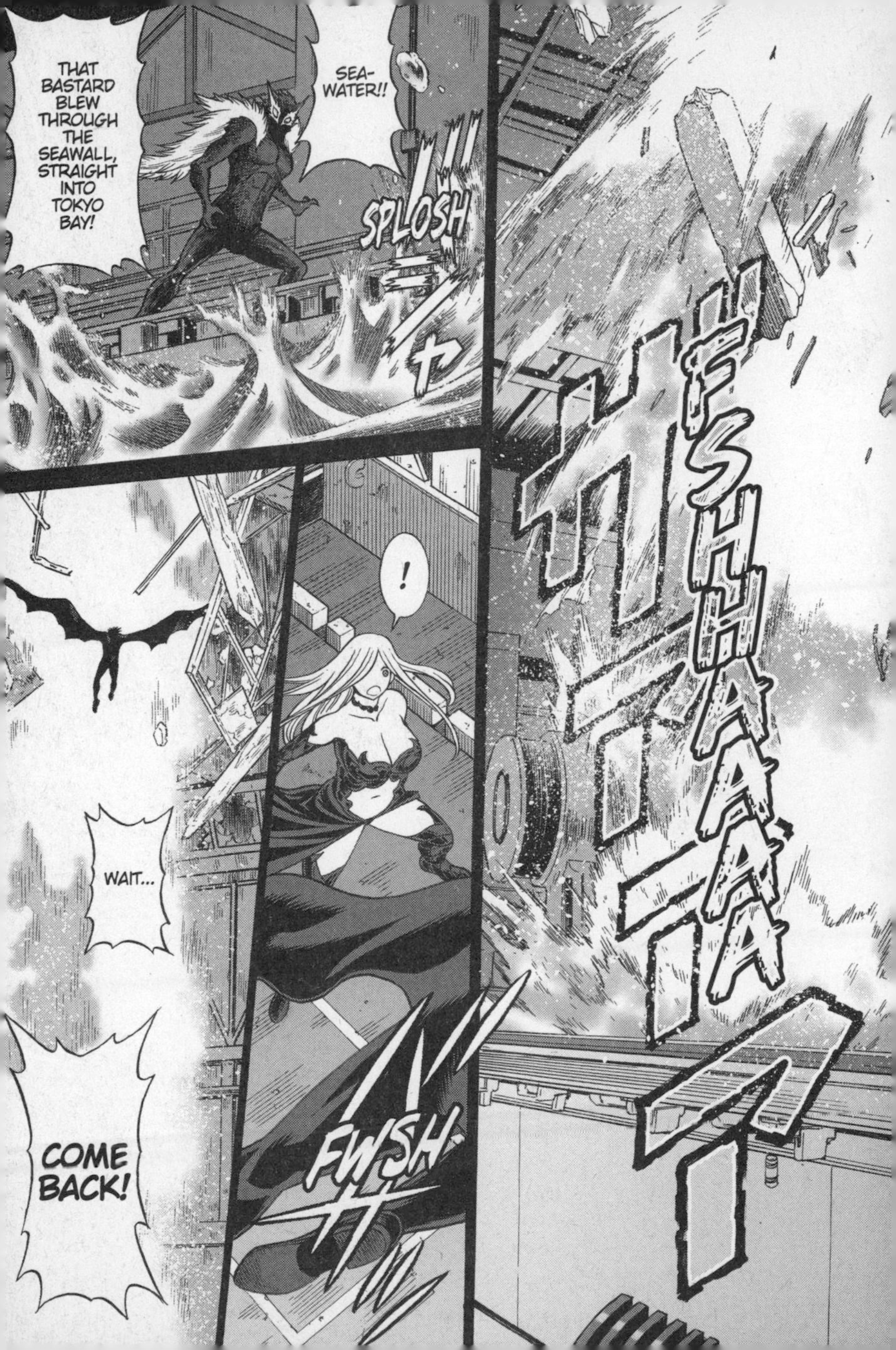
FSHHAAAA
SEA-WATER!!
THAT BASTARD BLEW THROUGH THE SEAWALL, STRAIGHT INTO TOKYO BAY!
SPLOSH
!
FWSH
WAIT...
COME BACK!

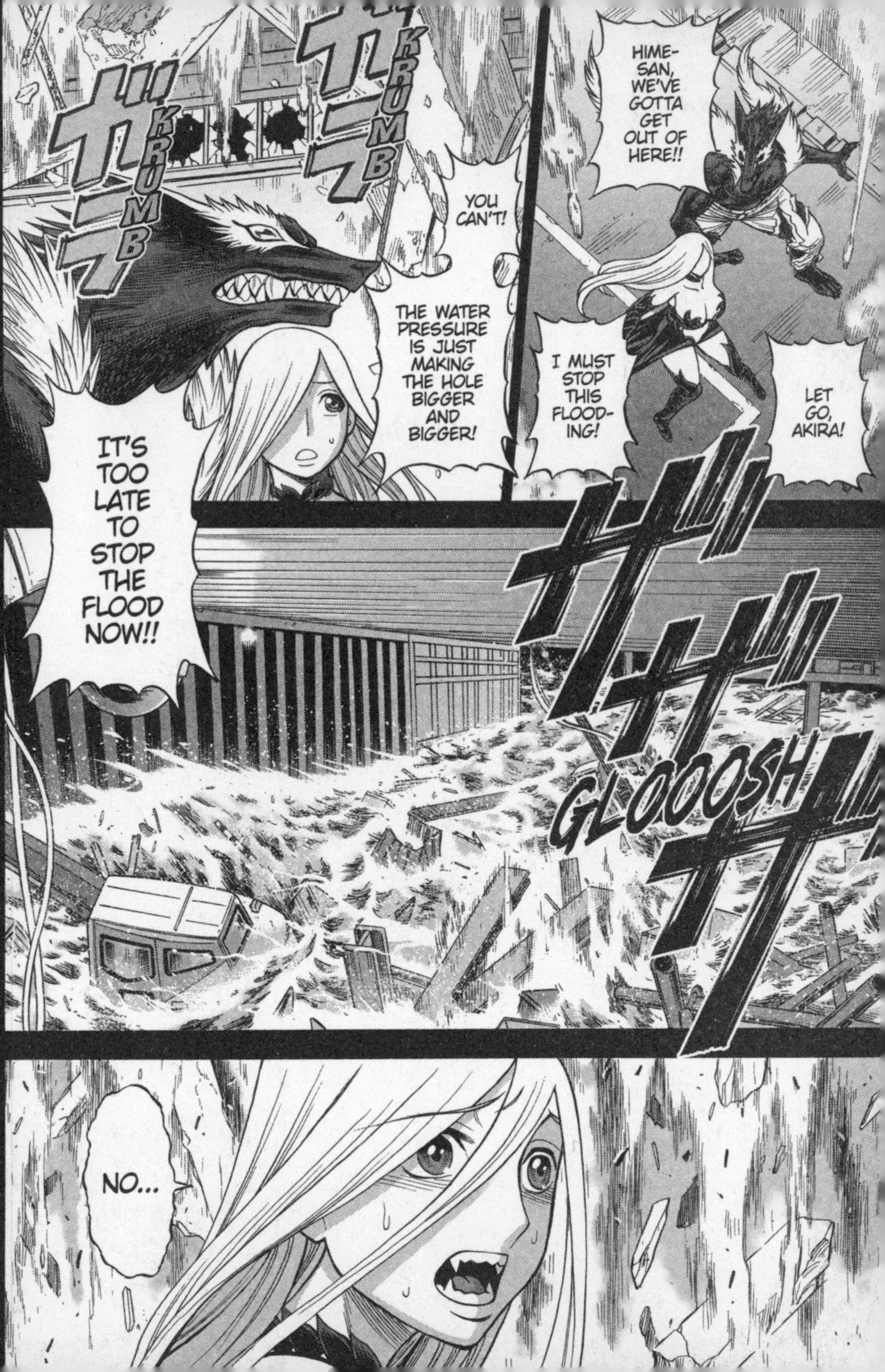
HIME-SAN, WE'VE GOTTA GET OUT OF HERE!!
LET GO, AKIRA!
I MUST STOP THIS FLOOD-ING!
KRUMB
KRUMB
YOU CAN'T!
THE WATER PRESSURE IS JUST MAKING THE HOLE BIGGER AND BIGGER!
IT'S TOO LATE TO STOP THE FLOOD NOW!!
GLOOOSH
NO...

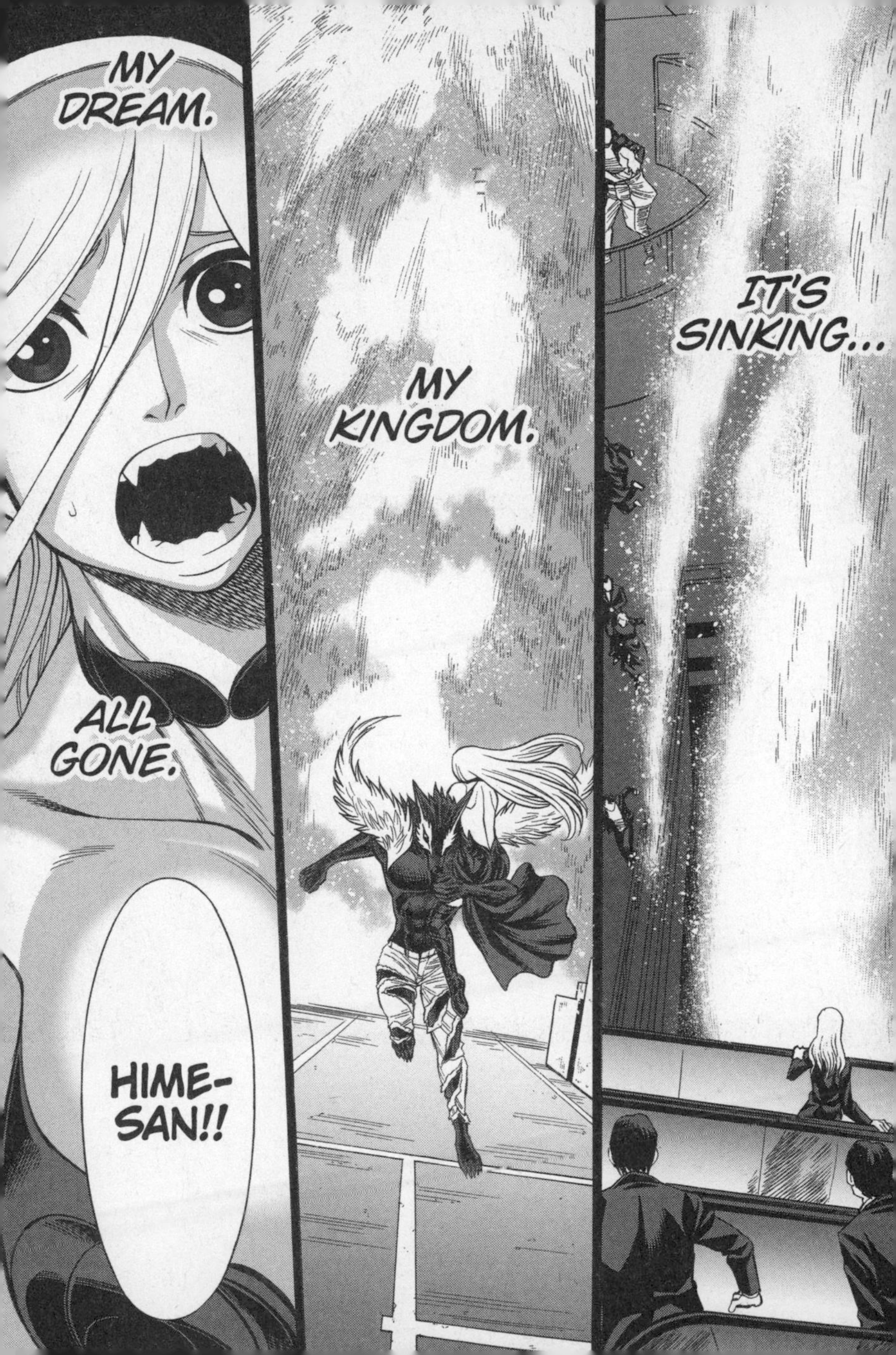
IT'S SINKING...
MY KINGDOM.
MY DREAM.
ALL GONE.
HIME-SAN!!

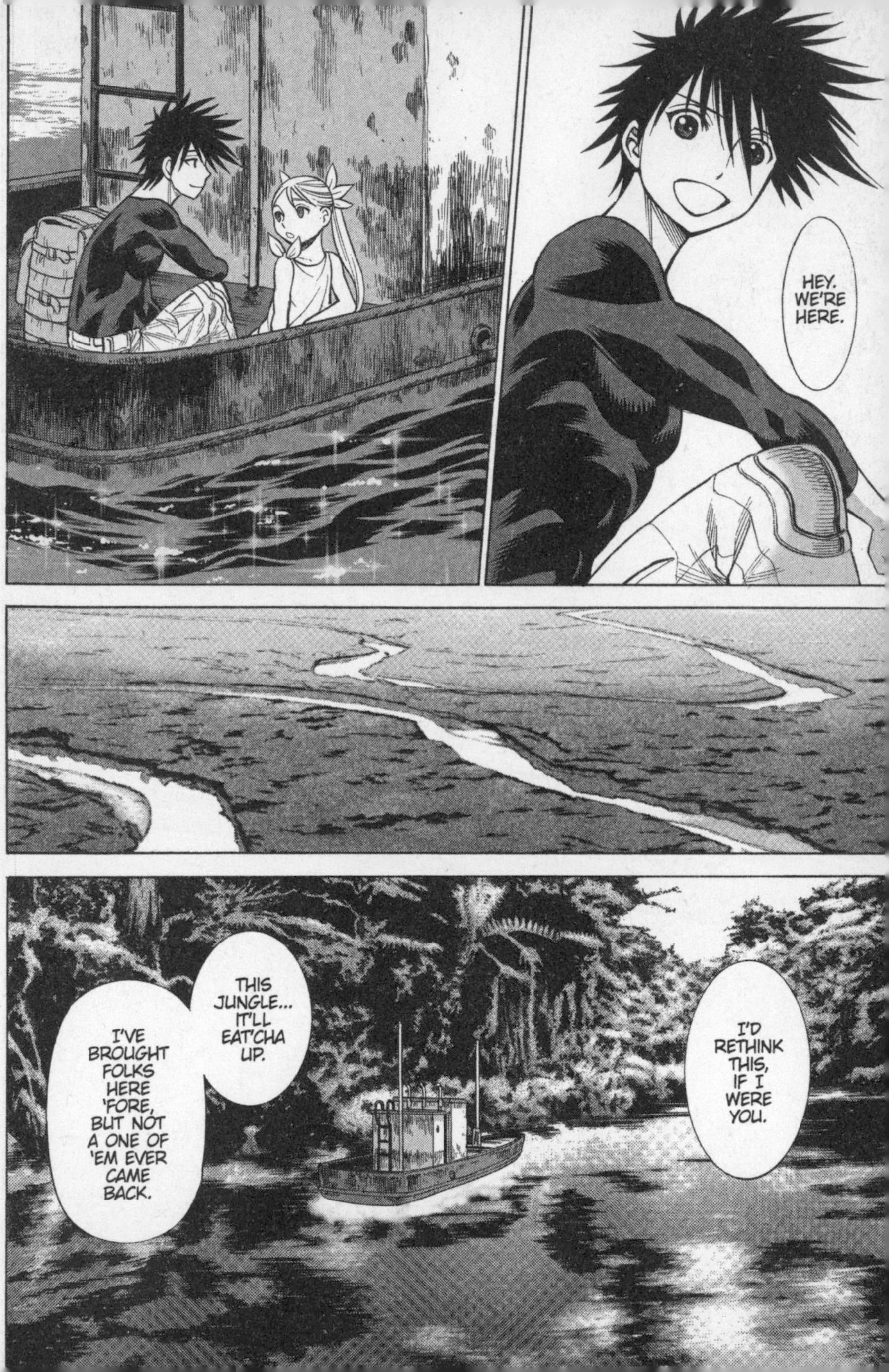
HEY. WE'RE HERE.
I'D RETHINK THIS, IF I WERE YOU.
THIS JUNGLE... IT'LL EAT'CHA UP.
I'VE BROUGHT FOLKS HERE 'FORE, BUT NOT A ONE OF 'EM EVER CAME BACK.

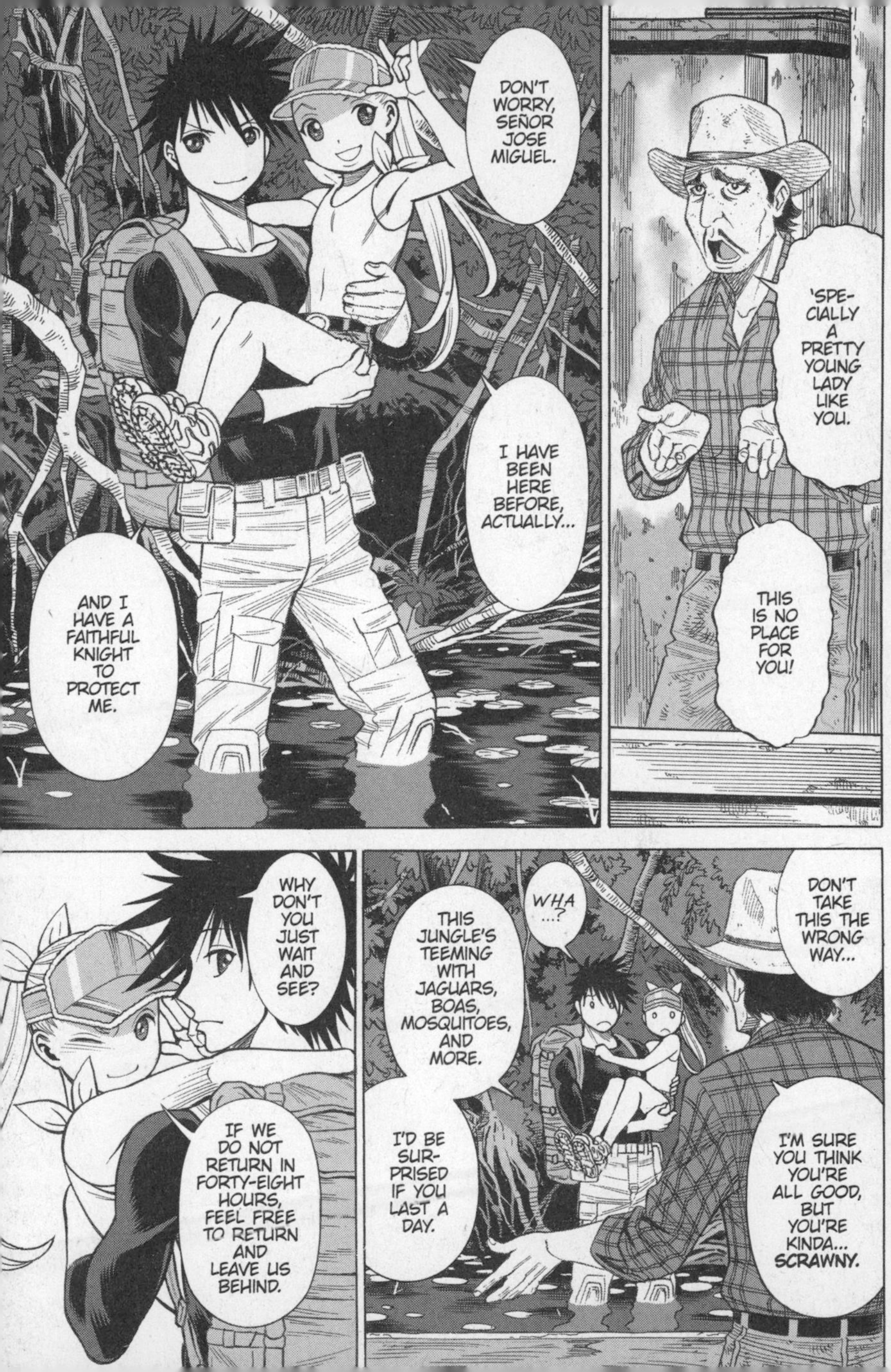
'SPECIALLY A PRETTY YOUNG LADY LIKE YOU.
THIS IS NO PLACE FOR YOU!
DON'T WORRY, SEÑOR JOSE MIGUEL.
I HAVE BEEN HERE BEFORE, ACTUALLY...
AND I HAVE A FAITHFUL KNIGHT TO PROTECT ME.
DON'T TAKE THIS THE WRONG WAY...
I'M SURE YOU THINK YOU'RE ALL GOOD, BUT YOU'RE KINDA... SCRAWNY.
WHA ...?
THIS JUNGLE'S TEEMING WITH JAGUARS, BOAS, MOSQUITOES, AND MORE.
I'D BE SURPRISED IF YOU LAST A DAY.
WHY DON'T YOU JUST WAIT AND SEE?
IF WE DO NOT RETURN IN FORTY-EIGHT HOURS, FEEL FREE TO RETURN AND LEAVE US BEHIND.

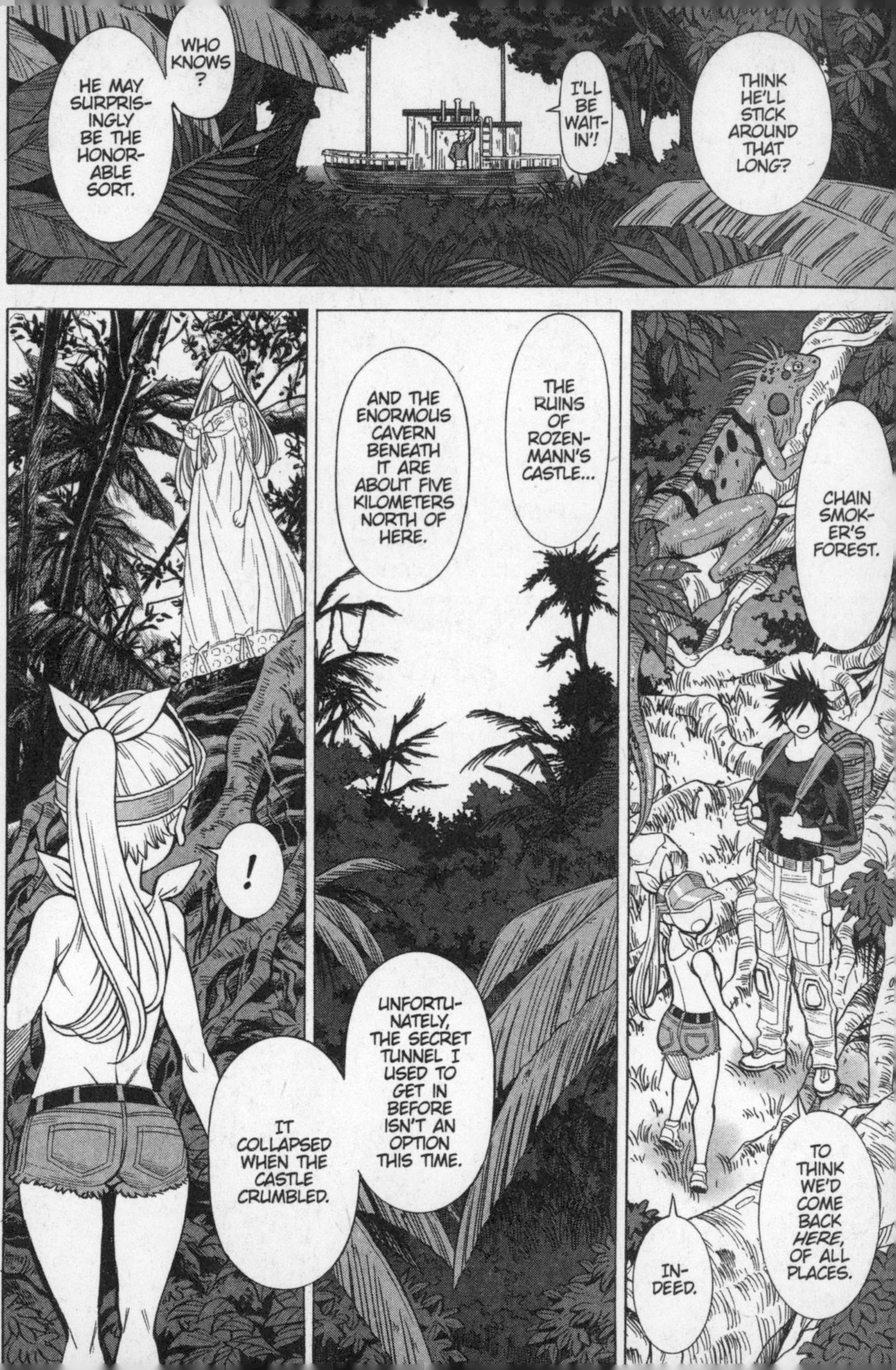
THINK HE'LL STICK AROUND THAT LONG?
I'LL BE WAITIN'!
WHO KNOWS?
HE MAY SURPRISINGLY BE THE HONORABLE SORT.
CHAIN SMOKER'S FOREST.
TO THINK WE'D COME BACK HERE, OF ALL PLACES.
INDEED.
THE RUINS OF ROZENMANN'S CASTLE...
AND THE ENORMOUS CAVERN BENEATH IT ARE ABOUT FIVE KILOMETERS NORTH OF HERE.
UNFORTUNATELY, THE SECRET TUNNEL I USED TO GET IN BEFORE ISN'T AN OPTION THIS TIME.
!
IT COLLAPSED WHEN THE CASTLE CRUMBLED.

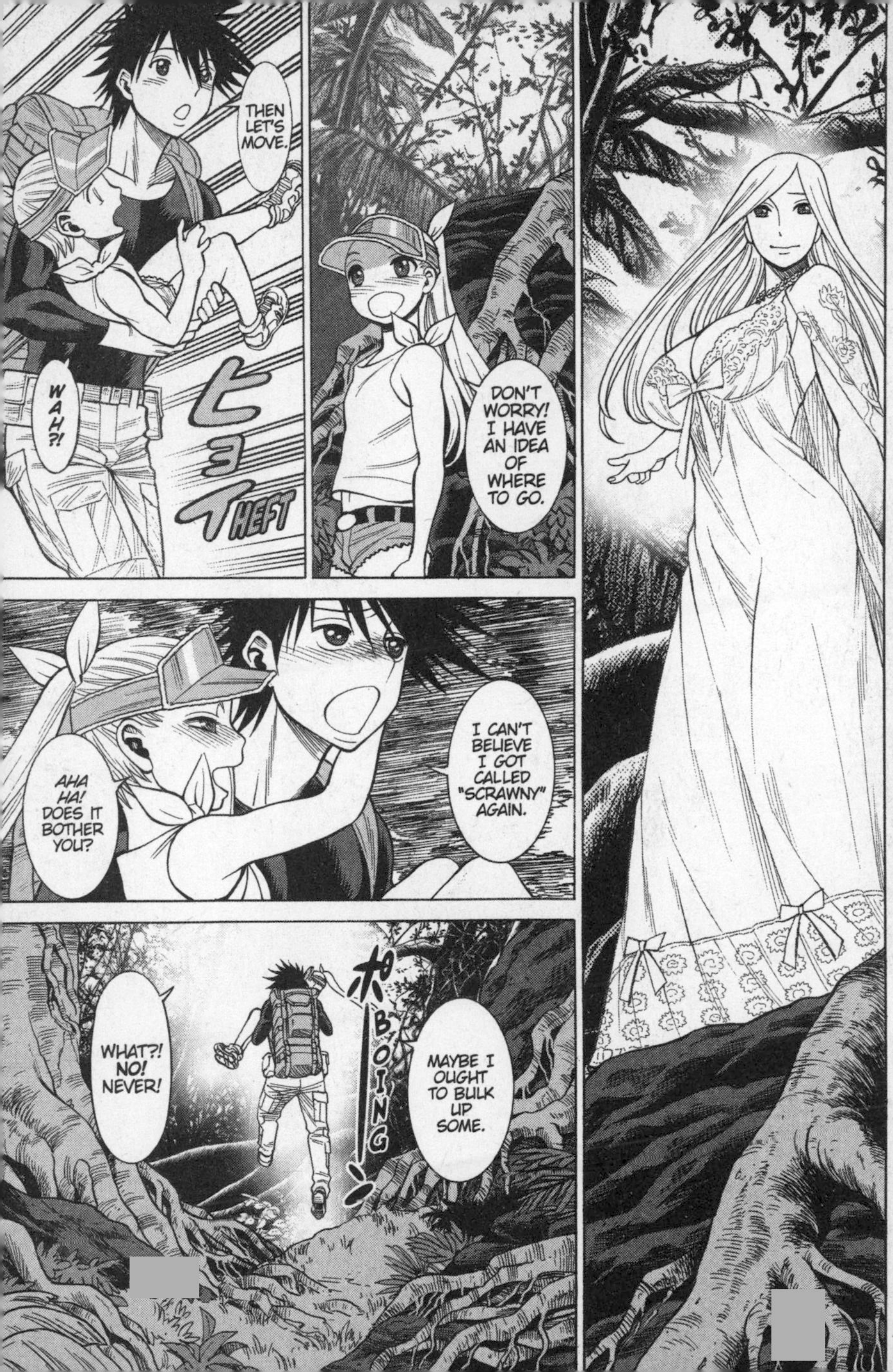

DON'T WORRY! I HAVE AN IDEA OF WHERE TO GO.
THEN LET'S MOVE.
WAH?!
ヒョイ
HEFT
I CAN'T BELIEVE I GOT CALLED "SCRAWNY" AGAIN.
AHA HA! DOES IT BOTHER YOU?
MAYBE I OUGHT TO BULK UP SOME.
BOING
WHAT?! NO! NEVER!

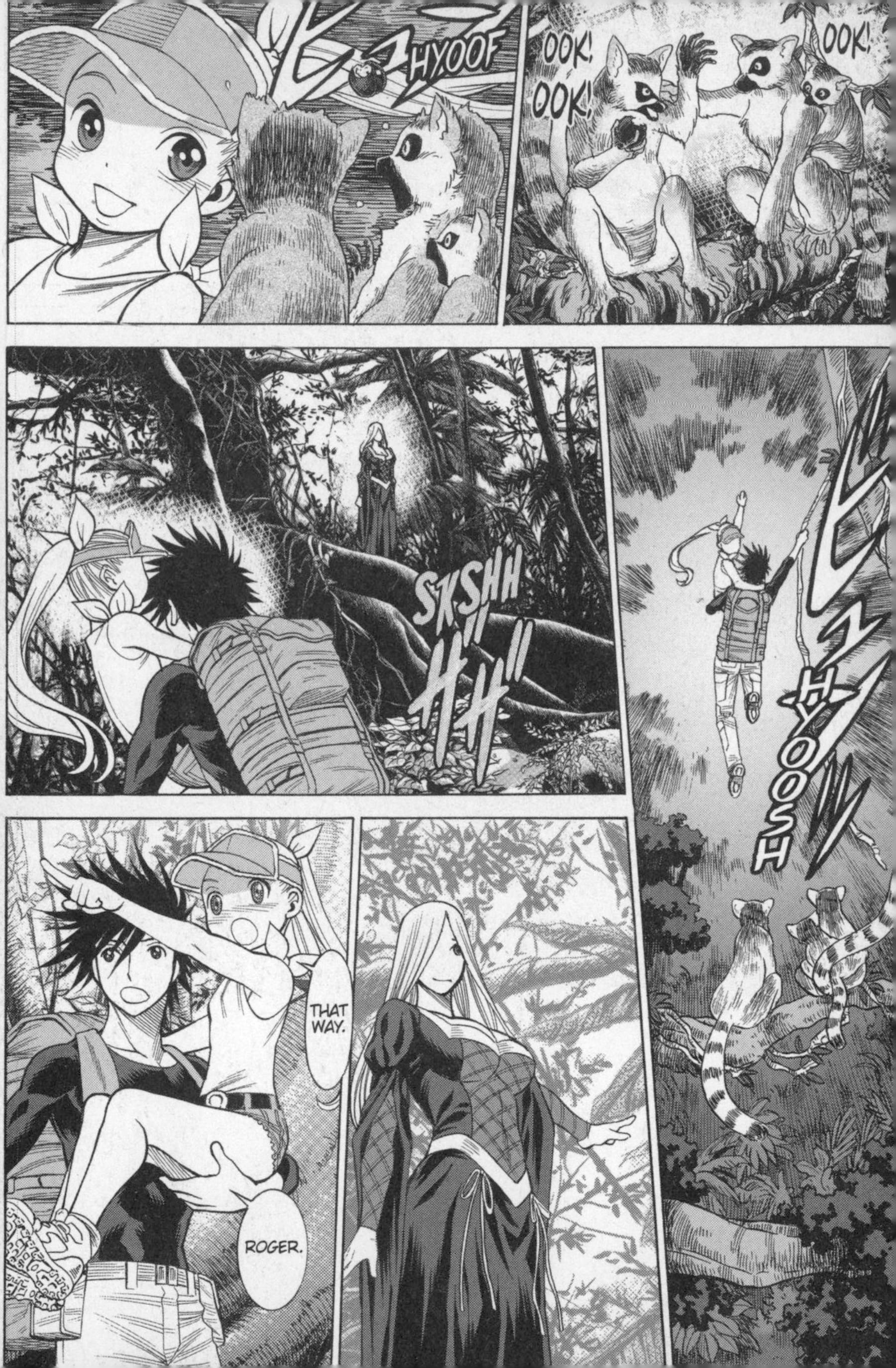
OOK!
OOK!
OOK!
HYOOF
HYOOOSH
SKSHHH
THAT WAY.
ROGER.

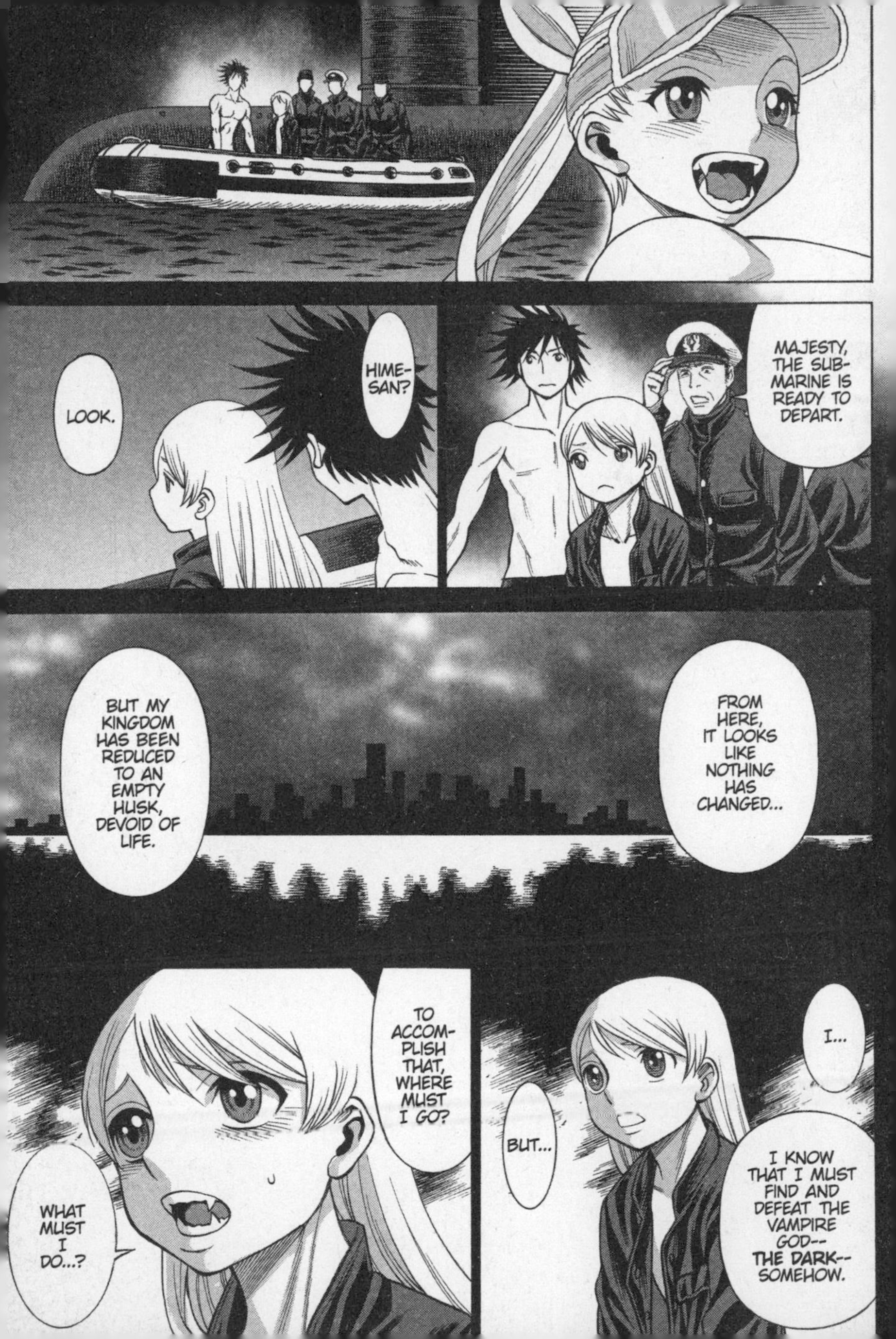
MAJESTY, THE SUB-MARINE IS READY TO DEPART.
HIME-SAN?
LOOK.
FROM HERE, IT LOOKS LIKE NOTHING HAS CHANGED...
BUT MY KINGDOM HAS BEEN REDUCED TO AN EMPTY HUSK, DEVOID OF LIFE.
I...
I KNOW THAT I MUST FIND AND DEFEAT THE VAMPIRE GOD-- THE DARK-- SOMEHOW.
BUT...
TO ACCOM-PLISH THAT, WHERE MUST I GO?
WHAT MUST I DO...?

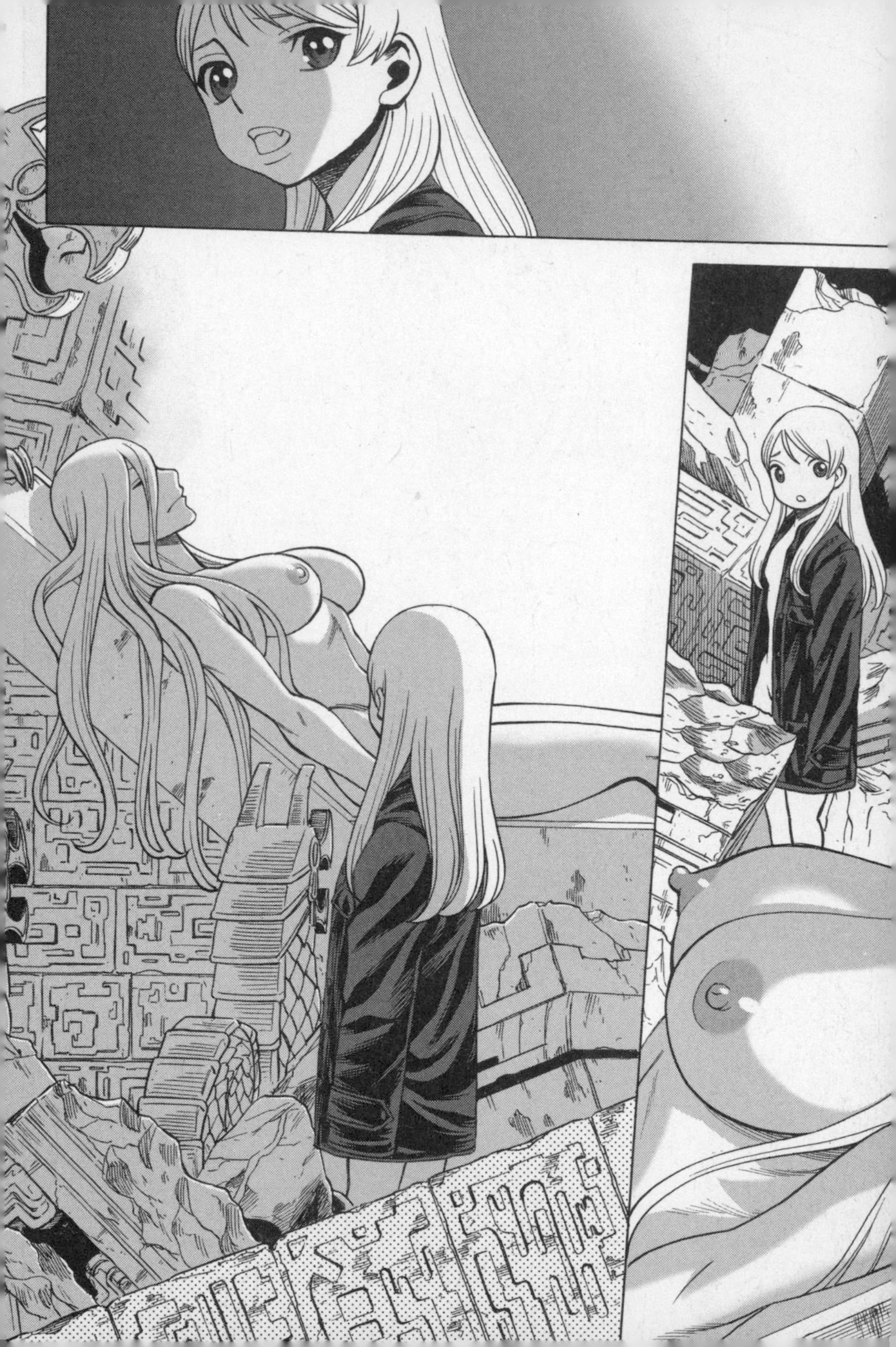

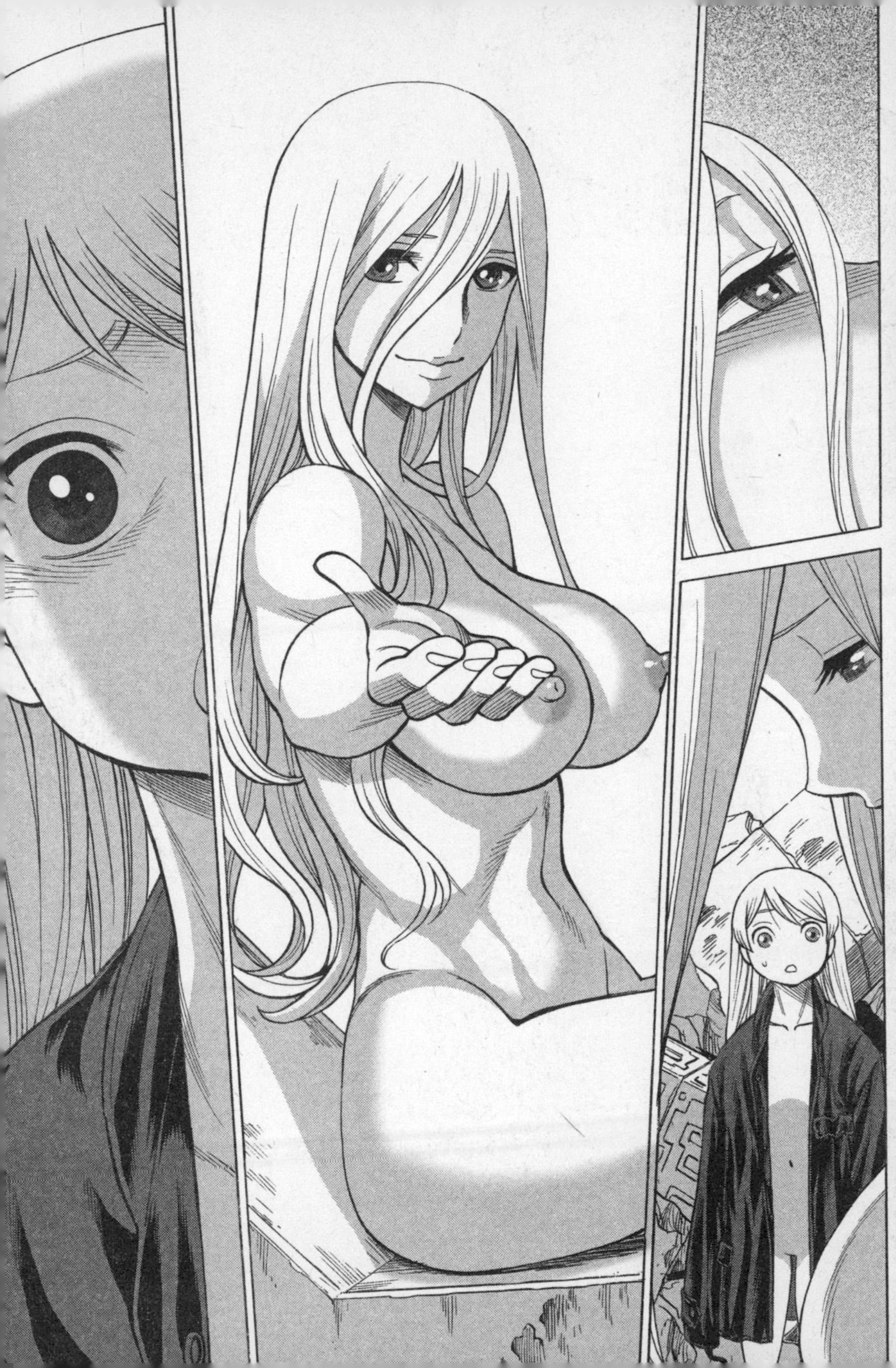

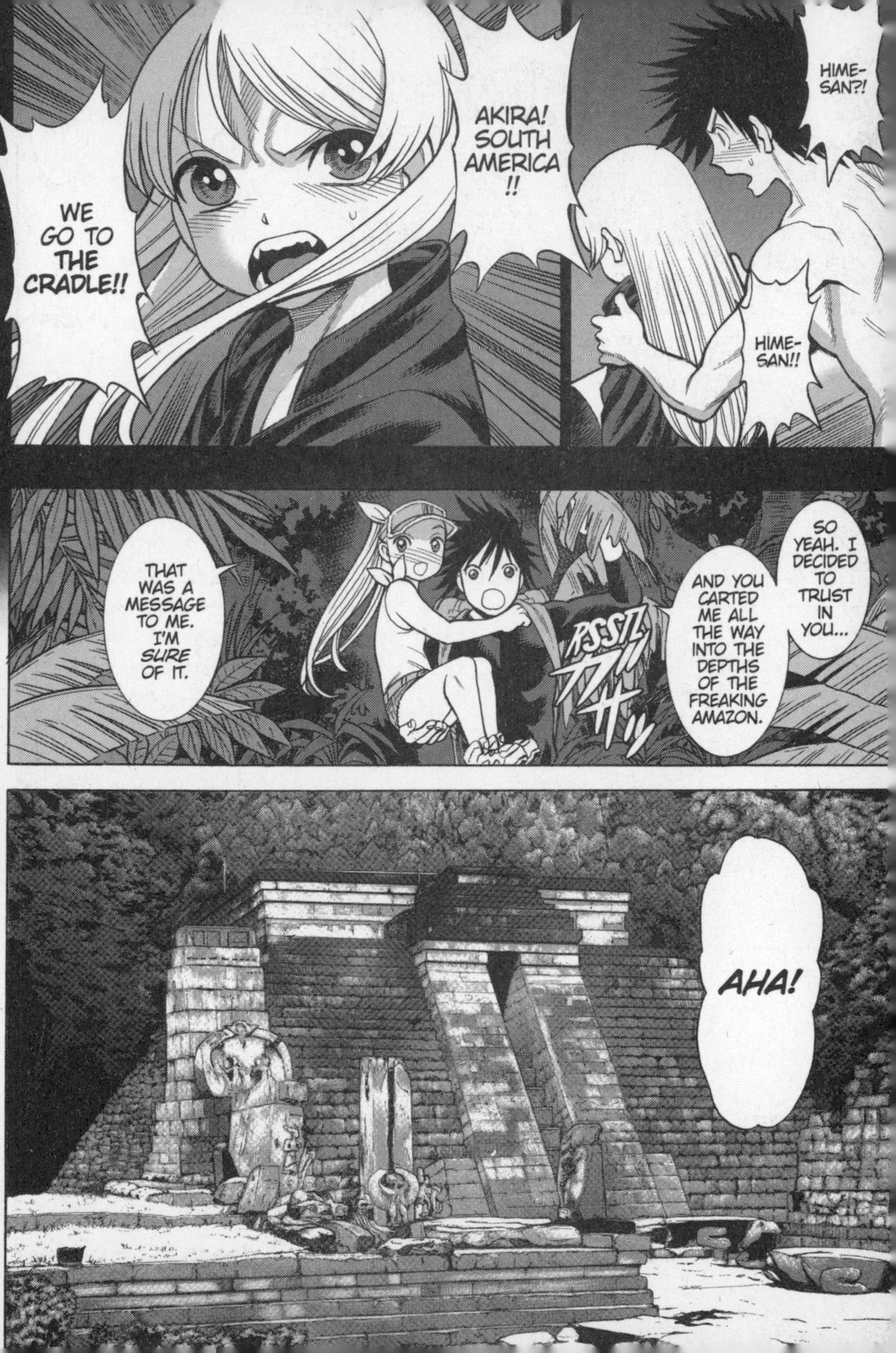
HIME-SAN?!
HIME-SAN!!
AKIRA! SOUTH AMERICA !!
WE GO TO THE CRADLE!!
SO YEAH. I DECIDED TO TRUST IN YOU...
AND YOU CARTED ME ALL THE WAY INTO THE DEPTHS OF THE FREAKING AMAZON.
RSSTL
THAT WAS A MESSAGE TO ME. I'M *SURE* OF IT.
AHA!

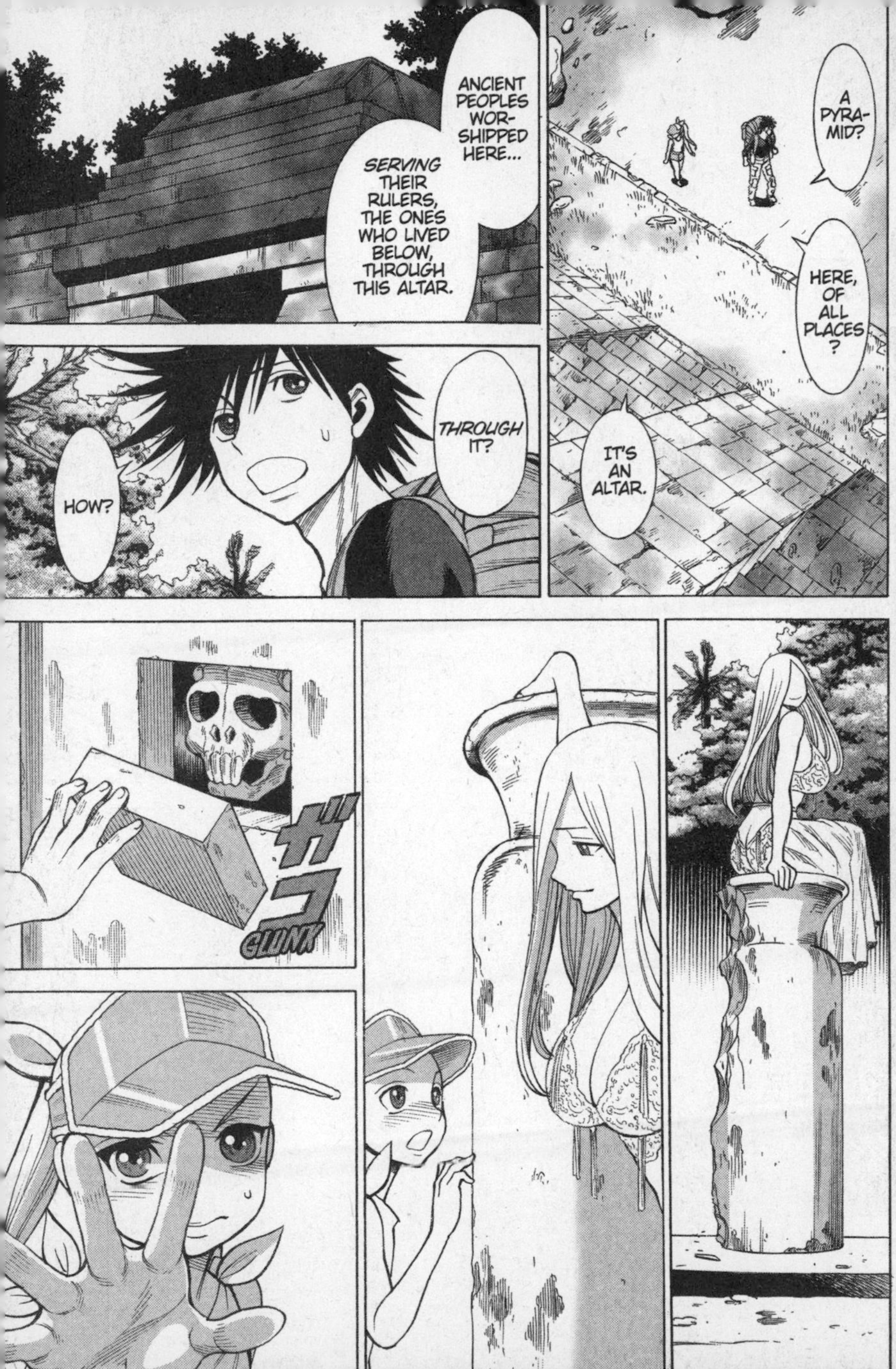
A PYRA-MID?
HERE, OF ALL PLACES?
IT'S AN ALTAR.
ANCIENT PEOPLES WOR-SHIPPED HERE...
SERVING THEIR RULERS, THE ONES WHO LIVED BELOW, THROUGH THIS ALTAR.
THROUGH IT?
HOW?
GLUNK

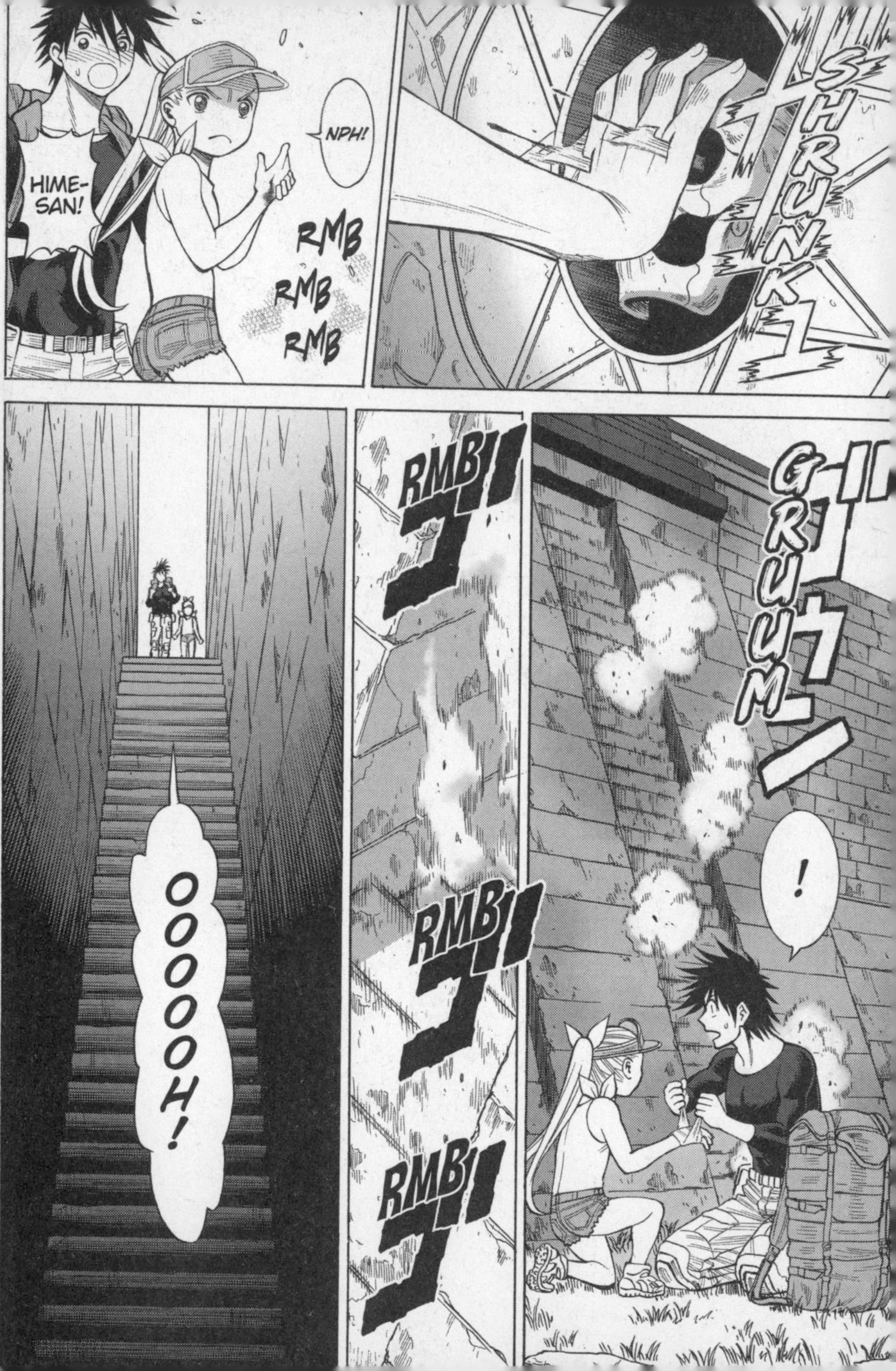
SHRUNK
NPH!
HIME-SAN!
RMB
RMB
RMB
GRUUM
!
RMB
RMB
RMB
OOOOOOH!

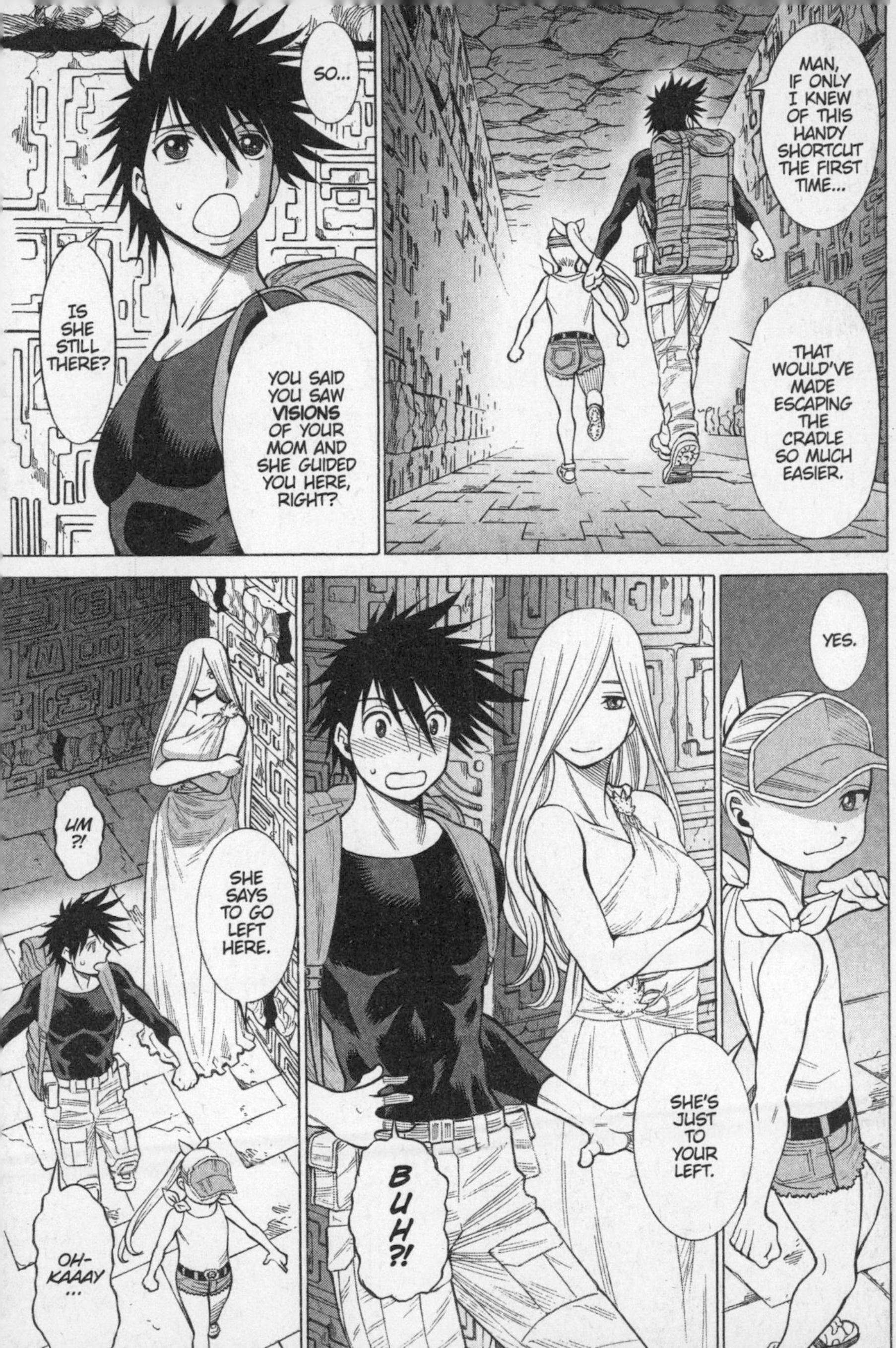

MAN, IF ONLY I KNEW OF THIS HANDY SHORTCUT THE FIRST TIME...
THAT WOULD'VE MADE ESCAPING THE CRADLE SO MUCH EASIER.
SO...
YOU SAID YOU SAW VISIONS OF YOUR MOM AND SHE GUIDED YOU HERE, RIGHT?
IS SHE STILL THERE?
YES.
SHE'S JUST TO YOUR LEFT.
BUH?!
SHE SAYS TO GO LEFT HERE.
UM?!
OH-KAAAY...

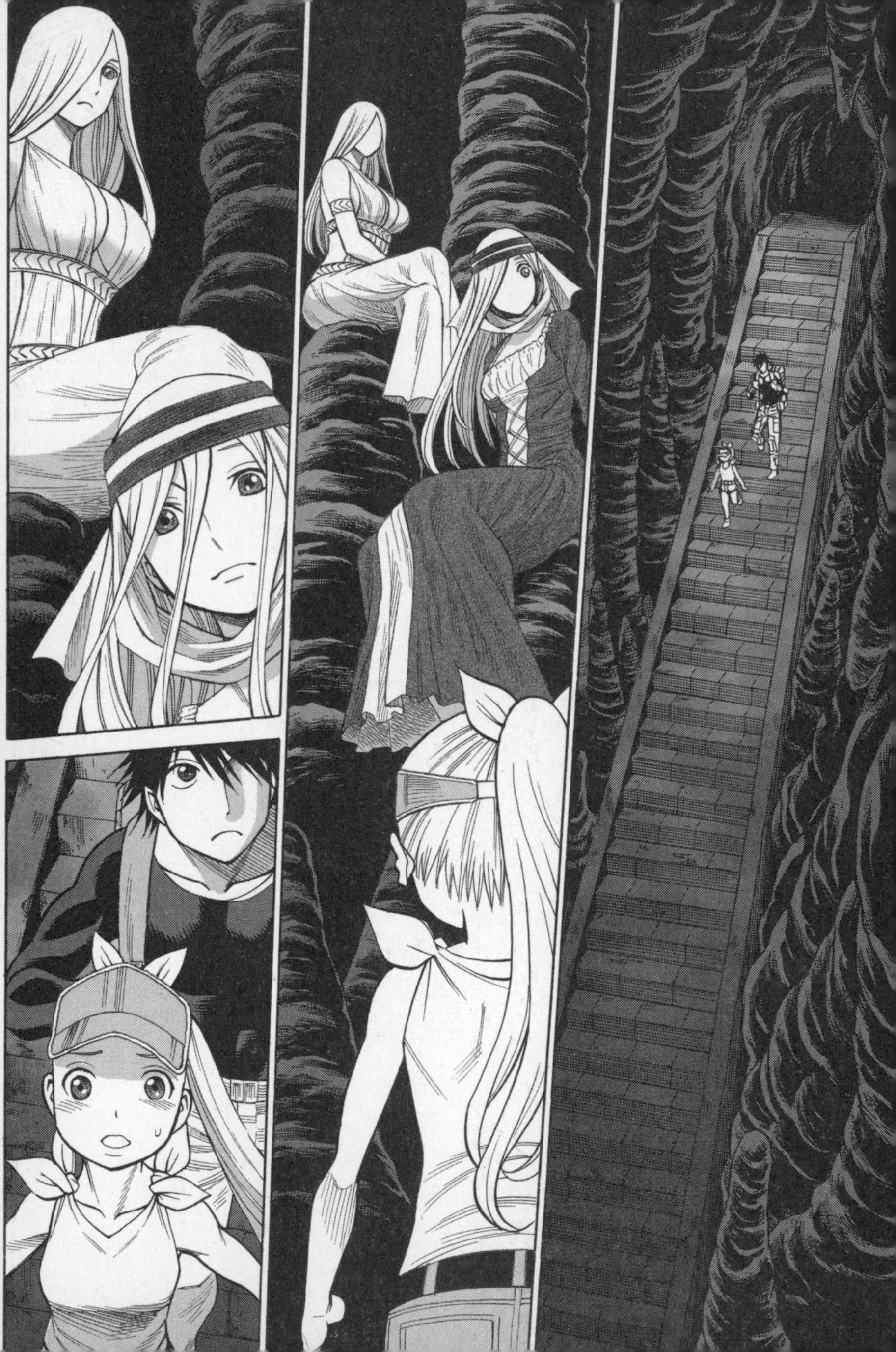

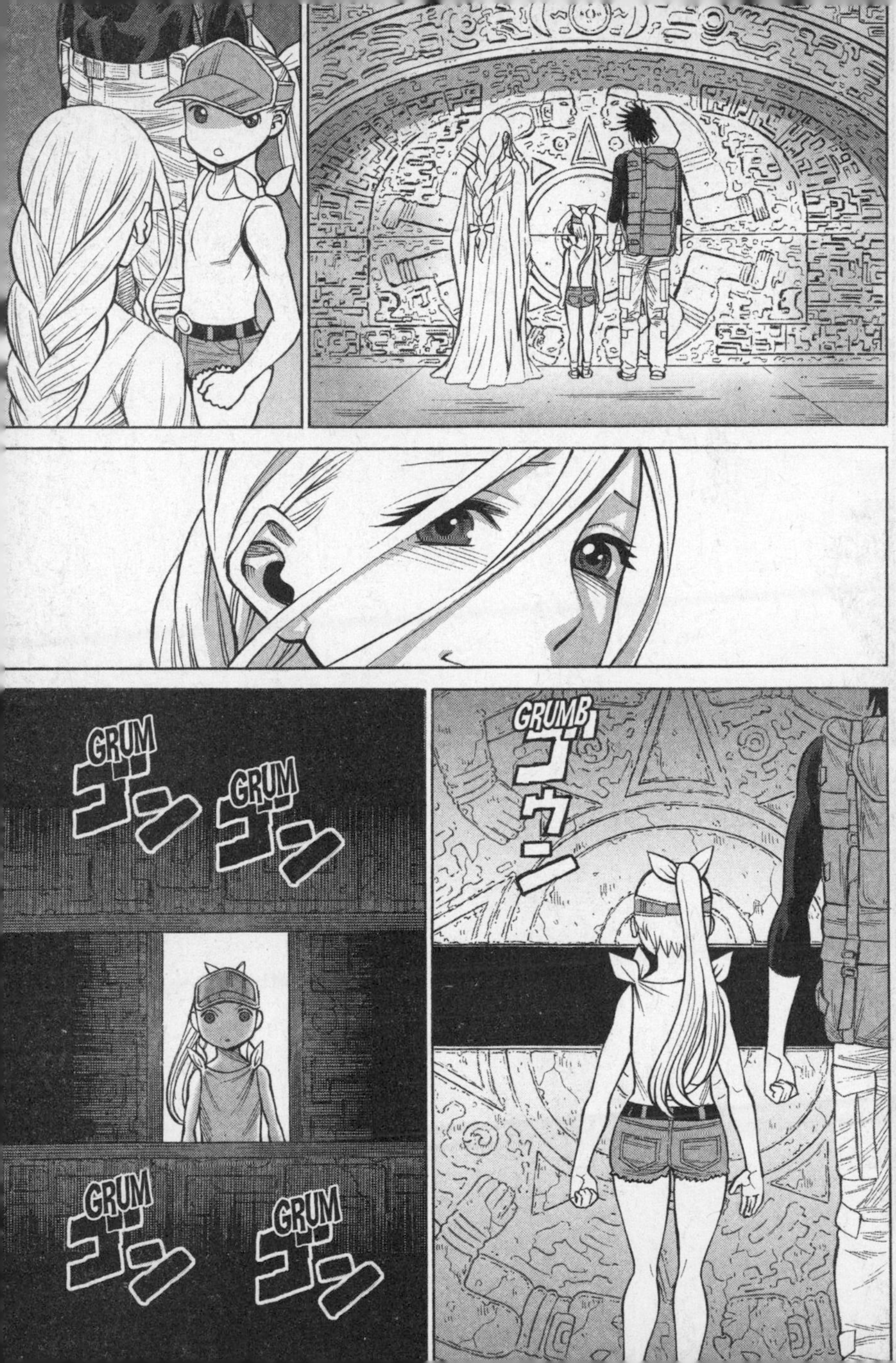
GRUMB
ゴウー
GRUM
ゴン
GRUM
ゴン
GRUM
ゴン
GRUM
ゴン

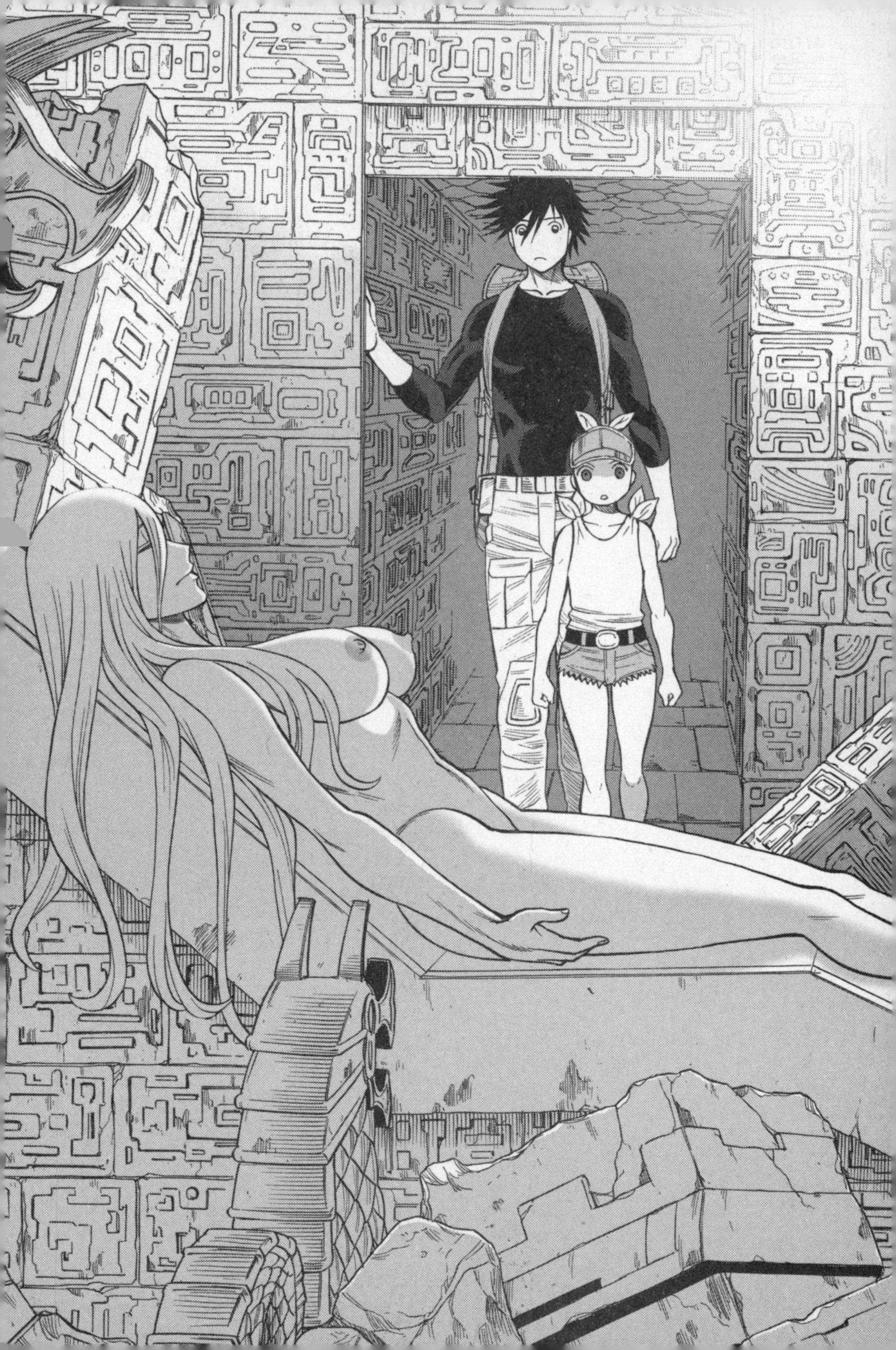

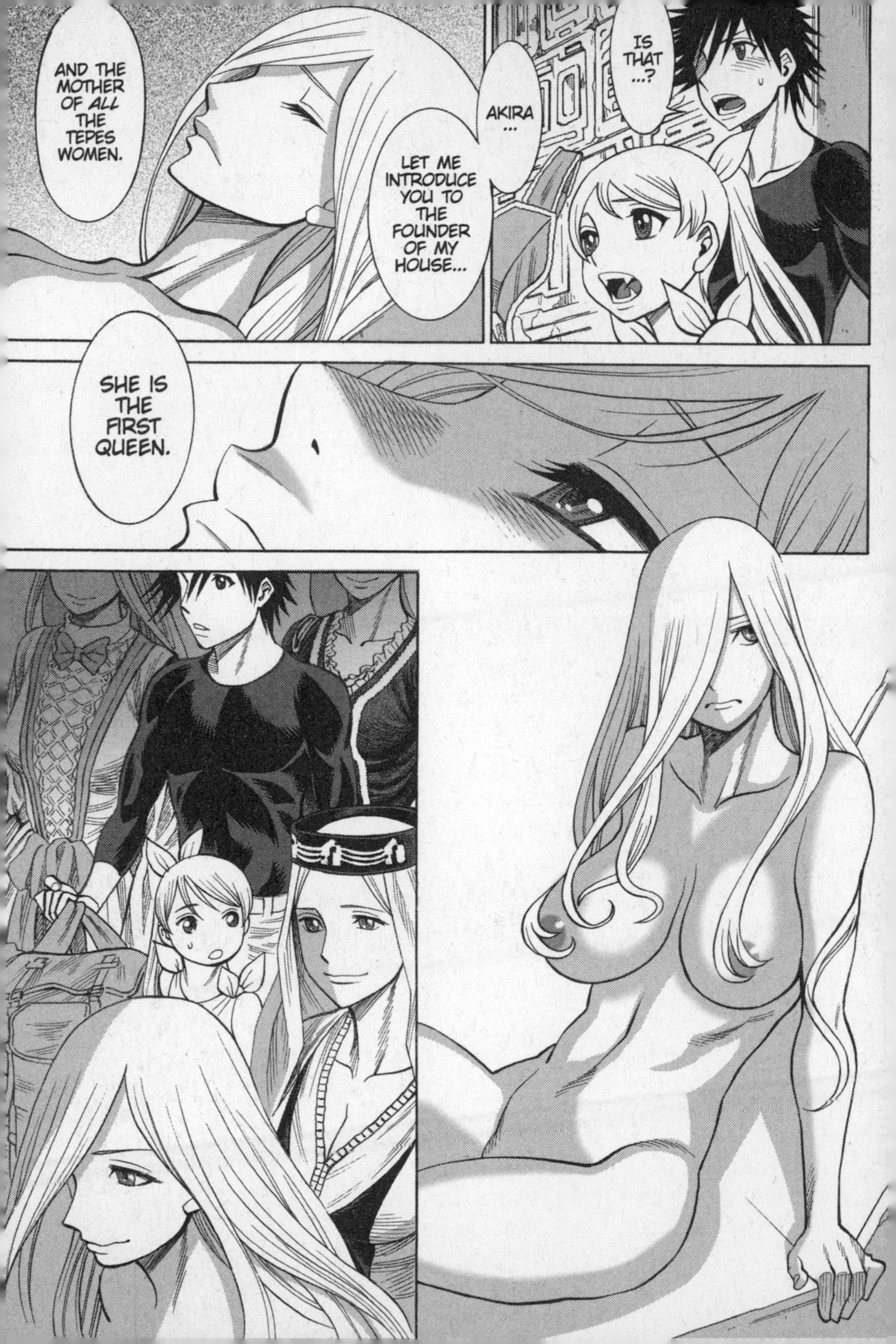
IS THAT ...?
AKIRA ...
LET ME INTRODUCE YOU TO THE FOUNDER OF MY HOUSE...
AND THE MOTHER OF *ALL* THE TEPES WOMEN.
SHE IS THE FIRST QUEEN.

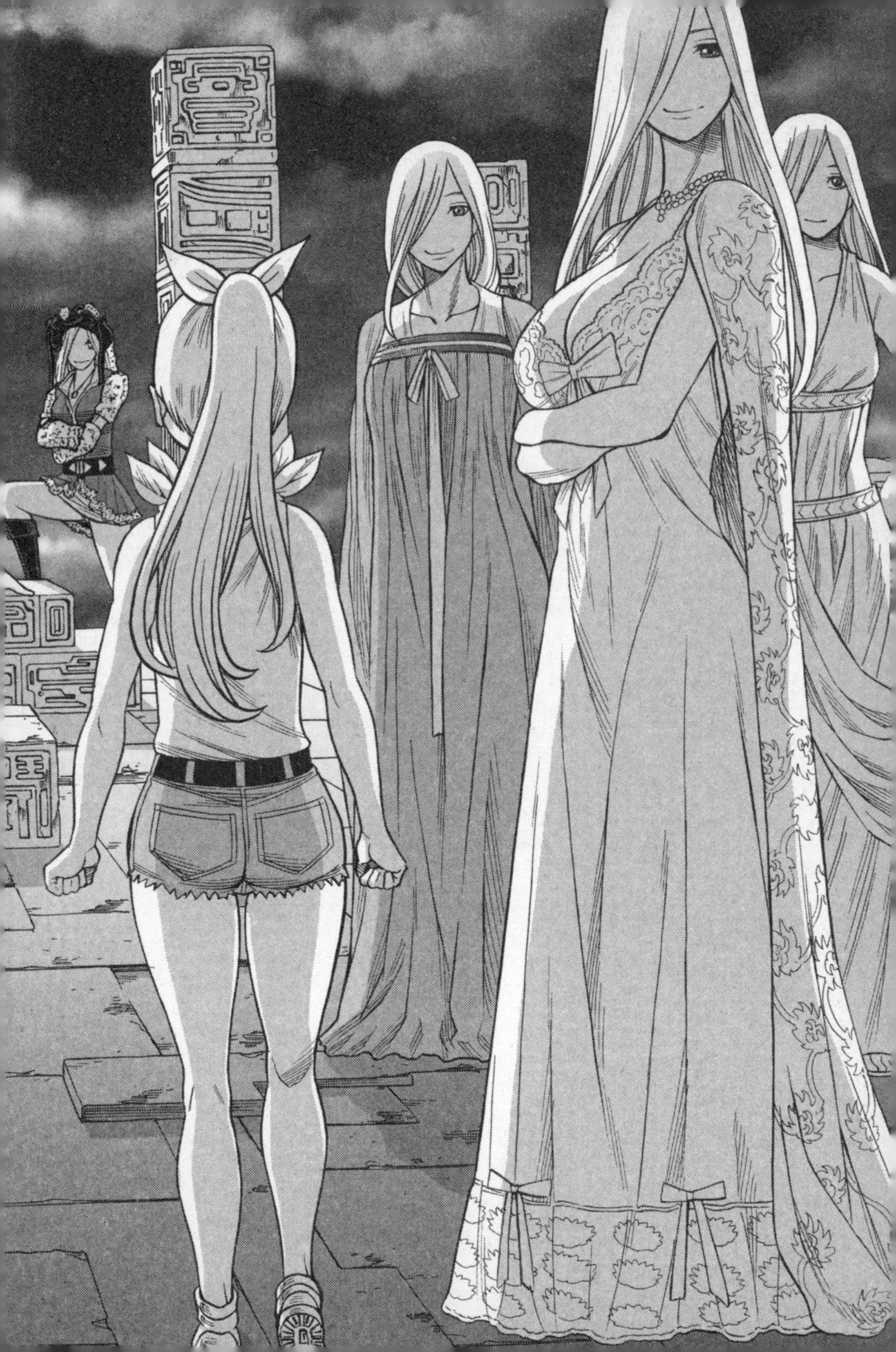

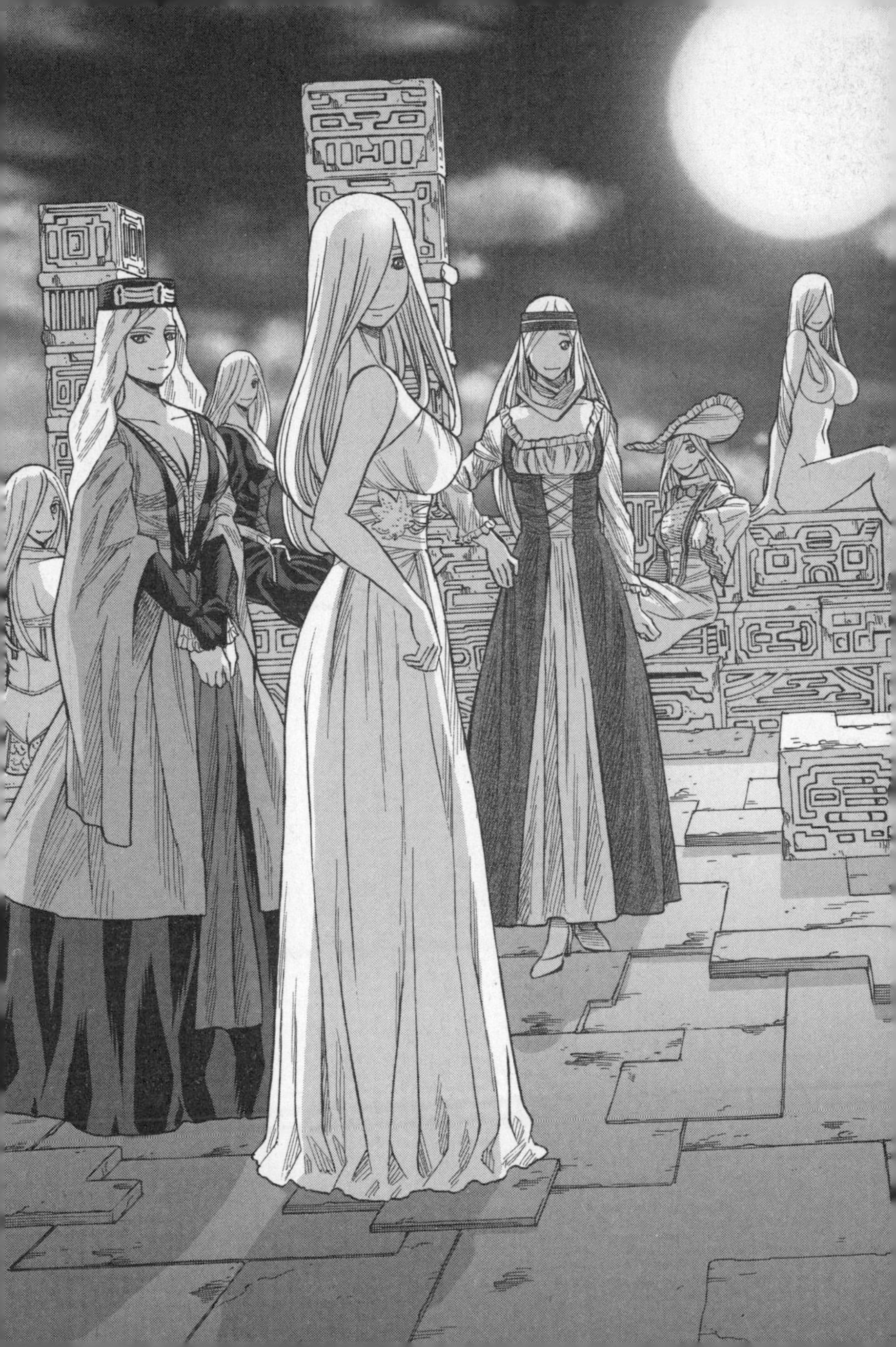

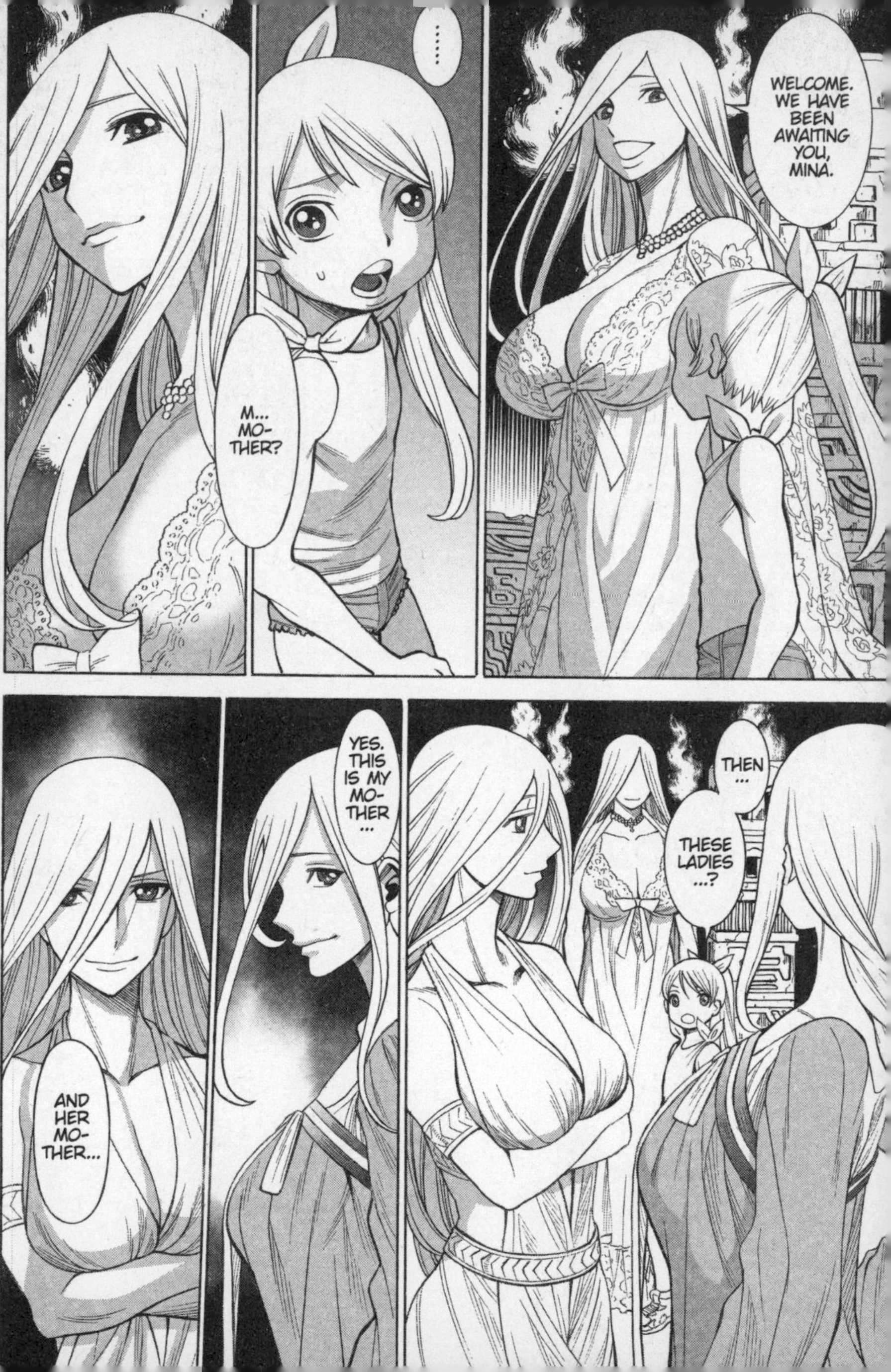
WELCOME. WE HAVE BEEN AWAITING YOU, MINA.
......
M... MO-THER?
THEN...
THESE LADIES...?
YES. THIS IS MY MO-THER...
AND HER MO-THER...

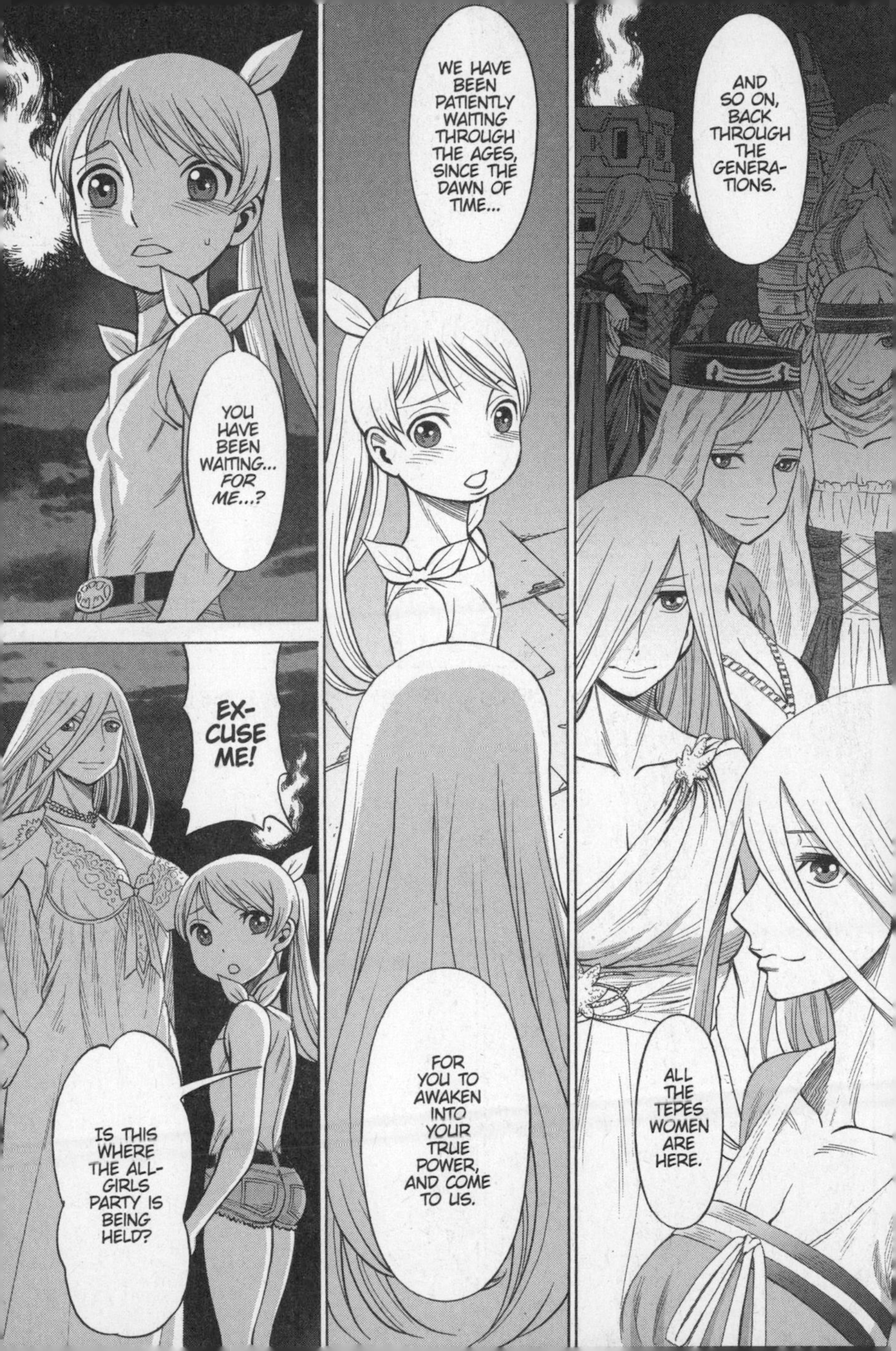
AND SO ON, BACK THROUGH THE GENERA-TIONS.
ALL THE TEPES WOMEN ARE HERE.
WE HAVE BEEN PATIENTLY WAITING THROUGH THE AGES, SINCE THE DAWN OF TIME...
FOR YOU TO AWAKEN INTO YOUR TRUE POWER, AND COME TO US.
YOU HAVE BEEN WAITING... FOR ME...?
EX-CUSE ME!
IS THIS WHERE THE ALL-GIRLS PARTY IS BEING HELD?

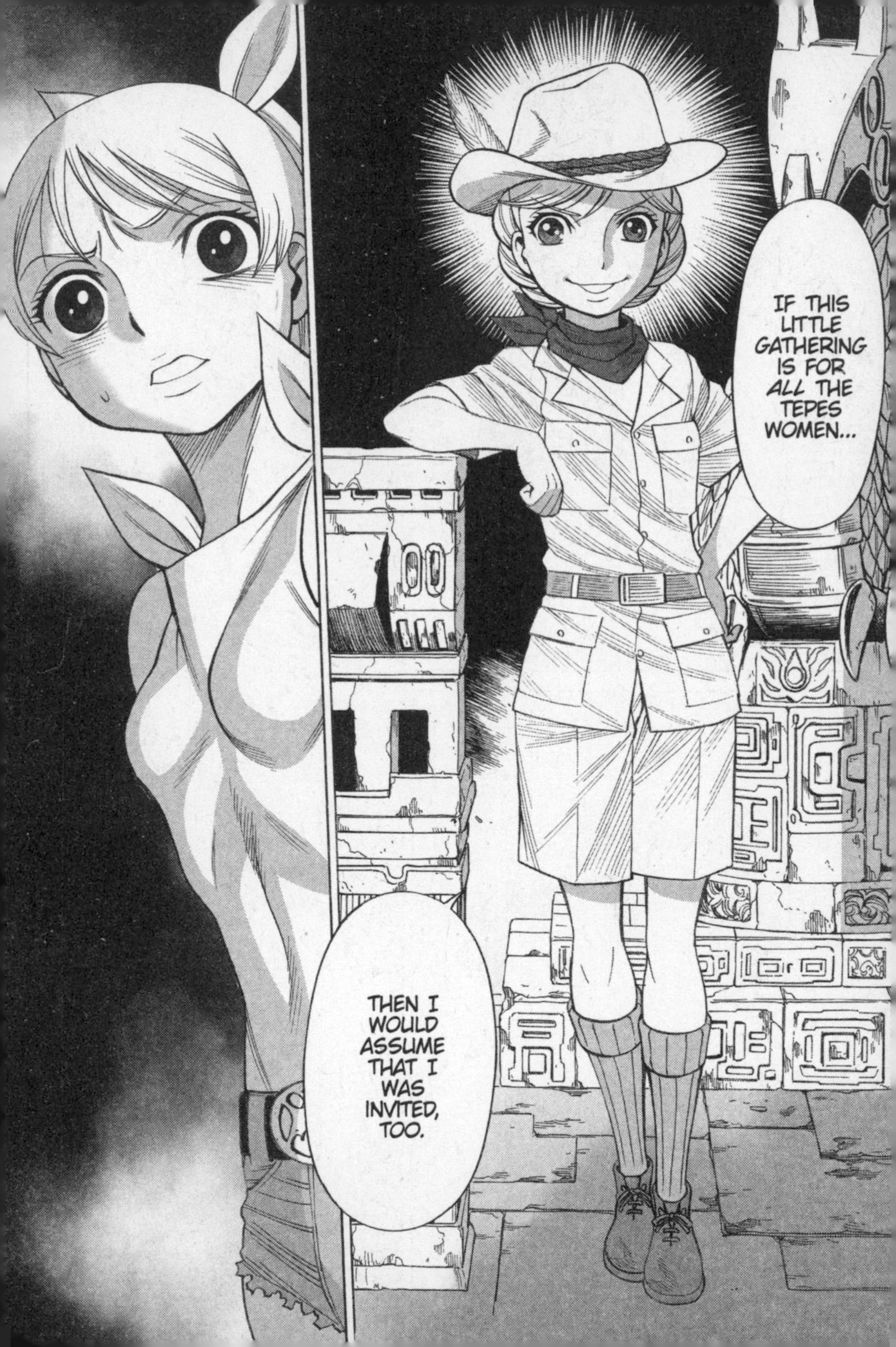
IF THIS LITTLE GATHERING IS FOR ALL THE TEPES WOMEN...
THEN I WOULD ASSUME THAT I WAS INVITED, TOO.

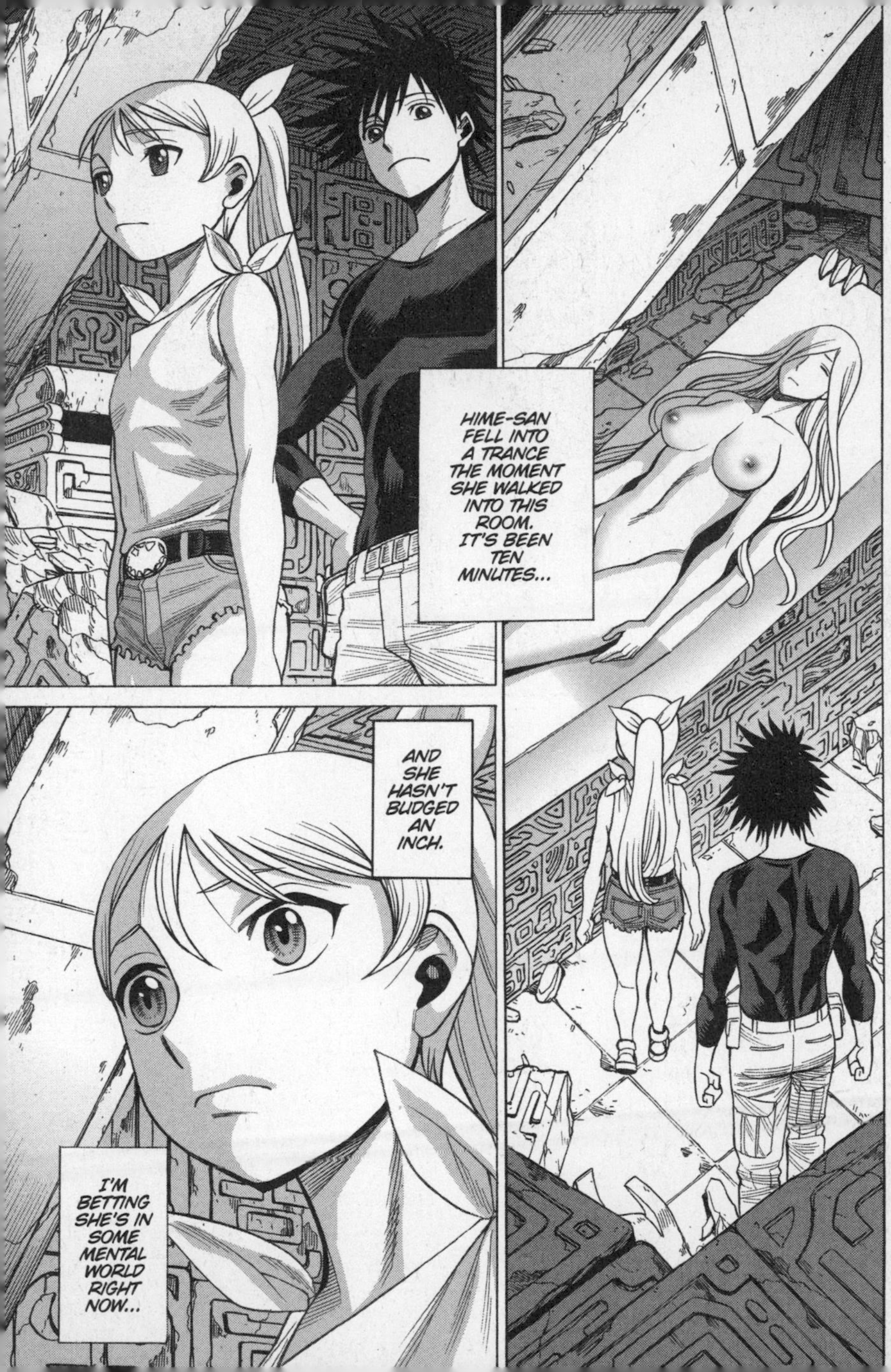
HIME-SAN FELL INTO A TRANCE THE MOMENT SHE WALKED INTO THIS ROOM. IT'S BEEN TEN MINUTES...
AND SHE HASN'T BUDGED AN INCH.
I'M BETTING SHE'S IN SOME MENTAL WORLD RIGHT NOW...

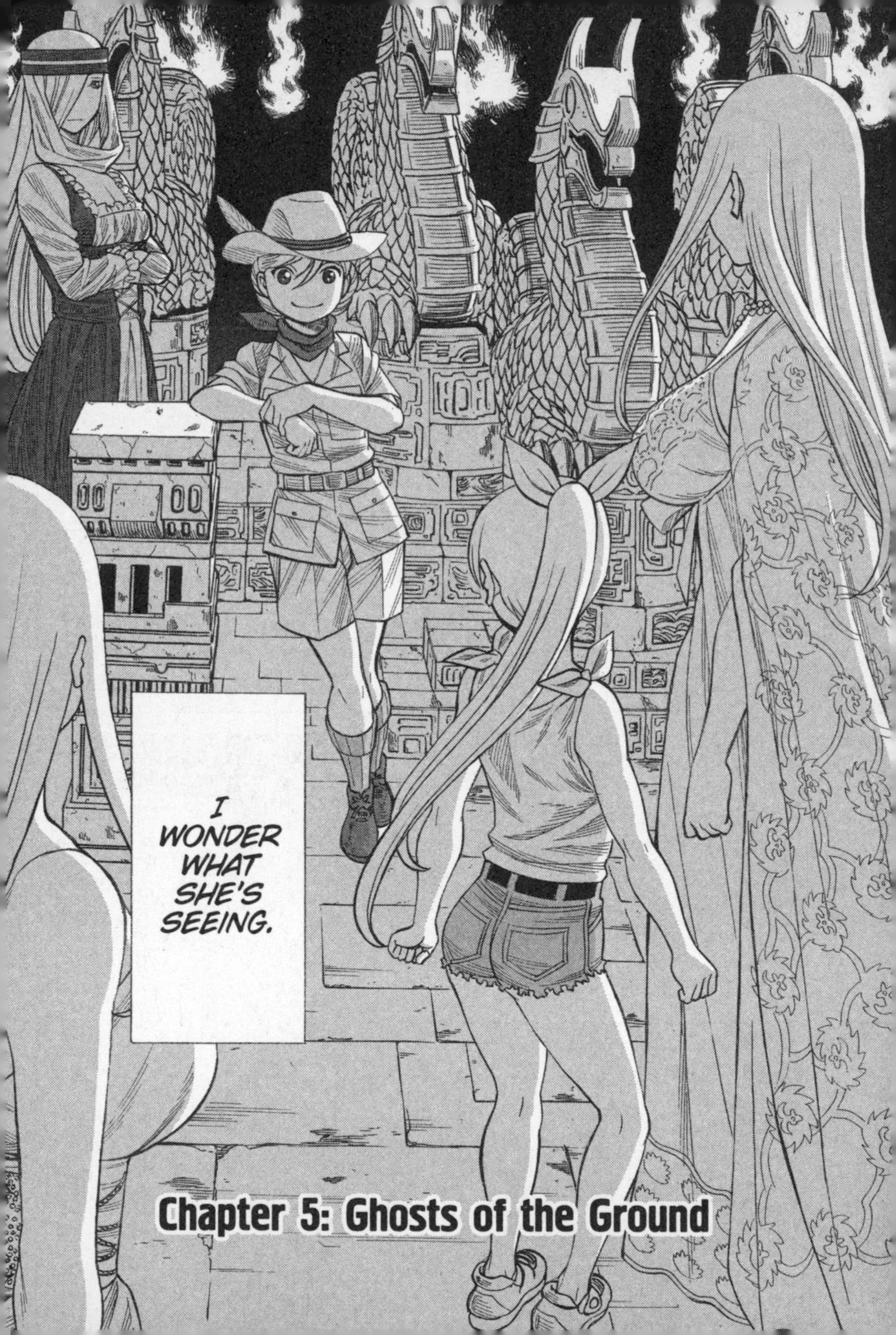
I WONDER WHAT SHE'S SEEING.
Chapter 5: Ghosts of the Ground

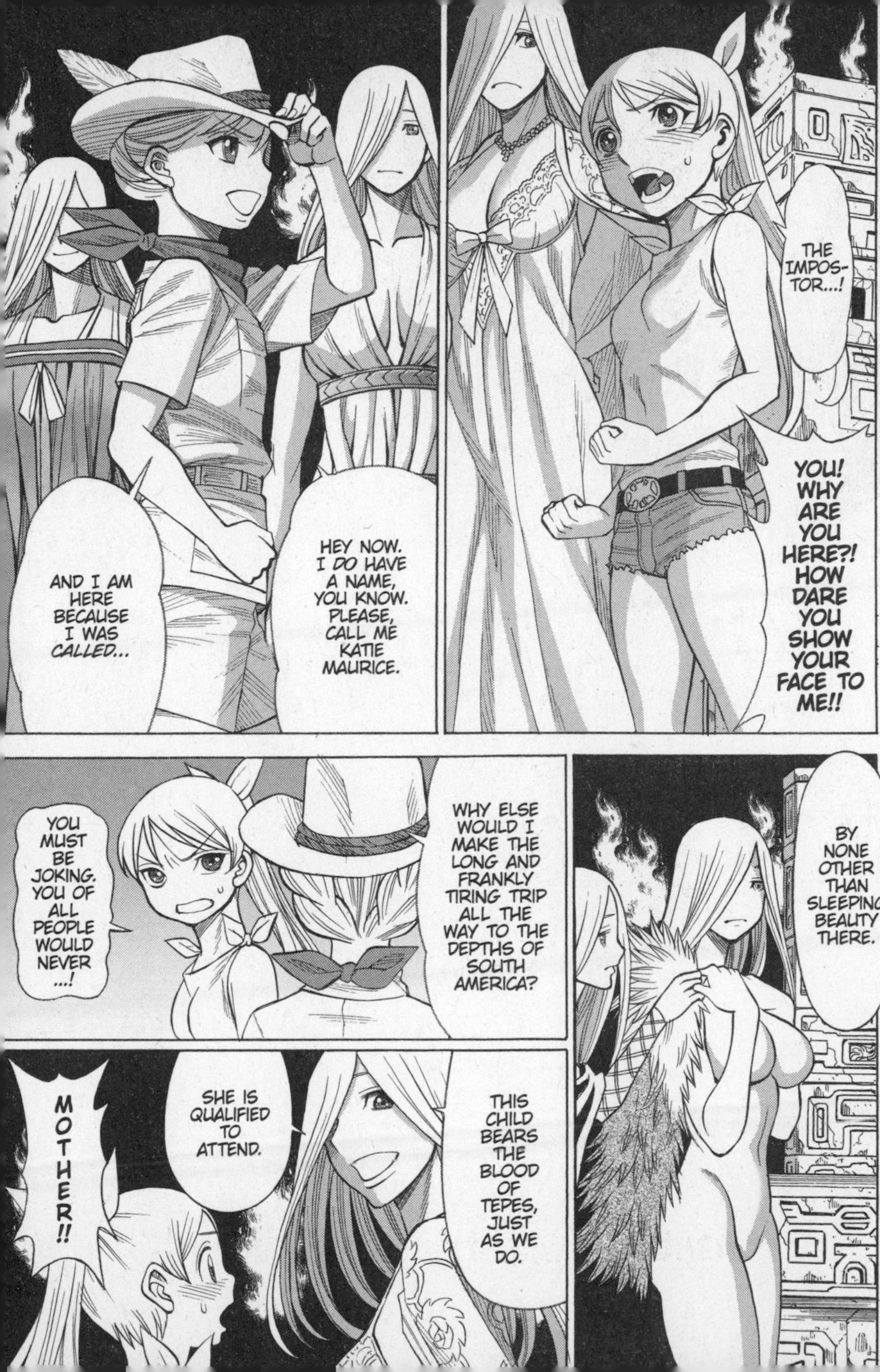
THE IMPOSTOR...!
YOU! WHY ARE YOU HERE?! HOW DARE YOU SHOW YOUR FACE TO ME!!
HEY NOW. I *DO* HAVE A NAME, YOU KNOW. PLEASE, CALL ME KATIE MAURICE.
AND I AM HERE BECAUSE I WAS *CALLED*...
BY NONE OTHER THAN SLEEPING BEAUTY THERE.
WHY ELSE WOULD I MAKE THE LONG AND FRANKLY TIRING TRIP ALL THE WAY TO THE DEPTHS OF SOUTH AMERICA?
YOU MUST BE JOKING. YOU OF ALL PEOPLE WOULD NEVER ...!
THIS CHILD BEARS THE BLOOD OF TEPES, JUST AS WE DO.
SHE IS QUALIFIED TO ATTEND.
MOTHER!!

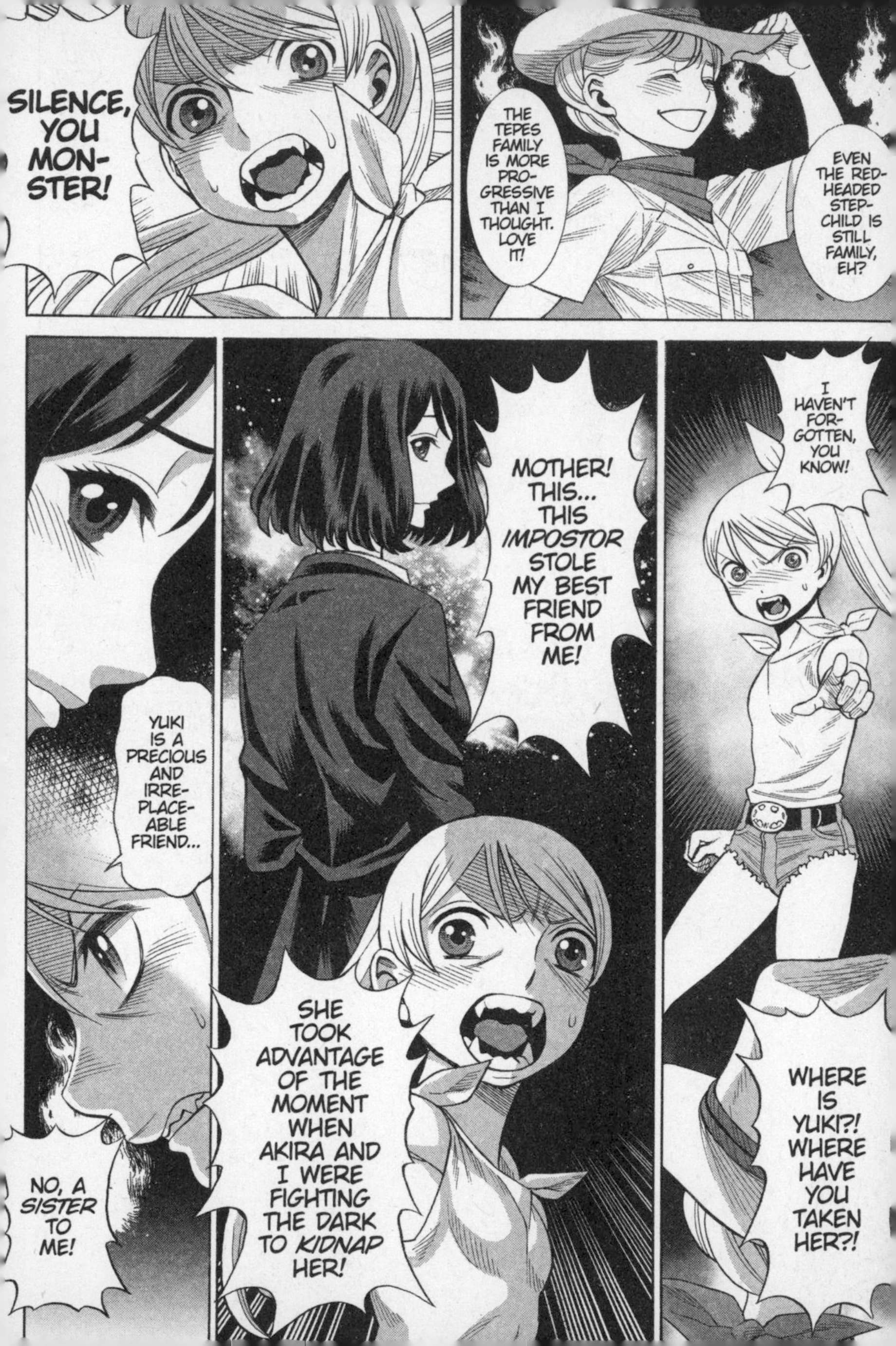
EVEN THE RED-HEADED STEP-CHILD IS STILL FAMILY, EH?
THE TEPES FAMILY IS MORE PROGRESSIVE THAN I THOUGHT. LOVE IT!
SILENCE, YOU MONSTER!
I HAVEN'T FORGOTTEN, YOU KNOW!
WHERE IS YUKI?! WHERE HAVE YOU TAKEN HER?!
MOTHER! THIS... THIS *IMPOSTOR* STOLE MY BEST FRIEND FROM ME!
SHE TOOK ADVANTAGE OF THE MOMENT WHEN AKIRA AND I WERE FIGHTING THE DARK TO *KIDNAP* HER!
YUKI IS A PRECIOUS AND IRREPLACEABLE FRIEND...
NO, A *SISTER* TO ME!

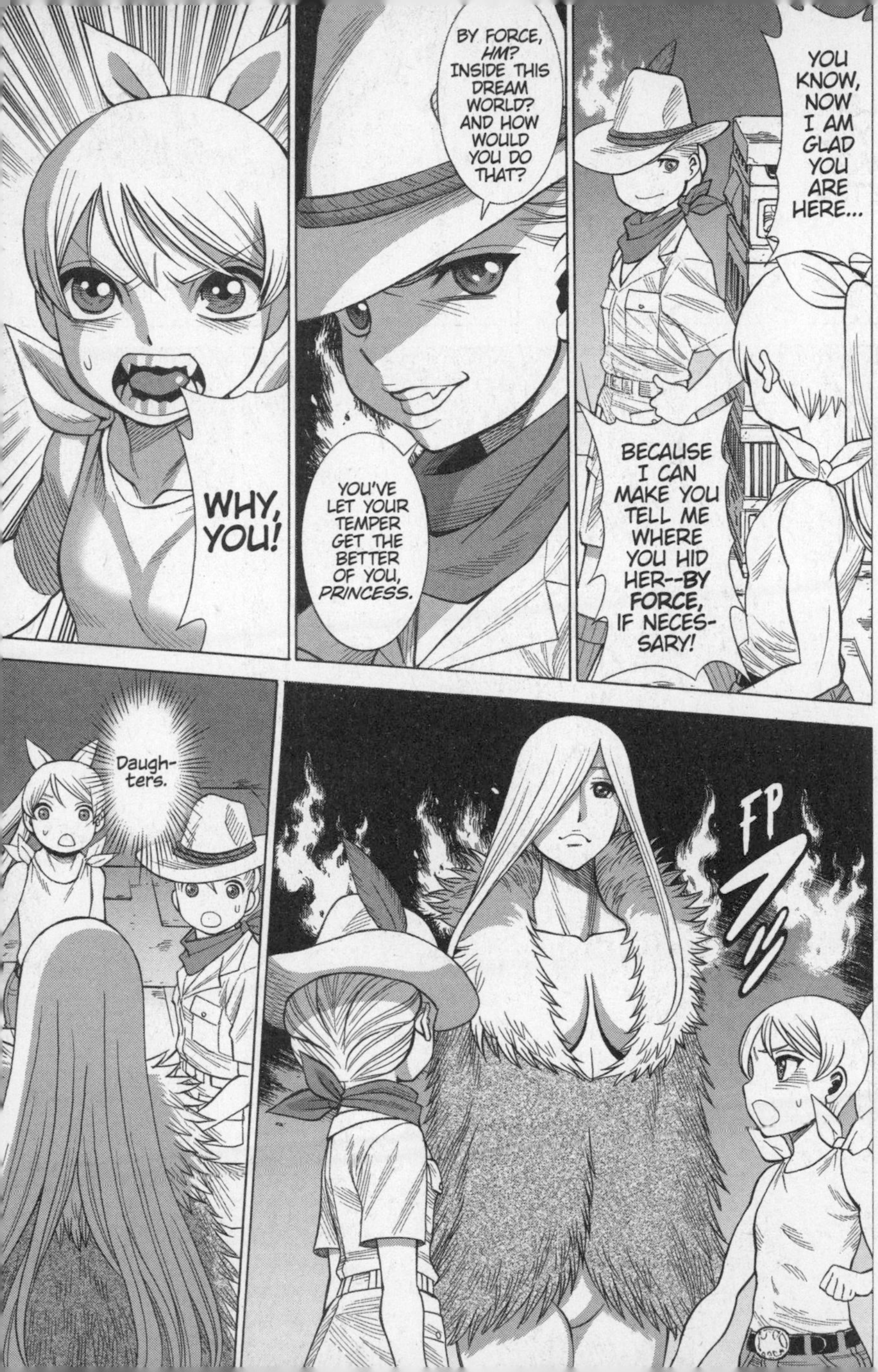
YOU KNOW, NOW I AM GLAD YOU ARE HERE...
BECAUSE I CAN MAKE YOU TELL ME WHERE YOU HID HER--BY FORCE, IF NECES-SARY!
BY FORCE, *HM?* INSIDE THIS DREAM WORLD? AND HOW WOULD YOU DO THAT?
YOU'VE LET YOUR TEMPER GET THE BETTER OF YOU, *PRINCESS.*
WHY, YOU!
FP
Daugh-ters.

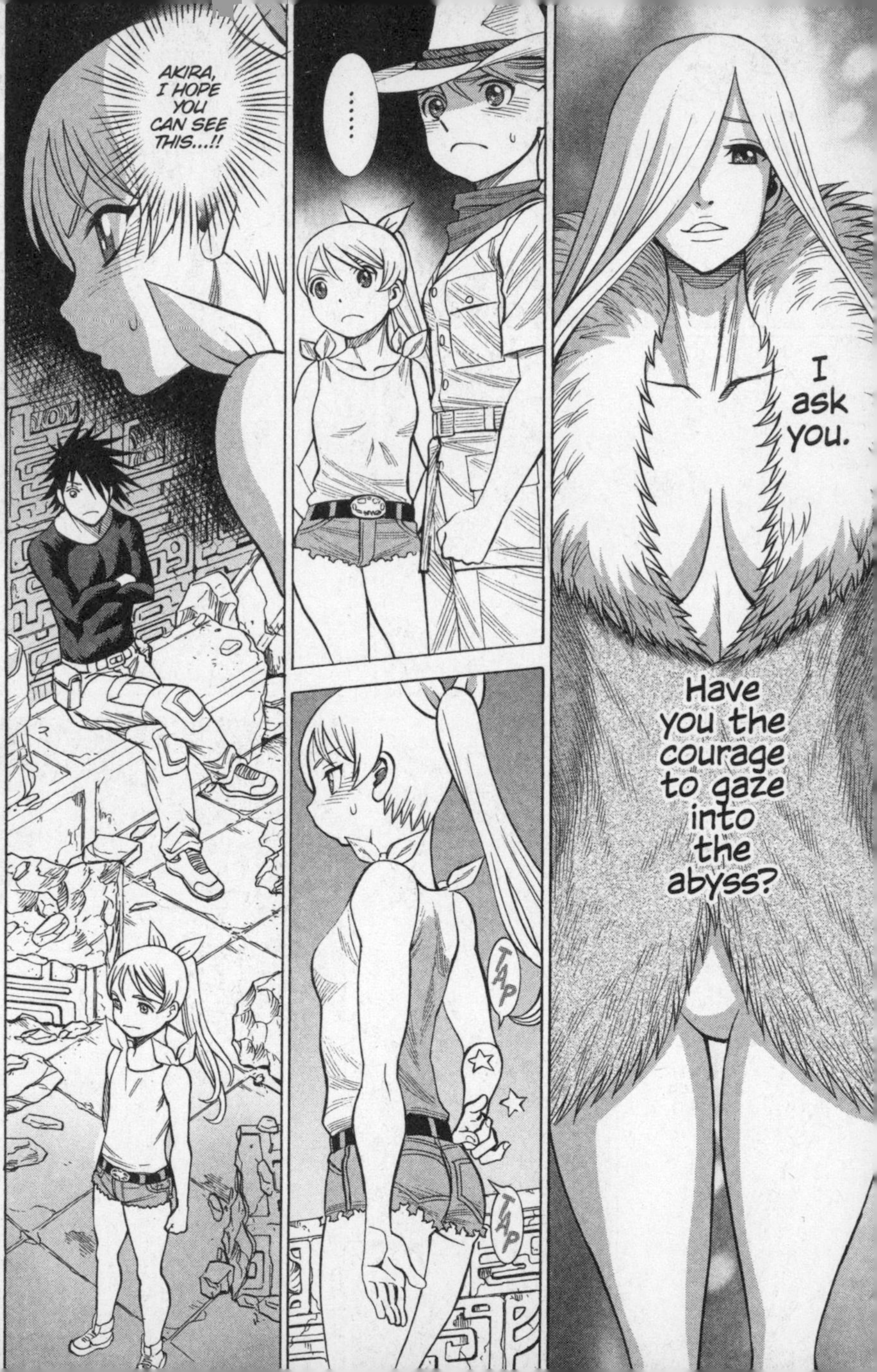
I ask you.
Have you the courage to gaze into the abyss?
......
TAP
TAP
AKIRA, I HOPE YOU CAN SEE THIS...!!

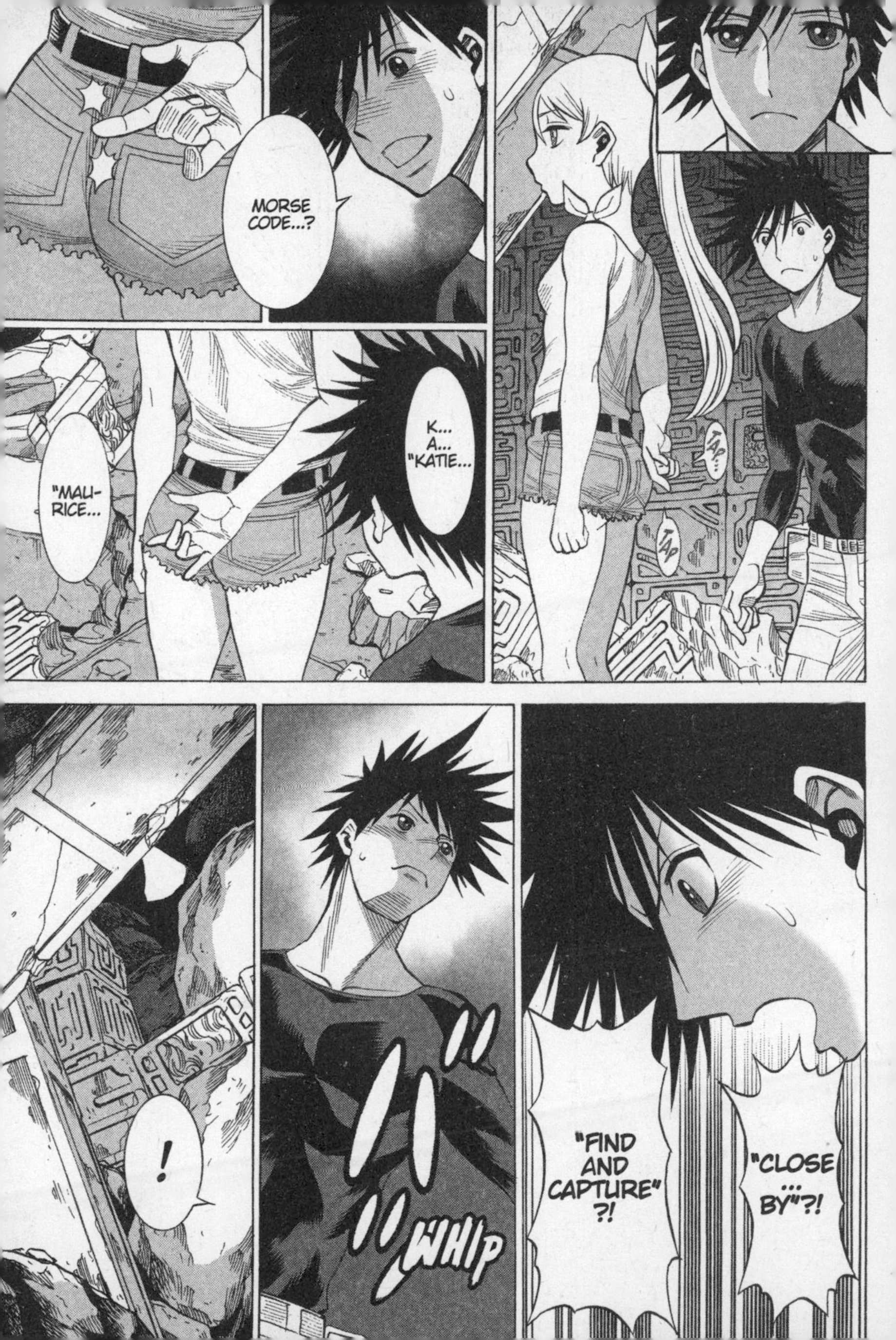
TAP
TAP
MORSE CODE...?
K... A... "KATIE...
"MAU-RICE...
"CLOSE ... BY"?!
"FIND AND CAPTURE" ?!
WHIP
!

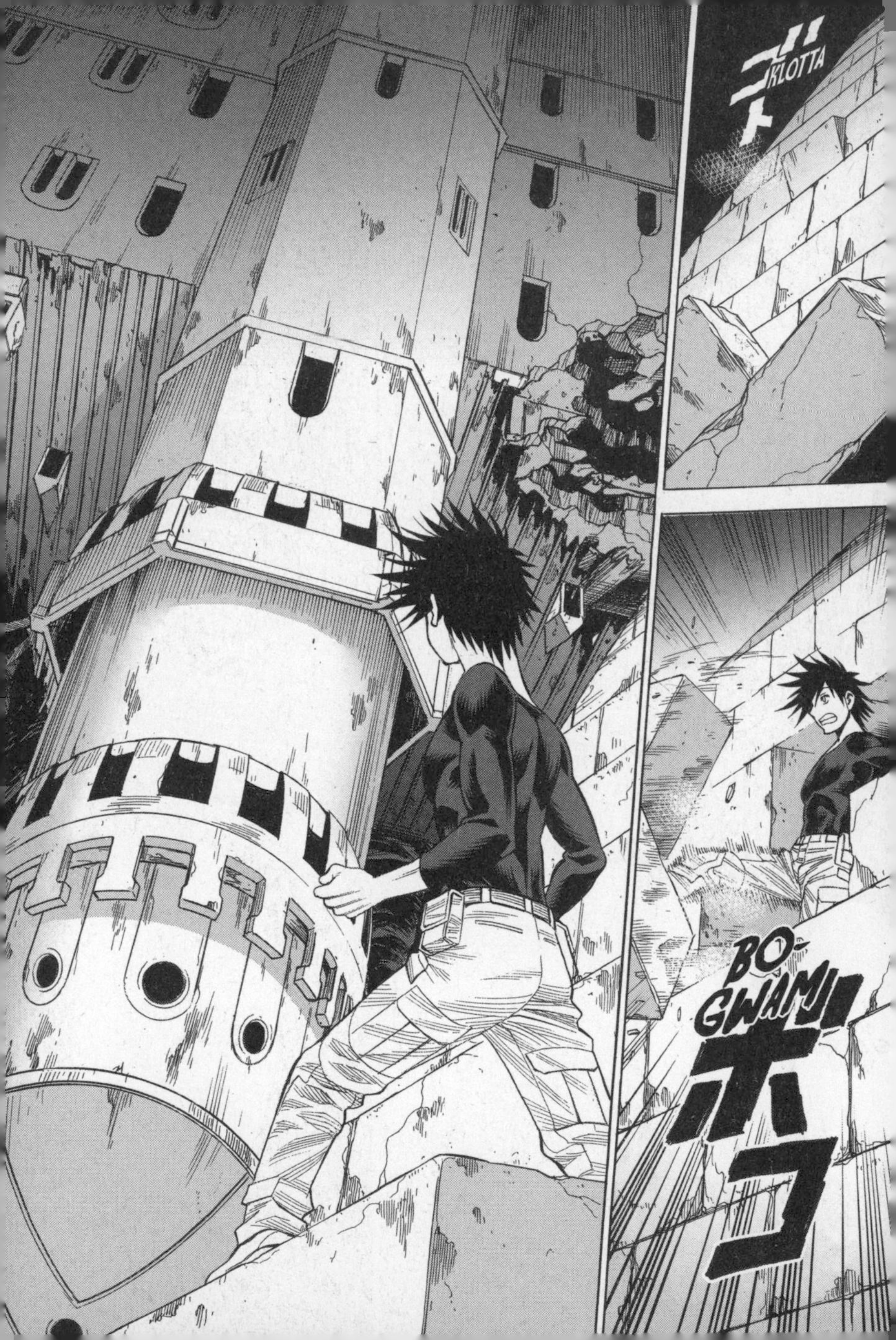
ゴゴ
KLOTTA
BO-GWAM!!
ボコ

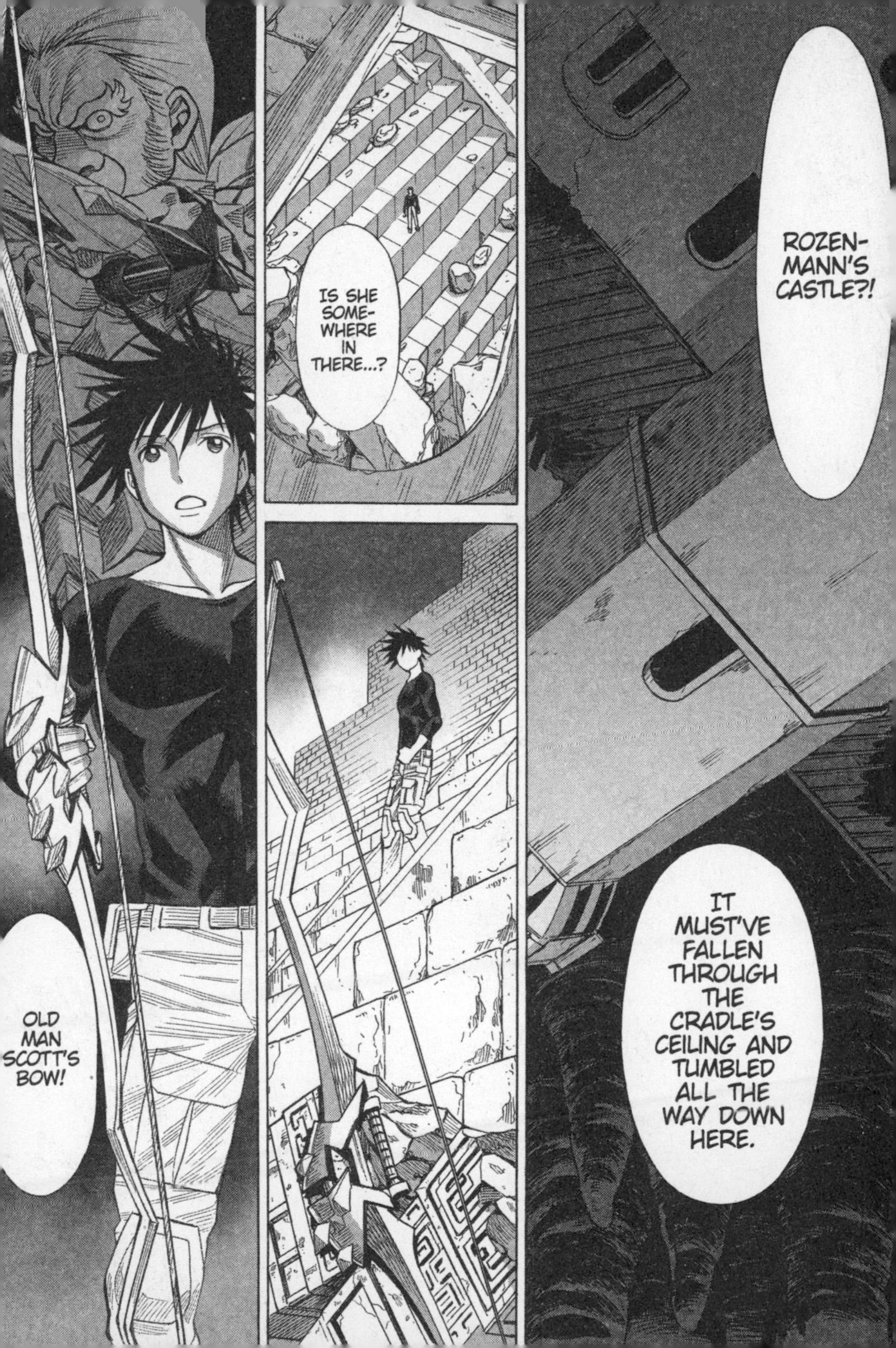
ROZEN-MANN'S CASTLE?!
IT MUST'VE FALLEN THROUGH THE CRADLE'S CEILING AND TUMBLED ALL THE WAY DOWN HERE.
IS SHE SOME-WHERE IN THERE...?
OLD MAN SCOTT'S BOW!

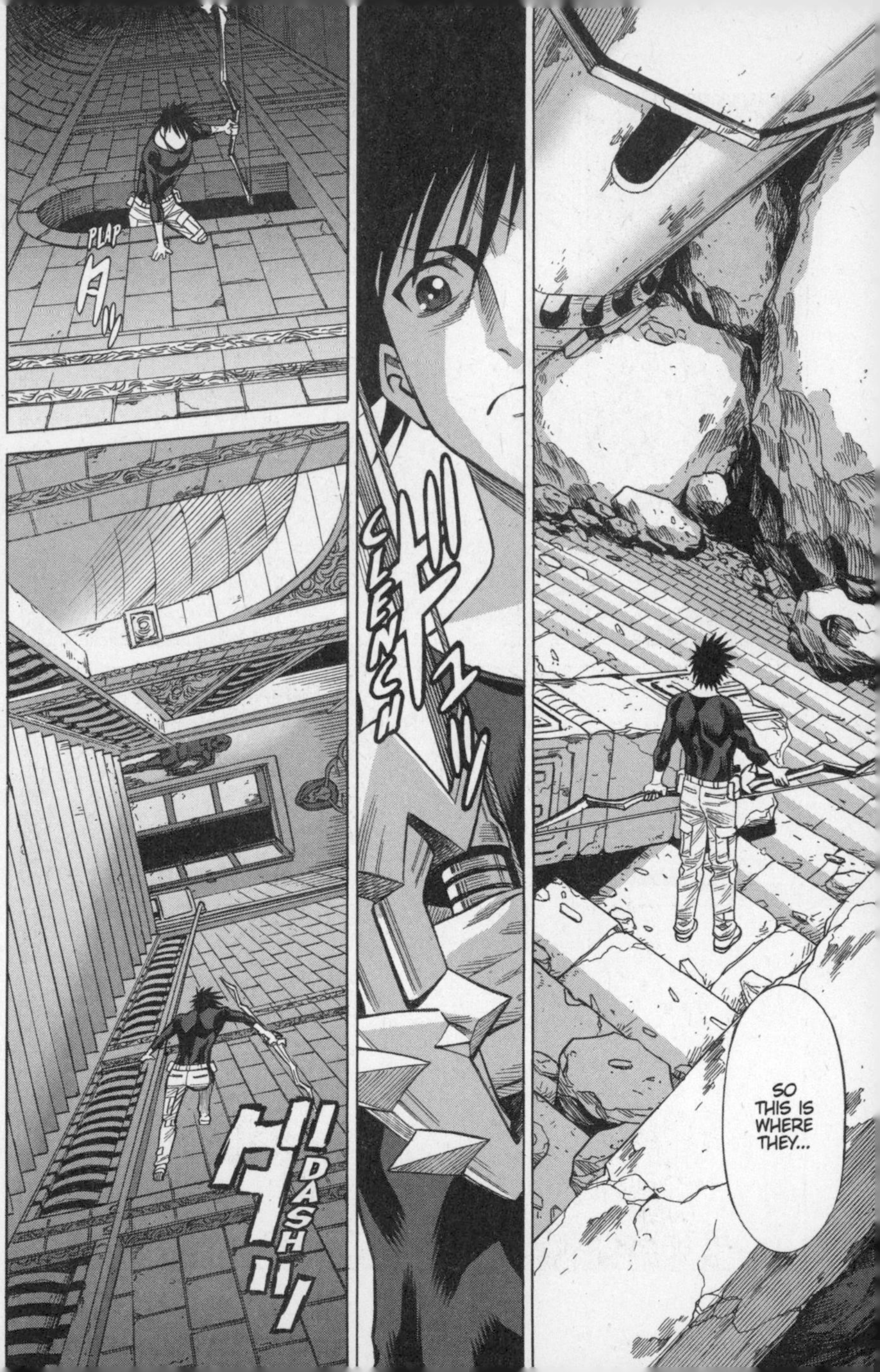
SO THIS IS WHERE THEY...
CLENCH
PLAP
DASH

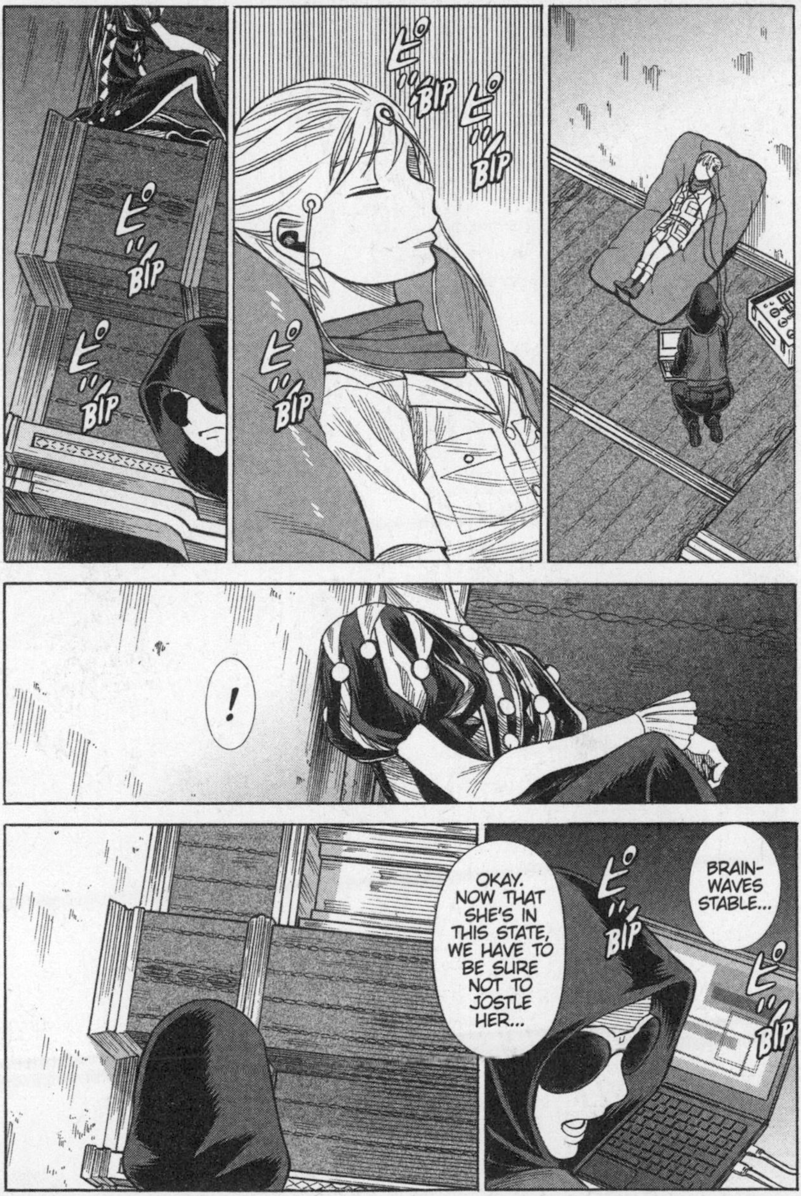
ピッ BIP
ピッ BIP
ピッ BIP
ピッ BIP
ピッ BIP
!
BRAIN-WAVES STABLE...
ピッ BIP
OKAY. NOW THAT SHE'S IN THIS STATE, WE HAVE TO BE SURE NOT TO JOSTLE HER...
ピッ BIP

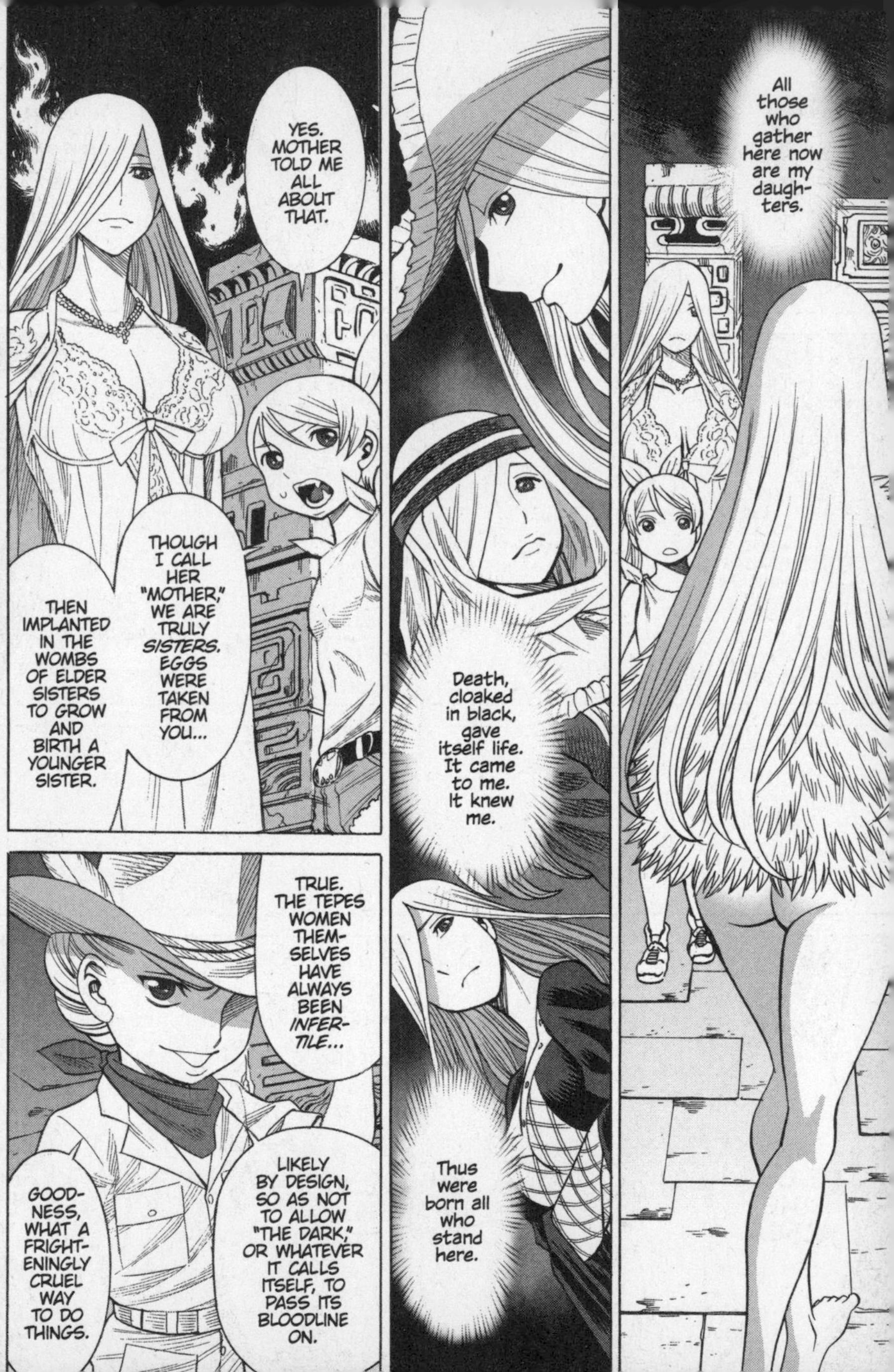

All those who gather here now are my daughters.
Death, cloaked in black, gave itself life. It came to me. It knew me.
Thus were born all who stand here.
YES. MOTHER TOLD ME ALL ABOUT THAT.
THOUGH I CALL HER "MOTHER," WE ARE TRULY *SISTERS.* EGGS WERE TAKEN FROM YOU...
THEN IMPLANTED IN THE WOMBS OF ELDER SISTERS TO GROW AND BIRTH A YOUNGER SISTER.
TRUE. THE TEPES WOMEN THEMSELVES HAVE ALWAYS BEEN *INFERTILE...*
LIKELY BY DESIGN, SO AS NOT TO ALLOW "THE DARK," OR WHATEVER IT CALLS ITSELF, TO PASS ITS BLOODLINE ON.
GOODNESS, WHAT A FRIGHTENINGLY CRUEL WAY TO DO THINGS.

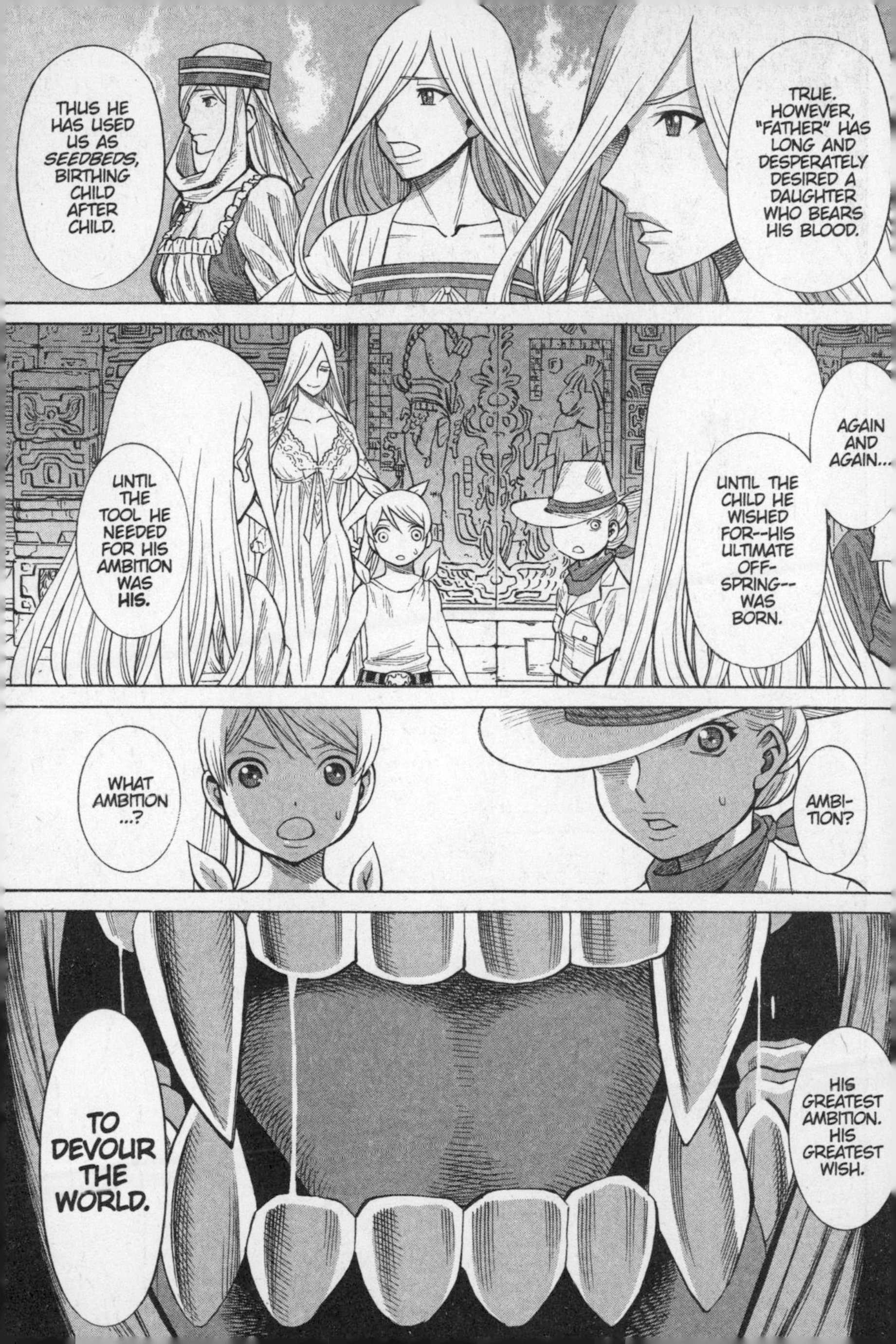
TRUE. HOWEVER, "FATHER" HAS LONG AND DESPERATELY DESIRED A DAUGHTER WHO BEARS HIS BLOOD.
THUS HE HAS USED US AS *SEEDBEDS*, BIRTHING CHILD AFTER CHILD.
AGAIN AND AGAIN...
UNTIL THE CHILD HE WISHED FOR--HIS ULTIMATE OFF-SPRING--WAS BORN.
UNTIL THE TOOL HE NEEDED FOR HIS AMBITION WAS **HIS.**
AMBI-TION?
WHAT AMBITION ...?
HIS GREATEST AMBITION. HIS GREATEST WISH.
TO DEVOUR THE WORLD.

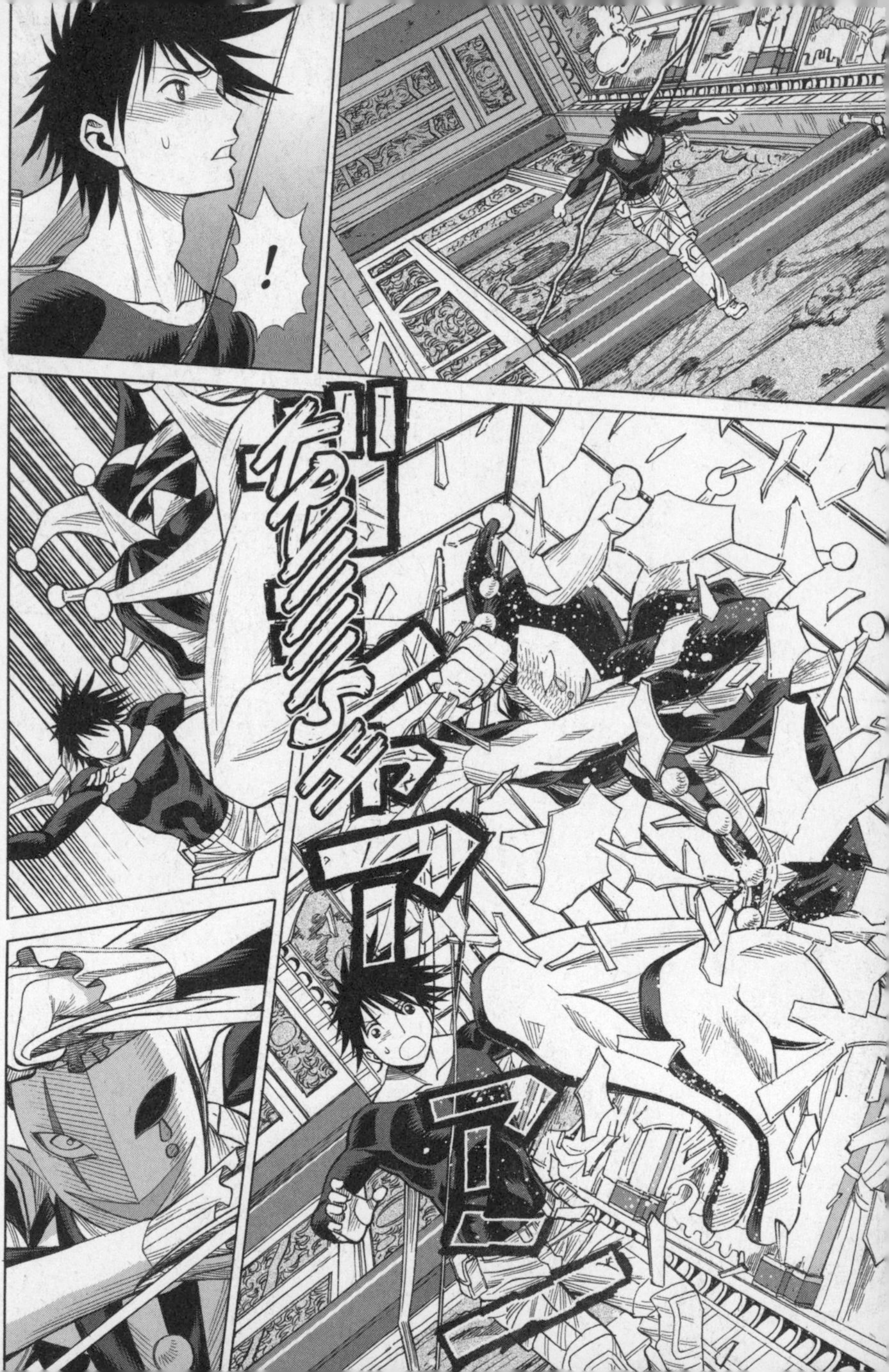
!
KRUUUSH!

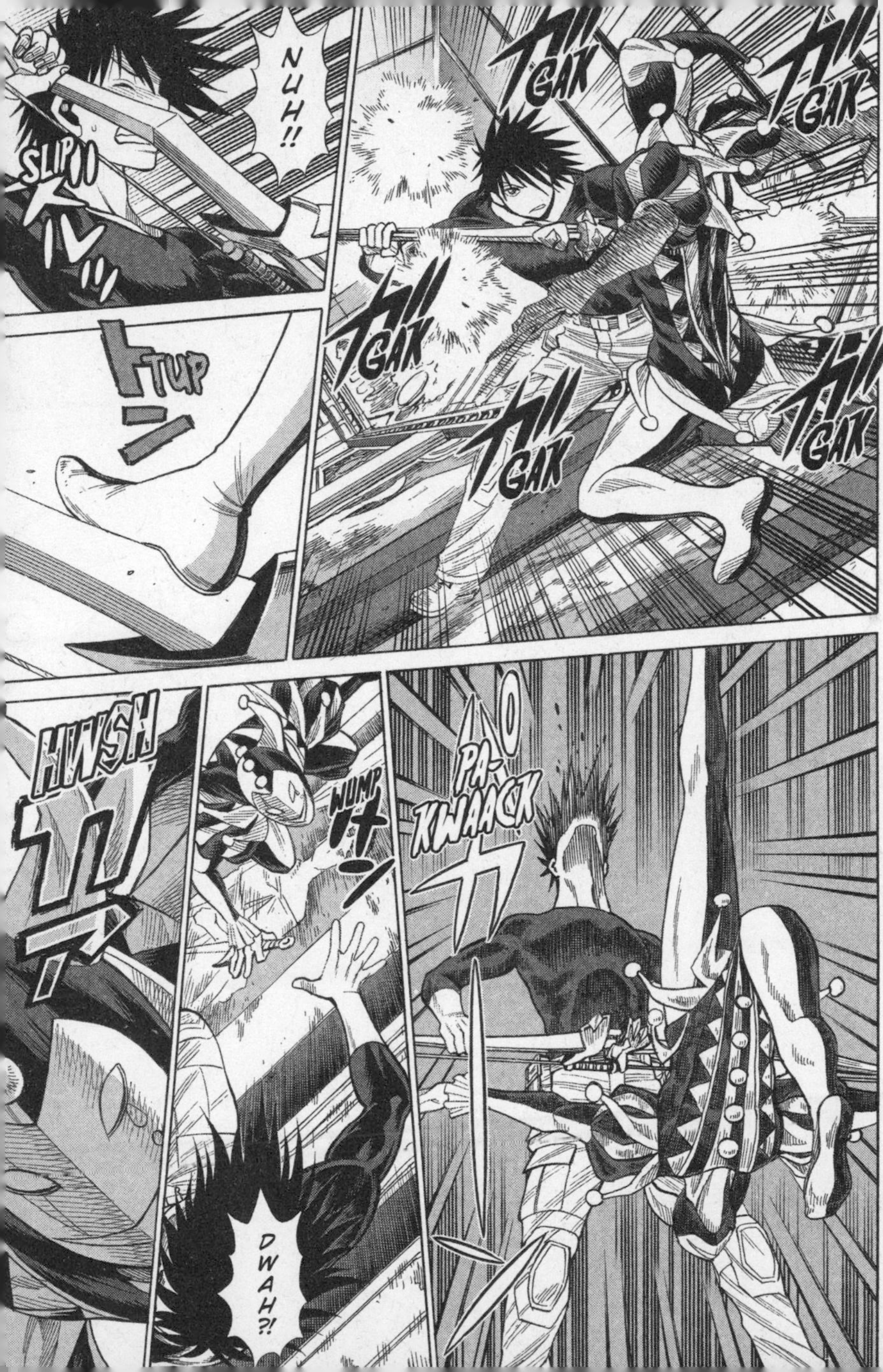
GAK
GAK
GAK
GAK
GAK
NUH!!
SLIP
TUP
PA-KWAACK
WUMP
HWSH
DWAH?!

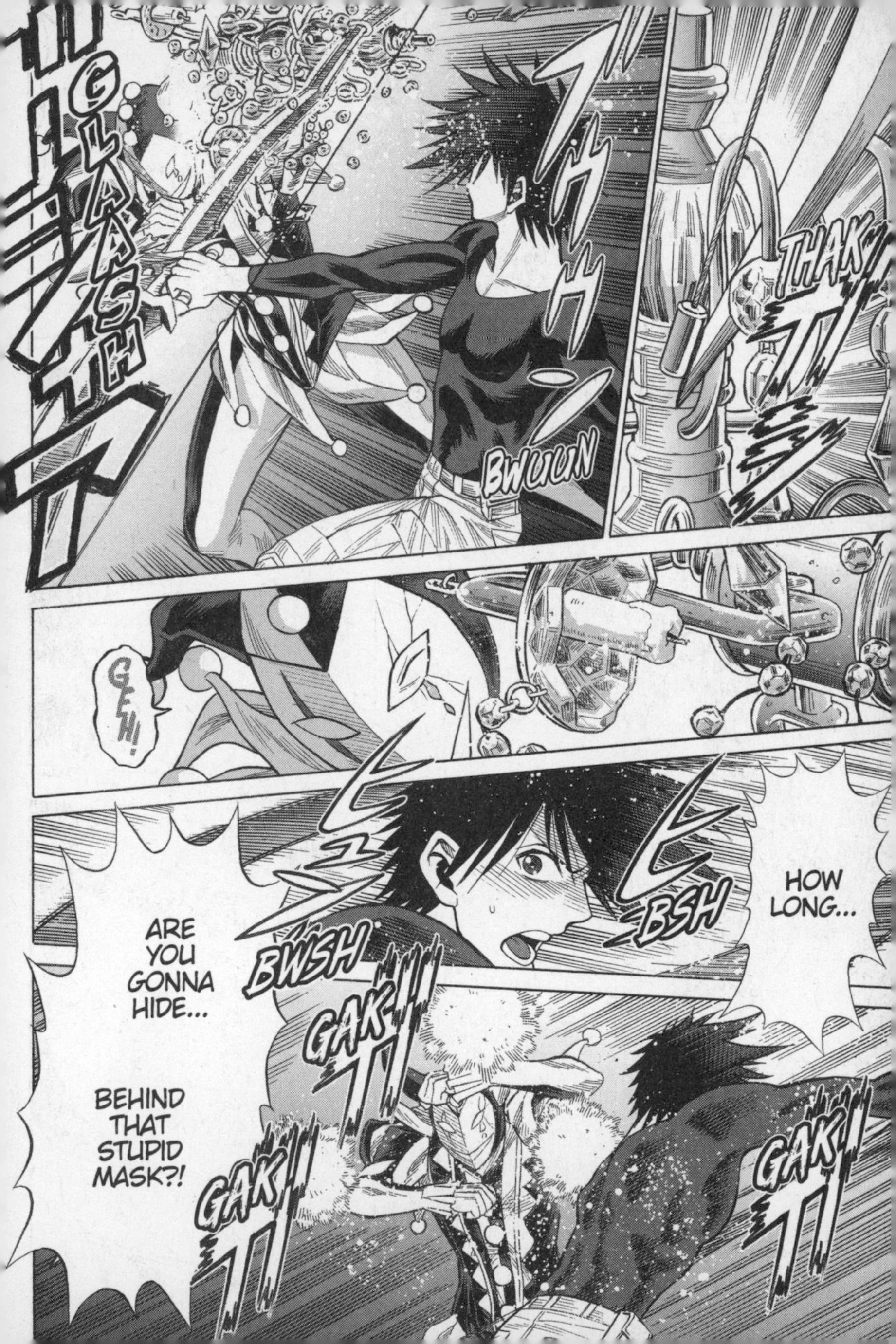
THAK
BWUUN
GLASH
GEH!
HOW LONG...
BSH
BWSH
ARE YOU GONNA HIDE...
GAK
GAK
GAK
BEHIND THAT STUPID MASK?!

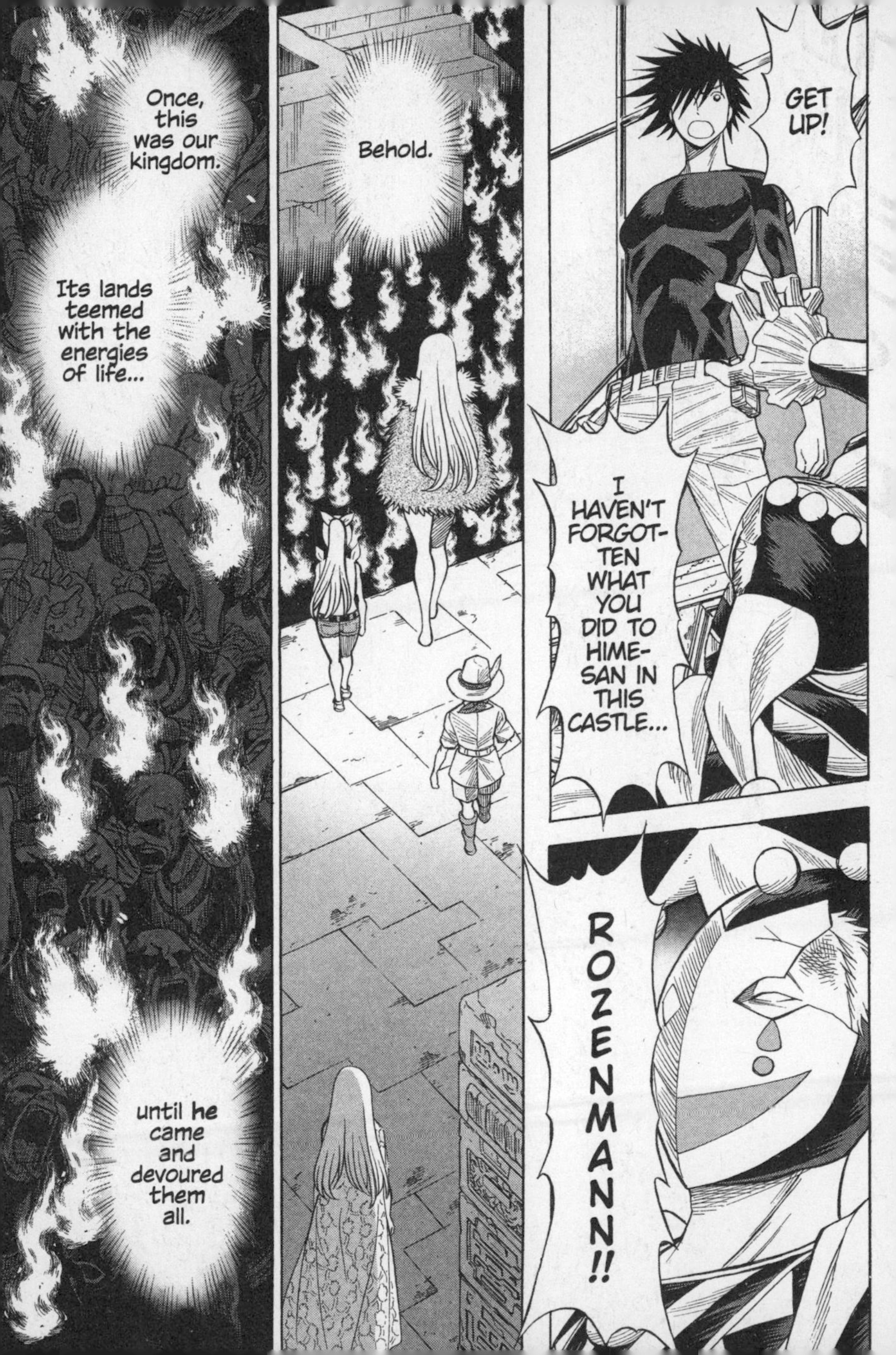
GET UP!
I HAVEN'T FORGOTTEN WHAT YOU DID TO HIME-SAN IN THIS CASTLE...
ROZENMANN!!
Behold.
Once, this was our kingdom.
Its lands teemed with the energies of life...
until he came and devoured them all.

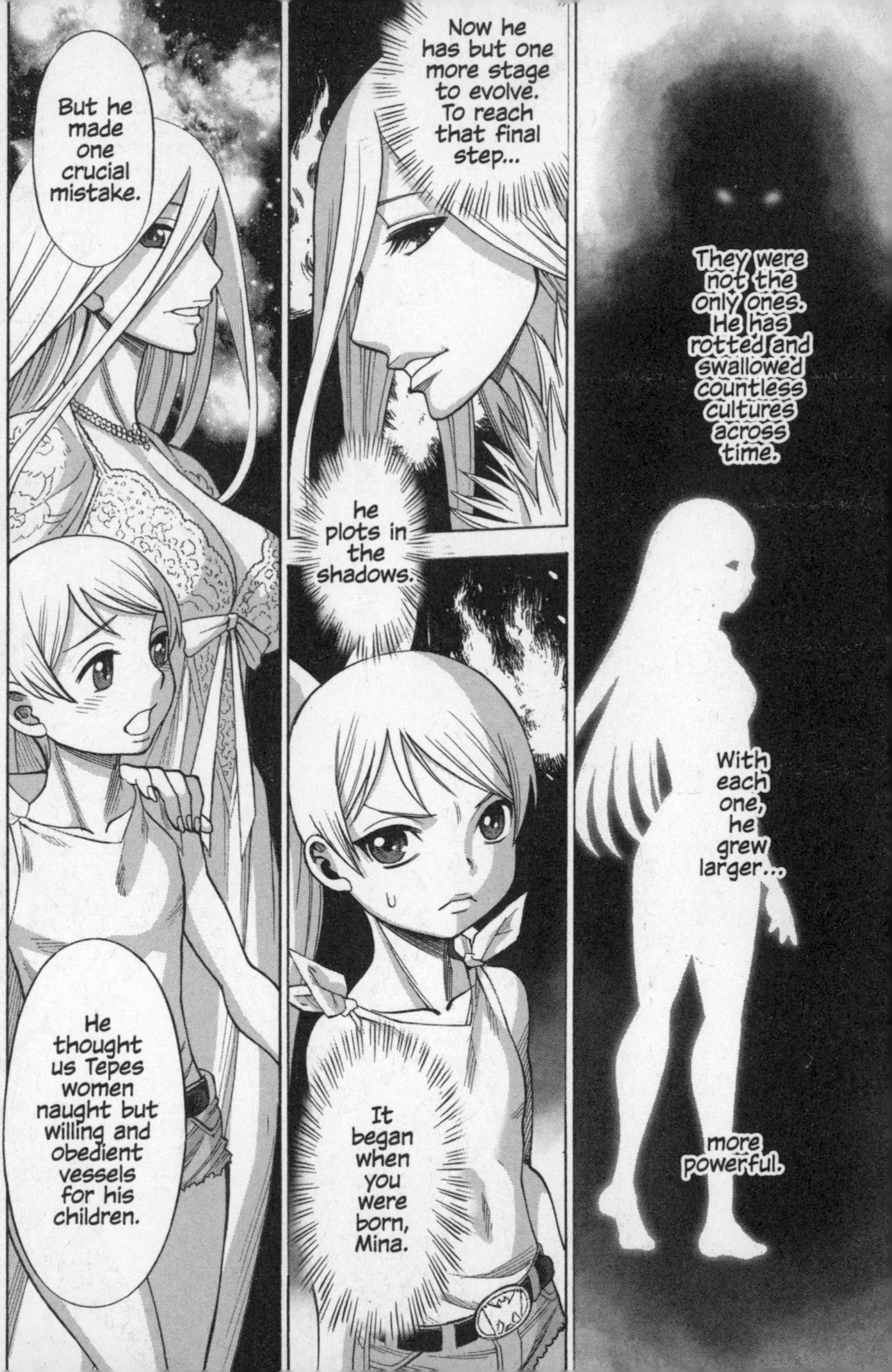
They were not the only ones. He has rotted and swallowed countless cultures across time.
With each one, he grew larger...
more powerful.
Now he has but one more stage to evolve. To reach that final step...
he plots in the shadows.
It began when you were born, Mina.
But he made one crucial mistake.
He thought us Tepes women naught but willing and obedient vessels for his children.

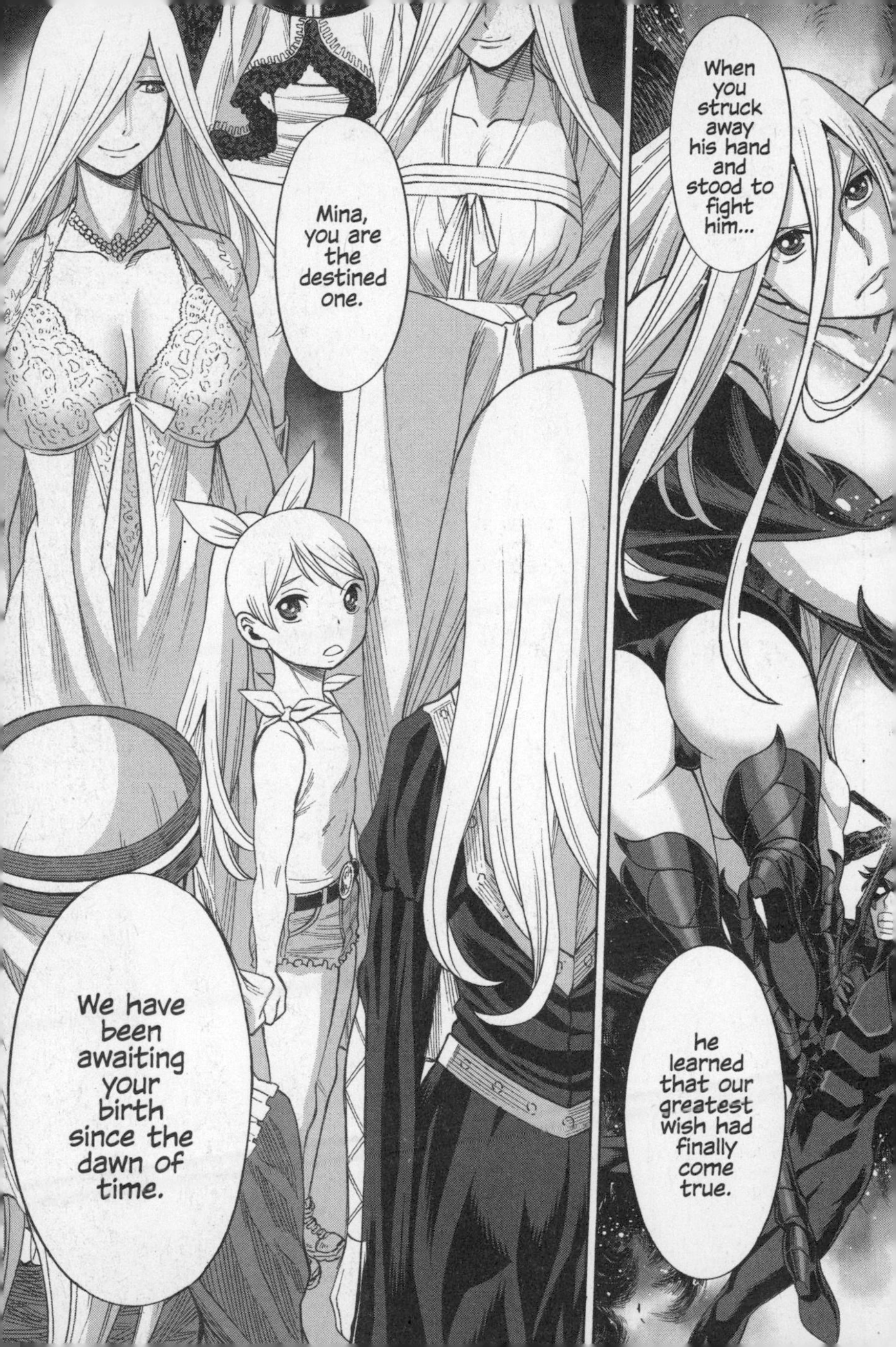
When you struck away his hand and stood to fight him...
he learned that our greatest wish had finally come true.
Mina, you are the destined one.
We have been awaiting your birth since the dawn of time.

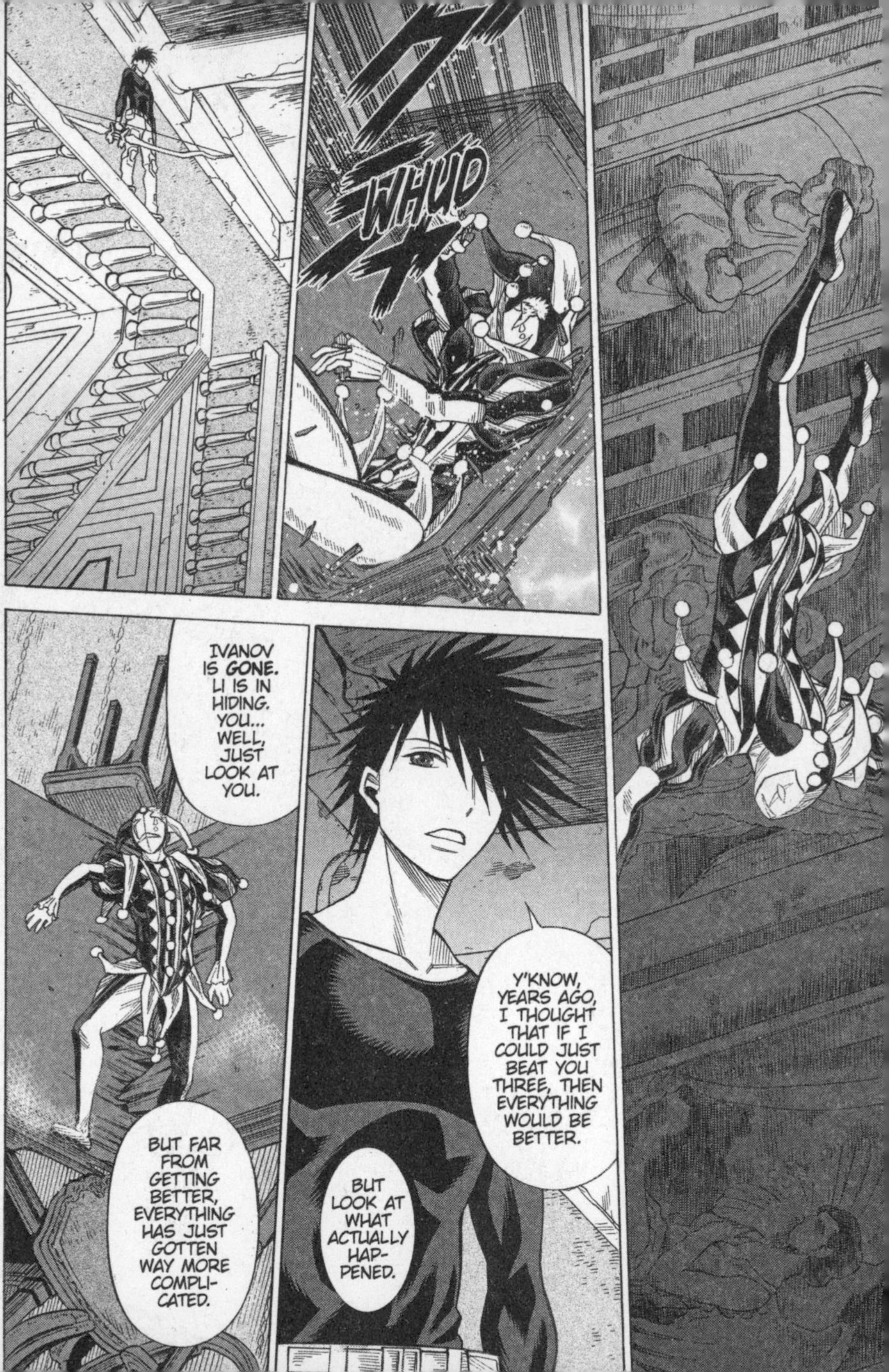
WHUD
Y'KNOW, YEARS AGO, I THOUGHT THAT IF I COULD JUST BEAT YOU THREE, THEN EVERYTHING WOULD BE BETTER.
BUT LOOK AT WHAT ACTUALLY HAP-PENED.
IVANOV IS **GONE**. LI IS IN HIDING. YOU... WELL, JUST LOOK AT YOU.
BUT FAR FROM GETTING BETTER, EVERYTHING HAS JUST GOTTEN WAY MORE COMPLI-CATED.

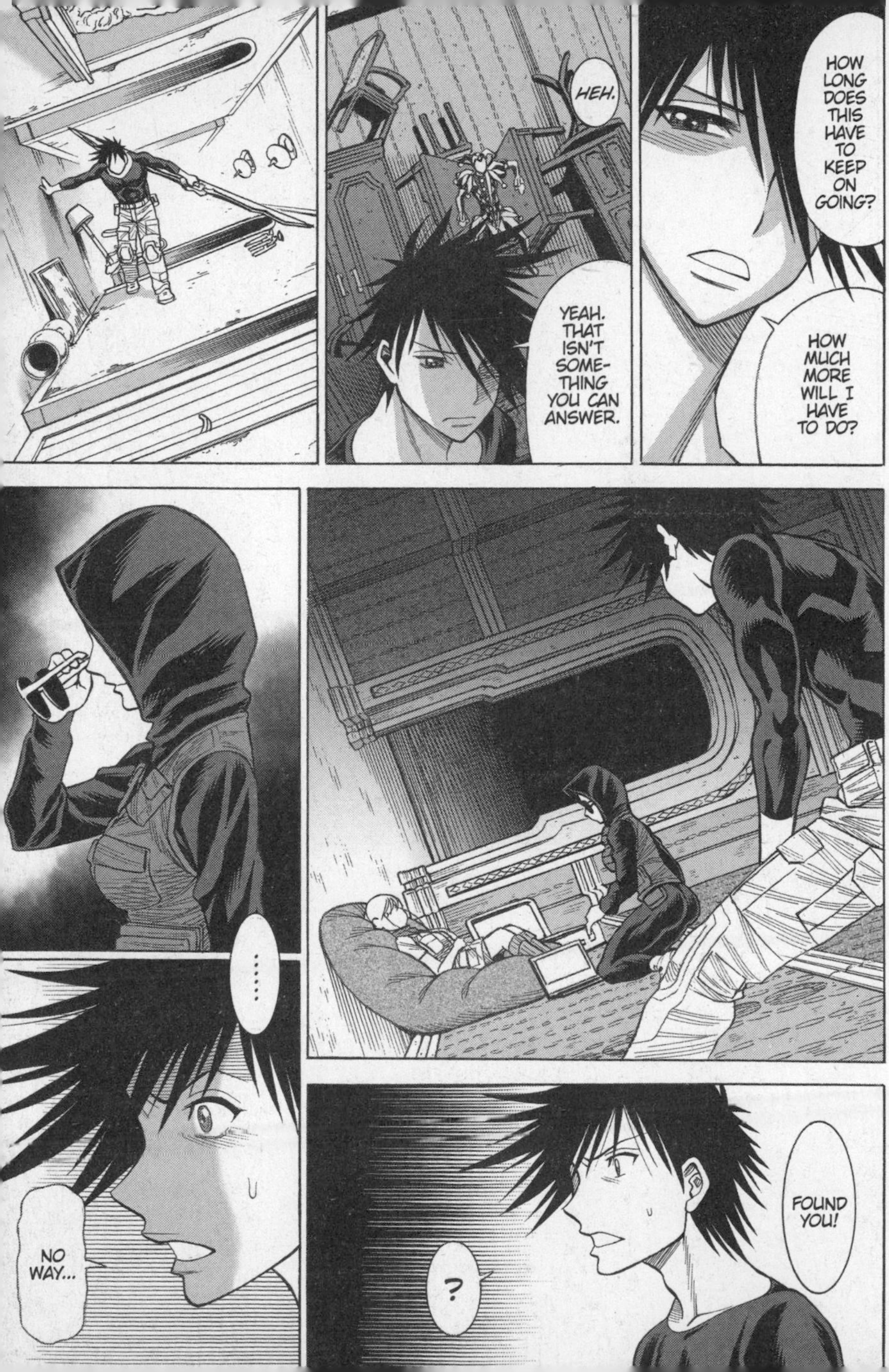
HOW LONG DOES THIS HAVE TO KEEP ON GOING?
HOW MUCH MORE WILL I HAVE TO DO?
HEH.
YEAH. THAT ISN'T SOME-THING YOU CAN ANSWER.
FOUND YOU!
?
......
NO WAY...

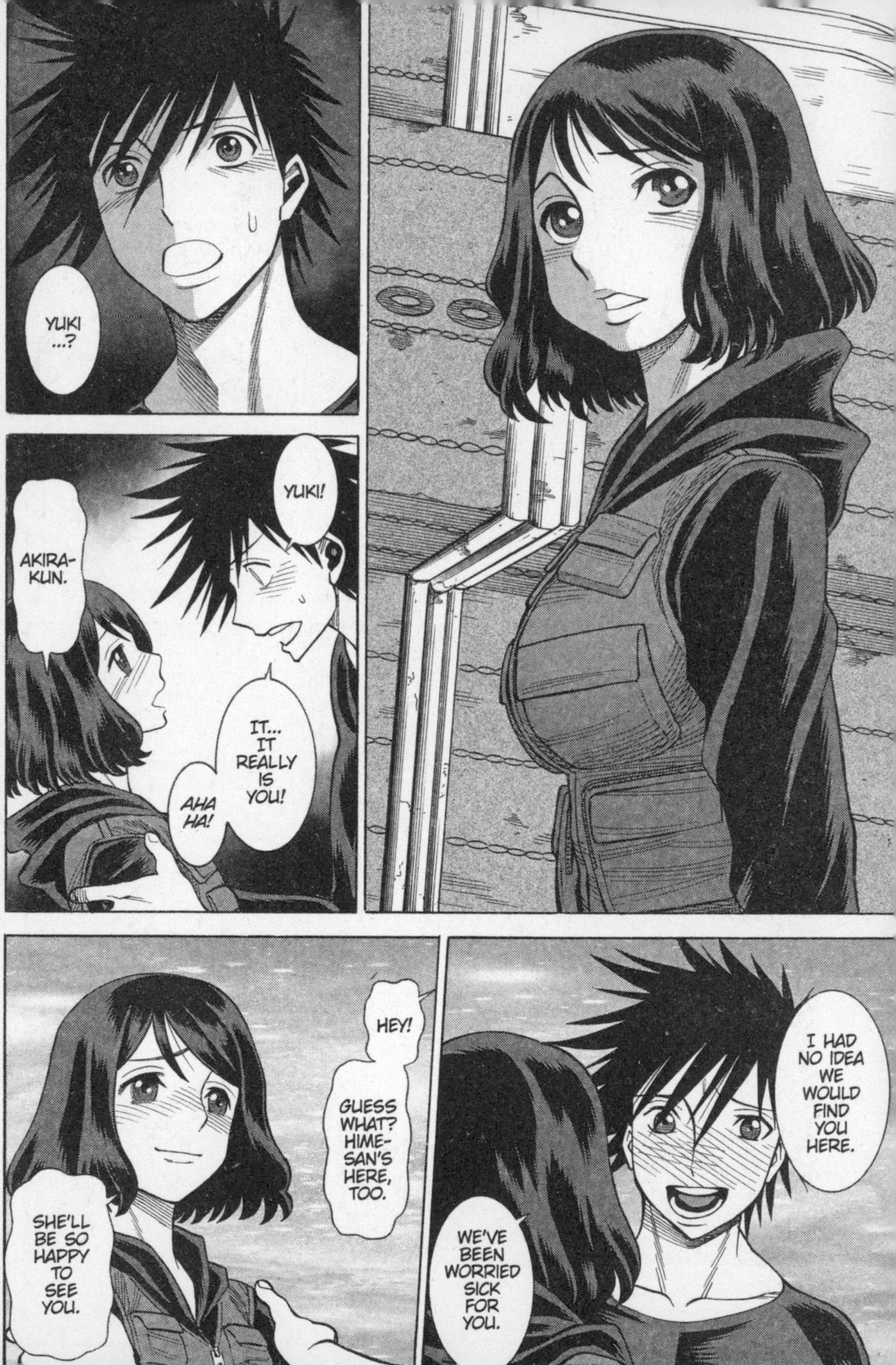
YUKI ...?
YUKI!
AKIRA-KUN.
IT... IT REALLY IS YOU!
AHA HA!
I HAD NO IDEA WE WOULD FIND YOU HERE.
WE'VE BEEN WORRIED SICK FOR YOU.
HEY!
GUESS WHAT? HIME-SAN'S HERE, TOO.
SHE'LL BE SO HAPPY TO SEE YOU.

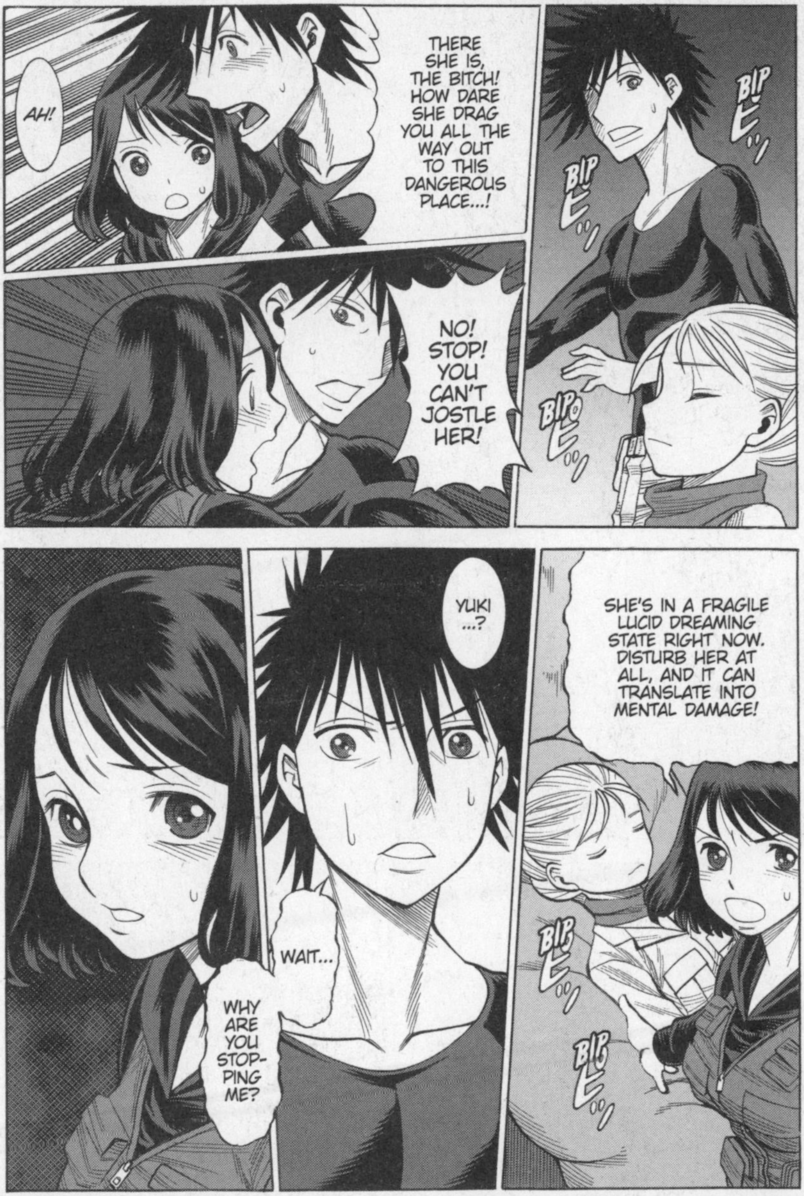
BIP
ビッ
BIP
ビッ
BIP
ビッ
THERE SHE IS, THE BITCH! HOW DARE SHE DRAG YOU ALL THE WAY OUT TO THIS DANGEROUS PLACE...!
AH!
NO! STOP! YOU CAN'T JOSTLE HER!
SHE'S IN A FRAGILE LUCID DREAMING STATE RIGHT NOW. DISTURB HER AT ALL, AND IT CAN TRANSLATE INTO MENTAL DAMAGE!
BIP
ビッ
BIP
ビッ
YUKI ...?
WAIT...
WHY ARE YOU STOPPING ME?

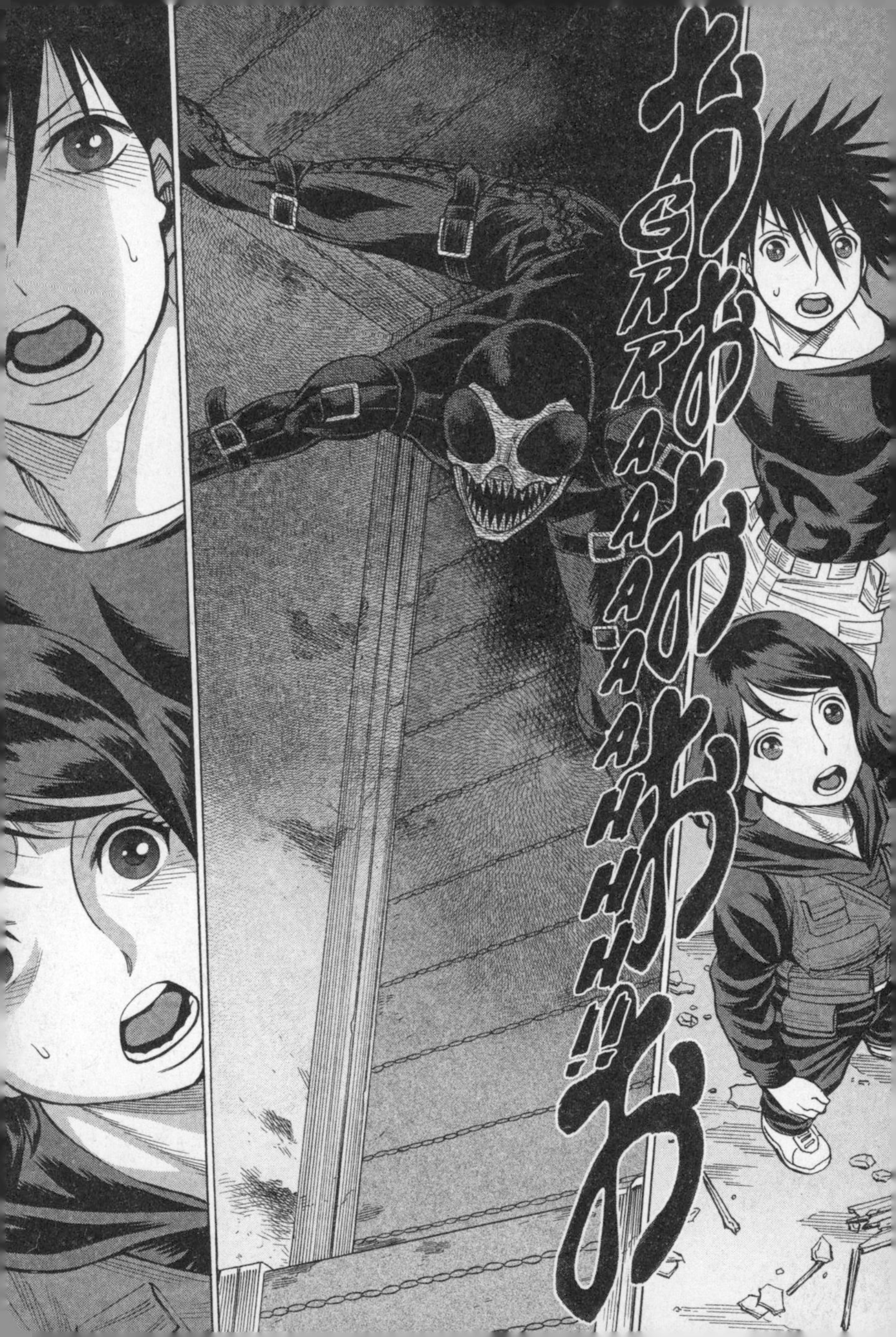
GRRAAAAAHHHH!!

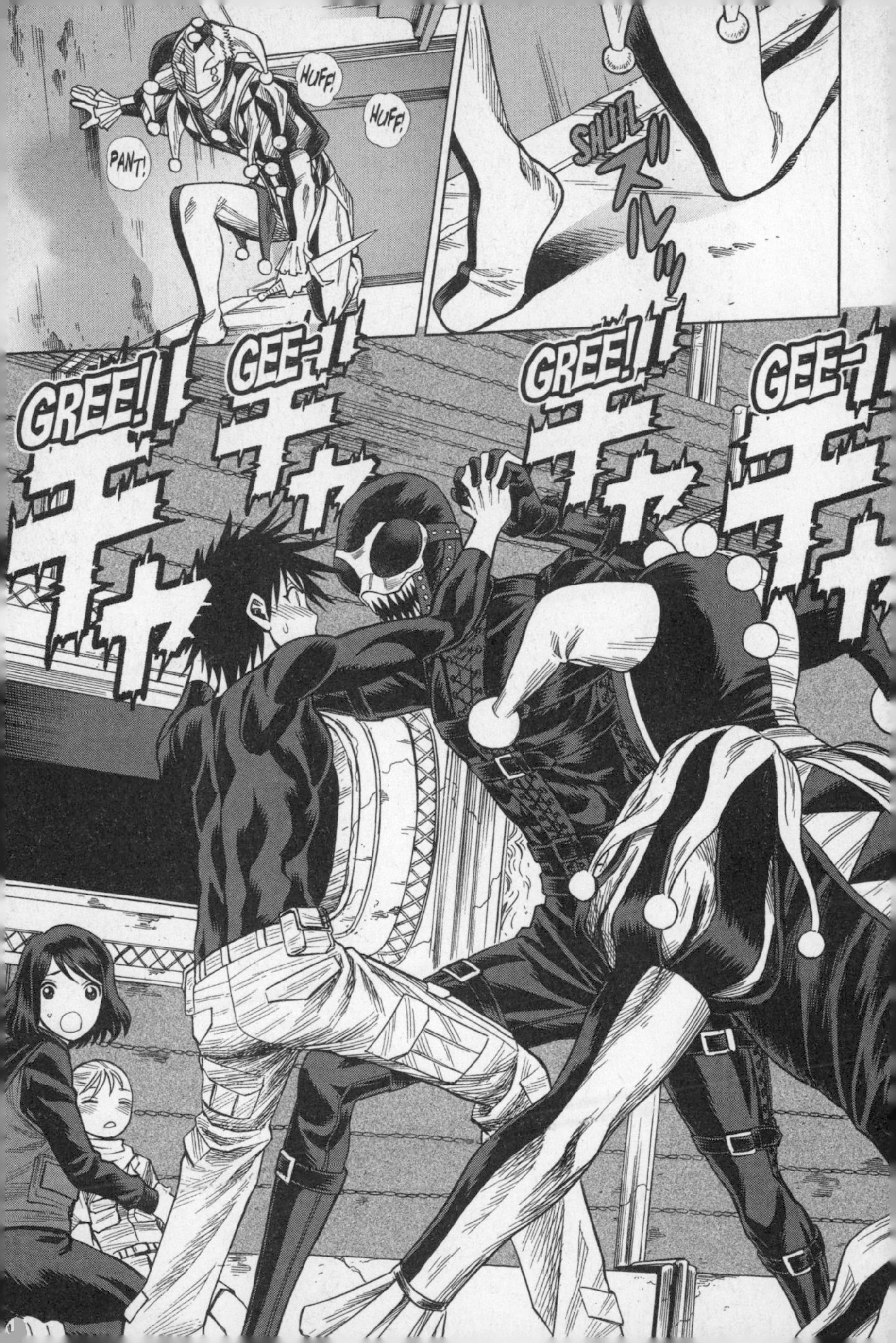

SHUFL
HUFF!
HUFF!
PANT!
GEE-!
GREE!!
GEE-!
GREE!!

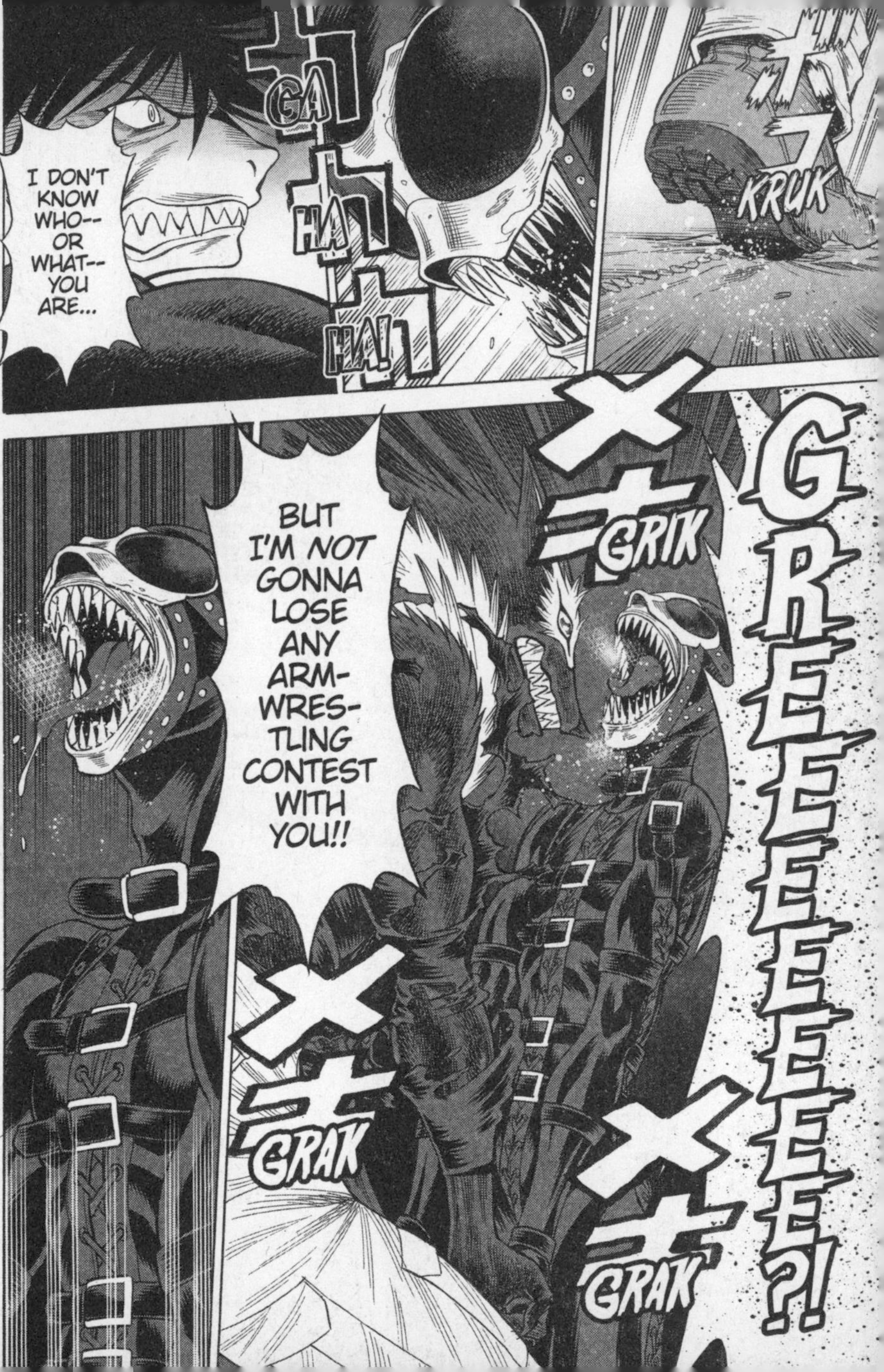
KRUK
GA
HA
HA!
I DON'T KNOW WHO-- OR WHAT-- YOU ARE...
GREEEEEEEE?!
GRIK
BUT I'M *NOT* GONNA LOSE ANY ARM-WRES-TLING CONTEST WITH YOU!!
GRAK
GRAK

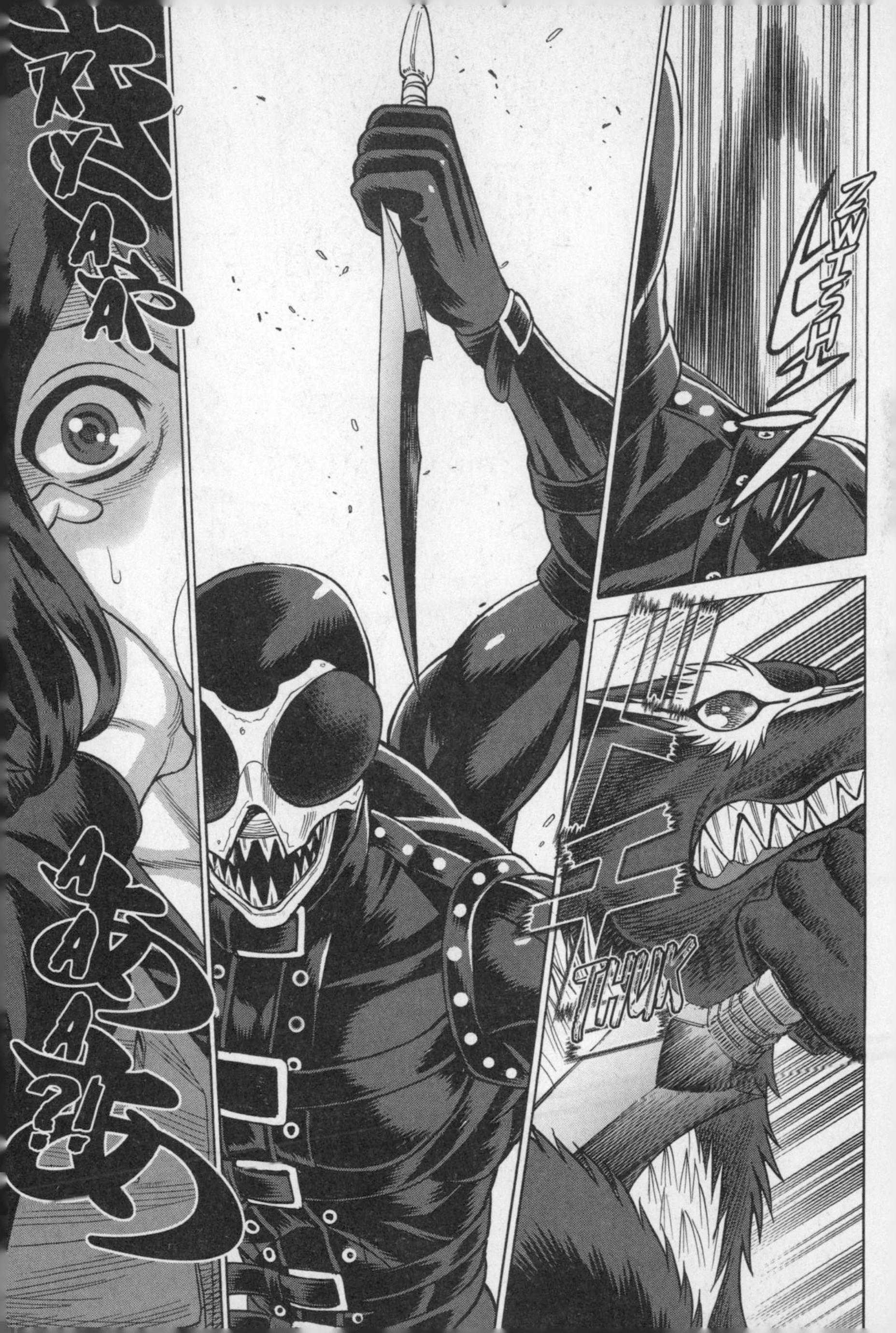
ZWISHH
THUNK
KYAAA
AAA?!

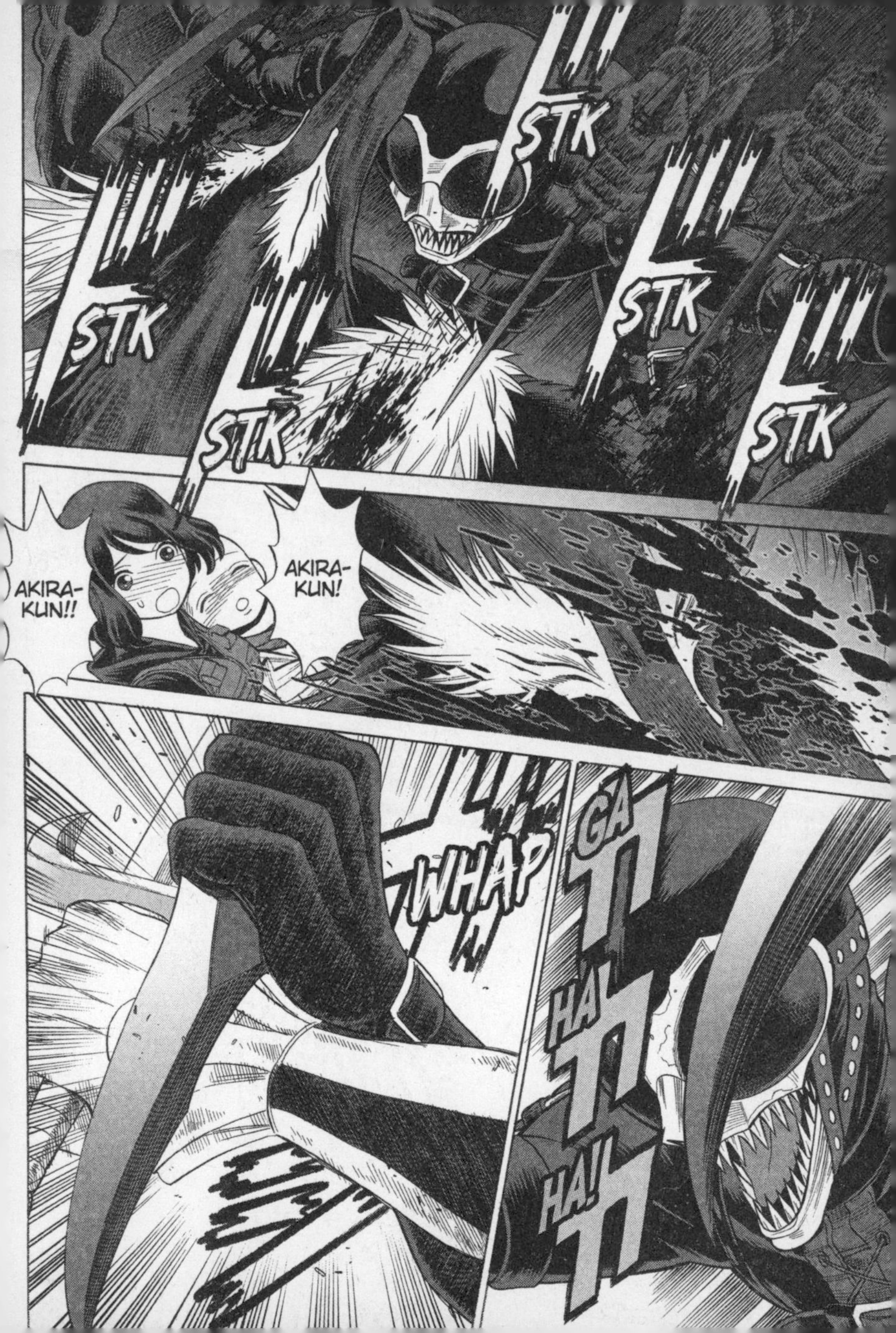
STK
STK
STK
STK
STK
STK
AKIRA-KUN!
AKIRA-KUN!!
GA HA HA!
WHAP

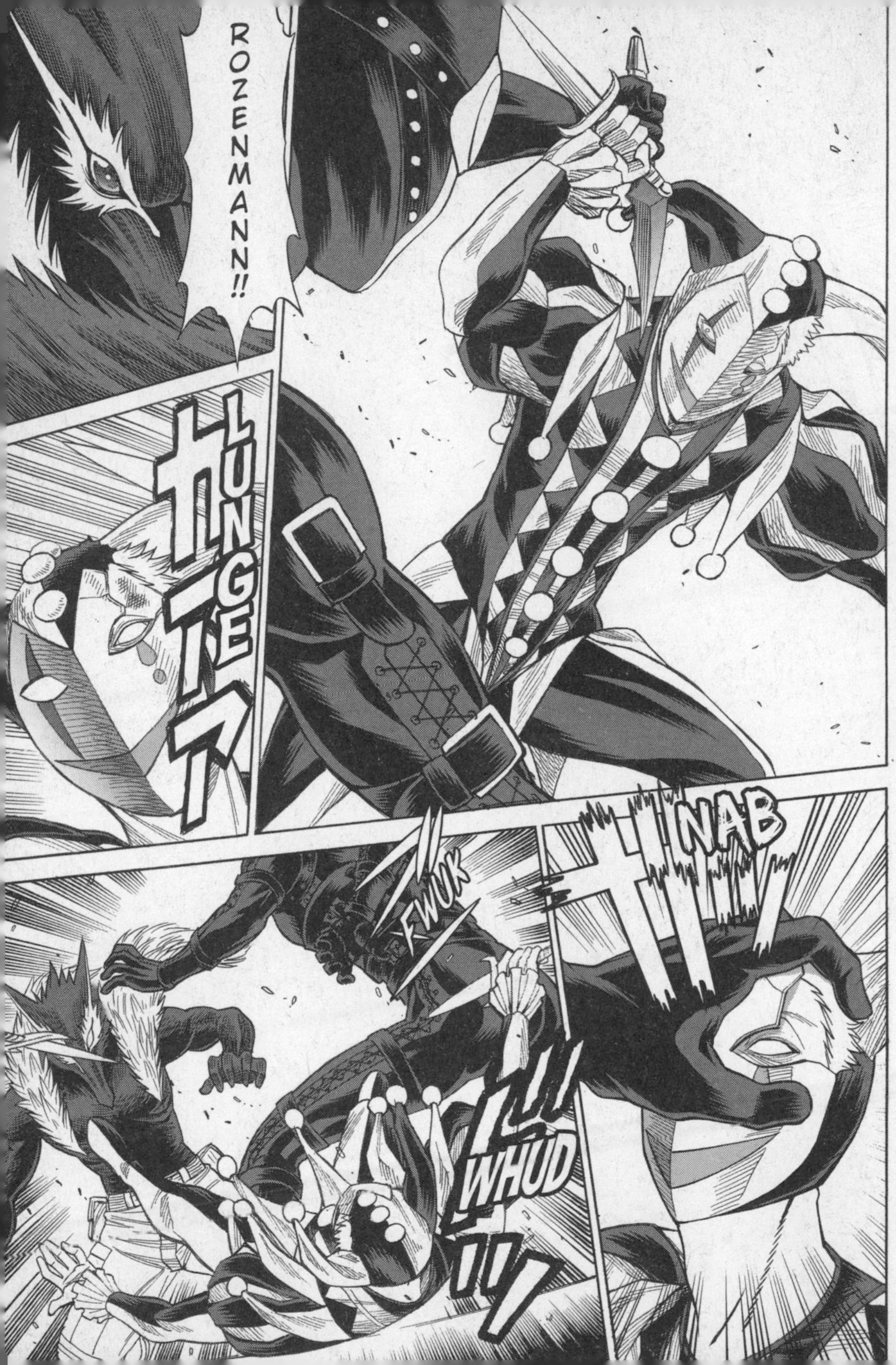
ROZENMANN!!
LUNGE
NAB
FWUK
WHUD

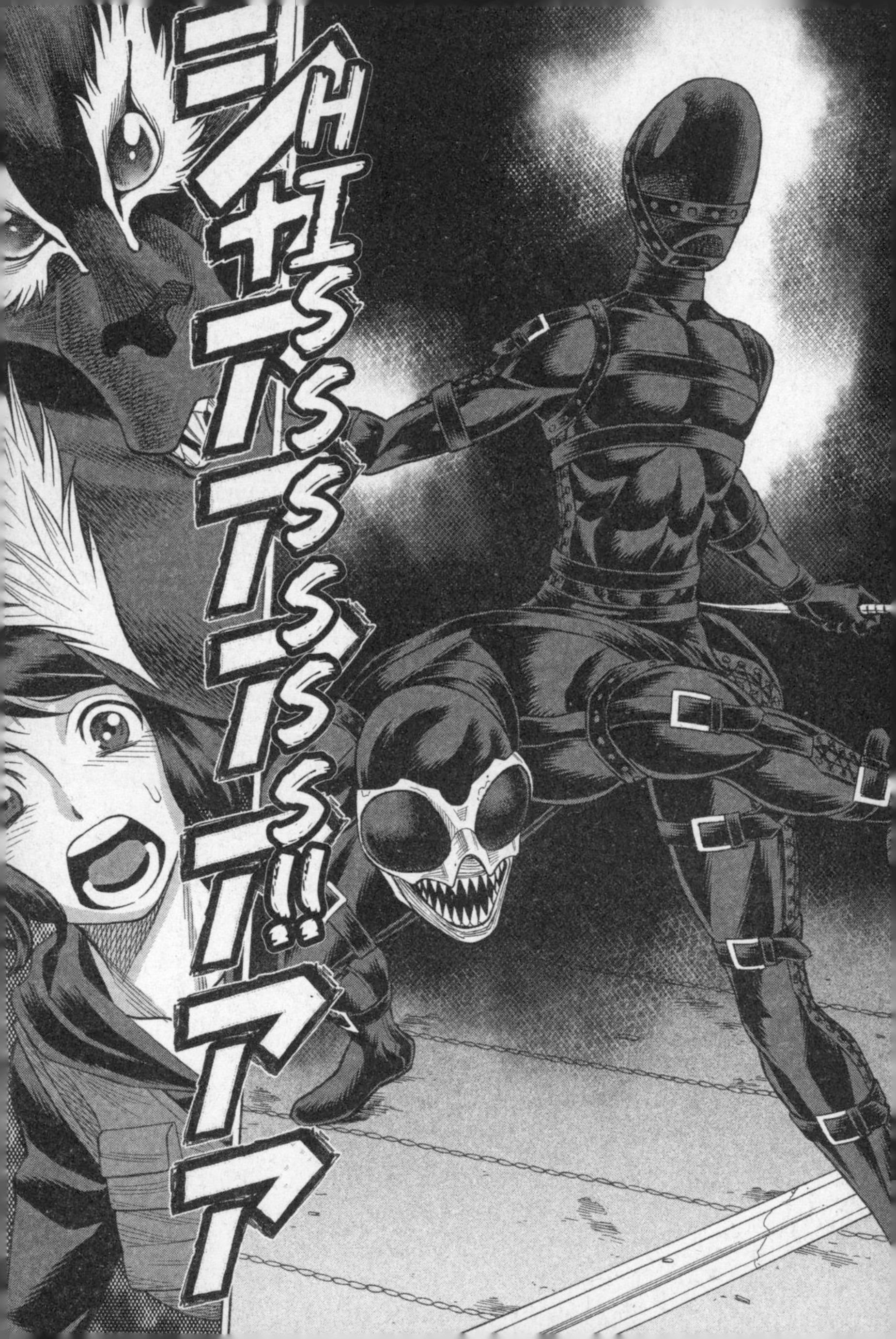
HISSSSSSS!!

Dance in the Vampire Bund
Vampire Bund
Age of Scarlet Order

Dance in the Vampire Bund
Age of Scarlet Order

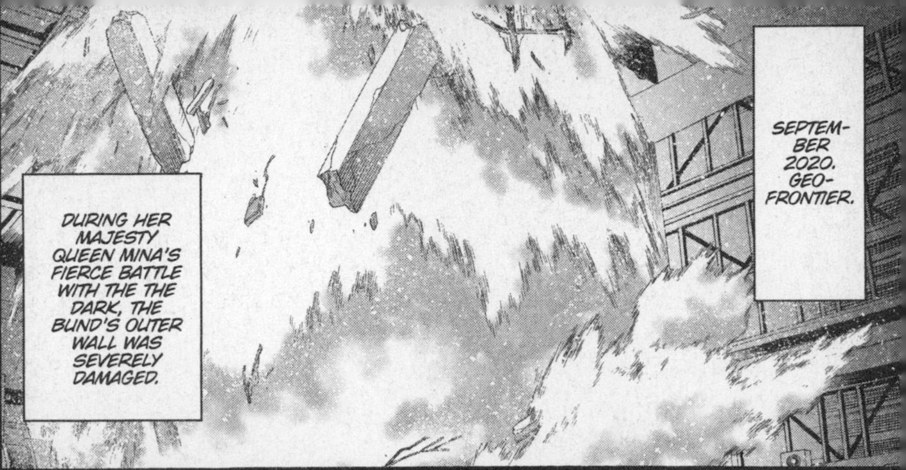
SEPTEMBER 2020. GEOFRONTIER.
DURING HER MAJESTY QUEEN MINA'S FIERCE BATTLE WITH THE THE DARK, THE BUND'S OUTER WALL WAS SEVERELY DAMAGED.

Dance with the Vampire Maids

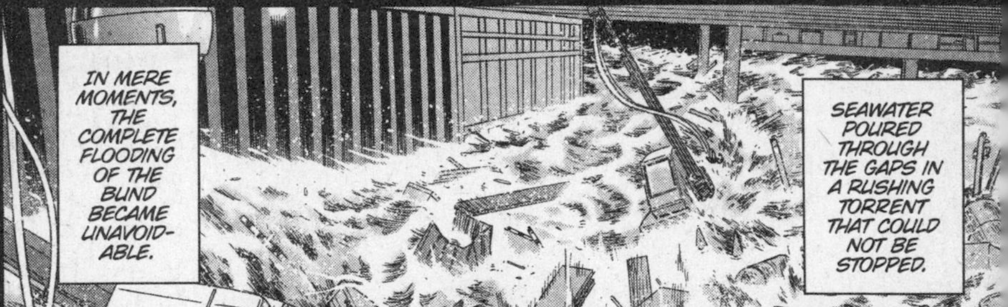
SEAWATER POURED THROUGH THE GAPS IN A RUSHING TORRENT THAT COULD NOT BE STOPPED.
IN MERE MOMENTS, THE COMPLETE FLOODING OF THE BUND BECAME UNAVOIDABLE.

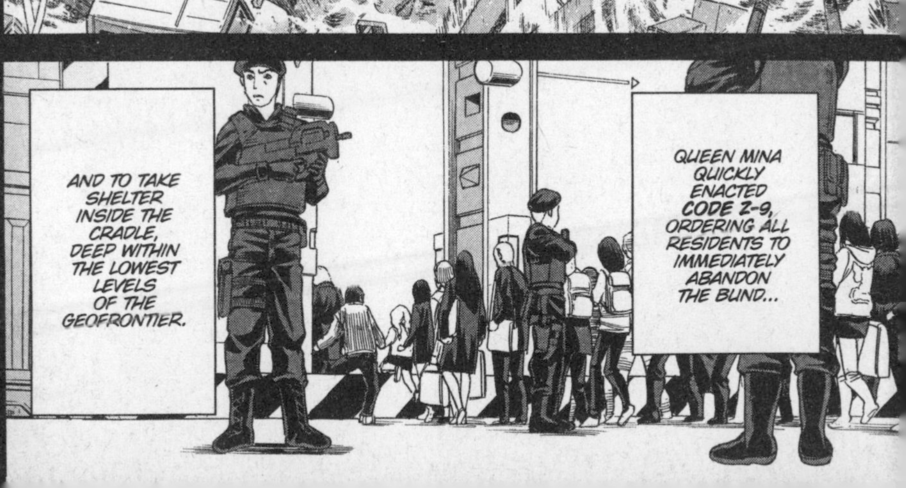
QUEEN MINA QUICKLY ENACTED **CODE Z-9**, ORDERING ALL RESIDENTS TO IMMEDIATELY ABANDON THE BUND...
AND TO TAKE SHELTER INSIDE THE CRADLE, DEEP WITHIN THE LOWEST LEVELS OF THE GEOFRONTIER.

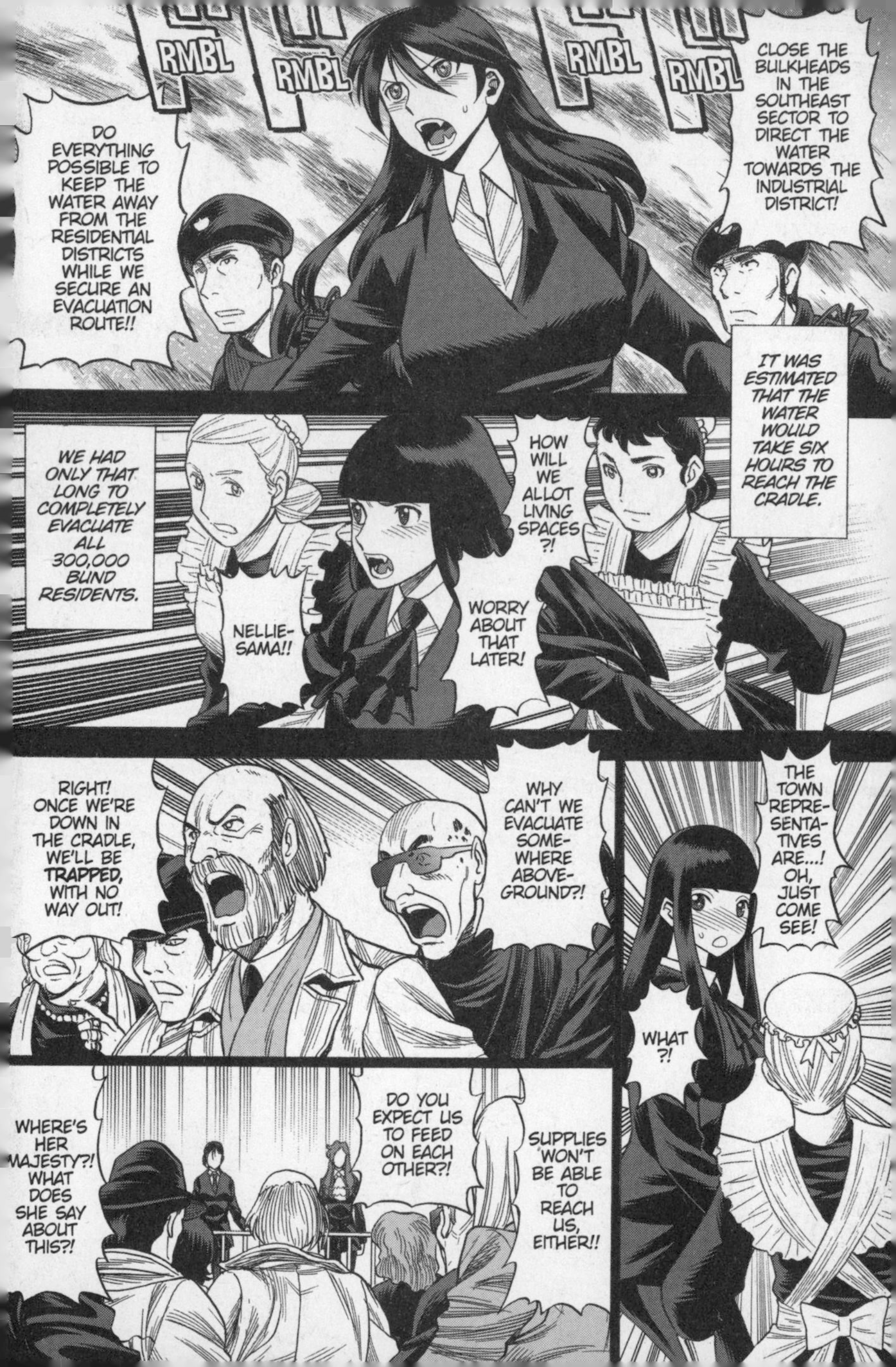
RMBL
RMBL
CLOSE THE BULKHEADS IN THE SOUTHEAST SECTOR TO DIRECT THE WATER TOWARDS THE INDUSTRIAL DISTRICT!
RMBL
RMBL
DO EVERYTHING POSSIBLE TO KEEP THE WATER AWAY FROM THE RESIDENTIAL DISTRICTS WHILE WE SECURE AN EVACUATION ROUTE!!
IT WAS ESTIMATED THAT THE WATER WOULD TAKE SIX HOURS TO REACH THE CRADLE.
HOW WILL WE ALLOT LIVING SPACES?!
WORRY ABOUT THAT LATER!
NELLIE-SAMA!!
WE HAD ONLY THAT LONG TO COMPLETELY EVACUATE ALL 300,000 BUND RESIDENTS.
THE TOWN REPRESENTATIVES ARE...! OH, JUST COME SEE!
WHAT?!
WHY CAN'T WE EVACUATE SOMEWHERE ABOVEGROUND?!
RIGHT! ONCE WE'RE DOWN IN THE CRADLE, WE'LL BE **TRAPPED,** WITH NO WAY OUT!
SUPPLIES WON'T BE ABLE TO REACH US, EITHER!!
DO YOU EXPECT US TO FEED ON EACH OTHER?!
WHERE'S HER MAJESTY?! WHAT DOES SHE SAY ABOUT THIS?!

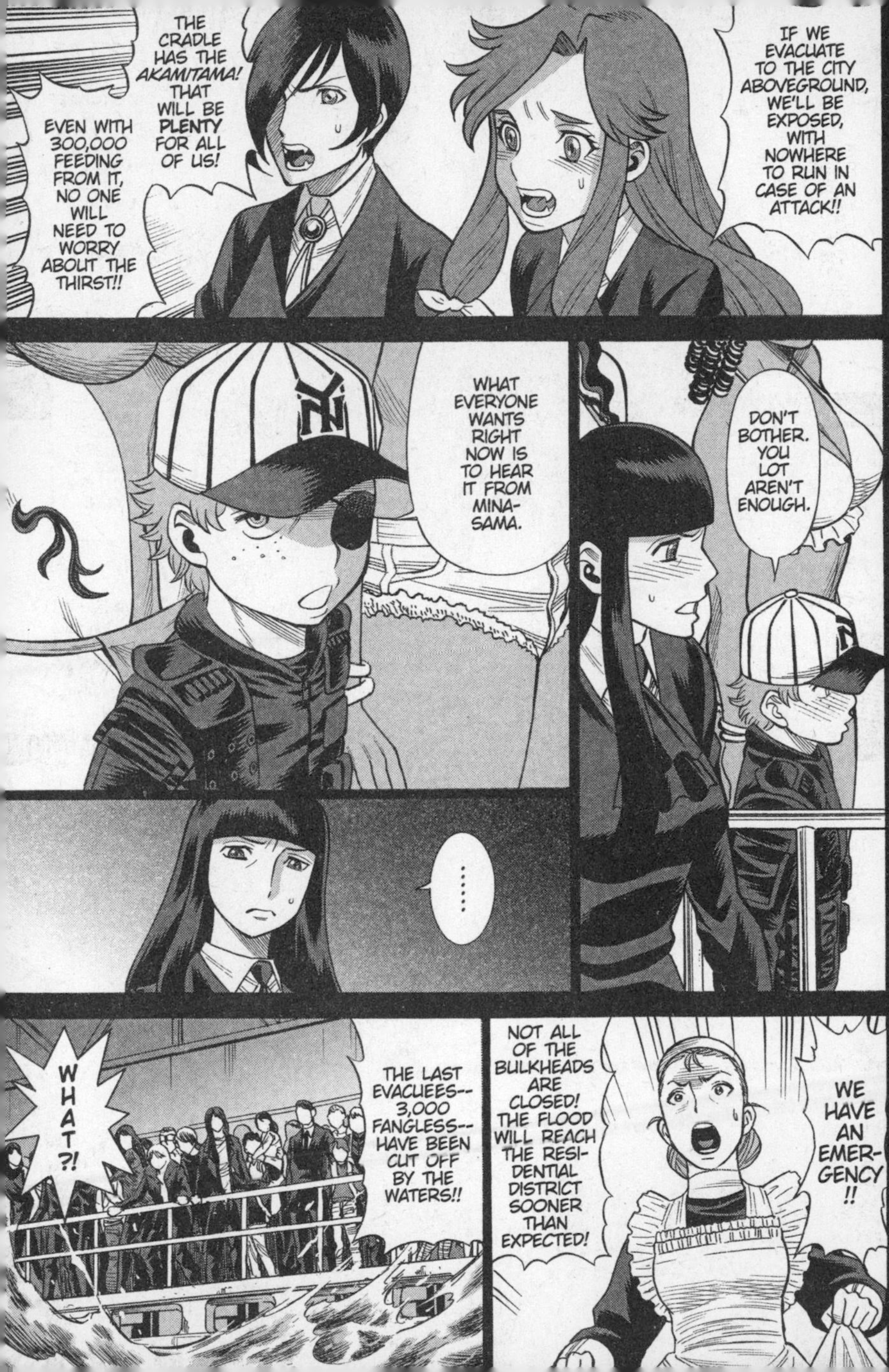
IF WE EVACUATE TO THE CITY ABOVEGROUND, WE'LL BE EXPOSED, WITH NOWHERE TO RUN IN CASE OF AN ATTACK!!
THE CRADLE HAS THE *AKAMITAMA!* THAT WILL BE **PLENTY** FOR ALL OF US!
EVEN WITH 300,000 FEEDING FROM IT, NO ONE WILL NEED TO WORRY ABOUT THE THIRST!!
DON'T BOTHER. YOU LOT AREN'T ENOUGH.
WHAT EVERYONE WANTS RIGHT NOW IS TO HEAR IT FROM MINA-SAMA.
......
WE HAVE AN EMERGENCY!!
NOT ALL OF THE BULKHEADS ARE CLOSED! THE FLOOD WILL REACH THE RESIDENTIAL DISTRICT SOONER THAN EXPECTED!
THE LAST EVACUEES--3,000 FANGLESS--HAVE BEEN CUT OFF BY THE WATERS!!
WHAT?!

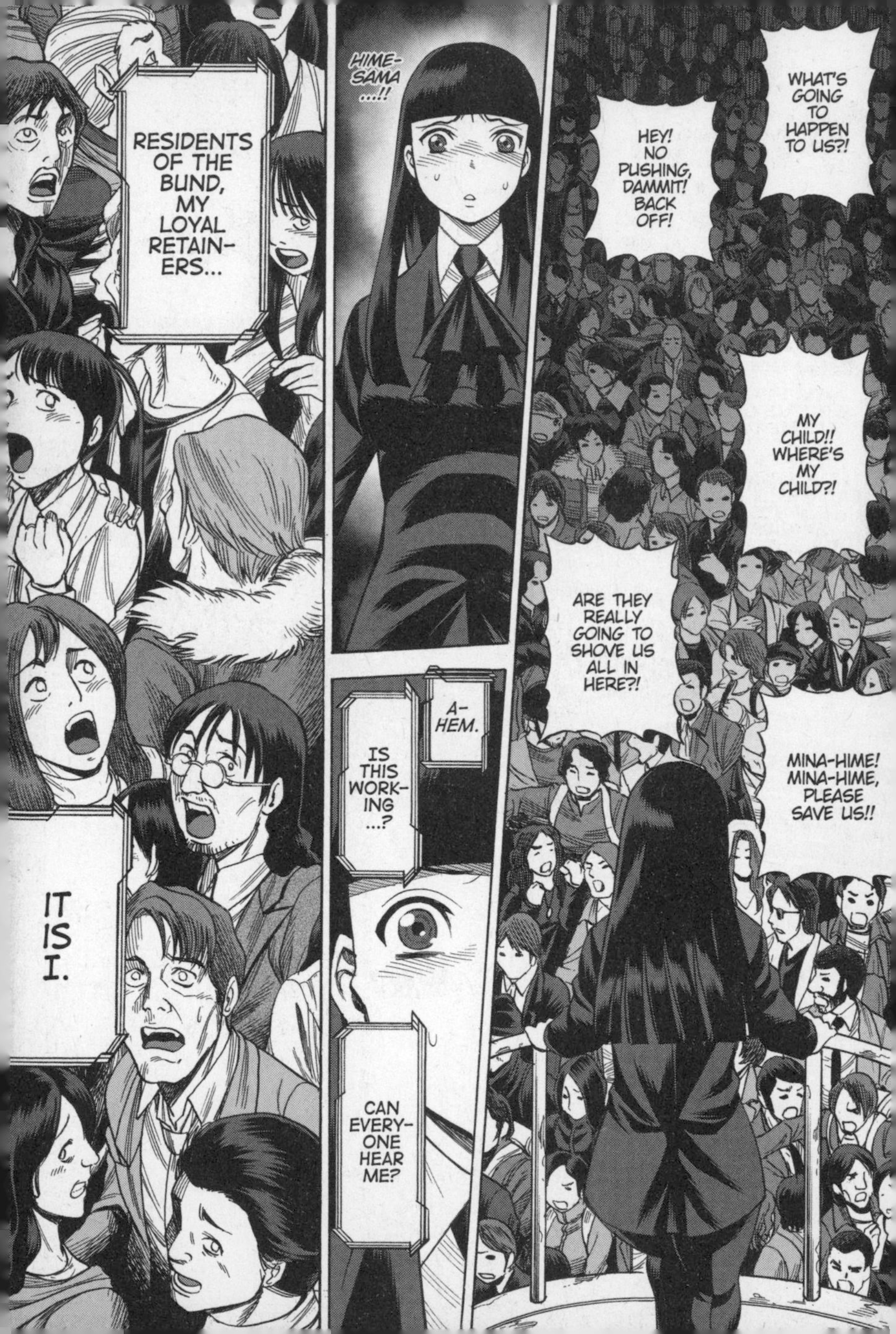
WHAT'S GOING TO HAPPEN TO US?!
HEY! NO PUSHING, DAMMIT! BACK OFF!
MY CHILD!! WHERE'S MY CHILD?!
ARE THEY REALLY GOING TO SHOVE US ALL IN HERE?!
MINA-HIME! MINA-HIME, PLEASE SAVE US!!
HIME-SAMA ...!!
A-HEM.
IS THIS WORKING ...?
CAN EVERYONE HEAR ME?
RESIDENTS OF THE BUND, MY LOYAL RETAINERS...
IT IS I.

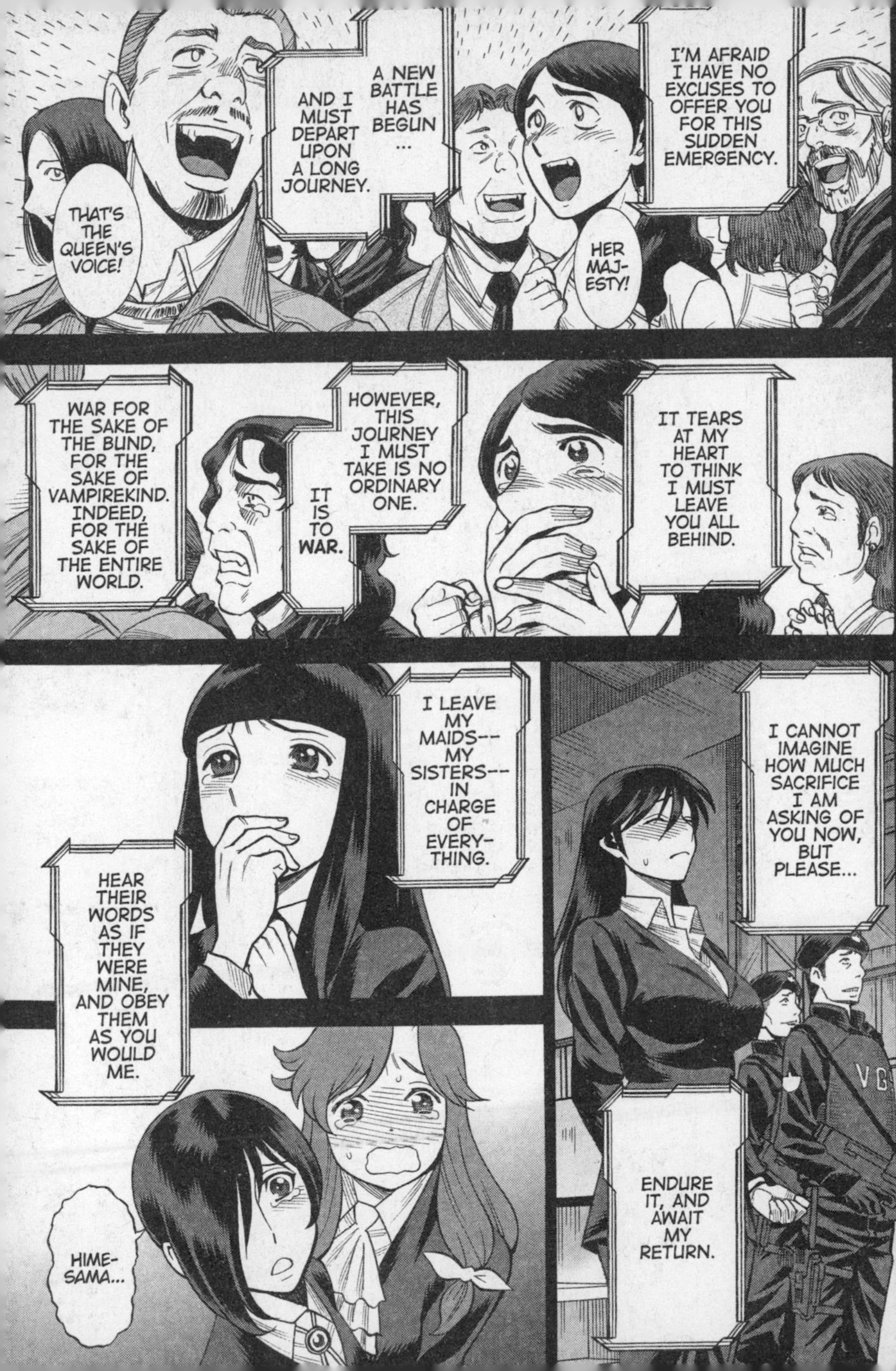
I'M AFRAID I HAVE NO EXCUSES TO OFFER YOU FOR THIS SUDDEN EMERGENCY.
HER MAJESTY!
A NEW BATTLE HAS BEGUN ...
AND I MUST DEPART UPON A LONG JOURNEY.
THAT'S THE QUEEN'S VOICE!
IT TEARS AT MY HEART TO THINK I MUST LEAVE YOU ALL BEHIND.
HOWEVER, THIS JOURNEY I MUST TAKE IS NO ORDINARY ONE.
IT IS TO **WAR.**
WAR FOR THE SAKE OF THE BUND, FOR THE SAKE OF VAMPIREKIND. INDEED, FOR THE SAKE OF THE ENTIRE WORLD.
I CANNOT IMAGINE HOW MUCH SACRIFICE I AM ASKING OF YOU NOW, BUT PLEASE...
ENDURE IT, AND AWAIT MY RETURN.
I LEAVE MY MAIDS--MY SISTERS--IN CHARGE OF EVERYTHING.
HEAR THEIR WORDS AS IF THEY WERE MINE, AND OBEY THEM AS YOU WOULD ME.
HIME-SAMA...

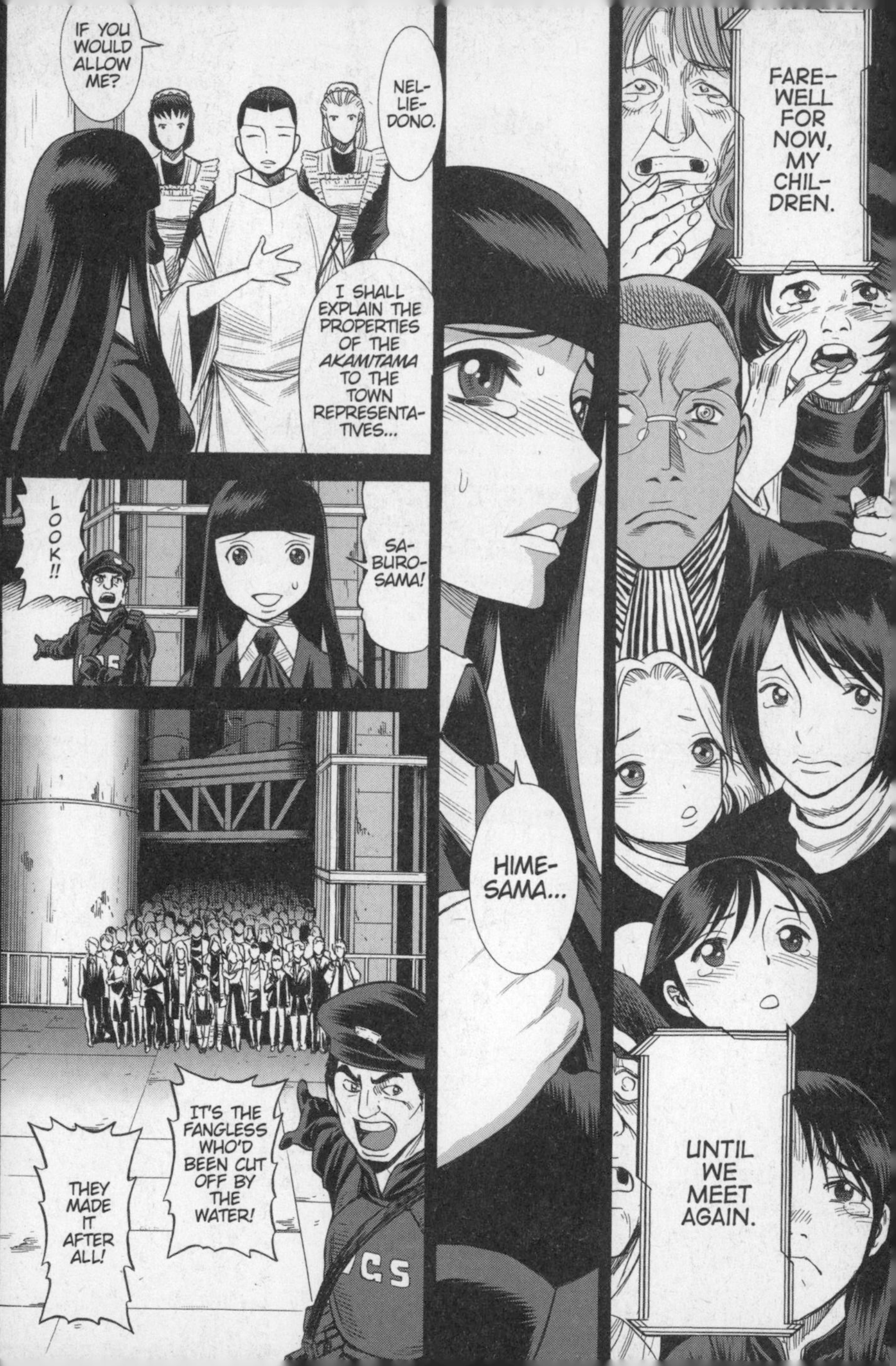
FARE-WELL FOR NOW, MY CHIL-DREN.
UNTIL WE MEET AGAIN.
HIME-SAMA...
NEL-LIE-DONO.
IF YOU WOULD ALLOW ME?
I SHALL EXPLAIN THE PROPERTIES OF THE *AKAMITAMA* TO THE TOWN REPRESENTA-TIVES...
SA-BURO-SAMA!
LOOK!!
IT'S THE FANGLESS WHO'D BEEN CUT OFF BY THE WATER!
THEY MADE IT AFTER ALL!

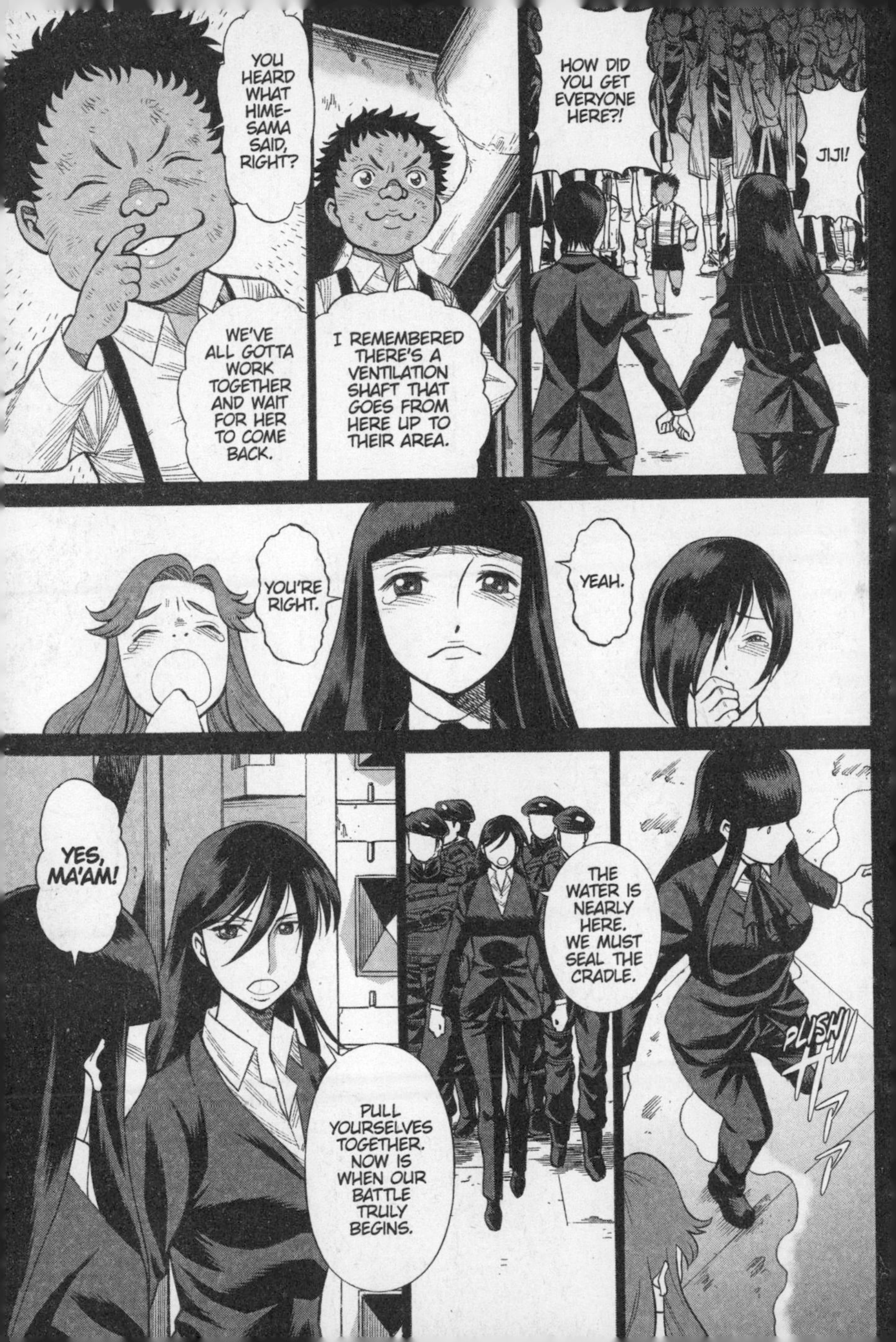
JIJI!
HOW DID YOU GET EVERYONE HERE?!
I REMEMBERED THERE'S A VENTILATION SHAFT THAT GOES FROM HERE UP TO THEIR AREA.
YOU HEARD WHAT HIME-SAMA SAID, RIGHT?
WE'VE ALL GOTTA WORK TOGETHER AND WAIT FOR HER TO COME BACK.
YEAH.
YOU'RE RIGHT.
PLISH
THE WATER IS NEARLY HERE. WE MUST SEAL THE CRADLE.
PULL YOURSELVES TOGETHER. NOW IS WHEN OUR BATTLE TRULY BEGINS.
YES, MA'AM!

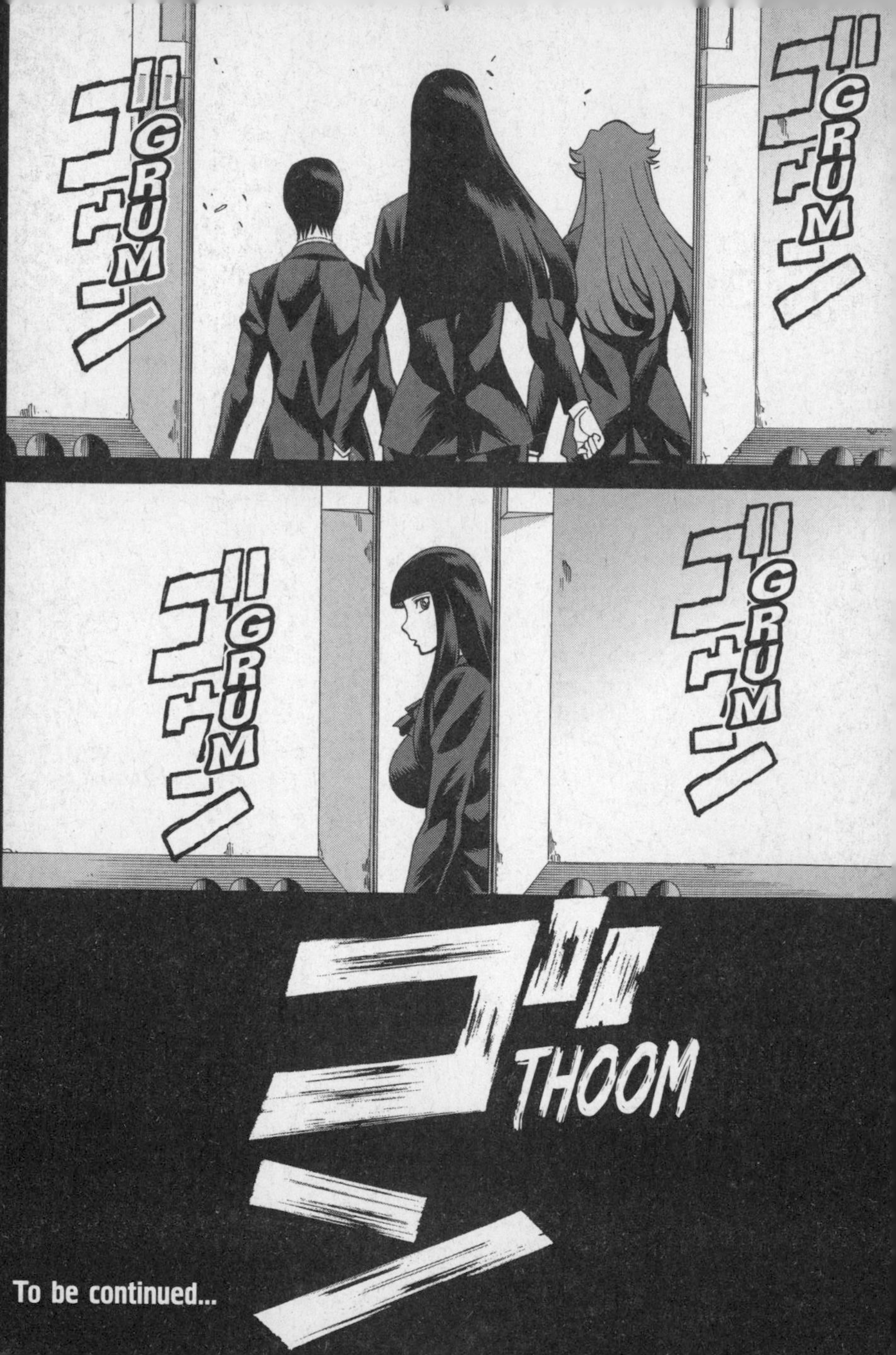
GRUM
GRUM
GRUM
GRUM
THOOM
To be continued...